CONSTITUTIONAL OPINIONS

CONST

TUTIONAL
OPINIONS

Aspects of the
BILL OF RIGHTS

LEONARD W. LEVY

New York   Oxford

OXFORD UNIVERSITY PRESS

1986

OXFORD UNIVERSITY PRESS

Oxford   London   New York   Toronto
Delhi   Bombay   Calcutta   Madras   Karachi
Kuala Lumpur   Singapore   Hong Kong   Tokyo
Nairobi   Dar es Salaam   Cape Town
Melbourne   Auckland

and associated companies in
Beirut   Berlin   Ibadan   Mexico City   Nicosia

Published by Oxford University Press, Inc., 200 Madison Avenue
New York, New York 10016

Library of Congress Cataloging in Publication Data

Levy, Leonard Williams, 1923–
   Constitutional opinions.

   Bibliography: p.
   1. United States—Constitutional history.   2. United States—Constitutional law. I. Title.
KF4541.L375 1986   342.73′029   85–7212
ISBN 0–19–503641–7   347.30229

Printing (last digit): 9 8 7 6 5 4 3 2 1

Printed in the United States of America

1-27-86

To My Daughters
Wendy Ellen and Leslie Anne
with love

Preface

An author who compiles an anthology of his own writings virtually waives his constitutional right to be free from the double jeopardy of a second exposure to critics. A preface conventionally is the vehicle for a display of modesty whose objective is to disarm critics. But an anthology of one's writings is an act of egotism, and the preface merely enlarges the target. This is, nevertheless, my second anthology. The first was entitled *Judgments*, creating the temptation to call this one *Misjudgments*, but my publisher balked at that. By calling this one *Constitutional Opinions*, I have at least reserved the possibility of entitling the sequel *Unconstitutional Opinions*.

This book, to quote Finley Peter Dunne's Mr. Dooley, is about what "some dead Englishmen thought Thomas Jefferson was goin' to mean when he wrote th' Constitution." I have always been fascinated by the most creative period in our constitutional history—the formative period; the origins and original meanings, as well as the development of constitutional provisions, especially of the Bill of Rights, have been an old and continuing preoccupation of mine as a scholar. This book is a small sampling of that interest on my part. The Bill of Rights, in particular, cements together most of these pieces, which deal mainly with First Amendment freedoms—freedom of religion, freedom from establishments of religion, freedom of speech, and freedom of the press. This book deals too with the related right from the Fifth Amendment which came into existence before the First Amendment freedoms. The right against compulsory self-incrimination originated because of inquisitions into beliefs and associations, especially political and religious ones. That right became a mainstay not only of our accusatorial system of criminal justice but of First Amendment freedoms.

Ours is an extraordinary system of government. We do not believe that the state is obligated to keep citizens from lapsing into politial and religious errors. We believe, rather, that citizens have the right and duty of preventing the government from falling into error. We sometimes forget, however, that we can secure our liberty only by preserving it for the most despicable and obnoxious among us, lest we set precedents that can reach us. Often, bad guys are responsible for posing constitutional issues that broaden the rights of all. As often, however, courageous individuals like John Lilburne, James Nayler, and

John Peter Zenger, all thorns in the heart of government, carry the standard of liberty at great personal cost but widen the bounds for posterity. This book is about them, as well as about the achievements of some of our noblest statesmen like Jefferson and Madison, who helped create a system in which regularized restraints on government augment our freedom. Sometimes directly, sometimes indirectly, the pieces in this volume are meant to illumine the reasons that, in the words of Justice Robert Jackson, "If there is any fixed star in our constitutional constellation, it is that no official, high or petty, can prescribe what shall be orthodox in politics, nationalism, religion, or other matters of opinion or force citizens to confess by word or act their faith therein."

Claremont, California   Leonard W. Levy
April 1985

Acknowledgments

I am thankful for permission to reprint the following:

"Freedom of Speech in Seventeenth-Century Thought" first appeared in *History 4*, copyright 1961 by Meridian Books.

"John Lilburne and the Rights of Englishmen" derives from my book, *Origins of the Fifth Amendment: the Right Against Self-Discrimination*, copyright 1968 by Oxford University Press.

"Quaker Blasphemy and Toleration" originally appeared in my book, *Treason Against God: the Offense of Blasphemy*, copyright 1981 by Schocken Books.

"Did the Zenger Case Really Matter?" initially saw print in the *William and Mary Quarterly*, 3rd ser., Vol. XVII, Jan. 1960; the revised version in this volume includes material from my book, *Emergence of a Free Press*, copyright 1985 by Oxford University Press.

"Constitutional History, 1776–1789" was written for the *Encyclopedia of the American Constitution*, eds. L. W. Levy and K. L. Karst, to be published in 1987 by the Macmillan Publishing Co. Inc. and is printed here with the special permission of that publisher, which holds the copyright.

"The Bill of Rights" originally appeared in the *Encyclopedia of American Political History*, ed. Jack P. Greene, copyright 1984 by Charles Scribner's Sons.

"The Original Meaning of the Establishment Clause" was first published in my book, *Judgments: Essays on Constitutional History*, copyright 1971 by Quadrangle Books, which transferred the copyright to me. The version published here was revised with the assistance of Thomas Curry for publication in *Religion and the State: Essays in Honor of Leo Pfeffer*, ed. James E. Wood, Jr., copyright 1985 by Baylor University Press.

"Liberty and the First Amendment: 1790–1800" originally appeared in the *American Historical Review*, Vol. LXVIII, Oct. 1962. The *American Historical Review* transferred the copyright to me.

"Jefferson As A Civil Libertarian" derived from my book, *Jefferson and Civil Liberties*, whose copyright I own as a gift of Belknap Press of Harvard University Press. The essay originally appeared in *Thomas Jefferson*, ed. Lally Weymouth, copyright 1973 by G. P. Putnam's Sons and is reprinted here by special permission of The Putnam Publishing Group.

"History and Judicial History: the Case of the Fifth Amendment" first appeared as "The Right Against Self-Incrimination: History and Judicial History," *Political Science Quarterly*, LXXXV, March 1969, copyright by the Academy of Political Science, which transferred the copyright to me. A revised version of the essay appears here.

ACKNOWLEDGMENTS

"Judicial Activism and Strict Construction" comes from my book, *Against the Law: the Nixon Court and Criminal Justice*, copyright by Harper and Row, 1974. The publisher vested the copyright in me.

Finally, this is the place to acknowledge my gratitude to my editor, Sheldon Meyer, whose encouragement, counsel, and confidence helped make this book possible as well as *Origins of the Fifth Amendment* and *Emergence of a Free Press*.

Contents

CONSTITUTIONAL OPINIONS

I

Freedom of Speech in Seventeenth-Century Thought

BELIEF IN THE EXISTENCE of witches, the flatness of the earth, and the divine right of kings are among the fighting faiths that have been discarded in the free exchange of ideas. The thick integuments of ignorance and prejudice are sometimes penetrated by the titanic blows of the moralist, sometimes by the detached empiricism of the scientist. But the indispensable condition of progress has always been intellectual liberty. We owe our philosophy of intellectual liberty to the seventeenth century—to Milton, Spinoza, and Locke above all. They taught us that even the best-warranted beliefs must be continuously tested in the crucible of criticism to determine their continuing validity. They taught us too that reliance upon authority is a poor test of truth. A proposition should not be accepted because Milton advanced it, but because he was right—if indeed he was right. On some major libertarian issues, he and his fellow philosophers of the seventeenth century were not "right." Although the thrust of their thinking supports an ever-broadening principle of intellectual freedom, we should recognize that much that passed for wisdom in their time may very well have passed out of date. Their position was neither the most libertarian nor their insights the best in the realm of political and religious expression. For they believed that the established order could be criminally assaulted by mere opinions, words and words alone, as contrasted with deeds. Present-day libertarians should therefore understand that romanticized images of Milton or ritualized endorsements of Locke—or, for that matter, of Jefferson and John Stuart Mill—may boomerang. More important, they should realize that there is a continuing need to revitalize and expand the philosophy of freedom of political discussion. As an initial step in this direction, the noxious encumbrances that have been inherited from the seventeenth century's most libertarian spokesmen must be discarded, like the belief in witchcraft, as a product of antiquated prejudice, understandable in its time, perhaps, but never valid.

Historians of libertarian theory have, in Mrs. Malaprop's phrase, too often "anticipated the past." They have succumbed to an impulse to recreate it so that it will yield a message that instructs the present and supports an authoritative and progressively unfolding tradition of freedom. It is comforting, of course, to have the past's wisest philosophies coincide with modern libertarian convictions that we know to be right. But it is precarious to rest those convictions on a narrow historicism, particularly if the "history" is not well founded. A case in point is the usual stress on the intentions of the framers of the First Amendment to abolish the common law of seditious libel and to give the utmost protection to freedom of speech and press. A related way to fortify the argument from the past is to parade the grandiloquent utterances of the theorists of intellectual liberty—Milton, Spinoza, and Locke among others. But one's convictions should not be based on convention; moreover, there is a very real possibility that the convention—a reliance on seventeenth-century libertarians —has frailties that too often are glossed over.

Freedom of speech had very little history as a concept, or a practice, prior to the First Amendment. The phrase itself until the last quarter of the eighteenth century referred both in England and America primarily to a parliamentary, not a civil, right. It signified, in the main, the legislator's immunity from punishment for anything said by him in his official capacity during a legislative session, rather than the citizen's personal right to speak his mind. The phrase originated in Anglo-American history in the struggle of Parliament to achieve the privilege of free debate. It did not imply the right of the citizen to broadcast seditious libel.

Freedom of speech could not become a civil liberty until the truth of men's opinions, especially their religious and political opinions, was regarded as relative rather than absolute; until kings and parliaments were sufficiently strong and stable to be able to ignore political criticism; and until the people were considered the source of sovereignty, the masters rather than the servants of the government. There could be no toleration of dissent when Catholics, Anglicans, and Puritans were profoundly convinced that the precise shade of belief which each respectively professed must be established as England's only true religion and that all be compelled to accept it for their own salvation as well as for the good of God and of the English nation. Whether the government was Catholic or Protestant, Anglican or Puritan, the compulsion of conscience for the sake of uniformity necessitated restraints upon freedom of expression. Moreover, the Reformation, by making the monarch the head of the established church, had converted every religious question into a political one and suffused government policies with religious overtones. As a result, heresy and nonconformity became virtually indistinguishable from sedition and treason. Criticism of the Church affected the State, and vice versa. The danger ascribed to wrong opinions was particularly great for several centuries after the emergence of the national state, when the life of the monarch was in jeopardy and the peace and security of the state were precarious. Freedom of religious and political expression was feared as a means of triggering conspiracies, internal disorders, wars, or revolutions that might pull down Church and State. Since the bad tendency of wrong opinions had become so magnified by the invention of printing, preventative censorship by means of a system of licensing all printed matter was established. Anything published without an imprimatur was criminal, and to make doubly certain that loopholes in the licensing system were plugged, the common law of criminal libel was developed.

By far the most repressive class of libel was seditious libel. It can be defined in a quite elaborate and technical manner in order to take into account the malicious or criminal intent of the accused, the bad tendency of his remarks, and their truth or falsity. But the crime was never satisfactorily defined, the necessary result of its inherent vagueness. Seditious libel has always been an accordionlike concept. Judged by actual prosecutions, the crime consisted of criticizing the government; its form, constitution, officers, laws, symbols, conduct, and so on. In effect, any comment about the government which could be construed to have the bad tendency of lowering it in the public's esteem or of disturbing the peace was seditious libel, subjecting the speaker or writer to criminal prosecution.

The philosophic principle of freedom of the mind had merely a slight influence on the expansion of freedom of speech or press. Libertarian expositions were abundant enough, but in England and America until the very late eighteenth century their libertarian quality was nearly as narrow as the common law in crucial respects. The result was that freedom of discussion for the thought that was hated or feared had no advocates on either side of the Atlantic before the 1790's.

To be sure, one can go all the way back to the ancients, especially the Athenians and the Romans of the early republic, and discover a few statements favoring an undefined broad liberty of expression. The plays of Euripides, for example, are a storehouse of allusions to the glories and values of free speech. The hero of *Ion*, to cite an instance, hopes that his unknown mother may be Athenian so that "by my mother may free speech be mine," else he "bears a bondman's tongue"; and a passage between Jocasta and Polyneices, in *The Pheonissae*, demonstrates the Greek understanding that unwise government results from a curb on the tongues of citizens. To a Greek statesman, declared Demosthenes, no greater calamity could befall a people than "the privation of free speech." Yet there is no evidence that even the most libertarian among the Greeks suffered oral or written sedition to exist with impunity. Plato's account of the punishment of Socrates by the freedom-loving Athenians for the crime of subversive utterances is the best-known case of its kind in history. Machiavelli might have been echoing the ancients as well as representing the best thoughts of the Renaissance when he qualified the right of every man to "think all things, speak all things, write all things." He pointed out that popular governments are aspersed because the people are free to "speak ill" of them, whereas princes, though wise to allow the citizen a "liberty to have and sustain the opinions which please him best," must be "talked of with Reserve and Respect."

Spinoza went as far as anyone up to his time in advocating that the state should permit the utmost latitude for men to speak their minds. In his neglected classic, *Theologico-Political Treatise* (1670), he presented as profound and sustained an analysis of freedom of thought and speech as had been offered, climaxing his work with a concluding chapter entitled "That in a Free State Every Man May Think What He Likes, and Say What He Things." From the premise that man is "by indefeasible natural right the master of his own thoughts" and cannot abdicate his "freedom of judgment," Spinoza concluded that diverse and contradictory opinions were inevitable; to compel men "to speak only according to the dictates of supreme power" would be disastrous to the state as well as to the individual. Believing, however, that "authority may be as much injured by words as by actions," he opposed an "unlimited concession" of free speech. He recognized that the individual and social interest in freedom had to be weighed against authority's competing claims: "we must, therefore, now inquire, how far such freedom can and ought to be conceded without danger to the peace of the state, or the power of the rulers."

Spinoza believed in the right to speak against the state, provided that no attempt is made to introduce any change on private authority and provided that verbal opposition is grounded in reason rather than "fraud, anger, or hatred." Argument that a law is unsound and deserves repeal should be permitted, as should any speculation concerning philosophy, religion, science, or "the liberal arts," even though falsehoods may proceed from unworthy motives; the possibility of abuse, contended Spinoza, ought not to warrant limiting the right. That right to "freedom of speech" should be recognized by the wise ruler so that resistance to him might be legitimatized and lessened and "so that men may live together in harmony, however diverse, or even openly contradictory, their opinions may be." The state that punished opinions injured itself. Acts "which alone are capable of offending," rather than the "opinions of mankind," should be brought to trial; the rights of rulers, argued Spinoza, in secular and sacred matters "should merely have to do with actions, but that every man should think what he likes and say what he thinks."

On the other hand, these libertarian notions on the scope of free expression proceeded from a premise that was shared by Machiavelli and Hobbes: the sovereign power, Spinoza wrote, has the "right to treat as enemies all men whose opinions do not, on all subjects, entirely coincide with its own"; but, he added, he was discussing the "proper" course of action for the state to follow, not its rights. Properly, it should punish only politically injurious speech as was tantamount to a seditious act. All "opinions would be seditious . . . which by their very nature nullify the compact by which the right of free action was ceded." Stirring up the people against their rulers, counseling civil disobedience, advocating the enactment of laws by unconstituted authority, teaching that contracts ought not be kept or that everyone should live as he pleases: these were, for Spinoza, criminal libels, exceptions to his rule that overt acts, rather than mere words, were alone punishable. Thus even Spinoza, for all his tolerance, drew the line at seditious utterances.

The same may be said of an equally libertarian group, the English Levellers, "who represented the first great outburst of democratic thought in history, with John Lillburne and Richard Overton leading the way." Almost any Leveller tract of the 1640's contained a passage condemning censorship and the licensing system, with an argument that freedom of speech and press were essential to the establishment of free government and personal liberty. "A Remonstrance of Many Thousand Citizens" (1646) asked Parliament to proclaim its legislative plans prior to enactment and to "heare all things that can be spoken with or against the same, and to that intent, let the imprisoned Presses at liberty, so that all mens understandings may be more conveniently informed. . . ." "The Humble Petition" of 1649, Overton's work in all likelihood, argued that when men's mouths were "kept from making noise" they are "robd of their liberties," truth suppressed, and the people kept ignorant and fit only to serve the unjust ends of tyrants. A free press was "essential unto Freedom" to prevent the nation from being placed in bondage, "for what may be done to that people who may not speak or write, but at the pleasure of Licensers." The government must "hear all voices and judgements" by removing the "least restraint upon the Press," for the people could not enjoy liberty without "speaking, writing, printing, and publishing their minds freely. . . ."

Despite such principled statements, there were moments when even Levellers advocated a more systematic enforcement of the licensing system—so long as it was not aimed at them. In *Englands Birth-Right* (1645), Lilburne himself, after criticizing press restraints and unlawful search and seizure of unlicensed Leveller material, complained of the freedom allowed to royalist publications and other "Malignant Books and Pamphlets tending to the ruine of the Kingdome . . . and freedome of People." Samuel Chidley, in a pamphlet attacking Lilburne's opponents, requested Parliament "to silence such Babblers . . ." and added: "I hold it one of the greatest abuses of the Commonwealth, that so many lying foolish Pamphlets have been, and are suffered to go abroad . . ."

William Walwyn, who has been called "the most consistently radical thinker among the Levellers," wrote a series of magnificent tracts on behalf of "the freedome of minde," liberty of conscience, and "freedome of discourse." At one point he went so far as to reject the bad-tendency test by arguing that criminal deeds alone should be punishable, but not expression. Yet even Walwyn confessed inconsistently, that words which were "scandalous, or dangerous to the State" had "upon good grounds" been prohibited by Parliament. In *The Compassionate Samaritane* (1645), he wrote, for example, in reference to "liberty of Conscience," which he thought the right of every man, that no one should be "punished or discountenanced by Authority for his Opinion, unless it be dangerous to the State," and he placed the identical restriction upon "the Presse."

Several Independent tractarians went as far, but no further, than their Leveller contemporaries in expanding the bounds of free expression. Roger Williams, for example, in his celebrated defense of toleration, *The Bloudy Tenent, of Persecution, for Cause of Conscience* (1644), exempted from the civil magistrate's jurisdiction all concernments of conscience, even "scandalous" doctrines in opposition to the establishment, but he broke into his argument to note parenthetically, "I speak not of scandal against the civil state, which the civil magistrate ought to punish. . . ." Henry Robinson, in his superb discussion *Liberty of Conscience*, was one of the rare writers to confront the problem of free expression for Roman Catholics without betraying his principles. When he contended that force or compulsion of any kind had no place in matters of religion and that reason and argument were the only allowable weapons, he expressly included "Papists, Jewes, Turkes, Pagans, Hereticks, with all Infidels & Misbeleevers." Religious "combat" was to be "fought out upon eaven ground, on equal terms, neither side must expect to have greater liberty of speech, writing, Printing, or whatsoever else, then the other." All men without exception were to have the "same privilege . . . to deliver their mindes freely both in speech and writing." Yet, Robinson defended an equal right of speech and press only in the context of an argument for freedom of religion. There is no evidence that he differed from Roger Williams or William Walwyn, no evidence, that is, that he countenanced any expressions scandalizing the government or that his tolerance of sectarian controversy extended to exclusively secular, particularly state, matters.

John Milton, at least in his famous *Areopagitica*, had a secularist approach to the problem of liberty of inquiry and expression, when compared to Robinson, Walwyn, and Williams. Milton, of course, is traditionally regarded as the great apostle of the free mind. Unquestionably, several passages of the *Areopagitica*, which are ritualistically quoted to the exclusion of all else, carry implications of majestic breadth, but no one who reads him with care should refer—as does Zechariah Chafee, Jr.—to Milton's "dream of free speech for everybody. . . .' Milton might cry out, "Give *me* liberty to know, to utter, and to argue freely according to conscience, above all liberties," but his use of the personal pronoun is significant, for his well-advertised tolerance did not extend to the thought that he hated. Indeed, it extended only, as he specified, to "neighboring differences, or rather indifferences," which in 1644 meant Protestantism in a variety of Puritan forms. He specifically excluded from his spectrum of neighboring opinions "Popery, and open superstition," which he thought "should be extirpat," and he banned also the "impious or evil" which "no law can possibly permit. . . ."

In a recent volume of essays littered with encomiums on Milton as the father of modern intellectual liberty, two contributions stand out as the only realistic appraisals. Salvador de Madariaga noted that as late as 1673 Milton was

> still putting forth authority, and not merely authority but Bible authority, as the standard of truth. . . . I believe that it is dangerous to listen to one who claims freedom of thought in the name of an orthodoxy. . . . There is yet another standard, the willingness to grant to others that freedom of thought that you want for yourself; and from that point of view I am not certain Milton satisfies us. Indeed, I am tempted to think he did not.

The very Reverend W. R. Matthews, Dean of St. Paul's, referring to the exaggerated notion of Milton's libertarianism held by those who have not recently read his book, pointed out that he "did not support freedom of religious debate for Catholics, Anglicans, Atheists or non-Christians," and concluded: "it is clear that Milton himself would have excluded not only the overwhelming majority of Christians but the greater part of the human race from the benefit of his tolerance." This Anglican statement is somewhat exaggerated, since Milton later transcended his Puritanism to encompass Anglicans in a proposed united front of all Protestants against Catholics. Yet the thrust of the exaggeration is in the right direction. Dean Matthews possibly had in mind the fact that the royalist writings which Milton deplored as a "court-libell against the Parlament" were Anglican in character. Milton thought that royalist writings should be censored, pointing out that if the licensing system had any justification, it would be in the performance of the "prime service" of preventing the circulation of such material. Milton did not, in other words, even oppose the licensing system unequivocally, despite his affirmation that free and humane government results only from "free writing and free speaking. . . .' Except for his criticism of royalist weeklies, he did not even interest himself in one of the chief issues in the controversy over freedom of the press at the time of the *Areopagitica*: the freedom of polemical news-writers. His silence on this issue helps explain the fact that in 1651 he was one of Cromwell's licensers or censors—despite his earlier and eloquent denunciation of such officials—since the works that came before him for his imprimatur were corontos or news books, partisan sheets of current news. In all likelihood Milton never intended that anything but the serious works of intellectuals, chiefly scholars and Protestant divines, should be really free. A later essay revealed the point rather explicitly when he noted that if open expression was feared because it might "unsettle the weaker sort," Latin, "which the common people understand not," would be a solution for having issues "discust among the Learned only."

In *A Treatise of Civil Power in Ecclesiastical Causes* (1659) Milton explicitly reserved the right of "a free and lawful debate" to all Protestants, thereby allowing even Anabaptists and Socinians on the left and Anglicans on the right to enjoy a privilege previously the prerogative of Puritanism only. But the "papist," whom Milton characterized as the "only heretic," was barred from participation, though not necessarily on religious grounds. Catholicism he thought to be less a religion than "a Roman principalitie . . . justly therefore to be suspected, not tolerated by the magistrate of another countrey." Although "just reason of state" may have been an understandable ground for restrictions on Catholic teaching and practice, at a time when the security of the government depended upon the maintenance of Protestant supremacy, Milton cut himself off from even this rationalization for intolerance. In 1673, in his tract *"Of True Religion, Heresie, Schism, and Toleration,* he wrote:

> As for tolerating the exercise of their [Catholic] Religion, supposing their State activities not to be dangerous, I answer, that Toleration is either public or private; and the exercise of their Religion, as far as it is Idolatrous, can be tolerated neither way; not publicly, without grievous and unsufferable scandal giv'n to all consciencious Beholders; not privately, without great offence to God, declar'd against all Idolatry, though secret. . . .

Having shown thus, that Popery, as being Idolatrous, is not to be tolerated either in Public or in Private; it must be now thought how to remove it and hinder the growth thereof, I mean in our Natives. . . . Are we to punish them by corporal punishments, or fines in their Estates, upon account of their Religion? I suppose it stands not with the Clemency of the Gospel, more then what appertains to the security of the State: But first we must remove their Idolatry, and all the furniture thereof, whether Idols, or the Mass wherein they adore their God under Bread and Wine: for the Commandment forbids to adore. . . . If they say that by removing their Idols we violate their Consciences, we have no warrant to regard Conscience which is not grounded on Scripture. . . .

These constricted views of freedom of religion influenced Milton's thought on freedom of speech and press. Writing at a time when his party was out of power and Catholic literature was being licensed under the Restoration, he complained of having to "suffer the Idolatrous books of Papists" and recommended against a policy of open debate with them. "Shall we condescend to dispute with them?" he asked and answered emphatically, "*we are not to dispute*." He appealed to all Protestants to join "on common ground against Popery," and to that end he pleaded the case of civil liberty—for Protestants only. Can one who based his religion exclusively on the Scriptures refuse with equity "to hear or read him, who demonstrates to have gained his knowledge by the same way? is it a fair course to assert truth by arrogating to himself the only freedom of speech, and stopping the mouths of others equally gifted?" In context, Milton's question demonstrates his limited support of free speech. Perhaps his narrow conception of intellectual liberty is best revealed by his own recommendation for the policy to be followed on press freedom. In the concluding section of the *Areopagitica* he endorsed a system of unlicensed printing, conditioned only upon the registration of all printers and authors; but he reserved the law of subsequent punishment for any abuse or licentiousness of the press: "Those which otherwise come forth, if they be found mischievous and libellous, the fire and the executioner will be the timeliest and the most effectuall remedy that mans prevention can use."

To Americans of the Framers' generation, Milton's reputation as a libertarian was rivaled only by John Locke's. In his *Essay Concerning Human Understanding*, Locke added a new dimension to the arguments for civil liberty. His predecessors had grounded their positions on the tyranny and futility of suppression, the morality of fairness and tolerance, the self-interest of sectarianism, the dictates of the Scriptures, the needs of scholarship and of Protestantism, and the certainty that truth would best falsehood in an open encounter. Although Locke employed these arguments too, he relied mainly on the contention that the mind is so frail, its understanding so limited, its beliefs so involuntary, that truth is inaccessible to it. All men, he admonished, ought to be skeptical of the validity of their own opinions, since they cannot know they are right and might very likely be in error. Opinions held with the "greatest stiffness" are more often than not the results of human incapacity—faulty judgment, prejudice, failure to examine one's own presuppositions, the inability to discover and use proofs, susceptibility to passion, and irrational habits of thought. Since men are forced to operate in a "twilight zone" of knowledge, whose truth and certainty is "scanty," it would be wisest, he wrote, for all

> to maintain peace and the common offices of humanity and friendship in the diversity of opinions. . . . We should do well to commiserate our mutual ignorance, and endeavour to remove it in all the gentle and fair ways of information, and not instantly treat others ill as obstinate and perverse because they will not renounce their own and receive our opinions, or at least those we would force upon them, when it is more probable that we are no less obstinate in not embracing some of theirs. For where is the man that has uncontestable evidence of the truth of all that he holds, or of the falsehood of all he condemns; or can say, that he has examined to the bottom all his own or other men's opinions? The necessity of believing without knowledge, nay, often upon very slight grounds, in this fleeting state of action and blindness we are in, should make us more busy and careful to inform ourselves than contain others.

Despite his elaborate analysis of the formation and nature of opinion, Locke as philosopher-psychologist did no more than endorse in principle toleration for diversity of opinions. He evinced sustained interest in the problems of freedom of expression only in connection with his preoccupation for protecting liberty of conscience, the subject of his four *Letters on Toleration*. Since he addressed himself mainly to freedom for sectarian rather than secular expression, his claim of writing in behalf of "ABSOLUTE LIBERTY" was overstated and even unjustifiable, considering the notable exceptions he made to principles that he supported in general. He could observe that the "opinions" of Catholics on Mass and of Jews on the New Testament, even though "false and absurd," were entitled to freedom because the business of the laws is to provide not for the truth of opinions but the safety of the Commonwealth as well as of every individual's goods and person. But he also believed that "no opinions contrary to human society, or to those moral rules which are necessary to the preservation of civil society, are to be tolerated by the magistrate."

Advocating that the intolerant should not be tolerated, Locke proposed punishment of any who "will not own and teach the duty of tolerating all men in matters of mere religion." In line with this view was a provision of the "Fundamental Constitutions of Carolina," which he framed, outlawing reproachful or abusive language of any religion as a disturbance of the peace. In an obvious reference to Roman Catholicism, he recommended prosecution of that church which taught that "faith is not to be kept with heretics." There was no inconsistency here with his thesis that the jurisdiction of the civil magistrate did not reach to religious belief or practice, since he affirmed that a right ended at the point that it prejudiced others, violated their rights, or jeopardized the peace of the state.

Locke, like Spinoza, would also punish those who taught that oaths and contracts were not binding, or that loyalty was not due to the ruler; and like Milton he regarded the opinions of atheists and the political implications of Catholic doctrine as seditious. He believed that the sanctions of the law should be invoked against the members of any church who arrogated to themselves the power of deposing kings or who professed doctrinal allegiance to another prince; for, he asked, did not their "doctrines signify, but that they may, and are ready upon any occasion to seize the government, and possess themselves of the estates and fortunes of their fellow-subjects; and that they only ask leave to be tolerated by the magistrates so long, until they find themselves strong enough to effect it?" The statement, although an allusion to the relations between English Catholics and the Vatican, applied in principle to persons of any party that advocated, even by tenuous implication, the overthrow of the government or whose opinions could be suspected of disloyalty.

Locke, in other words, drew a line at seditious utterances. At no point did he, nor did any of his libertarian precursors among the Levellers or Independents, criticize the common law of seditious libel. Indeed, he went out of his way, in the midst of an argument for complete liberty of conscience, to declare that if any person under color of freely exercising his religion, might behave "seditiously, and contrary to the public peace," he was punishable "in the same manner, and not otherwise than as if it had happened in a fair or market." That Locke meant mere verbal sedition, as well as overt action, is unquestionable, since he distinguished between peaceable and criminal "doctrine," and he listed slanderers, as well as the seditious, with thieves, murderers, and adulterers as deserving to be "suppressed." Moreover, one provision of his "Fundamental Constitutions of Carolina" stated: "No person whatsoever shall speak anything in their religious assembly irreverently or seditiously of the government or governors, or of state matters." The same constitution, incidentally, guaranteed freedom for "speculative opinions in religion," but was silent as to political opinions. A variety of personal rights were protected, but not speech or press.

Locke did not even defend a general freedom of expression when he lent his enormous prestige to those who successfully opposed re-enactment of the Licensing Act. In 1694 he drafted for the House of Commons a statement of eighteen reasons for ending the system of preventative censorship, not one a principled defense of liberty of the press nor a philosophical argument for the free mind. Locke argued that the lack of free competition injured the printing trades; that the Licensing Act was too vague and administratively unworkable; and that it was unnecessary, since the common law adequately protected against licentiousness. On these grounds of expediency, prior restraints died in England.

To suggest that Spinoza and Locke, or even Milton, were enemies of the free mind would be absurd; they were indubitably the most eminent defenders of civil liberty in their time. But they were *of* their time, and one of its a priori premises, unthinkable for anyone to attack, was the state's incontestable right to proscribe sedition—a commodious concept encompassing anything from mild criticism of public policy to attempted overthrow of the government. Neither Locke, Milton, nor their contemporaries ever indicated disagreement with the common law's spacious definition of unlawful discourse nor sought to limit its application. Subsequent generations of libertarians inherited from them and passed on to the American Framers in unaltered form an unbridled passion for a bridled liberty of speech. But the American Framers, however inconsistently, also inherited the principle of free speech to which they gave bold and unqualified constitutional recognition. It was the principle itself, not its originators' limiting glosses upon it nor its Framers' narrow understanding of it, that was meant to endure.

2

John Lilburne and the Rights
of Englishmen

LATE IN 1637 PURSUIVANTS of the High Commission arrested a young Puritan
named John Lilburne. He proved to be, by any standard, the most remarkable
person connected with the history of the origins of the right against self-
incrimination. Lilburne focussed the attention of the whole of England on the
injustice of forcing a man to be the means of his own undoing. His sensational
case was the immediate reason for the abolition of the oath *ex officio* and of the
courts which utilized it. In extraordinary abundance—everything about him
was extraordinary—Lilburne had an incomparable ability to dramatize himself
and his cause. He was a principled agitator with an incurably inflamed sense of
injustice which he knew how to communicate vividly to an audience.

Had Lilburne been the creation of some novelist's imagination, one might
scoff at so far-fetched a character. He was, or became, a radical in everything—
in religion, in politics, in economics, in social reform, in criminal justice—and
his ideas were far ahead of his time. From 1637 when he was but twenty-three
years old, a mere clothier's apprentice whose formal education had ended when
he was no more than fifteen, until his death twenty years later, he managed to
keep his government in a hectic state. In successive order he defied king,
parliament, and protectorate, challenging each with libertarian principles.
While others supported civil liberties to gain their own freedom and denied it to
their enemies, Lilburne grew more and more consistent in his devotion to the
fundamentals of liberty, and he was an incandescent advocate. Standing trial for
his life four times, he spent most of his adult years in prison and died in
banishment. Yet he could easily have had positions of high preferment if he had
thrown in his lot with Parliament or Cromwell. Instead, he sacrificed everything
in order to be free to attack injustice from any source. He once accurately
described himself as "an honest true-bred, freeborn Englishman that never in his
life loved a tyrant nor feared an oppressor." In his own days he was known as
Freeborn John because of his insistent references to the rights of every freeborn
Englishman.

Such men as Lilburne who make civil disobedience a way of life are

14

admirable but quite impossible. He was far too demanding and uncompromising, never yielding an inch of his ideals. He was obstreperous, fearless, indomitable, and cantankerous, one of the most flinty, contentious men who ever lived. As one of his contemporaries said, if John Lilburne were the last man in the world, John would fight with Lilburne and Lilburne with John. That trait helps explain his strength, but he was also a master of the arts of propaganda. He could convince and inspire his followers or confound his enemies with equal ease. No one in England could outtalk him, no one was a greater political pamphleteer. Lilburne, who was to become the leader of the Levellers, was the catalytic agent in the history of the right against self-incrimination. He appeared at the right moment in history.[1]

Lilburne's first offense was shipping seditious books into England from Holland, including several thousand copies of a pamphlet by Dr. Bastwick. On an order from the Privy Council, the case was turned over to Sir John Banks, the Attorney-General, for prosecution. Lilburne's guilt seemed certain, because two of his confederates had accused him in order to save themselves. One of them had made his accusation by sworn affidavit, naming Lilburne and John Wharton, an elderly book-dealer, as violators of the Star Chamber decree against importing unlicensed books. All that was needed were the confessions of Lilburne and Wharton. The Attorney-General's chief clerk examined Lilburne, who admitted only that he had been to Holland and had seen certain books and men there. Lilburne demanded to know the reason for questions which did not seem relevant to the cause of his imprisonment. "I am not imprisoned for knowing and talking with such and such men, but for sending over Books; and therefore I am not willing to answer you to any more of these questions, because I see you go about by this Examination to ensnare me: for seeing the things for which I am imprisoned cannot be proved against me, you will get other matter out of my examination." As for the charge against him, which the clerk clearly stated, he was innocent, he said, for he had sent no books from Holland to England (most likely a lie). Let his accusers be brought before him to accuse him face to face. Till then he would say nothing except that he would answer no "impertinent questions, for fear that with my answer I may do myself hurt." Lilburne at this stage had claimed a right "by the law of the land" to remain silent only to incriminating interrogatories that were not, in his opinion, germane to the charge. The charge itself he denied. The clerk revealed the specifics of the sworn affidavit against him, but he dismissed them as lies. The threat that he could be forced to answer left him unruffled. The clerk brought him to Attorney-General Banks who got no more from him.[2]

After holding him in jail for nearly two weeks, Banks sent Lilburne to the Court of Star Chamber, but failed to provide him with a bill of complaint setting forth the charges. The procedure followed in Lilburne's case was quite irregular; in "state" or "extraordinary" cases, the court was free to proceed at discretion. Ordinarily the crime was described in writing for the accused "with convenient certainty of the time, place, and person." He then took an oath truthfully to answer both the charges and any interrogatories that might subsequently be addressed to him. But he had ample time to answer in writing, initially with the advice of counsel. Of, if there was probable cause to think him guilty of a crime likely "to endanger the very fabric of the government," the court followed what William Hudson (*circa* 1636) called "an extraordinary kind of proceeding, more short and expeditious, which is called *ore tenus*"—an oral examination whose purpose was to elicit a quick confession. Some, said Hudson, censured that course of procedure "as seeming to oppose the Great Charter" because it bypassed all judicial proceeding, bill of complaint, and liberty to consult counsel. But there were supposed to be safeguards even in such a summary procedure. If the case involved a felony, "*nemo tenetur prodere seipsum*, but upon voluntary confession without oath." Neither oath "nor any compulsory means" was supposed to be used in an *ore tenus* proceeding on the theory that the confession must be strictly voluntary. If the accused denied the accusation, the court was supposed to proceed against him by bill of complaint and witnesses; should he confess but later repudiate the confession, even if he had signed it and members of the Privy Council testified to that fact, "so strictly held" was the rule of voluntariness that the court was supposed to proceed as if he had denied the accusation. The strange thing about Lilburne's case was the court's mixed procedure; there was no bill presented to him and no allowance of counsel, yet they demanded that he take the oath.[3]

The Star Chamber was following High Commission procedure, and Lilburne would have none of it. Several clerks examined him first. They tendered him a Bible and told him to swear.

"To what?"
"That you shall make true answer to all things that are asked of you."
"Must I do sir? but before I swear, I will know to what I must swear."
"As soon as you have sworn, you shall, but not before."

Lilburne persisted in his refusal to take the oath, fearing that they "went about to make me betray my own innocency, that so they might ground the bill upon my own words." Attorney-General Banks ordered Lilburne returned to prison.[4]

About two months after his capture, Lilburne was brought to trial before the Star Chamber, together with his accomplice, the book dealer John Wharton. Wharton, who was in his eighties, was a veteran of the Puritan wars against the High Commission; he had been imprisoned, according to his own testimony, no less than eight times for refusing the oath *ex officio*. He could quote both Sir Edward Coke and Archbishop Whitgift's Hampton Court statement against the oath. Lilburne, who was examined first, proved himself worthy of Wharton's company. Attorney-General Banks opened the proceeding against the prisoners with a verbal accusation that they had refused the oath, and then he read the affidavit of their confessed confederate who had turned state's evidence. On the principal charge, according to Lilburne's account, there was no discussion whatever beyond his simple allegation that the affidavit "is a most false lye and untrue." The Star Chamber appeared to be interested only in the fact that the prisoners would not swear the Star Chamber oath. Many men had refused the

High Commission oath, but refusal of the Star Chamber oath was rare if not unique because the requirement of swearing normally followed, rather than preceded, presentment by bill of complaint. The affidavit in this case may have served as a substitute for a bill, but it didn't satisfy Lilburne who wrote that he had refused "that which had never been refused before." He stated his reasons once again before the Lords of the Star Chamber, and Wharton followed his example. The court, failing to persuade them to change their minds, returned them to prison in solitary confinement.[5]

A week later, the two were brought again before the court. Lilburne claimed that the oath was "one and the same with the High Commission oath, which Oath I know to be both against the law of God, and the law of the land. . . ." Yet he knew his accuser and the charges against him. On his second appearance before the Star Chamber, they read aloud a second affidavit from his accuser, filled with more detail than the first. Lilburne continued to deny the accusation, yet would not deny it under oath. Nor would Wharton. Both tried to lecture the court on the immorality and unlawfulness of the oath *ex officio*. The court answered not by finding them *pro confesso* on the charges, but by finding them guilty of contempt for refusal to answer interrogatories under oath. "I was condemned," wrote Lilburne, "because I would not accuse myself." The court sentenced them to a five-hundred pound fine, punishment in the pillory, and imprisonment until they conformed themselves by taking the oath. In addition, Lilburne was to be whipped through the streets on the way from Fleet prison to the pillory.[6]

On April 18, 1638, the sentence of corporal punishment was carried out on Lilburne. Although he was almost beaten to death, he put on such a spirited show of defiance that he became famous overnight. The torturous two-mile walk from the Fleet to the pillory was a religious pilgrimage for him and many onlookers. People lined the streets to watch the spectacle, moaning as they thrilled to his beating and spiritual exaltation. Tied to the back of a cart and stripped to the waist, he was lashed every few steps with a three-thonged whip tied full of knots. Lilburne later estimated that he had been whipped at least two hundred strokes; an eye witness who walked the route swore that the number was not less than five hundred. Lilburne's shoulders "were swelled almost as big as a penny-loaf" and the "wales in his back . . . were bigger than tobacco-pipes." A "multitude" of people thronged about the pillory, shouting words of encouragement. The hole for his neck was so low that he was forced to stand stooped over, unprotected from an "exceedingly hot" sun. Despite his pain, Lilburne addressed the sympathetic crowd, rejoicing in his role as a Christian martyr. "I own and embrace" the pillory, he said, "as the welcome Cross of Christ, and as a badge of my Christian Profession." He spoke for about half an hour, reportedly keeping his audience spell-bound. It is almost beyond belief that anyone could have had the strength to do that after such a terrible beating, or that the authorities should have permitted him to stir up the crowd. He told them in detail the story of his trial and the reason for his suffering. Paul had found more mercy from the heathen Roman governors, for they had not put him to an oath to accuse himself. Lilburne described the "inquisition Oath" which he had refused as sinful and illegal, "it being the High-Commission oath, with which the prelates ever have, and still do, so butcherly torment, afflict and undo, the dear saints and servants of God. It is an oath against the law of the land (as Mr. Nicholas Fuller in his Argument doth prove): And also it is expressly against the Petition of Right . . . Again, it is absolutely against the law of God; for that law requires no man to accuse himself. . . ." On and on he went, condemning the oath. And then he launched into a long tirade against the prelates, pulling from his pocket three copies of Dr. Bastwick's book and throwing them to his fascinated listeners. "There," he cried, "is part of the Books for which I suffer, take them among you, and read them, and see if you find anything in them against the law of God. . . ."[7]

Lilburne's speech was interrupted at last by the Warden of the Fleet who commanded his silence. The martyr could not be intimidated, answering that he would declare his cause though he were to be hanged for it. The warden then ordered him gagged to shut him up, and they did it so cruelly, reported an eye witness, that it seemed as if they "would have torn his jaws in pieces." He bled profusely from the mouth. After Lilburne had been in the pillory for another hour and a half, he was taken back to prison. That same day the Star Chamber, on the report of the Warden of the Fleet, issued a new order to punish Lilburne for his behavior in the pillory. He was to be "laid alone with irons on his hands and legs" in the part of the prison "where the basest and meanest sort" were kept and be denied visitors, books, and writing materials. His physician later testified that he was "again and again" denied access to him, and when finally admitted found him "in an extreme violent fever . . . to the extreme hazard of his life." They kept him in a dungeon, chained and without a bed, for five weeks, and for the first ten days starved him. But for food smuggled through floor boards by his fellow prisoners, Lilburne would have perished. He claimed that his religion had sustained him through his terrible ordeal. After about four months he was released from solitary confinement and his prison conditions improved.[8]

He managed to smuggle out accounts telling the world how he had suffered for the sake of conscience because he would not accuse himself. The Star Chamber inexplicably seemed powerless to prevent him from writing his pamphlets or to locate the secret press that published them. Of the ninety-odd pamphlets that he published during his career, nine were written during his first imprisonment, which lasted almost three years. Aiming at the prelates, Anglo-Catholicism, the High Commission, and the Star Chamber, Lilburne helped bring a pustule of discontent to a head. Lord Clarendon, in his contemporary account, declared that Lilburne "afterwards confessed, in the melancholy of his imprisonment, and by reading the book of Martyrs, he raised in himself a marvellous inclination and appetite to suffer in the defence or for the vindication of any oppressed truth. . . ."[9]

. . .

The Long Parliament, dominated by Puritans and common lawyers, met on

November 3, determined to free victims of oppression, punish their oppressors, and institute reforms in church and state. Six days after the opening of Parliament, Oliver Cromwell, one of the new members from Cambridge, made his maiden speech on behalf of liberty for John Lilburne. A few days later he and other prisoners were set free. . . . On July 5, 1641, the king reluctantly assented to bills wholly abolishing the Courts of High Commission and Star Chamber.[10]

The act against the Star Chamber began with a recitation of chapter twenty-nine of Magna Carta and four thirteenth-century reconfirmations that endorsed common-law procedure as the only procedure when life, liberty, or property were at stake. Star Chamber proceedings and censures, said the act, had been found by long experience to be an intolerable burden on subjects and "the means to introduce an arbitrary power and government." Therefore it was enacted that that court be "absolutely dissolved," all trials to be determined "in the ordinary Courts of Justice and by the ordinary course of the law."[11]

The act against the Court of High Commission announced that the ecclesiastical judges, in accordance with royal letters patent, had fined, imprisoned, and exercised other authority not warranted by the Act of Supremacy, to the great oppression of the subjects—thus vindicating at last the theory of Coke and the common lawyers. Accordingly, Parliament abolished the High Commission. Moreover, the statute made it a criminal offense for any person exercising ecclesiastical jurisdiction to fine or imprison, or to force any person to take "any corporal oath, whereby he or she shall or may be charged or obliged to make any presentment of any crime or offence, or to confess or to accuse him or herself of any crime, offence, delinquency or misdemeanour, or any neglect or thing whereby, or by reason whereof, he or she shall or may be liable or exposed to any censure, pain, penalty or punishment whatsoever. . . ."[12]

Thus, finally, was abolished the oath *ex officio*, and the right against compulsory self-incrimination was established—but only in the ecclesiastical courts. A great victory had been won, but it in no way touched criminal procedure in the common-law courts. They employed no oath, of course, yet in the preliminary examination prior to indictment and arraignment, it was still ordinary practice to press a suspect to confess his guilt; and in the prosecution of an accused person before a jury, his interrogation was still the focal point of the trial, the objective to trap him into damaging admissions. Yet the common law was like a glass house whose residents—judges, lawyers, parliamentarians, and Puritan defendants alike—had been throwing a rock, the *nemo tenetur* doctrine, at the enemy: there had to be an impact. The common law had always regarded torture as illegal when its purpose was to extort a confession; it had long accepted the abstract principle that no man should be forced to incriminate himself. Chief Justice Hyde's remark in Fitz-Patrick's case in 1631 was an indication of that fact. But the principle and the practice were at considerable variance. There was not yet any recognition of the fact that refusal to answer an incriminating question did not imply guilt. The presumption of innocence had no real operation. Until there was respect in the courtroom for the claim that one had a right, enforceable by the court, not to incriminate himself, that right could not be said to exist.[13]

Sir James Fitzjames Stephen observed that after 1640 "the whole spirit and temper of the criminal courts, even in their most irregular and revolutionary proceedings, appears to have been radically changed from what it had been in the preceding century to what it is in our own days." In every case, he said, the accused had the witnesses produced against him and was allowed not only to cross-examine them, but to call witnesses of his own. "In some cases the prisoner was questioned, but never to any greater extent than that which it is practically impossible to avoid when a man has to defend himself without counsel. When so questioned, the prisoners usually refused to answer." These great changes, Stephen added, took place "spontaneously," without legislative enactment, and prevailed even in the political trials of the Restoration period. Stephen's view was generous. Criminal procedure undoubtedly became fairer before the Restoration, but the habit of addressing incriminating interrogatories to the defendant persisted. Without counsel he had to conduct his own defense, responding in some way, if he valued his life, to the accusations against him. Although the defendant could cross-examine the prosecution's witnesses, he could call his own only with the court's permission, and he could not subpoena their attendance nor have them testify under oath.[14]

Only the crown had a right to subpoena witnesses and take their testimony under oath. Sworn testimony was a privilege, for it added immeasurably to the credibility of the witness. Indeed, because sworn testimony was so highly regarded the accused himself was not permitted to testify under oath even if he wanted to. That the common law did not put him to oath, therefore, reflected at least in part an unfairness toward him. It prevented him from virtually exonerating himself by taking what in effect was a purgative oath. Much of the seventeenth century's praise of the common law for not putting the defendant to oath was somewhat misleading, unless it is understood that the oath referred to was the oath *ex officio*, that is, an oath to tell the truth *before* knowing the charges and accusers. But an oath to tell the truth after common-law indictment, could have been an advantage to the defendant and, it was thought, a great temptation to perjury. To a religious person, for whom an oath was sacred, as it was intended to be, an oath to tell the truth, even after he knew the charges and the identity of his accusers, put him in a terrible dilemma if he had in fact done the thing charged. The deed might be purely meritorious in his mind yet criminal as a matter of law, making the temptation to sin all the greater—and perjury was originally a sin. In the seventeenth century men did not take oaths lightly. That is why Lilburne, for example, a devout believer, though knowing the charges and his accusers, refused to make his denial under oath. And that is why he and his precursors, from Lambert to Cartwright, claimed that they should not be forced to testify against themselves. They had no choice, for their beliefs and actions were deemed criminal. As long as religious and political freedom did not exist, as long, that is, as there were crimes like nonconformity and seditious libel, men would have to claim in self-defense a right not to incriminate themselves. That right was a product of religious and political persecution. Like all rights associated with fair criminal procedure, it had to be fought for unceasingly. It did not develop "spontaneously," nor did any of the other rights that cluster around the concept of due process in criminal justice. Lilburne's later trials made that fact abundantly clear.[15]

· · ·

Lilburne had risen in the world after his release from prison. His pen and his persecution had brought him fame, and he was honored for both. The Commons voted his sentence to have been "illegal and against the liberty of the subject," and "bloody, wicked, cruel, barbarous and tyrannical" as well. Lilburne was filled with devotion to the parliamentary cause. When the civil war broke out between royalist and parliamentary forces, he enlisted as a captain. Captured in action, he was held a prisoner in chains, tried for treason, and sentenced to death. Parliament sent word that if Lilburne were executed, royalist prisoners would meet the same fate. He was reprieved and eventually freed in an exchange of prisoners; on his return to London, crowds greeted him, said Lord Clarendon, "with public joy, as a champion that had defied the King in his own court." He turned down a lucrative government post, saying that he would "rather fight for eightpence a day, till he saw the liberties and peace of England settled, than set him down in a rich place for his own advantage. . . ." He became a confidant of Cromwell, returned to the front, and rose to a lieutenant-colonelcy. As time passed, however, Lilburne became increasingly disillusioned with the parliamentary program, and in the spring of 1645 he resigned from the army, exchanging his sword for his pen.[16]

Puritanism, once a predominately moderate movement to reform the English church from within, had been pushed steadily toward radicalism by the pressure of persecution, war, and revolution. Presbyterianism of the sort once advocated by Cartwright and in control of Scotland had become ascendant in England, dominating the Commons. The Presbyterians favored the establishment of a new state religion, their own, in place of Anglicanism. Their impulse to coerce conformity was even more intense than that of the Laudian church; their bigotry extended not only to the Catholics and Anglicans but even to the hodge-podge of dissenting sects that had mushroomed within the Puritan movement. But the Presbyterians, though a marjority in Parliament, were divided on the question whether the state church, which they all wanted, should be controlled by Parliament or by the ministers and elders. Parliament itself was Erastian as well as Presbyterian, refusing to yield its supremacy on matters of religion. Its secular leaders were not only jealous of their own prerogatives; they understood better than the Presbyterian ministry the dangers of a policy of extreme coercion, for the highly individualistic sects were the backbone of the army.

The Puritan opponents of the Presbyterians were all known at first as the Independents, but they gradually fragmented into a center group, commanded by Cromwell, and numerous petty factions or "sectaries." Cromwell's group was not hostile to a Presbyterian establishment on condition that a large degree of toleration existed for other religions, Catholicism excepted. The rank and file of the army, where the sectaries were strongest, was as intolerant of Catholicism but fearful of any state establishment. Substantially Calvinistic in theology, like the dominant Presbyterian party, the sectaries were united in their opposition to any coercion of conscience (Protestant) and in their belief in the self-governance of each separate congregation. Largely in self-defense they were moving rapidly toward espousal of the principles of religious liberty and separation of church and state.

John Lilburne, who was something of a religious mystic, was moving in the same direction. He was appalled at the intolerance of Presbyterianism. In 1643 the Commons pledged itself to a Presbyterian church on the Scottish model, and in the following year acted to suppress assemblies of Antinomians and Anabaptists. Steps to establish Presbyterianism were taken in 1644 and 1645. Enforcement was spotty, but the evidences of intolerance were frightening. Roger Williams's plea for religious liberty, *The Bloudy Tenent of Persecution*, was ordered to be burned by the hangman, while laymen, the ministry of the sectaries—cobblers, peddlars, and ordinary people of all sorts who were moved by the spirit to preach the gospel—were forbidden to preach. Simultaneously Parliament acted to suppress religious and political controversialists who were advocating their views in print without check of any sort. The system of censorship having collapsed after the abolition of the Star Chamber and High Commission, the press had become free to anyone with a passion for expression. There were four "newspapers" in 1641, 167 in 1642, and 722 in 1645. There were only twenty-four pamphlets published in 1640, close to a thousand in 1641, and about two thousand in 1642. Every viewpoint from royalism and Anglo-Catholicism to democracy and Anabaptism showed up in print, bidding for public support. Harassed and outraged by the stream of criticism, Parliament established a licensing system designed to suppress seditious literature and to control the agencies of printing. The system of censorship which had formerly existed under royal auspices was revived with a difference: Parliament rather than Star Chamber governed the licensing as well as the detection and imprisonment of offenders. Milton's immortal *Areopagitica* of 1644 was merely one of many protests against official censorship. "The outstanding defender of Liberty of the Press during the Puritan Revolution," according to Siebert, the foremost historian on the subject, "was John Lilburne."[17]

Lilburne was quickly rising to the leadership of those who would be contemptuously called the "Levellers." His close friends William Walwyn and Richard Overton were more sophisticated intellectually, more original, more subtle, more rational, and even more radical than he; they greatly influenced his development. Yet he had a dramatic flair and personal magnetism that fitted him for leadership. In 1645 Dr. Bastwick, his former friend who had become an outstanding spokesman of the narrowest Presbyterianism, observed derisively that the "crowds and multitudes that run after him . . . look upon him as their Champion, applauding all his actions." Prynne, who sided with Bastwick, declared that Lilburne kindled "great combustion and tumults . . . among the

Ignorant Vulgar, who adore him as the onely Oracle of Truth," while Thomas Edwards, another Presbyterian stalwart, spoke of Lilburne as "an Arch-Sectary, the great darling of the Sectaries." Even before he quit the army to battle those who had "bitter designs against the poor people of God," Lilburne wrote a tract attacking Prynne and his party for religious persecution and censorship of the press. Commons' Committee on Investigation, a sort of House Committee for the Investigation of Un-English Activities, condemned Lilburne's "scurrilous, libellous, and seditious" pamphlet, and summoned him to answer for it. He defended his position vigorously before the Committee, in May 1645, denouncing Parliament for its intolerance, yet he was released. A month later the Committee re-examined him because of his authorship of another illegal, critical pamphlet, yet again overlooked both his offense and his offensiveness. But in July the Committee arrested him for libeling the Speaker of the House, William Lenthall.[18]

This time the Committee had a most unco-operative witness, for Lilburne obstinately refused to testify. He had decided to challenge the authority of Parliament to investigate his opinions or to subject him to incriminating interrogatories. Such behavior was unprecedented, but Lilburne saw in his case an issue that concerned the rights of every subject. Convinced that the Committee acted illegally, he flatly refused to answer questions against himself. Taking the offensive, he demanded to know the charges against him. His strategy was to demand common-law procedures from a legislative investigating committee, but the Committee scarcely felt itself bound by court-room requirements. It did not even agree that it was obliged to state the cause of Lilburne's commitment, although he claimed "a right to all the privileges that do belong to a free man as the greatest man in England . . . and the ground and foundation of my freedom I build upon the Great Charter of England." The Committee listened to him read chapter twenty-nine, his "birthright," satisfied itself that he would not testify, and sent him back to jail. Furious, he wrote a pamphlet depicting himself as the victim of tyrannical proceedings. Pridefully recounting his refusal to be a witness against himself, he explained to his readers that when a legislative investigating committee "sits upon criminal causes betwixt man and man concerning life, liberty, estate," it must honor the methods and rules of courts of justice. Its doors must be kept open to all the free people of England who wish to be present, and it must observe "that men should have the liberty of Magna Carta and the Petition of Right—for which I have fought all this while—and not to be examined upon interrogatories *concerning* themselves as we used to be in the Star Chamber, and for refusing to answer to be committed."[19]

Lilburne failed miserably in his novel effort to establish the right against compulsory self-incrimination in a proceeding before a House committee, but he would not abandon the principle for which he fought. In view of the fact that the Committee on Investigation had the authority to arrest, try, and convict him, his argument was not at all fantastic. There was no literal basis for it in the documents of fundamental law which he invoked, but it was reasonable to expect that a right which originated as a means of thwarting one species of inquisitorial examinations should apply to another. It was also reasonable to expect that a body having the authority of a court of law should follow the rules of such a court. The existence of the right itself in a court of law was something which Lilburne took completely for granted; his effort to extend the right was a case of necessity straining for an historical justification—chapter twenty-nine and the Petition of Right—that yielded new insights, however fictitious, on the meaning of fundamental law. If, as in Lilburne's thinking, the purpose of fundamental law was to protect the inviolability of the human personality and conscience, his argument, though inspired by revelation and intuition, made sense. But his much publicized claims worsened his situation. The Committee summoned him again to answer for his latest pamphlet; again he refused to testify. The Committee indignantly informed him that he had committed "the greatest affront and contempt that can be given to the authority of the House of Commons that when the House itself shall order that you shall be examined upon a business, you shall contemptuously say that you will answer to no interrogatories."[20]

Imprisoned in Newgate for what was technically the crime of breaching the privileges of Parliament, Lilburne wrote a new pamphlet, *Englands Birth-Right Justified Against all Arbitrary Usurpation, whether Regall or Parliamentary*. It showed the influence of Nicholas Fuller's *Argument* and of the commentaries on Magna Carta in the second volume of Coke's *Institutes*, both of which Lilburne had studied. He had become a jail-house lawyer. Indeed Prynne called him an "upstart monstrous lawyer" who "since he was called to the bar of Newgate, where he now practiseth, hath the Book of Statutes there lying open before him, which he reads and interprets to all the poor ignorant people that visit him. . . ." *Englands Birth-Right* argued that Parliament was limited by its own laws and could not justly punish any one who should "crosse some pretended Privilege of theirs." He claimed that the proceeding against him violated the act abolishing the Star Chamber, for its outlawed practices were not to be exercised by any other authority. In the Petition of Right which, he said, also bound Parliament, the true meaning of Magna Carta had been laid bare, because "amongst other things there expressed, it is declared to be contrary to law, to imprison a man without cause shewed or expressed, and also that it is contrary to *Law*, to force a man to answer to Questions concerning himself, or for refusall, to commit him to prison." By alleging a right not to be asked question *concerning* himself, he enlarged considerably the claim to a right which he did so much to establish.[21]

So obsessed had he become with the idea that no man should be forced to incriminate himself that Lilburne even believed that no one should be bound by law to answer to an indictment by pleading "guilty" or "not guilty." Questions to make him plead put him to "a criminall Interrogatory, concerning a mans selfe." It was a great snare to a conscientious man who could not lie, he argued. If he had committed the deed, he dared not plead "not guilty' for fear of lying, yet he destroyed himself contrary to the law of nature by pleading guilty to that which his adversaries might not be able to prove against him. From Fuller he got the notion that chapter twenty-eight of Magna Carta, like twenty-nine, buttressed the right for which he contended. The only course for a free man, he advised, was silence: let his adversaries state the charge against him and prove it to his face by witnesses. Christ himself by not answering had put off his enemies who sought to catch him by interrogatories. Hence, concluded Lilburne, justice demanded that Parliament not condemn a man for his refusal to reply to questions against himself. He acknowledged that it was "the usuall course of the COMMON-LAW" to put incriminating interrogatories to a defendant, but the question was, he asked—leaving no doubt of his answer—"whether that practise be just or no?"[22]

Englands Lamentable Slaverie, by Lilburne's friend William Walwyn, was published at about the same time. It was dedicated to Lilburne, the "Instrument of Englands Freedome." He lay in Newgate prison, said Walwyn "for refusing to answer upon Interrogatories to their Committee of Examinations, Contrarie to 1. The Great Charter of England, 2. The very words of the Petition of right. 3. The Act made . . . for the abolishing the Star-Chamber." Walwyn, who had already presented to the Commons a petition on Lilburne's behalf bearing over two thousand signatures, now extolled him in print for his valiant defense of the liberty of the subject. He had stood his ground when questioned by Parliament, alleging that it was against his liberty as a free-born Englishman to answer against himself, claiming Magna Carta as his justification: "you are the first indeed," applauded Walwyn, "that ever raised this new doctrine of MAGNA CHARTA, to prove the same unlawfull. Likewise, You are the first, that compareth this dealing to the crueltie of the Starre Chamber. . . ." Walwyn's pamphlet helped spread Lilburne's ideas, but it was Cromwell, the victorious general, who persuaded Parliament to liberate him. It would "discourage" the army, he said in a letter, "to censure an officer for his opinion in point of conscience; for the liberty whereof, and to free themselves from the shackles in which the bishops would enslave them, that the army had been principally raised." In October of 1645, after four months in jail, Lilburne was freed.[23]

The following March, the authorities arrested William Larner, whose illicit press had published Lilburne, Walwyn, and other sectaries. Larner "had learned so much of Lilburne's language," said the man who tracked him down, that he objected to questions tending to incriminate him. "I desire," said Larner, "the liberty of a Free-man of England not to answer to any interrogatories." He first made this claim before the court of the Lord Mayor and repeated it before the House of Lords. Two of his employees followed suit. Soon, the model of all this emulation joined Larner and his employees in prison. Lilburne had this time breached the privileges of Parliament by his criticism of a member of the House of Lords. Summoned for examination, he refused to testify and, as usual, compounded his affront by relating the whole story in a pamphlet. Magna Carta, he claimed, gave the Lords no jurisdiction to sit in judgment on a commoner in a criminal cause. Summoned again, he made a show of extravagant defiance, barricading himself in his cell; he had to be taken by force and dragged to the bar of the House. Once there he made a scene, refusing to kneel. The Lords retaliated by placing him in solitary confinement and—worst blow of all—denied him writing materials. A couple of weeks of such treatment simply aggravated his obstinacy. Summoned again to answer for his publications, he again refused to kneel and protested the proceedings. When the charges against him were read aloud, he stopped up his ears with his fingers. The Lords retaliated by sentencing him to a fine of two thousand pounds, and indefinite imprisonment in the Tower of London; they also disqualified him from holding any public office, civil or military, for the remainder of his life.[24]

Once more Walwyn rushed to Lilburne's defense with an eloquent review of his career entitled *A Pearl in a Dunghill*. Its purpose was to persuade readers that Lilburne's cause was their own, for he had done more than any man, Walwyn argued, to resist oppression and champion the liberties of England. Walwyn depicted the House of Lords as a new Star Chamber unjustly punishing free commoners by examining them as if the oath *ex officio* were still the law of the land. Richard Overton also spoke for Lilburne in 1646 in his influential *Remonstrance of Many Thousand Citizens*, "the most revolutionary tract that the Puritan Revolution had hitherto evoked." He too charged Parliament with behaving like the High Commission and Star Chamber: "Yee examine men upon *Interrogatories* and *Questions* against themselves, and Imprison them for refusing to answere." The pamphlet's frontispiece carried a portrait of Lilburne behind bars.[25]

Overton was soon behind bars, too. He wrote and smuggled out of prison an inflammatory pamphlet describing what had happened to him. Armed men, like pursuivants of the High Commission, broke into his house, "surprized me in my bed without any appearance or shew of any warrant," and brought him before a committee of the House of Lords. There, "being put High Commission like to answer to Interrogatories against my selfe," he refused to answer, not even to the question whether he was a printer, which was his trade. "But this is Lilburne-like," exclaimed one Lord. For his contempt the Lords sentenced Overton to indefinite imprisonment. Some months later their tyranny fell upon his family, too, because of their connection with the secret press which had not been silenced by the incarceration of Larner and Overton. Agents of the Lords' Committee on Examinations "rifled, plundered, and ransacked" his home in a search for evidence and arrested his wife and brother, all without warrant, he complained, or indictment, verdict of equals, lawful judgment, "or other due processe of Law proceeding contrary to the Fundamentall Laws of the Kingdom." His wife and brother, refusing to answer interrogatories concerning Overton, themselves, or "life, liberty, or goods," were also committed indefinitely. Overton, who did not usually share Lilburne's emphasis on legal rights and procedures, angrily detailed the various infringements of Magna Carta and the Petition of Right "which condemnes all High Commission like Interrogatory proceedings in a mans own cause. . . ." He accused Parliament of high treason, damned it as unrepresentative, and pleaded that conscience must be free of coercion. His *Appeal* was "one of his many classic statements of toleration." It was an appeal from the "degenerate" body of Parliament to the "free people in generall" and especially to members of the army. To the army alone he addressed his concluding recommendations, one of which was that no free commoner of England should be forced by the high court of Parliament, by any subordinate court of justice, or by any government authority, to take an oath "or to answer to any Interrogatories concerning himselfe in any criminall case, concerning his life, liberty, goods, or free-hold."[26]

The idea was certainly catching on. In 1646, according to the Presbyterian divine Thomas Edwards, who catalogued the "gangraena" in the realm, Andrew Wyke, a mechanic who became a Baptist minister, was brought before the local authorities in Suffolk because of his "Preaching and Dipping." Wyke "carried himself like Lilburne, Overton, and other fellow Sectaries, refusing to answer the Chair-man any questions . . . saying, I am a free man, and not bound to answer any Interrogatory, I will answer to no Interrogatory, either to accuse myself or any other." He was committed. His case is significant because like Larner, who first refused to incriminate himself before the common-law court of the Lord Mayor, Wyke's behavior before some 'committee' of Suffolk County, shows that the right was being claimed before all sorts of tribunals of criminal jurisdiction. It was being claimed, too, in the absence of an inquisitional oath and whether or not due accusation was made prior to interrogation.[27]

Lilburne, still in prison, though supposedly denied writing materials, was irrepressible. By bribing his jailors and in ways unknown, he managed to keep producing tracts, and they grew increasingly democratic in character. Religious liberty, freedom of the press, and the rights of the criminally accused were only part of his concern. He advocated social, economic, and political reforms that provoked the epithet of "Leveller" to be hatefully applied to him and his ideas. He rarely lost an opportunity to make his own case the case of the people. The titles of his pamphlets during this period suggest their incendiary nature: *The Just Mans Justification, The Freemans Freedome vindicated, Liberty vindicated against Slavery, Londons Liberty in Chains, An Anatomy of the Lords Tyranny*, and *The Charters of London* were part of his output of 1646, while he was imprisoned in Newgate. Attempts to silence him inexplicably failed, while the severe treatment accorded to him and his wife made him more contumacious, more provocative, more radical. Early in 1647 his house was raided, three loads of seditious papers and tracts were confiscated, and Mrs. Lilburne was taken into custody. John and she were both summoned before the Committee of Examinations, and she followed his lead in protesting that they had no right to demand her answers to incriminating questions. Lilburne told the world about this latest oppression, resolving in the *Resolved Mans Resolution* to defend his civil liberties "with the last drop of his hearts blood."[28]

The government's attempt to silence him was as impolitic as it was illegal by his standards. As one historian has observed, "By its injudicious treatment of the most popular man in England, Parliament was arraying against itself a force which only awaited an opportunity to sweep it away." During the winter of 1646–47, in London and in the army, the two sources of Leveller strength, the common people frenetically debated politics and religion. Like the essays of Tom Paine at Valley Forge in a later era, the essays by the Leveller leaders were avidly read, circulated, and discussed by the soldiers around their campfires. Richard Baxter, a Presbyterian leader, visited the army after the victory at Naseby and found a disturbing revolutionary spirit. A "great part of the mischief," he reported, was caused by the distribution of pamphlets by Lilburne, Overton, and Walwyn, whose work "seduced" honest men of ignorance into a "disputing vein" which made them argue "for Church democracy or State democracy . . . against the King and the ministry and for liberty of conscience." By the spring of 1647 a newswriter reported that the army was "one Lilburne throughout" and that the soldiers quoted his work as if it were law. That "law," which became their credo, taught them that it was un-Christian, un-English, and against fundamental liberties to oblige men to answer interrogatories against or concerning themselves.[29]

The spring of 1647 saw the publication of a democratic manifesto, the work of Walwyn, called "The Humble Petition of Many Thousands," which was addressed to the House of Commons. It by no means represented all the Leveller proposals, but it contained a program, as M. A. Gibb, Lilburne's biographer stated, "not for one Parliament, but for three hundred years" of Parliaments. Among its many recommendations was that Commons should permit "no authority whatsoever, to compell any person or persons to answer to questions against themselves," and it called for the release of all who had been imprisoned for their refusal. The right against self-incrimination which had begun as a protest against the coercion of conscience was growing as part of what Margaret Judson has called "the first great outburst of democratic thought in history, with John Lilburne and Richard Overton leading the way." One major Leveller document after another repeated with almost monotonous regularity an insistent demand for the right. It appeared, most importantly, in a clause drafted by Lilburne in the magnificent "Second Agreement of the People" of 1648, which anticipated so many fundamentals of the United States Constitution and Bill of Rights, and again in the equally prescient and democratic "Third Agreement of the People" of 1649. In these documents the Levellers proposed a written constitution to define the government of England, abolish arbitrary power, set limits to authority, and remove grievances. They advocated a unicameral legislature whose members would be apportioned among localities on the basis of population and be elected annually by all men over twenty-one excepting paupers and servants. There was to be freedom of religion and of the press; equality of all persons before the law; no judgment touching life, liberty, or property but by jury trial; no military conscription of conscientious objectors; no monopolies, tithes, or excise taxes; taxation proportionate to real or personal property; election of ministers by the people of their parish and voluntary support of public worship; election of all army officers excepting members of the general staff; the grading of punishments to fit the crime and the abolition of capital punishment except for murder; and the abolition of imprisonment for debt. This was the context of the insistent Leveller demand for a right against self-incrimination.[30]

The reason for the demand was simple enough. Parliament, the army's courts-martial, and Cromwell's Council of State all suppressed critical remarks as seditious speech, subjecting suspects to inquisitorial examination. In the absence of freedom of political discourse, the surest defense was the claim that no authority had the lawful power to address incriminating interrogatories. Nor were the Levellers the only victims and the only ones to invoke the right. In 1648, preliminary to Pride's purge of the Presbyterian majority of Parliament, a special subcommittee of a Joint Committee of Examinations was appointed to investigate in secrecy the loyalty of members whose religious and political opinions were offensive to the army leaders. The subcommittee concealed the names of accusers and examined Presbyterian members under oath as if it were the Star Chamber. Several indignantly refused to undergo oath or examination. Edward Baynton, for example, declared that it was "illegal to squeeze examinations out of a mans owne mouth; neither was a man bound to answer, where his words may condemn, but not absolve him. . . ." Clement Walker protested that no man could defend himself when the subcommittee carried on its business in the dark. We are called, he said, "to answer for our lives, *ore tenus*; and our accusation beginneth with the examination of our persons, to make us state a charge against ourselves, to betray ourselves, and cut our owne throats with our tongues, contrary to Magna Charta, the Petition of Right. . . . And no Witnesses are produced, nor so much as named." Walker recorded the episode in an understandably vehement tract.[31]

Another victim was John Maynard, whom the subcommittee also suspended and imprisoned in the Tower for his contumacy. *The Lawes Subversion: or, Sir John Maynards Case truly stated* denounced the proceedings. The passion of the Presbyterian author, John Holden, was worthy of Lilburne. Could anyone believe, he asked, that Parliament would have deviated so far from the rules of law and justice

> as to examine any man on interrogatories against himself in a criminal case? Would any have believed that this Parliament should have degenerated so far, as to indeavour to compel a man to destroy himself? Is it not a riddle surpassing all, that this monstrous age hath produced, that this Parliament, that hath deemed the Starre-Chamber and the Councell Tables names worthy to be a curse and a by-word to posterity, because of their cruelty in censuring men for refusing to answer interrogatories, that this Parl. I say, should urgently presse Sir Jo. Maynard to answer interrogatories against himself in a criminall case?[32]

Army control of Parliament benefited Lilburne and Overton who were released in August 1648. They remained true to their principles, denouncing tyranny whatever the source, even if from erstwhile friends. They had expected "things of an other nature" they declared sadly in a public petition to Parliament. They had expected that "you would have freed all men from being examined against themselves. . . ." Lilburne wrote *A Defiance to Tyrants, The Peoples Prerogative, The Lawes Funerall, A Plea for Common Right and Freedom*, and, early in 1649, *Englands New Chains Discovered* and *The Hunting of Foxes*. His disillusionment with Cromwell and the army leaders was bitter, his expression of it savage. England was once ruled by a king, Lords, and Commons; it was now ruled by General Cromwell, military courts-martial, and Commons—"and we pray you," he asked, "what is the difference?" One kind of oppression had been exchanged for another, the rule of an oligarchy based on military despotism. The Courts of High Commission and Star Chamber "are all alive in that Court, called the General Councel of the Army," which had court-martialed five soldiers who presented Leveller petitions. Each, Lilburne related, had been asked whether he had had a hand in the authorship of the petitions. One set a course which all others had followed, when he replied that he thought the court "had abominated the Spanish Inquisition, and Star-chamber practice, in examining him upon Interrogatories, contrary to their own Declarations; and he would rather lose his life, then betray his Libertie." A few days after this pamphlet appeared, Lilburne published a second installment of *Englands New Chains*, accusing Cromwell of having betrayed the revolution and all its principles. The general could stand no more. Parliament therefore declared that the pamphlet was "false, scandalous . . . highly seditious, and destructive to the present Government," its authors to be proceeded against as traitors.[33]

Several days later, on March 28, 1649, before five o'clock in the morning— an hour discreetly chosen to avoid the possibility of contending with a pro- Leveller mob—between one and two hundred armed men surrounded Lilburne's house, forced their way in, and took him prisoner. That same morning Cromwell's troops also arrested William Walwyn, Richard Overton, and Thomas Prince. The four prisoners were brought before the Council of State. John Bradshaw, the presiding officer, had served as Lilburne's counsel in 1645 when he had petitioned the House of Lords to join the House of Commons in voting his Star Chamber sentence illegal and award him reparations. On that occasion Bradshaw had condemned the Star Chamber sentence because it had been grounded on Lilburne's refusal to take the oath *ex officio*, "it being contrary," Bradshaw had said, "to the laws of God, nature, and the kingdom, for any man to be his own accuser." But in 1649 Bradshaw was in effect Lilburne's prosecutor; he asked the prisoner whether he had written *Englands New Chains*.[34]

Lilburne, "wondering at the strangeness of the question," answered that he was "amazed" at Bradshaw's having asked it. It had been only eight years since Parliament had annihilated the Star Chamber and High Commission "for such proceedings as these," less since Bradshaw himself had argued that incriminat- ing interrogatories were illegal. He would never, said Lilburne, commit so "un- Englishman-like" a deed as to answer. He would neither betray England's liberties nor himself. The Council should be "ashamed to demand so illegal and unworthy a thing of me as this." Bradshaw told Lilburne that they were not trying him, only seeking information for his trial. Lilburne would not even acknowledge their jurisdiction over him. Walwyn, Overton, and Prince in turn also invoked the right against self-incrimination. The four were herded into an ante-chamber while the Council debated their fate. Lilburne, listening at the keyhole, heard Cromwell bang his fist on the Council Table and shout, "I tel you Sir, you have no other Way to deale with these men, but to break them in pieces . . . if you do not break them, they will break you!" The four were committed to the Tower on suspicion of high treason. They promptly published a vivid account of their arrest and examination.[35]

In the succeeding months petitions flowed into Parliament demanding their release—some had as many as ten thousand signatures—and tracts written in the Tower flowed out. The four men were finally separated, kept in close confinement, and security regulations tightened to prevent their access to writing materials and the smuggling out of manuscripts. But their publications had already done a great deal of damage to the government, stirring resentments—so claimed the government—that led to mutinies in the army. In any case it seemed to be impossible to silence them even in the Tower. New pamphlets continued to appear. The "Third Agreement of the People," written by all four, was published on May 1, 1649, and by September Lilburne alone had written nine more tracts including *The Legall Fundamental Liberties* and the incendiary *Impeachment of High Treason against Oliver Cromwell and Henry Ireton*. The "Third Agreement of the People" had driven Cromwell to say that "the Kingdome could never be setled so long as Lilburne was alive." Cromwell blamed the army mutinies on Lilburne. *The Impeachment* provoked him to a fury; he vowed that either Lilburne or he must perish. In September 1649, a warrant issued from the Council of State for the trial of Lilburne by a special tribunal on the charge of high treason. In October a grand jury indicted him and he was put on trial for his life.[36]

John Lilburne was tried by a jury before an Extraordinary Commission of Oyer and Terminer consisting of eight common-law judges, the Lord Mayor of London, the Recorder of London, four sergeants-at-law, and twenty-six other special judges, including city aldermen and members of Parliament. The panel of judges was indeed extraordinary, but so was everything about the trial. All London focused on the event. The scene was the great Guild Hall of London, jammed with spectators. The streets near the courtroom were lined with troopers to prevent public demonstrations against the government, and soldiers kept Lilburne himself under constant surveillance during the trial. His own friends and supporters overwhelmingly outnumbered the government's adherents in the courtroom. One of his critics alleged, with probable exaggeration, that he had placed "hundreds" of his "myrmidons" in the audience to intimidate the court.[37]

Throughout his two-day trial Lilburne complained that he was being unfairly tried, but the trial was uncommonly fair by the standards then prevailing. Time and again the judges reminded Lilburne that he was receiving more favor than any prisoner charged with treason ever had, though he repudiated the court's "favors," saying that he claimed only the rights to which he was entitled by law, justice, and equity. The court was unbelievably patient with him, indulging his demands whenever the practices of the time permitted, because in a figurative sense, the government, too, was on trial; it was eager to prove before the bar of public opinion that it was lawfully constituted and just. Lilburne aimed at proving the opposite. Though he had no formal training in law, he had Coke's *Institutes* and other law books at his side, and had mastered them well enough to conduct his own defense as well as any attorney could. As long as he was permitted to speak—and there was no keeping him quiet—he outmatched all the judges before him. His great achievement at the trial was holding at bay the judges and Attorney-General Prideaux, his prosecutor, while he expounded to them and to his fellow citizens in the jury box and in the audience the fundamentals of fair criminal procedure from the time of arrest through trial. He placed the right against self-incrimination in the context of what he called "fair play," "fair trial," "the due process of the law," and "the good old laws of England."[38]

Lilburne's strategy was to challenge every step of procedure, pick to pieces each bit of evidence against him, depict the court as his oppressors, and appeal to the jury over the heads of the judges. From the moment the trial began, he sought to sabotage its proceedings in order to demonstrate unfairness or illegality or his pretended ignorance of law. Asked to hold up his hand so that he could plead to the indictment, he launched into a speech that spreads through thirteen pages of the report of the trial. The first words were that he was a freeborn Englishman who claimed his liberties. He demanded liberty to make exceptions to errors in the indictment before pleading to it. He claimed not to know the "formalities, niceties, and punctilios" of the law, though he proved himself to be far more adept than the court in excruciating quibbles. He had noticed that the doors of the courtroom had been closed and demanded that they be opened—which was done. He spoke of his record of patriotism, military valor, and championship of England's liberties. Citing Magna Carta, the Petition of Right, and Coke to prove that the court had no authority to try him, he insisted that he was entitled to trial by an ordinary court, rather than by an extraordinary, packed, and overawing tribunal. He, not the court, was overawing.[39]

He constantly associated the court with the Star Chamber and illegality. He related the story of his illegal arrest by armed men, Bradshaw's illegal interrogation when he was before the Council of State, and Bradshaw's earlier defense of his right not to be asked questions against himself. He even claimed a right not to be asked questions concerning himself. He had been denied, he protested, "'the undeniable privileges of the due process of the law from first to last." For months he had been held prisoner without the least pretense of a charge against him, though he was entitled to a speedy trial. Now that he was being put to trial he could find nothing in the "good old fundamental laws of England" that provided the least basis for the proceedings against him. Finally he demanded to know why he must hold up his hand—the request that provoked his long speech.[40]

When the judges sought to answer him and defend the lawfulness of his trial, he invariably interrupted them, alleging that they were taking advantage of him with "punctilios and niceties." When they tried to hush him up in order to proceed with the trial, he complained bitterly that they were denying him liberty of speech to defend himself when his life was at stake. When he finally permitted the indictment to be read, he discovered that the charge of high treason was not based on any of the writings or activities which had led to his arrest; the indictment was founded only on the tracts he wrote while in the Tower. Moreover, the indictment was founded on *ex post facto* statutes; they had been enacted after he was in custody and were tailored to punish his political propaganda. The accusation against him was that he had committed high treason by publishing that the government was tyrannical, usurped, and unlawful; by his writings he had sought to subvert the government and stir the army to mutiny. The nine-page indictment quoted generously from Lilburne's writings and when read in court stirred a commotion among the spectators. While the reading progressed, Lilburne noticed Attorney-General Prideaux whispering with one of the judges. He cried out that such whispering was "contrary to the law of England, and extremely foule and dishonest play"—he would have no more of such injustice. The judge defensively explained— Lilburne was always on the offensive, the court defensive—that it was necessary occasionally for the court to confer with the prosecutor. Not unless it be "openly, audibly, and avowedly," answered Lilburne; he would have no "hugger-mugger, privately or whisperingly."[41]

When at last the indictment had been read, Lord Keble, the presiding judge, asked Lilburne to plead guilty or not guilty. Instead Lilburne requested permission to make another speech. The court insisted that he plead. By the laws of England, he replied, "I am not to answer to questions against or concerning myself." "You shall not be compelled," answered Lord Keble, acknowledging the right to remain silent to incriminating interrogatories. But Keble had not realized that Lilburne was actually alleging that to require him to plead to the indictment was violative of his right, a view he had advanced three years earlier in *Englands Birth-Right*. One of the judges explained that by pleading to the indictment he would not accuse himself. By the Petition of Right, Lilburne replied, he did not have to answer any questions concerning himself, a familiar but strained Leveller interpretation of that great document which none of the judges corrected. Lilburne did not persist, however, in his unique refusal to plead. He would plead, he said, if afforded the privileges of the laws of England: he then requested a copy of the indictment, counsel to defend him, and "reasonable" time to consult with counsel even if it be "but eight or nine days." The court refused to breach precedent by granting his requests. He argued that he did not wish to plead until he had the opportunity of making exceptions to the indictment which was long, complicated, and in French and Latin which he did not understand. In fact, however, an explanation in English had been provided. When the court demanded that he plead, he burst out that they were trying to "ensnare and entrap" him. He demanded "fair play according to the laws of England." After a long wrangle, he offered to plead if the court would either provide him with counsel or promise not to take advantage of his ignorance of the law. Keble then promised him "fair play, and no advantage taken against you. . . ." At long last he pleaded not guilty. Excluding the reading of the indictment, the report of his trial covered twenty-five pages before reaching his plea; it should have been settled in a few minutes.[42]

The next step, the court informed him, was choosing a jury, but that proved to be a distant event, for the fiery Lilburne engaged the court in a long debate on his rights. He again demanded a copy of the indictment, the right to counsel, time to consult him, and the right to subpoena witnesses in his favor. Keble explained that the court would act as his counsel in matters of fact and that he needed no other counsel except for such matters of law that might arise. If they arose, he might have counsel. Lilburne insisted that the indictment involved matters of law. He complained that he had been in prison for seven months, could not have come to court prepared to defend himself against charges he had just heard for the first time, and he wanted to make exceptions to the indictment—for which he needed the aid of counsel. If the court would not grant his request, he asserted, "then order me to be knocked on the head immediately in the place where I stand, without any further trial, for I must needs be destroyed, if you deny me all the means of my preservation." He made such a fuss and so interrupted the judges who sought to answer him that Keble said, "Hear me one word, and you shall have two." Lilburne replied that because he was on trial for his life, he must have freedom to speak, but if they would not let him have counsel, he would say no more and they might as well murder him. Though the court tried to reason with him, he decried the injustice of it all. The prosecution and the judges, he said, had had months to "beat their brains together" with the assistance of his enemies to destroy him, yet took advantage of him by denying him counsel and a copy of the indictment—rights still half a century away. "O Lord!" he exclaimed, "was there ever such a pack of unjust and unrighteous judges in the world?" His counsel, a Mr. Sprat, was in the courtroom and declared that it would be easy to prove that the indictment involved matters of law which warranted the assistance of counsel. The court shut Sprat up. Lilburne burst out that the judges had reneged on their promise to give him a "fair trial." They aimed to kill him, he declared, despite his innocence; in a passion he called on God to deliver him from such tyranny and injustice.[43]

Lilburne had been offensively belligerent, obstructive, and abusive. It was his nature to be so, but it was also a clever stratagem. He finally prodded the court beyond endurance, provoking the long-suffering Keble to reveal his prejudice. The time had come, Keble said, to get on with the trial so that Lilburne's "secret actions" could be exposed to public view as "heinous." "You have had times to complot your treasonable venomous books, which shall be proved upon you; and till this be done, there is no matter of law to be looked at." When a man had "done such treasonable things," he must plead. Keble's speech proved, Lilburne answered, just what he thought. He knew that the judges had met several times over a period of months with Attorney-General Prideaux to plan his conviction. He wanted counsel to defend him. Prideaux asked the court to get on with the trial so that Lilburne could be "proceeded against for his notorious Treasons." That provoked Lilburne to a speech about the presumption of innocence. Until proved guilty and convicted by the jury, he was as innocent, he claimed, as those who called him traitor.[44]

The interminable altercation about his rights continued. He wanted not only counsel and a copy of the indictment; he demanded time to call witnesses. Keble said he should have brought his witnesses to court with him. How could he, Lilburne retorted, when he had just heard the indictment against him? The court gave him till seven o'clock the next morning to produce his witnesses. Some of them, he protested, lived a hundred miles away; others were "parliament men" and army officers who would not come voluntarily but must be subpoenaed. The court refused his request. The whole day had passed; it was time for adjournment. The court observed that all present should notice that "the prisoner at the bar hath had more favour already, than ever any prisoner in England in the like case ever had . . . the doors are wide open that all may know it." Lilburne sarcastically thanked the court, and they adjourned.[45]

The next day there was repeated squabbling between the defendant and the court, but at last a jury was impaneled and the case got under way. The prosecution called witnesses to prove Lilburne's authorship of the treasonable pamphlets, and he cross-examined them closely. At one point Prideaux asked Lilburne whether the manuscript of a tract was in his handwriting. Scornfully he refused even to look at the document, declaring he would answer no questions concerning himself. The court urged him to answer whether the handwriting was his, but he retorted that the judges were ignorant of the law on his rights. "My lord," said Prideaux, "you may see the valiantness of this champion for the people's liberties, that he will not own his own hand; although I must desire you gentlemen of the jury, to observe that Mr. Lilburne implicitly confesseth it." Stubbornly Lilburne declared again that the Petition of Right taught him to answer no questions "against or concerning" himself, and he had read "the same to be practised by Christ and his Apostles." A few minutes later, when a witness testified that he knew Lilburne's writing and identified as his the manuscript of *An Impeachment of High Treason against Oliver Cromwell*, Prideaux taunted Lilburne again for being "ashamed" to acknowledge his work. Again he invoked his right to remain silent, declaring that he was on Christ's terms and like Christ demanded that his accusers prove the accusation against him. Judge Jermin, interposing that Christ had said that he was the son of God, vainly urged Lilburne to confess also. The prosecution concluded its case by reading the statutes on which the indictment was based and some twenty pages of the most patently violative language from Lilburne's tracts.[46]

Lilburne's formal defense was that the prosecution had not proved his authorship. He neither denied nor affirmed his authorship; indeed, the most vehement tracts had his name on the title page. But he noted that whoever wrote them had done so after his imprisonment; moreover, that the treason statutes had been enacted after publication of some of the tracts charged against him. He insisted, too, that the tracts ascribed to him might be forgeries and that the treasonable passages might be part of the *errata!* Above all, he argued effectively that there was no proof that he was the author. In a few instances witnesses had testified to their knowledge of his authorship, but Lilburne claimed that in a legal sense they had proved nothing because two witnesses were required to each particular fact of treason. There was another long altercation between him and Prideaux on whether one witness to a pamphlet was enough. Although the court ruled in favor of the prosecution, Lilburne was interested in the opinion of the jury, not of the judges. He continually and deliberately wandered from the point to engage in a technically irrelevant argument which was his greatest strength—a passionate account of his illegal arrest and confinement, his war record, the unlawfulness of the court's authority to try him, his long struggle against injustice and tyranny, the refusal to give him a copy of the indictment or to allow him counsel, the persistent denial of due process and fair play, and the aim of the court to destroy him. Prideaux had done almost as much for Lilburne's cause by reading so extensively from his tracts against the government.[47]

It was a political trial, and Lilburne conducted himself as if public opinion on affairs of state and on matters of liberty and justice would be decisive. There was a reason why he repeated his remarks of the preceding day when he had spoken before the impaneling of the jury. On the second day of the trial he rehashed it all for the benefit of the jury. Against the authority of the judges, he openly appealed to the jury, telling them that they were the judges of law as well as of fact. The court, indignantly rejecting his aspersions on their authority, denied that the jury could decide matters of law. When Lilburne persisted in reading from Coke to teach the jury the law governing his case, the court tried to stop him, but it was impossible to shut him up. He would blare out against the "bloody judges" and call upon the jury to witness the fact that the court refused him freedom of speech to conduct his defense. He finally got his way and expounded law to the jury. During each altercation, when balked by the court he would accuse it of horrendous crimes against him, forcing Lord Keble apologetically to insist that he was getting "fair play." On one of these occasions, Keble assured Lilburne that no one previously had ever been tried before "so many grave judges of the law," thus allowing Lilburne again to denounce the irregularity of the court's commission to try him. He would rather, he said, be tried before one judge in an ordinary court, as was his right. If there had been "one judge, and no more," Keble foolishly answered, "and if you had not had this great presence of the court, you would have out-talked them; but you cannot do so here." Lilburne's retort proved that the "great presence" was no match for him. "Truly, Sir," he replied, "I am not daunted at the multitude of my judges, neither at the glittering of your scarlet robes, nor the majesty of your presence, and harsh austere deportment towards me, I bless my good God for it, who gives me courage and boldness." He had the boldness to complain whenever he was interrupted and even to claim that no one should talk when he was interrupting, because he was battling for his life.[48]

When Lilburne finally completed his defense with a long emotional appeal to the jury, the audience broke out in loud shouts of "Amen, Amen, and gave an extraordinary great hum," alarming the judges and the military commander who immediately sent for three more companies of foot-soldiers. Keble then gave a hanging charge to the jury—"your plot was the greatest that England ever saw, for it struck at no less than the subversion of this Commonwealth, of this state, to have laid and put us all in blood; your plot was such, that never such was seen in the world before to proceed from a private man. . . ." Lilburne interrupted to declare that there had never been such an unfair trial. Judge Jermin replied that never had judges been so badly abused before.[49]

The jury, after deliberating for an hour, returned a verdict of "Not Guilty." Pandemonium struck the courtroom. The reporter of the proceedings noted that "the whole multitude of people in the Hall, for joy of the Prisoner's acquittal, gave such a loud and unanimous shout, as is believed was never heard in Guildhall, which lasted for about half an hour without intermission." The acclamations for Lilburne's deliverance extended into the streets, where "the like hath not been seen in England . . . for joy the people caused that night abundance of bonfires to be made all up and down the streets." Two weeks later the Council of State, over the signature of President John Bradshaw, ordered Lilburne's release from the Tower. Overton, Prince, and Walwyn were freed with him.[50]

Notwithstanding Lilburne's triumph and popularity, or perhaps because of them, he was a man marked by the government for elimination one way or another. One of his pamphlets again provided the opportunity. Having intemperately assaulted the reputation of an influential member of Parliament, technically a breach of privilege, Lilburne was summoned before the bar of the Commons at the close of 1651. His enemies summarily convicted him without formal accusation, opportunity of defense, or semblance of trial. Retribution was swift and shockingly severe. By an attainder, they fined him seven thousand pounds, banished him for life, and sentenced him to death if he ever returned to England. Lilburne had always been quick to smear the epithet of "Star Chamber" on any procedure that fell short of his standards. But he had never been exposed to such monstrous injustice, nakedly violating every basic precept of English liberty. Yet he was helpless; he fled to Holland to escape the death penalty that automatically attached if he remained in the realm beyond twenty days.[51]

In June of 1653, after Cromwell had dissolved the Rump Parliament which had convicted Lilburne, the exile returned, confident that a changed political situation meant his safety. But the dictator, whose position was uncertain, could not permit the freedom of the realm to anyone as politically dangerous and popular as Lilburne, who had already announced that he would be peaceable only if England's liberties were re-established. The Council of State imprisoned Lilburne and put him to trial for his life, giving him every benefit of common-law procedure. After all, the government had only to prove that he was the John Lilburne mentioned in the bill of attainder in order to convict and execute him. But even Cromwell had underestimated his antagonist's amazing popularity and his legal ingenuity. "It is not to be imagined," said a contemporary, "how much esteem he hath got, only for vindicating the laws and liberties against the usurpations of his time." London rallied around him with petitions, pamphlets, and demonstrations of affection. Cromwell policed the streets with three regiments at the time of the trial in Old Bailey.[52]

The trial itself was long drawn out, in other respects much like the trial of 1649, with Lilburne using all his old tricks and demanding rights never before granted. This time, however, he succeeded in wresting from the court a copy of his indictment, and the assistance of counsel to challenge it. No one had ever before managed such a remarkable feat. Lilburne then attacked the indictment in such a way as to put the government on trial too, leaving the jury to choose between it and him. He reasoned that the indictment was based on his illegal conviction and bill of attainder of 1651; moreover, that the Parliament which had passed the bill had been an illegal body whose acts were not worthy of respect. Cromwell himself had dissolved that Parliament. If it had been a lawful and just body, then Cromwell's act was an unlawful usurpation, rendering illegal the very government that was prosecuting him. He backed up these bold "exceptions to the indictment" with a variety of formidable technicalities and shifty delaying tactics. When the court convened to hear the exceptions, after having capitulated to his demands for ample time to prepare them, he had already published a pamphlet, *The Exceptions of John Lilburne to a Bill of Indictment.*

Hundreds of his supporters were reported to be in and around the courtroom, armed and prepared for a rescue in the event of an adverse verdict. But Cromwell virtually had London under martial law. In Old Bailey the altercations between the prisoner and the court were stormy, filling the air with "furious hurley-burleys." Lilburne, as usual, would admit nothing, not even that he was the John Lilburne mentioned in the act of banishment. But he played his role as Freeborn John with gusto and drama, appealing once again to the jury to stand fast for English liberties. If he died on Monday, he told them, on Tuesday Parliament might pass sentence on every one of the twelve, on their families, eventually on the people of London and on all of England. The jury acquitted. The "joy and acclamation" of the spectators was so great that their shouts were heard "an English mile." The jubilation spread even to the troops who beat their drums and sounded their trumpets. Cromwell, "infinitely enraged," said Clarendon, regarded the verdict "as a greater defeat than the loss of a battle would have been."[53]

Parliament ordered the examination of the jury before the Council of State. The foreman would only say that he had acted in accordance with his conscience; he would answer no questions. Another juror, when asked to account for the verdict, replied, "What he can tell is one thing; but to accuse himself is another thing." He claimed that he did not think that the Lilburne before the court was the Lilburne mentioned in the attainder; when asked why, he replied that he was accountable only to God and would not answer. Another juror admitted that despite the ruling of the court, "He and the rest of the jury took themselves to be Judges of matter of law, as well as matter of fact"—proof that Lilburne had persuaded them to decide on the injustice and illegality of the 1651 bill of attainder, or of the prosecution of 1653, or both.

Most members of the jury would say only that they had decided according to conscience.[54]

Lilburne's courtroom triumph was his last. Cromwell had a tiger by the tail and simply could not let him go. The risk that he would spearhead intrigues against the government and promote discontent among the people was too great. In the dead of night, troops moved Lilburne from Newgate prison to the Tower—"for the peace of the nation." The government ordered the commander of the Tower to refuse obedience to any writ of habeas corpus in Lilburne's behalf. The prisoner was kept under such strict surveillance that he managed to produce only one more pamphlet, *An Hue and Cry after the Fundamental Lawes and Liberties of England.* He proved to be utterly intractable, rejecting overtures from the government to trade his silence for his liberation. Even in the Tower he was too much to endure. There were conspiracies against the government, even attempts on Cromwell's life, in which Lilburne's supporters were implicated. In the spring of 1654, therefore, Lilburne was transported out of London and out of the country, to a lonely exile in a prison fortress on the island of Jersey. Isolated from news, from intrigues, from visitors, from secret printing presses, he was, at last, a defeated man. He returned to religion, becoming a Quaker. The new faith suited him, for the Quakers were at that time a fighting sect of intense zealots, democratic in every respect and sensationally controversialist. The government imprisoned them by the hundreds. But Lilburne, cut off from the tumult, took refuge in the more spiritual aspects of Quakerism. Late in 1655 the government yielded to petitions and transferred him to Dover where the conditions of his imprisonment improved. But his health steadily deteriorated. In 1657, at the age of forty-three, he died. Two years later Parliament revoked his illegal sentence.[55]

The militant Christian democrat and libertarian had bequeathed to the English nation "his old buckler, Magna Carta," reconstrued to represent principles that free men would cherish and fight for. "I shall leave this Testimony behind me," he once predicted, "that I died for the Laws and Liberties of this nation." The outcome of his trial, he had predicted to the jury in 1653, would be a precedent for the good or evil of all the people of England. His entire career was a precedent for freedom, for freedom of religion, speech, press, and association. By his writings and his trials he sought to educate a nation on the relation of liberty to "fair play" in criminal procedure. Twice he convinced juries to decide on the injustice of laws used to prosecute political or religious prisoners. Accordingly he helped to make the jury the celebrated "palladium of liberty" so rapturously extolled by later writers. And more than any other individual he was responsible for the acceptance of the principle that no person should be compelled to be a witness against himself in criminal cases. Lilburne had made the difference. From his time on, the right against self-incrimination was an established, respected rule of the common law, or, more broadly, of English law generally.

3

Quaker Blasphemy and Toleration

IN THE 1650S THE RANTER and the Quaker were allied in antinomianism and opposed in all else. One was the libertine antichrist, self-indulgently reveling in sin, the other the primitive Christian self-righteously overcoming sin—and demanding, in the shrillest possible tone, that everyone else must find Christ exactly his way and no other. To the Quaker, no other way was possible. Linking Quakers with Ranters and even with blasphemy sounds preposterous to modern ears, but the Quakers of the mid-seventeenth century were not like their descendants. The first Quakers had the fiery temperament of Old Testament prophets, and they trumpeted the message of the New Testament as if no one had done so since Christ's apostles. They made extravagant claims that offended and infuriated people. In conduct and belief the first Quakers had about the same effect upon their contemporaries as Holy Rollers would have in a quiet Friend's meeting today.

The Quaker founder George Fox, and his captains, James Nayler, Francis Howgill, and William Dewsbury—all condemned for blasphemy—were pentecostal, puritanical, proselytizing zealots. Quakers obeyed no sacrament, no law, no ministry, and no custom that conflicted with the indwelling Light of Christ that guided their lives. They were militant, intolerant, and vituperative; they invited persecution, and they gloried in it as a sign of their witness to Christ. They saw themselves as the only true, infallible church and saw all Christians of the preceding sixteen centuries as apostates. The Protestants of England, whether Anglican, Presbyterian, Congregationalist, or Baptist, belonged, Fox said, to the "Synagogues of Satan."

> And therefore in the name & power of the Lord Jesus was I sent to preach the everlastinge gospell which Abraham saw & was preached in the Apostles days. . . . And since has the Apostacy gonne over all nations. . . . Nowe wee haveinge the false prophetts antichrists deceivers whore false Church beast & his worshippe in the dragons power betwixt us and the Apostles . . . I say to the everlastinge gospell must bee preacht againe to all nations & to every creature: which brings life & immortality to light in them that they may see over the Devill & his false prophetts & antichrists & seducers & deceivers & the whore & beast & before they was. And in this message of this glorious & everlastinge

gospell was I sent foorth to declare & thousands by it are turned to God & have received it & are come Into the order of it.[1]

Fox and his Quaker preachers engaged in "the Lamb's War." The Lamb, of Revelation 5:1–14, is the victorious Christ, exalted by God to govern the world after conquering the antichrist. Edward Burrough, one of Fox's soldiers for Christ, proclaimed that the Lamb "hath called us to make War in righteousness for His name's sake, against Hell and death, and all the powers of darkness. . . . And they that follow the Lamb shall overcome. . . ." Dewsbury spoke of the Lord's gathering a mighty host exalting Christ as King of Kings. The Quaker army raised in the north of England would march southward, reinforced by the mighty power of the word of God, as sharp as the two-edged sword, to cut down anyone, rich or poor, who disobeyed the righteous law. England would be conquered, but the victory would come "neither by sword nor spear, but by the Spirit of the Lord." Although the message was purely spiritual, its military coloration made the Quaker preacher, as Burrough acknowledged, look like a "sower of sedition, or a subverter of the laws, a turner of the world upside down, a pestilent fellow." No wonder that the members of Parliament thought that Theaurau John, the demented Ranter, was a Quaker when he flailed his sword against the great doors of the House of Commons.[2]

Quakers were not yet thoroughgoing pacifists, although they were incapable of harming anyone. While Fox was in Darby prison for his first blasphemy conviction, he demonstrated such charismatic qualities of leadership that he won the devotion of the common soldiers who heard him preach from his cell; the army offered him a captaincy if he would take up arms for the Commonwealth, but he declined, saying his was "the covenant of peace." His celebrated "flaming sword" was the sword of the Spirit, forged he said in the "pure fires" that lit up his soul. Still, he later censured the army for discharging Quakers as unreliable, and he lamented the army's failure to attack Spain, end the Inquisition, march on Rome itself, and continue into the lands of Islam, everywhere planting the true religion. Nayler, who had extensive military experience, presented the militant Quaker message most disarmingly when he wrote in his tract, *The Lambs War*, that everyone should discover Christ the Quaker way and so find a life of gentleness, faithfulness, and truth. The war was not directed against the government or the social order, and was only indirectly aimed against all the churches and sects of England. The war was, rather, directed at everyman; it was an inward war, exhorting the individual to crucify his spirit by confronting the Spirit of God within him and to find salvation.[3]

The Lamb's War was a full-time occupation for Quaker preachers. They were not Sunday Christians. Indeed, the sabbath day had no special significance for them. They abominated even the pagan names of the days of the week and months; when they redesignated the months and days as numbers (e.g., fourth day, second month), they were acting religiously. Matters of indifference to most people were for Quakers suffused with religious meaning. They rejected all oaths on the theory that a religious man would not perjure himself or affirm falsely; an oath implied that he spoke the truth only when he was sworn. But their first reason was that Jesus had said, "Do not swear at all" (Matt. 5:34). Quakers would not even swear an oath abjuring papal authority and the doctrine of transubstantiation, which they hated as they would the antichrist.[4]

"Moreover," Fox wrote, "when the Lord sent me forth into the world, he forbade me to 'put off my hat' to any, high or low; and I was required to Thee and Thou all men and women, without any respect to rich or poor, great or small." Quakers, who in the first generation almost invariably came from humble origins, enraged the gentry and magistrates by refusing "hat honor." Uncovering was the usual mark of deference or respect, but to the Quaker it was the sin of vanity. Similarly, they used "thee" and "thou" in addressing any individual, no matter how high his station, at a time when "thee" and "thou" were customarily used by superiors toward inferiors as marks of command and between equals as a mark of familiarity. "Plain speech," as the Quakers called it, was not a symbol of class warfare, nor a thing indifferent. Their refusal to kneel, remove their hats, use titles, or say "you" to a gentleman were deliberate acts of insubordination that conscience prompted. The Quakers were not really "levellers" in a political or social sense. Rather, they acted in the belief that God, before whom all were equal, was no respecter of rank. "Thee" and "thou" did not exalt the humble; the usage, like other Quaker customs, was an assault on the sin of false pride before God. Quakers owed loyalty only to the Spirit and to other "convinced" Quakers as signs of the Spirit. Every Quaker affront to a judge, a member of the gentry, a "priest," a government official, or an army officer was a self-testing by the regenerate against the unregenerate and a purposeful provocation of the unregenerate to see his own sins and thus become receptive to the Light of God within. Plain speech, plain clothing, and plain manners rebuked the world's vanities, set righteous standards, and, if necessary, led to the Cross.[5]

Quakers eagerly exposed themselves to martyrdom and suffered cruelly, needlessly in the minds of others, as proof that the Spirit within conquered one's own spirit or willful bent. "Being faithful to the Light," instructed John Audland, ". . . will lead you to the Death upon the Cross, and Crucifie you unto the World and wordly things, and raise you up into the pure Life, to follow the Lamb whethersoever he goeth." Self-crucifixion, figuratively, was a Quaker specialty—"follow the Lamb whethersoever he goeth . . . and therefore all come to the Cross and love it, and rejoyce in it." Prison became an almost normal form of Quaker self-crucifixion. Addressing a magistrate as "thee" instead of "your honor" or refusing to uncover before him could be taken as contempt of court. Quakers conscientiously opposed tithes for the support of an ungodly ministry, refused to pay fines, and failed to put up sureties for good behavior, and so they were jailed. They were stoned—the biblical punishment for blasphemy—and beaten by mobs so frequently and put into the pillory or flogged by court order so often that self-crucifixion became a way of life. In 1656 Fox estimated that "there were seldom fewer than one thousand in prison in this nation for Truth's testimony,—some for tithes, some for going to the steeplehouses, some for contempts, as they called them, some for not swearing, and others for not putting off their hats, etc." Included in Fox's "etc." was the woman who went to the "steeple-house," that is, challenged the parish minister for un-Christian teachings; she was tried for blasphemy and acquitted, but preferred to spend the winter in jail rather than promise that she would not disturb the worship of others.[6]

"Going to the steeple-houses" was probably the most provocative Quaker witness to the Spirit. Fox introduced the practice in 1649 when a steepled church in Nottingham appeared to him as an "idolatrous temple." The Lord instructed him, he reported, to "cry against yonder idol, and against the worshippers therein." Entering, he heard the minister say that the Scriptures decided all matters of religion, and Fox "could not hold, but was made to cry out and say, 'Oh, no, it is not the Scriptures,' and was commanded to tell them God did not dwell in temples made with hands." The Holy Spirit, he declared, had inspired the Scriptures and was the source of all religion. For disrupting divine service Fox was jailed, the first of many such occasions. Thereafter Fox and his converts to the indwelling Light invaded churches to denounce the preachers and their sinful congregations. God, the Quakers said, dwelt in the Spirit and the Spirit dwelt within every individual. The true church was a congregation of believers, not a building. Houses of worship, with or without steeples, became abominations to the early Quakers, as did ministers who taught falsely, or were ordained, or preached for money. Even the gathered churches of the separatist sects and their lay preachers, if paid, became targets of Quaker disruptions. "The disturbance of ministers in their sermons and alleged blasphemies," wrote William C. Braithwaite, the foremost historian of the early Quakers, "were the most usual grounds of complaint—the Quaker was frequently guilty of the first, and his innocence of the second, though clear to himself, was not easy of proof to a prejudiced and unsympathetic judge, who put the worst construction possible on unguarded statements about the indwelling life of Christ."[7]

William Penn entitled one of his books *Primitive Christianity Revived* (1696). That was Quakerism, or, rather, primitive Quakerism. Fox sought a return to the primitive church, as he understood it, purified of its accretions of sixteen centuries. Christianity in England was false, vain, and did not lead to the Cross, Fox preached. His mission was to bring the "pure religion" of Jesus to the people. One way of doing it was crying down and disrupting false worship, which the Quakers could not tolerate. There being so many souls that must be saved, errors in worship or in points of faith, "contrary to or different from the perfect Truth of the Gospel of Christ," required direct exposure and censure. Since the Lord accepted only His own worship, "here all Indifferency hath an end." Although the first Quakers were among the foremost advocates of liberty of conscience, it was not for them an end in itself but a means of propagating their faith. Their claim to infallibility matched that of the Roman Catholic church or of Calvinism, except that Quakerism made its advocates incapable of persecution. In the 1650s the Quakers had the same freedom of worship among themselves only; their faith compelled them to be missionaries among Christians worshipping falsely.[8]

Belief and action were inseparable to the Quaker. He must damn the antichrist in others and bring about conversions. "Hireling priests," the Quaker name for any ordained or paid minister, were too tolerant of sin and swollen with ceremonies and sacraments. Presbyterians and Independents won the particular contempt of Quakers because many of their ministers, having graduated from Oxford and Cambridge, knew less about the Spirit than common folk did. Herdsmen and fishermen, Quakers said, understood that the Spirit within man governed the interpretation of the Scriptures. Read literally, without the indwelling Light for guidance, the Bible became the "letter that killeth the Spirit." Fox liked to say that a believer needed no man to teach him, but only "an anointing within man to teach him, and that the Lord would teach his people himself." A Puritan preacher interrupted in his service could easily take such a statement as a rejection of the Bible, Christian sacraments, and Christian ministers.[9]

For all their talk about the love of God, Quakers used billingsgate, laced with biblical epithets, against other Christians. After spewing jeremiads, Fox would deny that he was railing; he spoke out of love, he said, while there was still time for repentance. Richard Baxter, the leading Puritan clergyman in western England, and no stranger to bitter religious controversy, wrote in 1657 that hardly a common scold in the past seven years had used against base people so many railing words as the Quakers used "against the faithful servants of Christ. . . . And no servant of Christ who hath learnt of Him to be meek and lowly can believe, if he be well in his wits, that this is the language of the Spirit of Christ." Long after, when Penn was succeeding Fox as the leader of the Quakers, Baxter noted their "extream Austerity," but insisted that their doctrines were

> mostly the same with the Ranters: They make the Light which every Man hath within him to be his sufficient Rule, and consequently the Scripture and Ministry are set light by: They speak much for the dwelling and working of the Spirit in us; but little of Justification, and Pardon of Sin, and our Reconciliation with God through Jesus Christ: They pretend their dependance on the Spirit's Conduct, against Set-times of Prayer, and against Sacraments, and against their due esteem of Scripture and Ministry. They will not have the Scripture called the Word of God: Their principal Zeal lyeth in railing at the Ministers as Hirelings, Deceivers, False Prophets, &c. . . .[10]

Cromwell, who could tolerate almost any Protestant opinion and did in fact tolerate Fox's refusal of hat honor and use of the familiar "thee," condemned the Quaker practice of violating the Christian worship of others. In 1655 he issued a proclamation of religious liberty "for all to hold forth and profess with sobriety, their light and knowledge therein, according as the Lord in His rich grace and wisdom hath dispensed to every man." The government would uphold liberty for "all persons in this Commonwealth fearing God, though of differing judgments," by protecting them against any who "abuse this liberty to the disturbance or disquiet of any of their brethren in the same free exercise of their faith and worship which himself enjoys of his own." Lately, declared the proclamation, "Quakers, Ranters, and others" had vilified and interrupted ministers and "daily" reproached congregations of Christians in public and private meetings. Hereafter, they would be prosecuted as disturbers of the peace. Until 1655 the law was that one might question a minister after his sermon, although the Quakers always did far more.[11]

Driven by religious exaltation and devotion to the Cross, they reproached other Christians by going naked in public "for a sign." Baxter acknowledged that it was "a Prophetical act," but he did not realize its significance. As Fox told the vicar of Ulverston in 1652, God made a Quaker "goe naked amongst you a figure of thy nakednese . . . before your destruction cometh . . . that you might see that your [you're] naked from the truth." The Quaker leaders did not reprove the practice, rooted in Isaiah 20:3, for it also showed a central trait of early Quakerism: the denial of self-will or the evidence of humility before the Cross. Each Quaker had to find God through Jesus Christ by learning to "give up self to die by the Cross. . . . Therefore keep in the daily cross, the power of God, by which ye may witness all that to be crucified which is contrary to the will of God, and which shall not come into his kingdom." To become a member of the "Children of Light" as the Quakers first called themselves, an individual must know his depravity by confronting the Light within. Conversion required a psychologically painful and prolonged encounter with self and God. Before one could be transformed as a person and become reborn as guiltless as Adam before the fall, he must acknowledge his sins, layer after layer, and personally experience divine wrath until it turned into love for the purified one.[12]

The very name "Quaker" reflected the fear and trembling a believer showed in the presence of the God of Jeremiah. The inward suffering produced intense physical agitation. "At first," Baxter recalled, "they did use to fall into Tremblings and sometimes Vomitings in their Meetings, and pretended to be violently acted by the Spirit; but now that is ceased; but now they only meet, and he that pretendeth to be moved by the spirit speaketh; and sometime they say nothing but sit an hour or more in silence, and then depart." Robert Barclay, writing about the same time, said in his book *Apology for the Quakers* (1675), that in the early Quaker meetings the "painful travail found in the soul" affected the body, so that "oftentimes, through the working thereof, the body will be greatly shaken, and many groans, and sighs, and tears, even as the pangs of a woman in travail, will lay hold of it; yea, and this not only as to one, but . . . sometimes the power of God will break forth into a whole meeting," everyone quaking, shaking, and groaning as he struggled with the evil in himself, until the Spirit brought serenity and thanksgiving. "And from this the name of *Quakers*, i.e., *Tremblers*, was first reproachfully cast upon us; which, though it be none of our choosing, yet in this respect we are not ashamed of it, but have rather reason to rejoice therefore. . . ." Fox himself attributed the origin of the name to a magistrate who scornfully used it while examining Fox for blasphemy in 1650, although the name in fact existed as early as 1647 to describe the spiritual behavior of others. After the victory at Dunbar in 1650 an officer rode back from his troop to discover the reason for a great commotion among his soldiers.

> When I came thither, I found it was James Nayler preaching to the people, but with such power and reaching energy as I had not till then been witness of. I could not help staying a little, though I was afraid to stay, for I was made a Quaker, being forced to tremble at the sight of myself. I was struck with more terror before the preaching of James Nayler than I was before the Battle of Dunbar, when we had nothing else to expect but to fall a prey to the swords of our enemies. . . . I clearly saw the cross to be submitted to. . . .

The curious aspect of this account is that Nayler, himself a veteran of the battle, had not yet met Fox and was not yet a Quaker.[13]

Primitive Quakerism was very much an embodiment of the youthful experiences of George Fox. In effect he demanded that others reenact his tormented conversion. He was born in 1624 in a tiny village in Leicestershire, the son of a weaver whom neighbors called a "Righteous Christer." The nickname more properly belonged to his son, who at nineteen, after his apprenticeship to a cobbler, left home to wander through the Midlands and learn more about religion. He listened to people of every Protestant persuasion, although he quickly abandoned "the high professors," the university-trained clergy, and consorted mainly with varieties of separatist sects, from whom he probably absorbed many ideas. He saw a turbulent and evil world. Finding no hope in institutions or men, he began receiving "openings" or insights directly from God. Between 1646 and late 1648 he shunned people as much as possible: he was "a stranger to all." So great was his misery he could not express it. But his description of his conversion and his commission to preach is one of the most agonizing and rapturous in English prose. By early 1649 he had "come up in spirit through the flaming sword into the paradise of God," relived the Creation, and by the indwelling Light reached Eden before the Fall. "But I was immediately taken up in spirit, to see another or more steadfast state than Adam's innocency, even into a state in Christ Jesus, that should never fall." His mission was to take others on the same journey. It was a dangerous mission because being taken "into a state in Christ Jesus" could be construed as antinomian blasphemy.[14]

Fox had little schooling and no formal divinity training; education would probably have ruined his ministry. No theologian, he expressed himself carelessly and overbluntly. He was a mystic, a firebrand, and inspired prophet, and, later, an organizer of a sect. But he had nothing new to offer in religious doctrine. Belief in the indwelling Christ who offered universal grace and perfection was certainly commonplace. Henry Lawrence, the president of the Council of State, told the House of Commons during a debate concerning Nayler's declaration that Christ was in him, "I wonder why any man should be so amazed at this. Is not God in every horse, in every stone, in every creature? Your Familists affirm that they are christed in Christ, and godded in God. . . . If you hang every man that says Christ is in you . . . you will hang a good many."

Even the Ranters had that "convincement," as Fox conceded, although he said they "fled the Cross."Edwards's *Gangrenae* and Pagitt's *Heresiography* were filled with examples of antinomian heresies. Behmenists, Familists, early Baptists, Diggers, Grindletonians, and many Seekers like William Erbury preached the Light within, the godded man, the reborn innocent. Fox grew up in that religious milieu, which was strongest in the north and west, where he began his mission. Unsophisticated rural folk on the geographic fringes of Puritan centers were most receptive to Fox's preaching. They found in it a way to salvation that was direct and familiar, and they discovered a range of emotional expression that was not otherwise permitted in daily life. Fox was a fundamentalist who suited their wants, and he conducted a great awakening in the style that later revivalist preachers copied.[15]

But Fox's extravagances in statement led him into trouble. In 1650, while traveling through Derby, he stopped with some followers at a "steeplehouse" where many "priests" congregated for "a great lecture." Fox waited for all to finish, then rose to speak about Christ's dwelling within. He and two friends were promptly arrested and brought before "Collonels and Justices and Priests," who examined them for eight hours. Fox told them that all their preaching, sprinklings, and sacraments would never sanctify a man. They asked him whether he was sanctified. "I said, sanctified? yes, for I was in the Paradise of God, and they said had I noe Sinne? Sinne said I Hee hath Taken away my sinne (viz. Christ my saviour) & in him there is noe sinne . . . & soe They committed mee upon That as a Blaspheamer. . . ." He was sentenced to six months' imprisonment for violating the provision of the act of 1650 against anyone claiming to be God or equal to God, or to have God's attributes, or to have God within him.[16]

The act of 1650 was framed for Ranters, whom Fox despised as filthy beasts. But the early Quakers were frequently mistaken for Ranters. A tract of 1652 condemned "Enthusiasts, Seekers, Shakers, Quakers, Ranters, etc." Ranterism and Quakerism were rival antinomian movements, and after the severe suppression of the Ranters in 1650–1, many converted to Quakerism; but old habits kept cropping out. A magistrate, Durand Hotham, told Fox in 1652 that the Quakers were saving England from being overrun by Ranters, but Hotham was a friend of Fox and privately admitted to him that he had believed in the indwelling Spirit for ten years. Others found blasphemy in such a belief. When Henry More, the Cambridge scholar, wrote that "Ranters and Quakers took their original from Behmenism and Familism," he was connecting the Quakers with blasphemy. Their enemies connected them with much more that was despicable—anarchists of the spirit, "levellers against magistracy and property," and the Anabaptists of Münster. One grand jury denounced "Ranters, Levellers and atheists, under the name of Quakers." Levelling might be inferred from Quaker plain speech and refusal to defer to rank, but the Quakers had no political program. To call them political radicals was absurd. But that Fox should have been condemned under the act against Ranters was not at all strange.[17]

When Fox's term in the Derby jail ended, the magistrate who had sentenced him demanded a steep bond of more than £200 for his release on good behavior. Relatives and friends raised the money, but Fox refused to pledge that he would not return to Derby and proclaim against its "priests." The magistrate, Gervase Bennett, who soon after became a member of the Council of State, furiously struck Fox and ordered him back in jail, this time in the dungeon, and there he stayed for over five months more. Immediately after his release he was preaching again.[18]

In Wakefield, to the north, he converted James Nayler, who became a leader of the early Quaker movement. Nayler, who was eight years Fox's senior, had left home in 1643 to serve in the army. After extensive combat experience he rose to become quartermaster of General Lambert's regiment. He left the army in late 1650 because of illness and took up farming. When Fox met him he was a member of an Independent congregation whose minister had been trained in Boston by John Cotton. Shortly after Nayler's conversion to Quakerism, he was "at the plow," he said, "meditating on the things of God, and suddainly I heard a Voice." It commanded him to leave his family and become a wandering Quaker preacher. Before Nayler left, Fox returned to his community and disputed Nayler's minister; there was a fracas, during which Fox was physically beaten by the congregants, although Nayler supported him. When Nayler left home to preach Quakerism, his minister excommunicated him for blasphemy. Fox and Nayler became intimate friends and remained so until 1656.[19]

That was the year of Nayler's disgrace, after the greatest blasphemy trial of the century. Nayler's death in 1660, shortly after his release from prison, and Fox's survival to 1691, dimmed the memory of Nayler's contribution to Quakerism. Within a few years of his conversion, he rivaled Fox. He was an equally powerful preacher, a superior prose stylist, and a prolific writer of tracts; and unlike Fox, who was abrasive and imperious, Nayler was gentle and considerate. When Baxter later reminisced about the Quakers, he mentioned Penn as their rising leader, did not refer to Fox at all, and said that Nayler had been "their chief Leader." Braithwaite, the leading Quaker historian, called Nayler "the most brilliant of the Quaker preachers," and a non-Quaker authority wrote that he was "a spiritual genius of a high order," whose "depth of thought and beauty of expression deserve a place in the first rank of Quaker literature."[20]

In 1652 Fox and Nayler preached together in northern Lancashire. On one occasion they were both nearly beaten to death by an enraged mob. They recovered at Swarthmore Hall in Ulverston. There Fox converted Margaret Fell, the wife of Judge Thomas Fell, who had been a member of the Long Parliament. Although Fell never converted, he used his influence to protect the Quakers and allowed his home to become their headquarters. Margaret Fell became one of the foremost Quaker missionaries and martyrs after the Restoration; following an imprisonment of four years she married Fox in 1668, although he was ten years younger. She treated him adoringly as the Messiah from the time they met, believing that he was possessed of the living Christ. If her early letters to him had fallen into the wrong hands, Braithwaite wrote, they would have "confirmed the belief that Margaret Fell was bewitched and that Fox was a blasphemer." Others addressed Fox with the same divine submission. He did not reprove them, but years later, when arranging his papers, he crossed out some idolatrous phrases. Even Nayler wrote, "Geo. Fox was denied as dust, but the Spirit that spoke in him is equall with God." Fox himself did not deny that, although on one occasion, when asked whether he was Jesus Christ, he replied, "No, I am George Fox."[21]

For their preaching around Ulverston, Fox and Nayler were charged with blasphemy in October 1652. Judge Fell managed to see that the warrant was not served, but Fox, accompanied by Fell and Nayler, insisted on riding to the Lancaster sessions to answer the warrant. Forty "priests" appeared as witnesses against Fox, but only three testified. The offense was serious, because under the act of 1650 a second conviction for blasphemy required banishment from the country. Shortly before, Fox privately told a friend that he was "the Sonne of God," although someone later changed Fox's manuscript account to read "a sonne of God." There is no doubt that he made unguarded oral statements. Fortunately for Fox, Fell was not the only sympathetic magistrate at his Lancaster trial, and the witnesses offered conflicting testimony about the defendant's exact words. To the first charge, that he had said he "had the divinity essentially in him," Fox denied having said "essentially," although he defended the doctrine of the indwelling Spirit. He also denied the charge of having said "he was equal with God," explaining that "He that sanctified and they that are sanctified are all of one in the Father and Son," and that all who were sanctified were the sons of God. He denied having claimed that he was "the judge of the world," although the testimony against him on that point was clear. To the charge that he had claimed to be as upright as Christ, he argued that "the saints," the true believers, "are made the righteousness of God" and shall be "like him"; Christ brought the saints to "perfection." One of the magistrates declared that Fox had blasphemed while presenting his defense in court. Another asked, directly, "Art thou equall with God?" Fox replied, "My Father and I are one, and as hee is, soo are wee in this present world." Nayler, quickly perceiving the danger in that reply, asked, "Dost thou aske him as a Creature or as Christ dwellinge in him?" When Fox insisted that Christ dwelt in him, Nayler added that nothing was sanctified but the Son, "and the Sonne being one in all, then the thinge sanctified is equal in all."[22]

Judge Fell, relying on the requirement that two witnesses must agree, said they had not; consequently, he quashed the warrant for blasphemy, leaving the issue unresolved. Orthodoxy sought satisfaction from a higher authority. Some Lancashire ministers, supported by a few local magistrates, petitioned the Council of State in London against the blasphemies of Fox and Nayler. All the old charges were repeated, and the Quaker leaders rushed an answer into print. Even as they denied the accusations, they exposed themselves more by saying, contrary to the act of 1650, "that God will dwell in man and walk in man." Braithwaite concedes that their vivid sense of personal union with Christ led them to identify with the Divine and advocate their own perfection. Tract writers replied and censured Fox and Nayler for blasphemy, but the busy Council of State took no notice.[23]

Nayler and Fox split up after the Lancaster trial, Nayler going into Westmorland where he met with violence and hatred, especially around Kendal. For blasphemous preaching about the resurrection, a warrant was issued against him. He was taken by force and tried by a lynch mob, presided over by a justice of the peace who struck off Nayler's hat with a pitchfork when he refused to uncover. For a while he submitted to theological questions put to him by local ministers. "I witness that Christ [is] in me," he said, but one minister answered that Christ was physically in heaven. He is in heaven spiritually, Nayler answered, not in the flesh. The armed mob was growing ugly, so the justice of the peace decided to remove the trial to a nearby tavern. There Nayler again refused to take off his hat and "thou'd" the magistrates, who immediately jailed him for contempt and vagrancy. Francis Howgill, a Quaker preacher, gathered a group of Friends to protest the treatment of Nayler, and Howgill was locked up with Nayler. The next day the two were transported under guard to the prison in Appleby, further north, to await trial.[24]

In January 1653, two months later, their case came to trial under the act of 1650. But the prisoners were in luck. One magistrate, Gervase Benson, was a local dignitary of great authority who had recently become a Quaker, and another, Anthony Pearson, was sympathetic. Others on the bench were hostile, but Benson and Pearson prevented a verdict of guilty. Pearson instructed the prisoners to remove their hats. They refused, Nayler explaining that they had no contempt for authority but honored God, who did not respect temporal distinctions in people. On a direct command from Pearson to uncover, Nayler pleaded "Conscience sake. . . . Where God commands one thing, and Man another, I am to obey God rather than Man." Benson called for the indictment to be read: the blasphemy consisted in Nayler's having preached "that Christ was in him, and that there was but One Word of God." Pearson asked, "Is Christ in thee?" "I witness him in me." "Spiritual you mean?" "Yea, Spiritual. . . ." "What difference then between the ministers and you?" They, Nayler answered, affirm that Christ rose with a "carnal body, but I with a spiritual." A colloquy ensued on the distinction between the Bible and "the Word of God." Nayler explained his doctrine that "the Word" is spiritual, not seen by the eyes of men but experienced by the Light within. At length, the magistrates fell to disputing with each other. Benson favored a directed acquittal on ground that there was no blasphemy in Nayler's teaching. Others disagreed. In the end, the court decided not to put the case before the jury but to render no verdict, and to keep Nayler and Howgill in prison indefinitely until they answered fresh accusations from local clergymen. The prisoners were not released until five months later. While they were still in the Appleby jail, Anthony Pearson, whose Puritanism had been unsettled by his encounter with Nayler, visited Fox at Swarthmore Hall; he left shaken but unconvinced. When Nayler was released, Person invited him to his home, and Nayler brought his judge into the Quaker fold. Pearson traveled with Fox that summer in 1653 and helped save him from another blasphemy charge.[25]

Fox was accused for the third time in Carlisle that summer. He was near the border of Scotland, in a Presbyterian stronghold, and had provoked disturbances on his way north. In Calisle, despite warnings from the magistrates, he "stood a-top" the cross in the middle of the market at midday and preached his gospel to a curious throng. Soldiers in the audience "were convinced" and protected him. He went to their garrison and convinced more, and on the next day, Sunday, he went to "the steeplehouse," the cathedral church. When the minister finished, Fox rose to speak. People "trembled and shook," he said, "and they thought the very steeple house shook and thought it would have fallen down." Friendly soldiers prevented a riot and surrounded Fox. Some were imprisoned for protecting him. But the town hall filled with "officers and justices" and "many rude people" that swore evidence against Fox, "for they were Independents and Presbyterians." Fox was summoned by a warrant.

> And one sware one thing and one sware another thing against me. They asked me if I were the son of God. I said, "Yes." They asked me if I had seen God's face. I said, "Yes." They asked me whether I had the spirit of discerning. I said, "Yes. I discerned him that spoke to me." They asked me whether the Scripture was the word of God. I said, "God was the Word and the Scriptures were writings; and the Word was before writings were, which Word did fulfil them." And so after a long examination they sent me to prison as a blasphemer, a heretic, and a seducer. . . .[26]

Fox was being held until the Assizes, when the county judges held trials with a jury. The news in the county was that Fox was to be hanged. The lord high sheriff, Sir Wilfrid Lawson, according to a letter from Margaret Fell, wanted to execute him at the first opportunity and spread word that he would be tried for his life. Fox reported that "great ladies" and "bitter Scottish priests" came to Carlisle "to see a man they said was going to die." In fact, however, when the Assizes convened, the judges refused to try Fox, leaving him to the local magistrates who had no power to condemn capitally. The judges who had that power probably believed that Fox was guilty of blasphemy; if he was convicted at the Assizes by a jury in a hostile town, the act of 1650 required banishment for the second conviction, and the expectation was that Fox would refuse, allowing no alternative under the act but execution. The judges of the Assizes did not want the responsibility of being the first civil officers to hang a man for his religion since the executions in 1612 of Legate and Wightman. So Fox languished in jail without a trial.[27]

He reported that the judges of the Assizes reviled him, left him to the town magistrates, and encouraged the latter to treat him cruelly, but in fact those whom he blamed probably saved his life. Anthony Pearson and Gervase Benson assisted him too. The two Quaker magistrates from Lancaster traveled to Carlisle, but the jailor refused to let them see Fox. He was transferred from a locked room to a foul dungeon with felons of both sexes, no toilet, and the prisoners "exceedingly lousy . . . almost eaten to death with lice." Pearson formally complained to the Assize judges, defending Fox from the accusations against him and protesting that he should not be left "to the rulers of this town who are not competent judges of blasphemy." Fox himself advertised his situation in letters to Friends and to the town magistrates, as did Pearson and Benson. Weeks passed, enough time for word to reach London. Cromwell and the Nominated Parliament then in session favored broad toleration. Parliament, Fox recorded, "hearing that a young man was to die for religion at Carlisle . . . writ down to the sheriff and magistrates." Carlisle set him free even before the writ arrived from London. After seven weeks of near starvation and brutal clubbings from his jailors, Fox returned to Swarthmore to recuperate, although on the way he turned "thousands" to Christ.[28]

During the next few years Quakerism penetrated southward throughout most of England, as its indomitable preachers worked county by county in pairs. The persecutions that followed them were severe but sporadic and local. By 1654 Fox was in London for the first time, preaching to huge crowds. Nayler, who joined him, was also received as a heroic figure. When Fox departed he left Nayler in charge. For the first time the Quakers were winning converts from better educated, prosperous city people. To eloquence Nayler coupled wit and warmth, and he had the civility of a gentleman with Fox's personal magnetism to boot. Quakerism almost became a London fashion, with Nayler lionized at parties attended by leading politicians and ministers as well as titled ladies. On a trip out of the city Nayler bested more than half a dozen "priests" in a public debate and the crowd shouted, "A Nayler, a Nayler hath confuted them all." But hints of spiritual travail within Nayler began peeping through his triumphs. He could not quash the sin of vanity. Some Quaker women were so smitten with him that they began to reverence him as more than a great preacher, and Nayler did not rebuke them. Nor had Fox when he received adoration. With Nayler, though, the problem became far more serious.[29]

Meanwhile the growing popularity of Quakerism made it the focus of rumors, some vicious, others absurd. William Prynn, the old mutilated Puritan martyr, was one of several who published the libel that the Quakers were really Jesuits and Franciscan friars in disguise sent by Rome to subvert the English people. The government flinched at plots, real and fancied. An officer arrested Fox on suspicion; when Fox would neither swear an oath abjuring Rome nor promise to return home and quit preaching, he was sent under guard to London and imprisoned. Cromwell required from him a pledge that he would not take up the sword against him or his government. Fox complied in a letter unlike anything Cromwell had ever seen. Calling himself "the son of God who is sent to stand a witness against all violence," Fox added, "My weapons are not carnal but spiritual and 'my kingdom is not of this world.' " The Lord Protector read the letter, interviewed its author, and sent him at liberty. As Fox left, Cromwell shook his hand and tearfully said, "Come again to my house; for if thou and I were but an hour in a day together we should be nearer one to the other." That was three weeks after Cromwell's declaration against Ranters and Quakers for disturbing Christian worship.[30]

As 1656 opened, Fox and his companions in Cornwall were thrown into Launceston prison "till the Assizes" in nine weeks. There was talk that the Quakers would be hanged, although their crime was not defined. The lord chief justice of England, John Glynne, presided when the sessions convened, but Glynne aborted the trial when he furiously ordered the Quakers back to prison because they would not uncover before him. At a rehearing, Fox managed to get the charges read—vagrancy, disturbance of the peace, refusal of the oath of abjuration, and perhaps sedition for that refusal. Once again, though, Glynne imprisoned them without trial for their contempt in refusing hat honor. They rotted in Launceston under horrible conditions—excrement was poured on their heads and the jailor beat them—until word reached London. Cromwell promised them liberty if Fox and his companions would go home. They refused; they also refused to pay court and jail costs. Hugh Peters, Cromwell's chaplain, observed that the government could not perform a greater service to the spreading of Quakerism than by making martyrs at Launceton. After eight months, they were freed.[31]

While Fox was at Launceton, Nayler's friends worried about Nayler's head being turned by reverential admirers in London; they persuaded him to travel to Bristol for a religious fair, but his worshippers followed. In Bristol, Nayler decided to visit Fox at Launceton. Fox had already heard about the strange goings-on around Nayler. In a letter of warning, Fox wrote, "Thou became a shelter for the unclean spirits, the beasts of the field, they made thee their refuge." In his *Journal* Fox recorded that Nayler and his companions "ran out into imaginations." A short distance from Lanceton, the Nayler group was arrested for vagrancy and jailed at Exeter. On Fox's release he visited Nayler at Exeter and "saw he was out and wrong." At prayers, as Fox admonished the Exeter prisoners, Nayler and his followers left the room—evidence, said Fox, of a "wicked spirit risen up among Friends." He spoke to Nayler the next day. Nayler, remorseful, would have kissed Fox in the Quaker fashion, but "seeing he [Nayler] had turned against the power of God," Fox extended his foot for Nayler to kiss: "the Lord God moved me to slight him and set the power of God over him." So ended the Fox-Nayler relationship. In Exeter prison Nayler was moody, ill, exhausted, and scarcely ate for weeks at a time.[32]

Letters from admirers intending to comfort him aggravated the growing delusion, which he found disturbing, that he James Nayler was a special sign from God. A Quaker, when impelled by the Light within to serve as a sign, experienced spiritual torment and exaltation. To reject the sign implied self-will, a reproach to the divine prompting that betokened the sign. Nayler read the admiring letters, and although they sent a fear through him, he kept them. One follower described him as "King of Israel and Son of Most High." The writer of another letter wished she could present him with gold, frankincense, and myrrh. Still another called him the "son of Zion, whose Mother is a Virgin, and whose birth is immortal." One woman saluted him as the "Prince of Peace" and "fairest of ten thousand, thou only begotten Son of God," and her husband added the postscript, "Thy name is no more to be called James but Jesus."[33]

The "miracle" in Exeter prison involving Dorcas Erbury magnified tenfold the overpowering sense that the God in him had chosen him for a special mission. Dorcas, the daughter of William Erbury the Seeker, had fallen into unconsciousness and seemed dead for two days. Nayler entered her cell, placed his hands on her, and commanded her to rise—and she did. Fox himself had exercised healing powers. Once he cured a deformed boy by laying his hands on him, and on another occasion he claimed that he "raised up" a woman and her child who were dying. Francis Howgill had once called upon the power of God that raised Jesus to make a lame boy walk, and when the miracle failed, Howgill was surprised. No Quaker had raised a person from death, until Nayler seemed to do so in Exeter. His success intensified the hysteria among his worshippers. Fox wrote, "James, thou must bear thy owne Burden, and thy Companyes with Thee, whose Iniquity doth increase, and by thee is not cried against." In late October 1656, Nayler and the Exeter Quakers who had been arrested for vagrancy were freed.[34]

He and eight of his followers traveled from Exeter to Bristol. Their sensational entrance into the city drew crowds even in a downpour. Nayler sat on his horse as if in a trance, while the others, bareheaded, surrounded him and led him through the mud, singing "Holy, holy, holy, Hosannah, Lord God of Israel." They spread their sodden cloaks for his horse to walk upon as he passed through the city streets. The deliberate reenactment of Jesus' entry into Jerusalem on Palm Sunday was intended as a symbol of the imminent coming of Christ—a common enough millenarian belief. The whole group was arrested and sent to the Guildhall for an examination. Ordinarily, local Quakers— Bristol had a thousand—turned out to show sympathy for a Friend in trouble, but Fox had passed through Bristol and sent letters there warning the Quakers not to support Nayler's extravagances. Not one appeared at the Guildhall.[35]

There, before the mayor, the local magistrates and ministers, and the townspeople, Nayler and his followers were searched. The "incriminating" letters of adoration were found on him, used as evidence, and published in lurid accounts. One of the women in his company had in her pocket a description of Jesus that fit Nayler closely; a formal report of Parliament later took notice "how much he resembled . . . the picture usually drawn for our Saviour." During the examination in the Guildhall, the women prisoners sang, cried hosanna, and one kissed Nayler's hands before the horrified magistrates. If any were guilty of blasphemy, they were the Quakers offering worship to Nayler. Whether they believed that he was Christ incarnate is uncertain, but they worshipped the Christ whom they believed to be patently manifest within him. Nayler himself was neither an imposter, as many then believed, nor a fool, nor was he crazy as some historians have thought. He was guilty of bad judgment, excessive zeal, and an incapacity to see himself as others—Fox as well as non-Quaker Christians—saw him. He was the reluctant Jesus in a Passion Play because he had become convinced by the agony of his spirit that God intended him as a sign, both of Immanentism and of Imminence.[36]

The Quakers of the 1650s saw their time as the edge of the Apocalypse.

They expected the Lamb's victory over everybody during their lifetime. Much of Quaker preaching was a gloomy prediction that the wrathful day of the Lord was near. "Who waits upon the Lord in his Light," wrote Margaret Fell, ". . . shall see this fulfilled and shall be preserved." Naturally the Second Coming would be preceded by signs of all sorts; Nayler, in a judgment misrepresented by his worshippers, thought he was such a sign, because the strong Light within him made him God's instrument. But he did not believe he was the only sign, the only instrument, the only man through whom the Light worked its mysterious wonders. His interrogators at the Bristol Guildhall, not understanding, quite reasonably saw blasphemy. The misunderstandings between Nayler and them are clear from his examination.[37]

In response to questions he said that he made his extraordinary entrance into Bristol at the command of the indwelling Christ. He did not rebuke those who sang praises, because they were praising the Lord, not him as a man. Promptings from God were not his to rebuke; people about him heeded the Spirit within. No, he was not the "Fairest of Ten-Thousand." He could not help looking as he did, but he denied that his physical appearance was an "attribute" of any sort.

Q. Art thou the only Son of God?
A. I am the Son of God, but I have many brethren.
Q. Have any called thee by the name of Jesus?
A. Not as unto the visible, but as Jesus, the Christ that is in me.
Q. Dost thou own the name of the King of Israel?
A. Not as a creature, but if they give it to Christ within, I own it, and have a kingdom but not of this world; my kingdom is another world, of which thou wotest not.
Q. Whether or no art thou the Prophet of Most High?
A. Thou hast said, I am a Prophet.
Q. Dost thou own that attribute, the Judge of Israel?
A. The judge is but one, and is witnessed in me, and is the Christ, there must not be any joined with him: if they speak of the spirit in me, I own it only as God is manifest in the flesh, according to God dwelleth in me, and judgeth there himself.[38]

The answers were pure Quakerism. Fox had said the same things to Cromwell. The only christological note that Nayler introduced was his answer "Thou has said it." But pure Quakerism was blasphemy to those who believed that Christ was not within people but physically in heaven. And Nayler's replies lent themselves to misinterpretation. When, for example, they asked him whether he was "the everlasting Son of God," he replied that any in whom Christ dwelt was the everlasting Son, "and I do witness God in the flesh; I am the Son of God, and the Son of God is but one." He meant, as he had said earlier, that he had "many brethren." For Nayler, Christ was the only Son of God and the Son "is but one" dwelling in many. When asked whether he or any of his followers blasphemed, he declared, "What is received of the Lord is true."

Q.   Was Dorcas Erbury dead two days in Exeter, and didst thou raise her?

A.   I can do nothing of myself: the Scripture bearest witness to the power in me which is everlasting; it is the same power we read of in the Scripture. The Lord hath made me a sign of his coming: and that honour that belongeth to Christ Jesus, in whom I am revealed, may be given to him, as when on earth at Jerusalem, according to the measure.

They called that blasphemy, and his answer, "Who made thee judge," also reflected his own refusal to judge his worshippers: "I ought not to slight anything which the spirit of the Lord moves." The entire examination made him seem arrogant beyond belief, if not worse, yet for his part he was reflecting the humility he felt before his God. Any miracle he had performed he attributed to the indwelling Christ; any worship directed at him he had received on the same behalf. Only at the end of the examination did he lose his self-control and violate Quaker precepts. Nayler had offered excessive tenderness to a woman whom Fox had rejected as unclean in spirit; on learning that Nayler favored her, Fox reproved him for treating her like "the mother," that is, the Virgin Mary. The Bristol examiners asked Nayler why he had called her "mother, as George Fox affirms." Nayler exclaimed, "George Fox is a lyar and a firebrand of hell; for neither I, nor any with me, called her so." Long after, Nayler declared that that was the only answer he regretted.[39]

Nayler's worshippers when examined did not make the distinctions that he did, and their testimony did him harm, as if he were guilty of their blasphemies. One woman acknowledged that she should worship him on her knees because "James Nayler will be Jesus, when the new life is born in him." If there was any ambiguity in her statement, she resolved it when she added that Nayler had the spirit of Jesus in him "above all men." Dorcas Erbury's evidence was the most damaging. She insisted that Nayler raised her from the dead and therefore was Jesus. They asked whether Jesus Christ did not sit at the right hand of God, and she replied, "He, whom thou callest Nayler, shall sit at the right-hand of the Father. . . ."[40]

The Bristol magistrates, believing that they were confronted by more than they could cope with, sent a transcript of the proceedings under seal to their deputy in the House of Commons. He reported it to the house, which appointed a committee of fifty-five to investigate and propose action. The committee summoned Nayler, three women including Dorcas, and the man who called Nayler Jesus. Five members of the committee interrogated them in even greater detail than had the Bristol officials. Nayler, of course, was the center of attention. In the end the committee of fifty-five agreed on two charges against him: that he assumed "the gesture, words, honour, worship, and miracles of our blessed Saviour," and that he had assumed His "names and incommunicable attributes."[41]

Nayler replied to the committee as candidly as he had in Bristol, yet the committee took every point as "proved" against him by his own words. They reported that he did not deny being "the only begotten Son of God," although he insisted, "I am the Son of God, but I have many brethren." When the question was asked whether he was the "only begotten Son," he replied, "Thou has said it. . . . Do not ensnare the innocent." The committee resolved that he claimed the title of "the Prophet of the most high God," although he declared, "There be other Prophets besides me." Similarly the committee resolved that he claimed to be king of Israel, when in fact he denied all titles "as a creature," although he acknowledged that the Christ in him was king. When he conceded that others gave the name Jesus "to the Christ that is in me," they resolved that he had assumed the name; yet he denied that he ever used the name for himself. They insistently misconstrued his meaning. At one point he stated, "Nay, do not add to my words; I speak as plain as I can, that all the glory may be given to God, and none to the creature . . . and none to me, as you look upon me as a creature." If his companions attributed anything to James Nayler that belonged to God, "then it is reprovable." He took their remarks as honoring the Lord; otherwise he would have "utterly denied" them. After the committee had examined him for the third and last time, they allowed him a final statement. It was a sockdolager:

> I do abhor that any of that honor which is due to God should be given to me, as I am a creature: But it pleased the Lord to set me up as a sign of the coming of the righteous one; and what hath been done in my passing through the towns, I was commanded by the power of the Lord to suffer such things to be done to the outward as a sign. I abhor any honour as a creature.

Thomas Bampfield, a man respected enough to become the next speaker of the house, reported to the House of Commons on behalf of the committee that Nayler was guilty of blasphemy and various misdemeanors.[42]

From the moment that the House of Commons had taken jurisdiction of Nayler's case, his conviction was certain and Cromwell's policy of toleration was in jeopardy. Under the 1653 Instrument of Government, by which Cromwell had become protector, most Christians were free to worship as they pleased. The protectorate was a Puritan Commonwealth tempered by a very broad measure of toleration, even more in fact than in law. Article 35 of the Instrument "recommended" the Christian religion as the religion of the nation and provided for its support, but article 37 protected anyone professing faith in God through Jesus, "though differing in judgment from the doctrine, worship, or discipline publickly held forth." At the time of Nayler's case, no doctrine, worship, or discipline had been defined. The Instrument of Government provided that except for "popery or prelacy" and "licentiousness," no one should be restrained in his religion who did not use his "liberty to the civil injury of others" or "actual disturbance of the peace." The Instrument, which reflected the wishes of Cromwell, his Council of State, and the army, was imposed upon a reluctant Parliament. From the outset Parliament sought to narrow Cromwell's policy of toleration. Members of the house were appalled by his courtesies toward Quakers, his talks with Fifth Monarchists, his dignifying Anglican priests, and his refusal to enforce laws against both Roman Catholic worship and Anglican use of the Book of Common Prayer. Cromwell's policy prevailed because the army backed him. He would have liked the Protestant clergy to agree on a national church comprehensive enough to take in all Protestants, from the sectarians to peaceable Anglicans like Archbishop Ussher. Cromwell drew the line against Socinians, who repudiated the divinity of Christ, and against Ranters, whom he believed opposed to all religion.[43]

Cromwell's hope for a comprehensive national church foundered on sectarian divisions. The Protestant clergy of England bitterly disagreed among themselves; they could not even concur on the fundamentals of the Christian faith. Not even the Presbyterians and Independents could agree, though they were all Puritans; indeed, members of the same sect conflicted among themselves. As time passed the Congregationalists had emerged as the strongest Independent sect, and they grew increasingly conservative. The Independents opposed a national church and uniformity in religion. By the time of the protectorate, the Congregationalists, like their counterparts in New England, favored state support of religion and religious guidance of the state. As time passed the Congregationalists grew closer to the Presbyterians than to the separatistic and voluntary churches of the sects from which Congregationalism had sprung. But even the Presbyterians were divided between latitudinarians like Richard Baxter and those like Samuel Rutherford who looked to Scotland. The principal difference between Congregationalists and Presbyterians was that the former believed that individual churches should be self-governing, while the latter preferred a centralized ecclesiastical polity of church synods. Both Congregationalists and Presbyterians, who dominated Parliament in the 1650's, strongly favored an establishment of trinitarian Protestantism along Calvinist lines, and they supported the continuance of tithes. Cromwell too favored tithes till some better substitute might be found.[44]

Cromwell's toleration policy, by seeking to please almost everyone, antagonized the most powerful alliance in Parliament—Congregationalists and Presbyterians. The protector's settlement allowed each parish to choose its minister from lists approved by committees that certified ministerial fitness. Congregationalists, other Independents, Presbyterians, and a few Baptists controlled the committees of certification. In effect England had a plural establishment of various Puritan churches that was wedded, reluctantly, to a constitutional policy of toleration for the numerous gathered churches that supported themselves and existed outside the establishment. It was a strange and divided confederation of Protestant denominations, plus the sects, without doctrines or rites beyond profession of Christ. Anglicanism labored under repressing legal disabilities, but in practice the government in the 1650s— Cromwell and his council—connived at allowing religious liberty for them and any Christians (Socinians always excluded) who did not disturb the state or the worship of others. The persecution of the Fifth Monarchists was centralized but motivated purely by political considerations. The persecution of the Quakers was locally inspired, not centrally, but only because Parliament could not dominate the religious settlement of the Commonwealth, try as it might. Catholics, a despised and untolerated minority, to Parliament's alarm were left unmolested even in London, as were Anglicans, if they worshipped quietly, although the worship of both violated the law. The Venetian ambassador in 1655 reported that the English were "divided into as many faiths as there are heads, and the number of religions equals the number of men." The protector, he observed, favored no sect and it, "suits his policy that 246 religions should be professed in London . . . differing greatly from each other and incompatible. This division into so many sects makes them all weak, so that no one [sect] is strong enough to cause his apprehension."[45]

Most Puritans in and outside of Parliament abhorred the sects, abhorred tolerating them officially, and abhorred the de facto toleration of Anglicans and Catholics. And Parliament represented, in the main, the Puritans. They divided on religious matters but not radically on the issue of toleration, and on this issue Parliament probably represented the nation more accurately than did the executive branch and the army. If Cromwell's first protectorate Parliament had had its way, it would have produced what the quarreling divines could not—a confession of faith that subverted the Instrument of Government. If Parliament had had its way, it would have disposed of John Biddle under the Blasphemy Act of 1648. If Parliament had had its way, it would have excluded from the scope of toleration many of the self-supporting gathered churches that used lay ministers. Parliament was particularly rabid in condemning "atheism, blasphemy, damnable heresies, popery, prelacy, licentiousness, and profaneness," all of which it moved to bring exclusively within its jurisdiction and definition. Parliamentary intolerance, representing a Puritan phalanx of conservative Independents, Congregationalists, and Presbyterians, plus a few Particular Baptists (Calvinists), was deadly opposed to the tolerance of the executive and the army. In a blistering attack on their bigotry, Cromwell dissolved his first Parliament in January 1656, after it sat for five months. By dissolving Parliament he saved Biddle and prevented the formation of a national or uniform confession of faith determined by the Commons.[46]

Cromwell's second protectorate Parliament, which met in September 1656, was even more conservative than the first on religious matters. Of 460 who were elected, approximately one hundred were so objectionable that the Council of State, under a power wrested out of the Instrument of Government, excluded them. About fifty more failed to take their seats. The remainder were loyal to Cromwell, but not to the latitudinarian religious provisions of the Instrument. This was the Parliament that passed by a two-to-one majority a severe recusancy act intended to disable the practice of Roman Catholic worship. The same Parliament, which offered the crown to Cromwell, forced a change in the constitution of England by altering the religious provisions of the Instrument. The new constitution of 1657 provided for a "Confession of Faith," to be jointly approved by the protector and Parliament; "no other" profession or worship should "be held forth and asserted" as the public profession, but orthodox trinitarians who believed the Scriptures as the revealed word of God would be tolerated. Socinians, irreligious persons, "Popery," and "Prelacy" would not be tolerated, nor would any who should "revile or reproach the Confession of Faith," or blaspheme, or behave licentiously. By implication Quakerism and dozens of obscure sects, including Familists, Sabellians, Muggletonians, Seventh Day Baptists, Fifth Monarchists, and Ranters, were proscribed.[47]

And this was the Parliament, the "Nayler Parliament," so called by the historian Thomas Carlyle, who floridly satirized it as follows:

> To Posterity they sit there as the James-Nayler Parliament. Four-hundred Gentlemen of England, and I think a sprinkling of Lords among them, assembled from all the counties and Boroughs of the Three Nations, to sit in solemn debate on this terrific Phenomenon; a Mad Quaker fancying or seeming to fancy himself, what is not uncommon since, a new Incarnation of Christ. Shall we hang him, shall we whip him, bore the tongue of him with hot iron, shall we imprison him, set him to oakum [making hemp]; shall we roast, or boil, or stew him;—shall we put the question whether this question shall be put; debate whether this shall be debated;—in Heaven's name, what shall we do with him, the terrific Phenomenon of Nayler? This is the history of Oliver's Second Parliament for three long months and odd.[48]

Carlyle's parody lacked understanding, because the Nayler case raised fundamental constitutional questions that received serious consideration by Parliament. Moreover, the case really tested the limits of tolerance in a Christian commonwealth that enjoyed a greater degree of free exercise of religion than England had ever known, and many members of Parliament, including some rabid ones, sought to rationalize their positions. Not since the Servetus case had there been so important a blasphemy trial, and this one produced the greatest debate on the meaning of blasphemy, and thus on the limits of toleration, in English history. In the end Parliament exercised its *judicial* powers to condemn Nayler for "horrid blasphemy" and sentenced him to grisly corporal punishment followed by an indeterminate period in prison. But the end was not a foregone conclusion. The key votes were close, and the issues so complex that many members could not make up their minds; almost one-third of the house abstained from voting.

From the beginning there was no certainty that Nayler had violated any law or, if he had, what that law was. Was it parliamentary law, common law, natural law, moral law, or biblical law? Was his crime, if he had committed one, divine impersonation, seduction, idolatry, or blasphemy? Was an offense against religion an offense against the state when the head of the state was not the head of a national church? In the absence of ecclesiastical courts, which had been abolished since 1641, was an offense against religion merely a sin, which was cognizable only by God? If Nayler had committed blasphemy, and it was a high crime against God, comparable to treason, could or should the state vindicate the honor of God? What did blasphemy mean? Were there differing degrees and kinds of blasphemy, some capital in nature and others not? If blasphemy was a crime punishable by the state, did jurisdiction over it lie with the regular criminal courts or could Parliament intercede? A trial court had sentenced William

Franklin for claiming to be Jesus, in 1650, prior to the enactment of the statute against the Ranters; but no determination had ever been made by the King's Bench, the high court of criminal jurisdiction, that blasphemy was an offense at common law. That did not happen until 1676. The House of Commons had tried and convicted Paul Best for blasphemy in 1646, but they had no law for their action, and even after imprisoning him they never reached a formal decision of a judicial or a legislative nature. The house kept John Biddle in jail without even trying him. During the debate on Nayler's case no one dissented from those who pointed out that Parliament had not judged Biddle in a legal sense. As Lord Chief Justice Glynne told the "Nayler Parliament," "This is a new case before you, and it will be a precedent." He and many others would have let the courts decide the precedent." For Parliament to decide it, some legalists believed, was "dangerous."[49]

Under the Instrument of Government of 1653, which was the Constitution of Great Britain, "the supreme legislative authority" was vested in the lord protector, assisted by a Council of State whose approval he required. Parliaments were to be called every third year, consisting of one house only. Bills enacted by Parliament required the consent of the executive, who might dissolve any Parliament after it had sat for five months. The Instrument vested no judicial authority in Parliament. The House of Lords before its abolition in 1649 could act as the highest court of the land. Did its judicial authority somehow devolve upon the Commons, authorizing them to take jurisdiction of Nayler's case? If so, what law had he broken? A judicial body can apply only the standing law; it cannot otherwise punish. Did Nayler violate the Blasphemy Act of 1648? Significantly, no one during the entire debate on Nayler's case relied on that statute; it was a dead letter. Some members tried to wrest precedents against Nayler from the Bible and even from the act of 1401 for the burning of heretics, *De Haeretico Comburendo*, but not a member even referred to the act of 1648. They seemed to assume that the Blasphemy Act of 1650 against the Ranters had superseded that of 1648. Francis Rous, a member of Cromwell's council, sought Nayler's death, but declared, "The laws against blasphemy and Ranters are in force, and you may proceed upon them," forgetting that the courts had jurisdiction under that statute and that the penalty for a first offense was only six months. John Thurloe, the secretary of state, declared, "I know no law in force this day against blasphemy; unless it be that of the Old Parliament"—the act of 1650.[50]

Could Parliament proceed against Nayler under its *legislative* authority? If so, Cromwell could veto any bill. Parliament might pass a bill of attainder, that is, a legislative declaration of guilt against the accused and a sentence against him; but all the precedents seemed to show that attainders had been based on some standing law—that, at least, was the legal theory. Alternatively, Parliament might proceed by an ex post facto law, making criminal an act committed earlier and not at the time illegal. Some declared that any attainder in this case must be retroactive, but many warned against the injustice of ex post facto laws. "You are launching into a matter of great consequence," warned Major General

Howard. "Whatever you do in this, it may be of ill consequence to posterity." "To take away a man's life by a subsequent law, it is of dangerous consequence," warned Colonel William Sydenham, a councillor. Another councillor, Walter Strickland, urged, "I would have every Englishman be careful in this case. It has been our happiness to be governed by a known law." One theme that ran continuously throughout the debates was that Parliament had no law for what it was doing. Yet some took the view that "Parliament is so sovereign, that it may declare that to be an offence, which never was an offence before." When, however, Major General Thomas Kelsey said, near the end, "This is a new business. . . . You have no law for what you do," he was technically correct.[51]

Because the case was unprecedented, there was no knowledge for sure how to proceed or what to call the crime. Government spokesmen had no fixed position, except perhaps that death was too severe a punishment. Those who insisted that Nayler had committed a "horrid" blasphemy demanded death; avenging the honor of God required an exemplary vindication before the whole nation. That too was a major theme of debate, reiterated monotonously. One of the revengers was Bampfield, who chaired the committee report. He called the moderates the "merciful" party. Although Cromwell was the leader of the merciful party, he kept aloof from the affair until after Parliament rendered its judgment. Only then, when demanding to know by what authority the members had acted, did he reveal that not even he could extenuate Nayler's conduct. He detested giving the least countenance "to persons of such opinions and practices, or who are under guilt of such crimes as are imputed to the said person. . . ." But he did not want Nayler executed. Yet his elder son and successor, Lord Richard Cromwell, announced at a state dinner, well before Parliament voted against capital punishment, that "Nayler deserves to be hanged." The members of the Council of State who held seats in Parliament, although tending to oppose death, reflected a spectrum of opinion ranging from broad toleration to bloodthirsty prejudice.[52]

The lord president of the council, Henry Lawrence, was the one who declared that God was in "every horse, in every stone, in every creature," and added, "If you hang every man that says, 'Christ is in you the hope of glory,' you will hang a good many." Every Quaker said that, he observed. He understood and accepted as tolerably Christian Nayler's distinction between the historical Christ who died in Jerusalem and the Christ that was "in him in the highest measure." Lawrence thought it was a "sad" opinion, no more. He could not call it blasphemy of any sort. "It is hard to define what is blasphemy," he remarked. Doubtless, members thought Arianism was blasphemy, and so too was denying the divinity of Christ, but people's private opinions were not an affair of Parliament. Lawrence acknowledged that he knew Quakers, discoursed with them about religion, and read some of their books. He hoped that most Christians knew "the mystery of Christ manifest in the flesh." Still, he thought that Quakers tended too much toward Arminianism and he would restrain them. But not by punishing for blasphemy.[53]

Major General Philip Skippon was also a member of the council. He called himself "the Christian Centurion," although one scholar called him a bigot and a typical Presbyterian. Skippon recommended that Nayler be "hanged, drawn, and quartered." His views represented nearly half the members who voted. The "growth of these things," he said of Quaker practices, "is more dangerous than the most intestine or foreign enemies. I have often been troubled in my thoughts to think of this toleration. . . . Their [Quaker] great growth and increase is notorious, both in England and Ireland; their principles strike at both ministry and magistracy." Skippon was jealous of God's honor and zealous for it. Nayler's blasphemy was "horrid." The Mosaic law governed the nation, Skippon held, and all who blasphemed should be accountable under it. He raged against "these Quakers, Ranters, Levellers, Socinians, and all sorts" who "bolster themselves under [Articles] thirty-seven and thirty-eight [of the Instrument] of Government, which, at one breath, repeals all the acts and ordinances against them." Nayler was the product of the Instrument's liberty of conscience, and so were the sects. "If this be liberty, God deliver me from such liberty. It is to evil, not to good, that this liberty extends." God's glory had been trampled enough by it.[54]

Major General William Boteler, an Independent, agreed with Skippon, and backed his case with biblical precedents, many far-fetched, to prove that Nayler should be stoned to death. As if they were theologians, soldiers and lawyers vied in construing arcane passages from the Scriptures to support of their arguments that Nayler had committed horrid blasphemy, or ordinary blasphemy, or some other offense. The Bible carried more weight by far than the common law, even more than parliamentary law, because the offense was against religion; Puritans knew their Bible and it yielded more precedents to construe than their secular law. George Smith, one of the judges who hanged Jock of Broad Scotland earlier that year, offered the case of several who were hanged in the sixteenth century for speaking against the Book of Common Prayer; and he reminded Parliament, its laws imposed death on a man who stole a shilling. "Yet we make nothing of robbing God of his glory." If the secular law failed, Judge Smith proposed, the Bible showed the way: death by stoning.[55]

Skippon's rant against Quakers, other sects, and liberty of conscience mirrored a theme of the revengers. They used Nayler's case to discredit the burgeoning sects generally and Quakerism in particular, which they found execrable. As of 1656 Nayler loomed larger and more dangerous than George Fox. Skippon believed that only "Biddle and his sect" were as dangerous as Nayler's. In and outside Parliament Nayler was described as "the chief of the Quakers," "a most eminent Ringleader," and "worst of all the Quakers." One member claimed that Nayler "writes all their books." His prominence, especially in London where he had proselytized so successfully, marked him as a target. After Parliament had sealed Nayler's fate, Colonel Sydenham of the council marvelled at how zealous members were against Nayler, yet were so merciful to his four companions whom Parliament also held in the Gatehouse prison. Bampfield, who had brought in the committee report, recommended that the four be sent "to the House of Correction for three months, and [you] rid your hands of them." And yet, Sydenham declared, they were the greater offenders; they had actually committed idolatry, whereas Nayler "denied all honour to himself." With "no law at all for it," Parliament had "opened a gap to prostitute both life, member, and liberty" by the "arbitrary" power of men who had the votes to do whatever they wanted.[56]

The reason for the distinction in treatment between Nayler and his companions is obvious: he appeared to be the great leader. "Cut off this fellow, and you will destroy the sect," one member urged. Anthony Ashley Cooper of the council sensibly replied that if Parliament killed Nayler, it would make him a martyr and multiply Quakerism. Although Cooper was of the merciful party and spoke abstractly for toleration, his Presbyterianism surfaced when he urged, "I would have you use some endeavour to suppress the growth of them in general." Griffith Bodurda, who found no blasphemy in Nayler, believed that "Millenaries" of "this sort of Quakers" should be "suppressed" as dangerous. Major General William Goffe, a prodigious Bible expert who advocated "amity, love, and charity" while urging death for Nayler as a horrid blasphemer, charged that all the Quakers "go about and revile the ordinances and ministers of Christ, and would tear the flesh off the bones that profess Christ." They were all "beasts" and deserved to die. Judge Smith lamented that England had the reputation among nations as "the great nursery of blasphemies and heresies." Colonel Briscoe too was sure that Quakers "are destructive to human society. . . . Do not they all hold against the essence of Government?" Sir George Downing, alarmed because Ranters and Quakers had increased by the "thousands," recommended that Parliament should "take them all off by a law." If it did not execute Nayler. "It is high time to take a course with them," chimed in Glynne, the chief justice; he knew from his experience that they contemned magistracy, and now "they grow to a great number."[57]

Whether the sects should be tolerated was the broad issue of the Nayler case. A few speakers, including Councillors Walter Strickland, Gilbert Pickering, and William Sydenham, like Henry Lawrence, the head of the council, defended toleration of the sects, Quakers included. "If Nayler be a blasphemer," said Sydenham, "all the generation of them are so, and he and all the rest must undergo the same punishment." Yet, "The opinions they hold," he declared, "do border so near a glorious truth, that I cannot pass my judgment that it is blasphemy." Those who defamed the sects and spoke alarmingly about their growth used the instance of James Nayler to reproach the Instrument of Government's toleration. His blasphemy, they claimed, proved that its lax policy easily degenerated into spiritual anarchy, fanaticism, and gross immorality. The result threatened the safety of the nation and of the Protestant religion. Skippon was correct about Article 38, for it held "null and void" all laws against religious freedom that conflicted with Article 37; but Article 37 only roughly defined that freedom. Captain Adam Baynes, one of the tolerationists who did not believe that Nayler had blasphemed, declared, "the Instrument of Government says, all shall be protected that confess faith in Jesus Christ, which, I suppose, this man does." But Colonel Francis White, in support of the same cause, corrected Baynes by quoting the Instrument to show that Article 37 set a proper limit on religious freedom by restricting it to those who did not injure others or practice licentiousness. Downing, a revenger, hoped that the Instrument would not stand in the way of death for a horrid blasphemer; and Goffe claimed that although he would give his life for the Instrument, "Yet if it hold out anything to protect such persons I would have it burnt in the fire."[58]

Lord Strickland, a tolerationist, called attention to the fact that wherever the Gospel flourished, "most prodigies of heresies and opinions" will be found, "which will happen always, unless you restrain the reading of the Scriptures." The right of each person to think for himself about the Scriptures was at stake, and that was what the Instrument protected. Banish Nayler if you must, Strickland observed, but nothing more. Even banishment would be a "dangerous precedent to posterity. It is against the Instrument to proceed. . . ." Bodurda, on the same side, objected to admitting the power of the civil magistrate in matters of religion. Those who demanded Nayler's death, he declared, kept claiming that the mind of God was clear in this matter, and they repeatedly resorted to biblical texts for various proofs; but, said Bordurda, he was sure that Nayler "would also say, 'The mind of God was clear to him,' and it may be proved just, by as many texts." Colonel Holland summed up the tolerationist view: "Consider the state of this nation, what the price of our blood is. Liberty of conscience, the Instrument gives it us. We remember how many Christians were formerly martyred under the notion of blasphemy; and who can define what it is."[59]

Many definitions were offered and applied to the case, but every member shaped his argument to suit the outcome he sought. By no means were all of the "merciful" party tolerationists. Not that anyone opposed toleration in the abstract. Even Skippon and the other revengers favored their brand of it. The real tolerationists were those who opposed finding blasphemy in the case and construed the Instrument and anything else at hand—the Bible, the examples of Holland and Poland, natural law, moral law, common law, and parliamentary law—to prove their point. All the tolerationists were merciful men, but not all the merciful men were tolerationists. Indeed, most who opposed the revengers opposed death or a brutal sentence, but not a lighter sentence. Few openly claimed that Nayler was guiltless or deserved no punishment whatever. But the revengers took the lead, from the moment Bampfield presented the committee's report, and the others resorted to all sorts of maneuvers to oppose whatever motions the vengeful recommended.

At the very beginning, when the committee reported on December 4, 1656, the revengers wanted to condemn Nayler on the basis of the report, while their opponents demanded witnesses, sworn testimony, and a fair trial. For two days Parliament debated whether Nayler should be given an opportunity to speak against the charges, although they had not agreed on the charges. Those who argued for due process voted with many who confidently expected Nayler to hang himself by confessing his guilt. Most members had never seen him and were curious. Major General John Lambert, a councillor, had known Nayler well. "He was two years my quartermaster," Lambert recalled, "and a very useful person. We parted with him with great regret. He was a man of unblameable life and conversation, a member of a very sweet society of an independent church. How he comes . . . to be puffed up to this opinion I cannot determine."[60]

On December 6 Nayler was brought before the bar of the house. He refused to kneel or remove his hat; they had expected that and agreed that he might stand, but the sergeant-at-arms took off his hat. The clerk read to him the main sections of the committee's report. Thomas Burton, who recorded the parliamentary debate, was one of the vengeful. He recorded that Nayler, "in effect, confessed," and some historians accepted Burton's judgment. However, Nayler's words show only an admission that the committee had accurately reported what he had said. Nayler hoped that Parliament would not misconstrue his meaning. When questioned for less than half an hour, he told the same story as before, denying any worship paid to him. "I abhor it, as I am a creature." If Christ was in him, they asked, how did he pray to the Christ who died at Jerusalem? To questions on this problem Burton recorded none of Nayler's answers, noting only that he "answered pretty orthodoxly."[61]

After Nayler withdrew and awaited judgment in the Gatehouse prison nearby, the debate rambled and raged for nine long days before the decisive voting. The revengers demanded and won immediate acceptance of the committee's report. "Seeing Nayler must die," one member promptly said, "I desire to know what manner of death it must be." Members roared objections. Questions of procedure and jurisdiction remained to be resolved, let alone the character of the offense; talk of punishment was quite premature. On the evening of December 8, the revengers won another victory when Parliament resolved, without a vote count, that Nayler "upon the whole matter, in fact, is guilty of horrid blasphemy." Not even that was conclusive, because they continued to argue as if every question were still open; often more than one question was before the house at a time, and members, on getting the floor addressed several issues. Everything—procedure, jurisdiction, the offense, its punishment— seemed interwoven. But the overriding issue was clear to all: Would death be the punishment?[62]

When the revengers recommended the use of Parliament's legislative power by passing either an attainder or an ex post facto law, the merciful and the tolerationists demurred at the injustice as well as the danger to posterity. When the revengers recommended Parliament's judicial power as the basis for its sentence, the others claimed that no such power existed, or, if it did, it could not extend to life or limb. When a vengeful Ashe located the source of parliamentary judicial authority in *De Haeretico Comburendo*, the act of 1401 for the burning of heretics, the reply shot back, we will never rake out those ashes; under that law we must all burn as heretics and blasphemers. When the revengers claimed that Nayler had blasphemed and that Parliament should not trifle about the law that authorized the death penalty, the others looked to lesser offenses.[63]

When the revengers insisted that Nayler's blasphemy was "horrid," the others ridiculed the distinction between blasphemy and horrid blasphemy, although they adeptly made distinctions of their own to suit their purposes. Those distinctions between blasphemy and lesser offenses saved Nayler's life. The vengeful claimed that Nayler's offense was the "crime that deposes the majesty of God Himself, *crimen laesae maiestatis*, the ungodding of God," was Major Beake said. The vindictive Downing asserted that blasphemy was the highest offense: "treason against Heaven." No one commented on the blasphemous irony in his reminding the house that Nayler would not remove his hat, "though you be gods in one sense." But the other faction denied that Nayler had blasphemed at all. He had exalted himself, Councillor Strickland admitted, but neither he nor any of his followers claimed that he was Jesus or Christ. He did not allege that "the essence of Christ is in him." He was scandalous, overproud, and sinful, but not a blasphemer, because he honored God; a blasphemer would curse or revile Him. All the mercifuls and tolerationists agreed on that point. Leviticus 24:15–16 proved that capital blasphemy consisted only in reviling God.[64]

Bulstrode Whitelocke, the lord commissioner of the treasury and an eminent jurist, studied the Hebrew text and patiently explained it. He defined the Hebrew words, concluding that this was not a case warranting death. Indeed if those lusting for Nayler's blood had understood the very text that they claimed as the basis for their judgment, they would have known that in Hebrew law the crime of blasphemy could not be committed at all unless the very name of God was cursed. Some divines, Whitelocke conceded, disagreed whether the sacred name must be the express object of the curse, but all agreed that without speaking evil of God and making imprecations against Him, there was no blasphemy. At worst, Nayler's offense came within the fifteenth, not the sixteenth, verse of Leviticus 24, and so merited only a whipping. With a lawyer's fine sense for punctilios, Whitelocke noted that the motion to condemn Nayler for "horrid blasphemy" did not specify that it was blasphemy "against God." In any case, God's mind in the matter was not knowable, and His law did not require death. Nayler's claim that Christ dwelt within him did not constitute blasphemy. That claim, Whitelocke observed, was not uncommon, for even the Lutherans believed in "the ubiquity of Christ." Whitelocke recommended that Parliament turn the case over to the Upper Bench; let the highest judges grapple with the problem. Parliament ought to do nothing more. "One Parliament may count one thing horrid blasphemy, another parliament another thing. The word blasphemy may be as far extended as was heresy." Whitelocke hoped not. Once, opposition to tithes was heresy, and now some said that having compulsory tithes was heresy. Learn from past mistakes. Whitelocke urged. If Nayler died, no man might be safe in the future. Whitelocke's long speech was a marvel of erudite learning in law, religion, and history. If any of his listeners had been undecided, they must have been influenced by his proofs that no law—Mosaic, Gospel, moral, natural, national, or international—supported the death penalty.[65]

But Whitelocke persuaded no one whose mind was already convinced. The vengeful members, challenged time and again to defined the particular nature of Nayler's blasphemy, replied that Nayler had assumed the honors and attributes of God or Christ, or they misstated the facts by claiming that he had passed himself off as Christ. Every misstatement provided the others with a chance to correct the record. Those who worshipped Nayler were idolaters, said Pickering, but not Nayler. "Take well what he said for himself as well as against." Pickering recalled that the late John Selden, the greatest parliamentarian, after listening to Paul Best the Socinian, had remarked that Best was a better man than he thought himself to be. "That may be this man's case," Pickering added. Nayler simply gave himself out to be "a prophet, a type, a sign, to warn men of the second coming of Christ. . . .' Samuel Highland stressed that Nayler not only did not revile God; he worshipped Christ. Where was the blasphemy?[66]

To that the revengers replied that because Nayler was a Christian, his assuming the attributes of Christ magnified the offense. The tolerationists responded that he did not say Christ dwelt wholly or exclusively in him, and one member reminded the others that Christ himself said that blasphemy should be forgiven (Matt. 4:19). To the revengers, however, the doctrine of the indwelling Christ was blasphemous in and of itself. Blasphemy, they admitted, might in its literal sense mean speaking evil of God, but its commonsense meaning was that no person could call himself Christ. Major General Packer replied that if the crime was against God, no man could decide for Him. Many of us, like Job, are blasphemers, he said. As for Nayler, he adored, not vilified; he believed in the Father, the Son, and the Holy Spirit. Let him repent, even if it was only a "show" of repentance. Those wanting his death misinterpreted his words in such a way as to require the destruction of all the sects. The Christian way was moderate and tolerant. "You may as well condemn a Papist," said Packer, "for worshipping Christ in the bread and wine, as in this case of Nayler's." Cooper saw in Nayler a dark carriage and a strong delusion, but not blasphemy, surely not horrid blasphemy. If there was horrid blasphemy, did that mean there was blasphemy "more horrid, and most horrid? I offer it to you, whether it were not a greater blasphemy to say he were very Christ." Cooper dared not say it was blasphemy at all. Nayler, he noted, made a "nice distinction, a vast difference between Christ Jesus dwelling in us, and being worshipped in a creature." Still others seeking to save Nayler said he acted without malice, was only a seducer or an imposter, merely disturbed the peace, had high delusions, or set up signs like an idolater. But he was no blasphemer, let alone a horrid one.[67]

On December 16, the members were finally ready for a conclusive vote. A motion that Nayler be executed lost by a vote of ninety-six to eighty-two. The debate suddenly collapsed. Rapid motions were introduced on lesser punishments—that his long hair be cut, that he be branded with a "B," that his tongue be slit—and were voted up or down. Finally the motions that passed, all without recorded vote, were stitched together to produce a sentence:

> Resolved, that James Nayler be set on the pillory, with his head in the pillory, in the New Palace Westminster, during the space of two hours, on Thursday next, and be whipped by the hangman through the streets of Westminster to the Old

Exchange, London; and there, likewise, to be set upon the pillory, with his head in the pillory, for space of two hours, between the hours of eleven and one, on Saturday next; in each of the said places, wearing a paper containing an inscription of his crimes: and that at the Old Exchange, his tongue shall be bored through with a hot iron, and that he be there also stigmatized in the forehead with the letter B.; and that he be, afterwards, sent to Bristol and conveyed into and through the said city, on a horse bare ridged, with his face back, and there also publickly whipped, the next market-day after he comes thither: and that from thence he be committed to prison in Bridewell, London, and there restrained from the society of all people, and kept to hard labour till he be released by the Parliament: and, during that time, be debarred of the use of pen, ink, and paper, and have no relief but what he earns by his daily labour.

The boring of the tongue, implicitly, and the branding with "the letter B," explicitly, signified the crime of blasphemy. The sentence was entered as a judgment of Parliament, that is, a judicial sentence not subject to review by the courts, thus preventing appeals, bailing, or release on habeas corpus.[68]

Debate resumed on the question of whether Nayler should be recalled to the bar to hear the sentence. The vengeful members opposed that, although Chief Justice Glynne had never heard of a case in which a convicted man was not given an opportunity to say why judgment should not be passed against him. A compromise was arranged: they voted to call him back to hear their judgment but not to let him speak against it. Sir Thomas Widdrington, the speaker, told Nayler he had escaped death: "They desire your reformation rather than destruction." Nayler asked what his crime was; he tried several times to say more but was cut off. The speaker pronounced the sentence. As Nayler was led away he said, "God will, I hope, give me a spirit to endure it." Some members were bitter that an Englishman should have been denied his right to speak about the judgment against him.[69]

The first part of the sentence was executed on December 18. "The eyes of the whole nation are upon you in this business," revengers had repeated during the debate. Now the eyes of London were on Nayler. He stood in the pillory near Parliament with a paper pinned to his hat, inscribed "For horrid blasphemy and being a Grand Impostor and Seducer of the People." Although the weather was unusually cold, the bailiff stripped him to the waist after they took him down from the pillory, and bound him to the back of a cart which they drew to the Exchange. The executioner, using a whip of seven cords, each knotted, lashed Nayler at every step. He took 310 lashes. Colonel Holland reported to Parliament that the women who later nursed Nayler's wounds told Holland "there was no skin left between his shoulders and his hips." A Quaker, who watched the punishment and walked alongside the cart, reported that he did not cry out.[70]

In Parliament that day members presented petitions against Quakers from various cities and counties. The revengers wanted a statute against them generally and also a new act against blasphemy. The Quakers were all "levellers," said one, against authority and property. Whitelocke opposed either bill.

Sydenham agreed: "It is like the word Lollards or Puritans, under the notion whereof, many godly people are now [buried] under the altar, their blood being poured out. It is of dangerous consequence." Strickland would have no act against blasphemy; punish only disturbers of the peace, he argued. "We may all, in after ages, be called Quakers." Laws against Papists, he reminded, had been turned against "the best Protestants." The proposed bills were consigned to a committee which let them die, although in the following year, 1657, Cromwell accepted from Parliament a new constitution that constricted the liberty of conscience guaranteed by the Instrument of Government.[71]

Londoners, having watched Nayler receive the first part of his punishment, petitioned Parliament to suspend the rest of it. General Lambert, affirming that Nayler was too sick to undergo the remainder, urged that a physician be sent to him. Parliament decided to send "some godly ministers" instead, but postponed the next dose of the punishment for another week. On December 20 crowds were at the doors of Parliament with petitions on behalf of Nayler. After a debate whether to receive some prosperous burghers, the house by one vote allowed thirty to enter. They represented about one hundred; their spokesman was once a chaplain in the New Model Army. They were honest, godly persons who disowned the crime, Lambert said. None was a Quaker. Their petition spoke for "Conscience-Liberty." They claimed that the state should not pass judgment on religious error or blasphemy, and that corporal punishment in such a case was wrong. They had signed the petition, they said, out of "tenderness to the cause of spiritual and civil liberty." Resting their case on Article 37 of the Instrument, they requested that the remainder of the sentence be cancelled. When they withdrew, a debate flared anew on the basic question of whether liberty of conscience meant protection for blasphemers, but "being weary of it," the house adjourned for lunch.[72]

The same petitioners, joined by many others, turned to Cromwell. One petition forwarded to him at this time came from George Fox; it was less a petition than a theological statement of the Quaker position on Immanence written when Parliament first took custody of Nayler. Fox did not mention Nayler by name. the only point of pertinence was a cryptic postscript: "If the seed speake which is Christ . . . it is not blasphemie but truth, but if the seed of the serpent speake and say he is Christ it is the Liar and the blasphemie and the ground of all blasphemie. . . ." Cromwell offered no support to the petitioners for "spiritual and civil liberty." He intervened only with a terse letter to Parliament asking for their grounds of the sentence against Nayler. That provoked a two-day debate on constitutional issues bearing on the adjudicatory powers of Parliament and touching only incidentally on the issue of blasphemy. In the end Parliament proved incapable of formulating a response to the protector. But some of the mercifuls tried to use the issue to obtain a decision on the petition to cancel the rest of the sentence. They lost overwhelmingly, 113 to 59. Members knew that when the deputation of ministers had met with Nayler on Christmas Day, he had still defended his beliefs. Downing shouted, "We are God's executioners. . . . Had you anything from himself, of recantation, it were something. But, as the case is, if ten thousand should come to the door and petition, I would die upon the place before I would remit the sentence you have already passed." Even some of the mercifuls made much of the fact that Cromwell had not asked for a remission of the sentence. And Nathaniel Fiennes, a councillor who had stood with the mercifuls, argued that the petition for remission was "dangerous," because it would "debar the civil magistrate in matters of religion. . . . That is too much liberty."[73]

On December 28th Nayler underwent the second part of the sentence. Burton, one of the revengers, was present among the crowd of "many thousands." They were strangely quiet and sympathetic, and those who were closest and could see the spectacle stood bareheaded. Burton recorded that he went

> to see Nayler's tongue bored through, and him marked in the forehead. He put out his tongue very willingly, but shrinked a little when the iron came upon his forehead. He was pale when he came out of the pillory, but highcoloured after tongue-boring. He was bound with a cord by both arms to the pillory. Rich, the mad merchant [a Quaker] sat bare at Nayler's feet all the time. Sometimes he sang and cried, and stroked his hair and face, and kissed his hand, and sucked the fire out of his forehead. Nayler embraced his executioner, and behaved himself very handsomely and patiently. A great crowd of people there . . .

A week later Nayler still could not speak.[74]

The final part of the sentence was executed in mid-January in Bristol, as a burlesque of Nayler's entrance there about three months earlier. They transported him to that city sitting on a horse with his face to the rear. In Bristol, they stripped him for the whipping. This time, however, the Quakers of the city turned out en masse to support him; many wept. Bristol had more compassion than Westminster. The authorities allowed one of Nayler's friends to hold the executioner's arm to check his lashes. From Bristol, soldiers conveyed him back to London's Bridewell prison to begin a perpetual imprisonment. He was put to hard labour in solitary confinement and denied a fire to keep him warm in winter.[75]

In February 1658 Nayler, who had been gravely ill, repented by acknowledging that he had been possessed by a dark spirit and had received idolatrous worship. The Spirit of Jesus in him now dictated "lowness, meekness and longsuffering." He wanted Fox's forgiveness, but Fox was unyielding. On September 8, 1659, after nearly three years, the Rump Parliament released Nayler. The army, by then, had deposed Richard Cromwell as the second protector, and it freed many Quakers. Nayler, subdued, returned to preaching. At a London meeting arranged by common Friends, he and Fox appeared on the same platform, but Fox was distant. In 1660, thirteen months after his liberation from Bridewell, Nayler at the age of forty-four, a sick and broken man, died— the victim of a system that could not allow "too much liberty." In that year the Stuart Restoration began. Soon after, the Puritan "priests" who had shrieked for Nayler's life, as well as the Quaker preachers who had reviled those priests, were jailed by the tens of thousands, fellow prisoners.[76]

4

Did the Zenger Case Really Matter? Freedom of the Press in Colonial New York

THE PERSISTENT IMAGE of colonial America as a society which cherished freedom of expression is a sentimental hallucination that ignores history. The evidence provides little comfort for the notion that the colonies hospitably received advocates of obnoxious or detestable ideas on matters that counted. Nor is there reason to believe that rambunctious unorthodoxies suffered only from Puritan bigots and tyrannous royal judges. The American people and their representatives simply did not understand that freedom of thought and expression means equal freedom for the other fellow, particularly the one with the hated ideas.

To be sure, the utmost freedom often existed on the frontier. The test of free speech, however, is not the right of a man to soliloquize or shout his outrageous opinions from the top of a lonely mountain; it is, rather, his right to speak openly and with impunity among his neighbors. Colonial America may have been the scene of the most extraordinary diversity of opinion on religion, politics, and other vital subjects, but each community, especially outside the few "cities," tended to be a tight little island clutching its own orthodoxy, willing to banish or extralegally to punish unwelcome dissidence. As John P. Roche says so strikingly, "Colonial America was an open society dotted with closed enclaves, and one could generally settle with his co-believers in safety and comfort and exercise the right of oppression."[1]

When vigorously expressed nonconformist opinions were suffered to exist by the community, they were likely to run afoul of the law. In colonial America, as in England, the common law of seditious libel was strung out like a chicken wire of constraint making the open discussion of public issues hazardous, if not impossible, except when public opinion opposed administration policy. However, the judiciary in America, particularly in the eighteenth century, was not the agency that menaced those who would disturb an acquiescent public opinion. It is traditional, of course, to state that colonial times were troubled by a continuing struggle between "the royal judges" and American writers and printers who demanded freedom to criticize the government. The celebrated trial in 1735 of John Peter Zenger for seditious libel of the governor of New York is invariably presented in the context of such a struggle, and Zenger's acquittal is construed as a great victory against the judges and for freedom of the press.[2] No such struggle really existed. Moreover, the Zenger case had no appreciable effect upon the freedom, or rather lack of freedom, of the press in colonial New York.

Nevertheless, the verdict of history is correct in regarding this case as a watershed in the evolution of freedom of the press, not because it set a legal precedent, for it set none, but because the jury's verdict resonated with popular opinion. The widely read and frequently reprinted report of the case strengthened a widespread belief that the law of seditious libel derived from Star Chamber doctrines, belied common sense by denying truth as a defense, and denigrated the role of juries, thus jeopardizing the honest expression of opinions. The Zenger verdict made people exult both in liberty and the relationship of liberty of the press to liberty itself. Just as people understood the difference between gods and God, so too this case gave them a lucid understanding of what they knew instinctively, that a gulf existed between legal liberties and liberty. It invigorated their understanding that citizens—and Zenger's attorney spoke of "citizens," not just subjects—should distrust an unjust government that sought to overawe them. It fortified their conviction that in a season of tyranny, citizens must be forthright in their censure of that government and should enjoy impunity for their courage in speaking out truthfully. It made them believe that intemperance in governing justified intemperance in expression and that intemperate criticism of an arbitrary or corrupt administration, if true, should not be a crime. As a writer in the *Philadelphia Gazette* declared about the popular verdict, "if it is not law, it is better than law, it ought to be law, and will always be law wherever justice prevails."[3]

The Zenger case originated in a power struggle between New York's governor, William Cosby, and the political faction led by Lewis Morris, who determined to check Cosby's arrogant, mendacious, and illegal regime. Soon after his arrival in New York in the summer of 1732, the royal governor antagonized the local establishment. Rip Van Dam, a leading merchant who was the senior member of the Council, had acted as governor until Cosby arrived. Cosby demanded half the salary that the Council voted for Van Dam. When Van Dam refused to pay, Cosby sued him in the provincial supreme court, after first authorizing its judges to sit as a court of equity, which functioned without a jury. Chief Justice Lewis Morris accepted the arguments of Van Dam's lawyers, James Alexander and William Smith, that an equity court created solely by the governor was illegal, but the other two judges, James DeLancey and Frederick Philipse, supported the governor. Cosby fired Morris and elevated DeLancey to the chief justiceship, without the Council's consent. DeLancey's commission authorized his court to determine both civil and criminal cases. By contrast, in England the judges of the King's Bench, the supreme criminal court, possessed no civil jurisdiction, and the judges of the highest civil court, the Court of Common Pleas, exercised no criminal jurisdiction. Moreover, judges traditionally held office during "good behavior," but Cosby had appointed DeLancey and Philipse to serve at his "pleasure."

Morris, a nabob of New York, joined forces with Van Dam, Alexander and Smith, his two lawyers, Philip Livingston, and Cadwallader Colden, the colony's scientist-politician, and formed a "Popular Party" to challenge the judicial commissions, expose the arbitrary malfeasance of the governor, and regain political power. But the opposition faction needed a voice to shape and mobilize public opinion. Cosby controlled the sole newspaper of the province, the *New-York Gazette,* run by William Bradford, "The King's Printer." The solution was the founding of an opposition newspaper. Thus the *New-York Weekly Journal,* printed by John Peter Zenger, originated as a propaganda vehicle for the Morris faction. Zenger himself, a poorly educated German immigrant, was neither the editor nor writer of his paper; he was merely the printer and had scant understanding of politics or of the opinions that filled the columns of his newspaper. In effect James Alexander was the managing editor and chief editorial writer; Morris, Smith, and Colden, as well as Alexander, posing as pseudonymous readers, contributed letters to the editor scalding the governor and his appointees as villains who had no respect for law, liberty, or private property. Even the advertisements in the newspaper ridiculed the Cosbyites.

The *Weekly Journal* also published extracts from Whig theorists, chief among them John Trenchard and Thomas Gordon, the authors of *Cato's Letters: Or Essays on Liberty, Civil and Religious.* Zenger's paper, as the first independent and truly free press in America, engaging weekly in the dangerous practice of opposing the administration of the province, needed a theory to legitimate its editorial practices. The reading public as well as Crown officers had to be educated. *Cato's Letters* served to castigate Cosby, to broadcast Whig theory, and to rationalize freedom of the press.

In the second issue of the newspaper, in late 1733, Alexander wrote the first of several essays in which he developed a libertarian theory of freedom of the press to justify the newspaper's actual practice of that freedom. At the same time Alexander excoriated Cosby by innuendo. Explaining why freedom of the press was a necessary part of the British constitution, Alexander observed that some people believed that might made right, and "if such an over grown Criminal, or an impudent Monster in Iniquity, cannot immediately be come at by ordinary Justice, let him yet receive the lash of satire, let the glaring truth of his ill administration . . . render his actions odious to all honest minds." Two months later the *Weekly Journal* referred to a governor who had turned "rogue."[4]

Cosby decided to stop Zenger's press by imprisoning the printer for his seditious libels. Chief Justice DeLancey failed, however, to convince a grand jury to indict, and he failed again nine months later in October 1734, despite a strong charge on the meaning and dangers of seditious libel.[5] Cosby's Council then urged the Assembly to concur in an order that certain issues of Zenger's newspaper be burned by the common hangman, that a reward be offered for the authors of the libels, and that the printer be prosecuted. The Assembly refused, as did the city's Court of Quarter Sessions. The Council then commanded the sheriff to see to the burning of the papers. On November 17, 1735, Zenger was imprisoned on a warrant issued by the Council charging him with having published "several seditious libels . . . tending to raise factions . . . among the people . . . inflaming their minds with contempt of His Majesty's government, and greatly disturbing the peace thereof."[6]

Although Zenger had the best lawyers in the colony, James Alexander and William Smith, they could not prevent the chief justice from setting bail impossibly high, thus keeping his prisoner in jail. In January 1735 DeLancey failed for a third time to obtain a grand jury indictment. Richard Bradley, the attorney general, then charged Zenger by an information for having published "false, scandalous, malicious, and seditious" libels.[7] That is, on his authority as prosecutor, the attorney general bypassed the grand jury system and single-handedly preferred charges, an "information" against Zenger before the court, which then ordered a trial. Prosecution by information was legal, though unpopular. Fortunately for Zenger, Bradley's information contained the word "false," which ultimately proved to be the key to his defense. Zenger's lawyers, knowing that a court consisting of DeLancey and Philipse was biased against their client, challenged the legality of the commissions of the judges. DeLancey, outraged, summarily disbarred Alexander and Smith. In their place he appointed a young but able lawyer, John Chambers, to defend Zenger. Chambers, although an opponent of the Morris faction, pleaded Zenger not guilty and diligently challenged prejudiced jurors. The original panel of jurors included Cosby appointees, enemies of Morris, and Cosby's "baker, tailor, shoemaker, candlemaker, joiner, etc." DeLancey, confident that the prosecutor could easily prove that Zenger had published the libels, supported Chambers's motions, with the result that a neutral jury was impaneled to try the case.[8] Meanwhile, as Zenger spent nine months in prison awaiting his trial, his wife tended his press and Alexander supervised the continued publication of the *Weekly Journal*.

August 4, 1735, was the day of the trial. After the attorney general opened the prosecution's case, Andrew Hamilton of Philadelphia surprised the court when he rose in the audience and introduced himself as Zenger's counsel. Chambers yielded. James Alexander had engaged Hamilton, an old friend, to defend the printer and in so doing obtained the services of a man reputed to be the best advocate in America. Hamilton had been attorney general of Pennsylvania and at the time of the trial was speaker of the Pennsylvania Assembly. His case was ready-made for him, because Alexander had prepared a masterful brief.[9]

Hamilton opened the defense with Alexander's daring gambit of confessing Zenger's responsibility for the allegedly libelous articles. Hamilton added, however, that Zenger had a right to publish the truth. The attorney general, believing that the confession virtually awarded the verdict to the prosecution, accurately declared that because Zenger had admitted the publications, "the jury must find a verdict for the King, for supposing they were true . . . the law says their being true is an aggravation of the crime."[10] Hamilton disagreed; for the publications to be libelous, he argued, they must be false. Bradley, thinking to impress the jury, reviewed the publications against the governor, concluding that they stirred up sedition and disturbance of the peace by disquieting the minds of the people. Hamilton insisted, however, that the charges against Zenger included the word "false," without proof of which no libel existed; only if the Crown proved the falsehood would he concede the libel. When the Crown attorney refused to offer such proof, on ground that he was not obliged to do so, Hamilton shrewdly offered to prove that the alleged libels were true, knowing that if he persuaded the jury, Cosby in effect would have been convicted. Accordingly the chief justice swiftly intervened: "You cannot be admitted, Mr. Hamilton, to give the truth of a libel in evidence," because it was a libel even if true. "The law was clear," DeLancey correctly stated, "that you cannot justify a libel," and for the second time he quoted Sergeant William Hawkins's authoritative book, *Pleas of the Crown*, in support of his ruling.[11]

Hamilton retorted that the court's law derived from the tyrannical Court of Star Chamber, long since dead, to the good fortune of English liberty; he squeezed precedents to buttress his view of the law that it permitted truth as a defense to a charge of libel. Hamilton could not satisfy DeLancey, because the great legal luminaries of England—Coke, Hale, Holt, and Hawkins—had proved that the common-law courts perpetuated and accepted Star Chamber doctrine. Nevertheless, Hamilton managed to exploit the doubt in the minds of the jurors whether the law made good sense. Mercilessly Hamilton scored the doctrine that truth aggravated a libel; were the jurors supposed to believe that "truth is a greater sin than falsehood"?[12]

When DeLancey stopped Hamilton from arguing further that truth was a defense to a charge of libel, Hamilton necessarily abandoned his reliance on Alexander's brief and shifted his strategy. "Then, gentlemen of the jury," he declared, "it is to you we must now appeal for witnesses to the truth of the facts . . . and are denied the liberty to prove." Boldly he played to the jury over the head of the court, concocting an argument that was destined to survive first in public opinion and ultimately in the law itself. He reminded the jurors that as citizens of New York, they knew the facts concerning the supposed libels about the governor's administration. The facts, he declared, were "notoriously known to be true."[13] When a difference arose as to whether Zenger's words should be understood as malicious, seditious, and tending to breach the peace, DeLancey remarked that those who had to judge would understand the words properly. Hamilton told the jurors that they, not the court, were the judges; if they did not understand the words to be false, the publications were not criminal. DeLancey then ruled that the jury's only task was "to find that Zenger printed and published those papers, and leave it to the Court to judge whether they are libelous . . . it is in the nature of a special verdict where the jury leave the matter of law to the Court."[14]

Hamilton, addressing the jury, then launched into an argument of several hours. The court's rule, he said, "renders juries useless," a result he again traced to rulings of the "terrible Court of Star Chamber." A free people, having a sense of justice, knew when a governor abused power. They would protect the innocent from him because they were not obliged "to support a governor who goes about to destroy a province . . . or their privileges." Legal restraints on the right of freemen to protest extended only to "what is false." Hamilton admitted that although truth alone could excuse complaints about a bad administration, "nothing ought to excuse a man who raises a false charge or accusation, even against a private person, and that no manner of allowance ought to be made to him who does so against a public magistrate." The attorney general, Hamilton reminded the jury, regarded government as above criticism and insisted that licentiousness could not be tolerated, because it brought rulers into popular contempt. Hamilton did not disagree except that he did not regard truth as licentious. He called attention to the fact that government officials who abused power caused injustice and oppression, thereby deserving the contempt of the people. Thus, if the jury believed that Zenger had published the truth, the verdict should be in his favor.[15]

Hamilton knew that the law was against him and that Zenger was guilty as a matter of law. So he had used the jury as a court of public opinion and turned the case into a trial of Cosby. Hamilton's best defense turned out to be an aggressive assault. Summoning his forensic gifts, he then turned his case into one that would endure as long as people cherished liberty and trusted juries. Ascending the heights of eloquence, he declared in his peroration that Zenger's was not a "small" case:

> . . . the question before the Court and you gentlemen of the jury is not of small nor private concern, it is not the cause of a poor printer, nor of New York alone, which you are now trying. No! It may in its consequences affect every freeman that lives under a British government on the main of America. It is the best cause. It is the cause of liberty; and I make no doubt but that your upright conduct this day will not only entitle you to the love and esteem of your fellow citizens; but every man who prefers freedom to a life of slavery will bless and honor you as men who have baffled the attempt of tyranny; and by an impartial and uncorrupt verdict, have laid a noble foundation for securing to ourselves, our posterity, and our neighbors that to which nature and the laws of our country have given us a right—the liberty—both of exposing and opposing arbitrary power (in these parts of the world, at least) by speaking and writing truth.[16]

Although both the attorney general and chief justice again reminded the jury that scandalous reflection on the government that stirred popular odium was a crime, Hamilton got in a parting shot. He apologized for having been carried away in the cause of freedom. The jury had heard enough. After withdrawing "a short time," they returned a general verdict of not guilty, "upon which there were three huzzas in the hall, which was crowded with people." Zenger left the courtroom a free man.[17]

Despite the verdict, the common law remained the same. Moreover,

Hamilton never conducted a frontal assault on the concept of seditious libel. He never argued that publications tending, however remotely, to breach the peace or to lower the public's esteem of the government should be free from prosecution. His argument, rather, was that truth should be a defense against a charge of seditious libel.[18] When the court rejected this proposition, Hamilton retreated to the argument that the jury should not return a special verdict on the question whether the defendant had, as a matter of fact, published the statement charged and thereby leave the court to rule, as a matter of law, whether the words were criminal per se. He urged instead that they should return a general verdict, deciding the law as well as the facts.[19]

Hamilton did not consider that truth is a mischievous, often an illusory, standard that often defies knowledge or understanding and cannot always be established by the rules of evidence. He did not consider that one man's truth is another's falsehood or that political opinions, which notoriously differ, may not even be susceptible of proof. Nor did he consider that a jury in a case of seditious libel is a court of public opinion, often synonymous with public prejudice, and hardly adequate as an instrument for measuring the truth of an accusation that the government, or its policies, or its officials, may be unjust, tyrannical, or repugnant to the public interest. Accusations of the latter order, without exception, were the subject of prosecutions for seditious libel. When judges were dependent tools of the state, a jury of one's peers and neighbors might seem to be a promising bulwark against the tyrannous prosecution of seditious libel by the administration and its judges. But juries, with the power of ruling on the guilt or innocence of alleged libels, as events later proved, could be as influenced by prevailing passions as judges when deciding the fate of defendants who had expressed unpopular sentiments. In England, where the power of juries in libel cases was secured by Fox's Libel Act of 1792, the most repressive prosecutions were, with very few exceptions, successful.[20] In America only one verdict of "not guilty" was returned in the numerous prosecutions under the Sedition Act which entrusted criminality to the jury and admitted truth as a defense.[21]

Embattled libertarians of the eighteenth century belatedly discovered that they had mistaken a prop of straw for brick by accepting Hamilton's position rather than repudiating the concept of seditious libel. His argument, which hinged on the fact that public opinion was opposed to the administration, had its limitations as a libertarian defense of the press and, despite the jury's verdict, left the law unchanged. Indeed, judging from its impact on the bench, Hamilton's argument was like the stagecoach ticket inscribed, "Good for this day only." As late as 1804 Chief Justice Morgan Lewis of New York, a Jeffersonian no less, was of the opinion that truth does not constitute a defense against a charge of criminal libel.[22]

The fame of the Zenger case derives in part from the fact that it was so isolated—and well publicized—a phenomenon. Except for an obscure trial of a New Yorker in 1745 for "singing in praise of the Pretender"[23] and another insignificant prosecution in South Carolina at about the same time,[24] Zenger's case was the last of its kind under the "royal" judges.[25] Altogether there were probably not more than half a dozen prosecutions for seditious libel in the whole of the American colonial period.[26] Indeed, the maligned judges were virtually angels of self-restraint when compared with the intolerant public or with the oppressive governors who, acting in a quasi-judicial capacity with their councils, were more dreaded and active instruments of suppression than the common-law courts. The most suppressive body by far, however, was that acclaimed bastion of the people's liberties, the popular elected assembly. That the law bore down harshly on verbal crimes in colonial America was the result of the inquisitorial propensities of the governors and legislatures, which vied with each other in ferreting out slights upon the government. The law of seditious libel was enforced in America primarily by the provincial assemblies exercising their power to punish alleged "breaches of parliamentary privilege." Like the House of Commons which they emulated, the assemblies, needing no grand jury to indict and no petty jury to convict, zealously established the prerogative of being immune to criticism. An assembly might summon, interrogate, and fix criminal penalties against anyone who had supposedly libelled its members, proceedings, or the government generally. Any words, spoken or printed, which were imagined to have a tendency to impeach an assembly's behavior, question its authority, derogate from its honor, affront its dignity, or defame its members, individually or collectively, were regarded as seditious and punishable as a breach of parliamentary privilege.[27]

Had John Peter Zenger attacked the New York Assembly instead of a despised royal governor, he would have been summarily convicted at the bar of the house, jailed, and in all likelihood, forgotten by posterity. Instead, he was tried by a jury and acquitted because he symbolized a popular cause. The Assembly had refused to support the prosecution and so had the Court of Quarter Sessions, the upper house of the city's legislature consisting of the mayor, recorder, and aldermen sitting in a judicial capacity. That body, dominated by the partisans of Lewis Morris, believed itself bound to preserve "as much as they can, the liberties of the press, and the people of the Province, since an Assembly of the Province and several Grand Juries have refused to meddle with the papers."[28]

The Zenger case at best gave the press the freedom to print the "truth," but only if the truth were directed away from the assembly. The power of the assembly to punish nonmembers, as well as members, for breach of privilege, enabled it to control the press. Indeed, long after the right to publish without first obtaining government approval or license had been won, the assembly continued to regard the unlicensed publication of its votes and proceedings as a breach of privilege. This information of the most vital public interest could be printed only after first being submitted to the speaker of the house for his examination and signature. The governor, too, was finicky about publications concerning him.

Events in colonial New York demonstrate that the press was still not free after the Zenger case. James Parker, the colony's official printer, knew as well as anyone that he was under the restraints of the government. In 1747 he found himself caught between hammer and anvil, under contradictory orders from the governor on the one side and the assembly on the other. Governor George Clinton had sharply criticized the assembly for its failure to appropriate sufficient funds for the prosecution of King George's War. The assembly, angrily retorting that the Governor's criticism tended to the "subversion" of its rights, drew up a long remonstrance in its defense. Clinton, in an effort to prevent the publication of reflections upon him, then commanded Parker not to print the remonstrance in the licensed proceedings of the assembly. The printer helplessly turned to the legislature for instructions, thereby giving that body an opportunity to masquerade as the defender of freedom of the press. Unanimously the legislators voted: "That it is the undoubted Right of the People of this Colony, to know the Proceedings of their Representatives . . . That any Attempt to prohibit the printing or re-printing, any of the Proceedings of this House, is an infringement of the Privileges of this House, and of the People they represent . . . That his Excellency's Order to forbid the printing or reprinting the said Remonstrance, is unwarrantable, arbitrary and illegal, and . . . tends to the utter subversion of all the Rights and Liberties of this House, and of the People they represent."[29] The assembly then ordered Parker to print its remonstrance and deliver ten copies to each member so that the people might be apprised of their representatives' "firm Resolution to preserve the Liberty of the Press."[30] Confronted by this popular stand, Clinton shrewdly took no action against Parker; there was no sense in further antagonizing the assembly from which adequate defense measures were still to be wheedled.

The legislature's professed commitment to the principle of a free press was abandoned a few years later, in 1753, when the printer, Hugh Gaine, believing the royal instructions to the new governor and the latter's speech to the assembly to be a matter of public interest, published them in his New York Mercury. The assembly, upon learning that Gaine had "presumed" to print part of its proceedings without license, summoned him to its bar and demanded to know by what authority he had dared to breach its privileges. Gaine, astonished and intimidated by the turn of events, most abjectly humbled himself. He had done wrong, he claimed, only out of ignorance; profusely sorry for having given offense, he "humbly asked their pardon." Mollified by this proper display of contrition, the assembly magnanimously released him after formal censure, a warning, and exaction of the costs of the case.[31]

In 1756 James Parker became the next victim of parliamentary privilege. He had published in his New York Gazette an article on the distressed condition of the people in Orange and Ulster counties which the house took to be "greatly reflecting" upon it and calculated "to irritate the People of this Colony against their Representatives. . . ." Parker and his associate, William Weyman, were voted to be guilty of a "high misdemeanour" and contempt of authority. Taken into custody by the sergeant at arms of the house, they were interrogated before the bar. A most co-operative witness, Parker revealed that the offensive article had been written by the Reverend Hezekiah Watkins of Newburg. The publishers confessed their fault for printing the article, denied any intention of giving affront, and humbly begged the pardon of the honorable house. The honorable house kept its prisoners in jail for a week before discharging them. The Reverend Mr. Watkins, who had been promptly arrested, confessed his authorship but pleaded that he had acted out of a mistaken zeal for the welfare of the people rather than from disrespect for the house. He was heartily sorry, he declared, and pleaded to be forgiven, but was jailed anyway. The next day, however, he was officially reprimanded and discharged after being forced to pay the costs.[32]

In 1758 the speaker of the house received a letter from one Samuel Townsend, a justice of the peace in Queen's County, asking legislative relief for certain refugees quartered on Long Island. The speaker, presenting the letter to the house, termed it "insolent," whereupon that body commanded Townsend's appearance. When he daringly failed to show up, he was cited for contempt, and a warrant was issued for his arrest. Hauled before the bar, he was examined in the usual intimidating fashion, but showed no signs of repentance. The assembly then voted that, because his letter reflected on its "Honour, Justice and Authority," he was guilty of a "high Misdemeanour and a most daring Insult." The gloomy prison in which he found himself provoked Townsend to reconsider his position. He sent the house a petition expressing his deep sorrow for having written the letter which had inadvertently cast reflection on the house. He promised faithfully to avoid committing such misdeeds in the future and concluded by asking for the house's "Compassion." Moved by this respectful submission from a judge, the assembly released him from jail and discharged him after an official reprimand from the speaker.[33]

As New York approached the revolutionary controversy, its press was only as free as its legislature permitted. In practice, all political comment was tolerated as long as criticism did not in any way touch the people's representatives. The courts were merely a formal threat against unfettered discussion, as the Zenger case demonstrated. It was the legislature, with unlimited discretion to scotch supposed breaches of parliamentary privilege, which actively exercised repressive power. The frequency of the cases and the incidence of punishment scarcely suggests tyranny, but the house's arbitrary use of its prerogative was sufficiently restrictive to have a smothering effect on the free expression of opinion relating to legislative matters and measures. Libertarian theorists had argued that freedom of speech and press had the salutary effect of checking evil or incompetent rulers and stimulating responsible government. But in New York the legislature never permitted this libertarian theory a chance to be put into practice. The royal governor, his policies, and his administration were almost always fair game for popular disapprobation; the Zenger case proved that, but little more. In the struggle of the colonial assembly for independence from the governor, most antiadministration criticism played into the hands of the assembly and the "popular" party. "Freedom of the press," in other words, was a useful instrument for the expansion of legislative prerogative, but in any clash between parliamentary privilege and liberty of discussion, the former was deemed the superior value and emerged the victor.

The limited experience of colonial New York with broad freedom of the press matched the limited thinking of libertarian theorists on the scope of permissible expression. No one even dared to criticize the assembly's restraints on the press. And Andrew Hamilton himself, in his defense of Zenger, had confessed that a "false" charge against the administration merited punishment as seditious libel.[34] Indeed, Hamilton, in 1729, as a member of the Governor's Council in Pennsylvania, had helped send the printer, Andrew Bradford, to jail for having published an article offensive to the government.[35] James Alexander, who deserves credit for having provided Hamilton with his winning argument in the Zenger case,[36] published an essay on freedom of the press in 1737,[37] expressing the most libertarian sentiments that may be found in colonial America. Yet Alexander also believed that "to infuse into the minds of the people an ill opinion of a just administration, is a crime that deserves no mercy. . . ."[38] The colonial understanding of the scope of free expression was further revealed in 1753 by an editorial in the *Independent Reflector*, the voice of the New York "Triumvirate"—William Livingston, John Morin Scott, and William Smith—young lawyers with republican ideas and a passion to be heard. When an opposition paper had refused to publish a rejoinder composed by one of them, they published their credo on liberty of the press: "A Printer ought not to publish every Thing that is offered him; but what is conducive of general Utility, he should not refuse, be the Author a Christian, Jew, Turk or Infidel. Such refusal is an immediate abridgment of the Freedom of the Press. When on the other Hand, he prostitutes his Art by the Publication of any Thing injurious to his Country, it is criminal. . . . It is high Treason against the State. The usual Alarm rung in such Cases, the common Cry of an Attack upon the LIBERTY OF THE PRESS, is groundless and trifling. The Press neither has, nor can have such a Liberty, and whenever it is assumed, the Printer should be punished."[39]

The most willing tool of the crown could hardly have disagreed with this definition of a free press by the republican patriots from the colony identified with Zenger. On the other hand there could be no greater danger to open political debate than the vague crime of constructive treason, especially if it could be committed by mere words. Even a crown lawyer knew that the law ruled out treason in any case where words against the government were unconnected with some treasonous project for carrying them out; such words were criminally punishable only as a seditious libel, a distinction of importance since the latter was a mere misdemeanor, while treason was a capital crime. That fact reveals the severity of the remarks by New York's Whig lawyers.

A few years after they had published their credo on the liberty of the press, James Parker, who had been their printer and editor, wrote a broadside opposing a stamp tax on newspapers that was being proposed by the New York Assembly (1759). Parker announced that in countries "where Liberty truly reigns, every one hath a Privilege of declaring his Sentiments upon all Topicks with the utmost Freedom, provided he does it with proper Decency and a just Regard to the Laws."[40] Yet "the Laws" provided for the punishment of words that tended, however remotely, to disturb the peace, to lower the government in the esteem of the public, or to breach parliamentary privilege. Parker's statement was a neat way of saying that all opinions short of illegal ones were free, an epitome of the American view of the matter.

The New York General Assembly, which had intimidated a printer and his journeyman in 1766 for inadvertently publishing an address of the house with two typographical errors,[41] proved that it was capable of dealing effectively even with a radical of the patriot party. In December 1769, the assembly had voted to supply provisions for the King's troops in New York City in return for Governor Cadwallader Colden's signature to an act authorizing the emission of needed bills of credit.[42] Three days later a handbill addressed "To the Betrayed Inhabitants of New York," signed by a "Son of Liberty," blanketed the city. The author condemned the Assembly for abandoning the liberties of the people by passing the provisions bill, and he called upon the public to rise against unjust measures. The next day another broadside appeared, over the name of "Legion," urging the public to attend a mass protest meeting. Fourteen hundred turned out and were addressed by the radical agitator, John Lamb. The Asssembly retaliated by declaring each broadside to be "a false seditious and infamous Libel" and called upon the governor to offer rewards for information leading to the discovery of the author or authors. The Assembly had passed the provisions bill by a bare majority, but unanimously passed its resolves against the seditious writers. Governor Colden gladly complied with the Assembly's request and issued proclamations offering one hundred and fifty pounds in reward money.[43]

Dazzled by so much money, a journeyman printer in the shop of James Parker betrayed his employer as the printer of "To the Betrayed." Parker, who in 1756 had been jailed for a week by the Assembly for printing a reflection, now charged with having published a seditious libel, suffered arrest and an inquiry by the governor and Council. The Sheriff took into custody all his apprentices and journeymen for questioning at the same time. Their testimony substantiated that of the informer and also revealed that one Alexander McDougall had corrected the proofs at the printing office. Parker himself balked at naming the author, but he could not withstand the threats of imprisonment and dismissal from his post as comptroller of the post office. He made a deal with the Council, buying immunity against prosecution and loss of his post by identifying the author and pledging to appear against him as a government witness.[44]

Parker identified the man as Alexander McDougall, a local merchant who with Lamb and Isaac Sears was one of the commanders of the Sons of Liberty. Later McDougall would serve in both the First and Second Continental Congresses and as a major-general during the Revolution. He died in 1786 a pillar of conservatism, the first president of the Bank of New York and founder and head of the Society of Cincinnati in New York.[44] In February of 1770, he was arrested on a charge of seditious libel against the Assembly. With Parker as a witness of his authorship, the legislature had a sure-fire case and turned the prisoner over to the common-law courts. McDougall, on examination before Chief Justice Daniel Horsmanden, remained silent except to demand a trial by jury. The judge set bail at the inordinately high sum of five hundred pounds, which McDougall refused to pay, although Governor Colden called him "a person of some fortune." He preferred waiting in jail as a martyr while awaiting the action of the grand jury.[45]

McDougall remained in jail for two and a half months. His imprisonment did more to publicize the cause of liberty of the press than any event since Zenger's trial. Alexander's account of that trial was republished for the third time in New York, and Parker's paper and Holt's *New York Journal* courageously plumped for McDougall and freedom of discussion. The editor and the prisoner against whom he was to testify wrote hortatory articles urging all the colonies to enact statutes abolishing the "tyrannical Tenets" of the common law of seditious libel which was invariably associated with the infamous Star Chamber. Yet neither ever attacked the concept of seditious libel. They made no suggestion that government could not be criminally assaulted by its citizens' opinions. Beneath the epithetical rhetoric lay only the proposition that truth be accepted as a defense.[47] The *New York Mercury*, however, defended the common law and backed the Assembly against McDougall.[48] The editor of conservatism's voice was Hugh Gaine, who in 1753 had been forced by the Assembly to humble himself in order to avoid prosecution for having printed its proceedings without prior license. Gaine's principal statement on freedom of the press was the following:

> Among the Objections which to blind the Credulous, have been raised against this Prosecution, the most considerable are, that it is an Invasion of the *Liberty of the Press*, and of the *Right of the People to convass the Conduct of Government; and that the Paper itself is not offensive or criminal*. No man, 'till this Day of constitutional Light, has pretended, that the Press could sanctify every Production, however atrocious or malignant. Sufficient it is, that a *Printer* enjoys equal Privileges, with his fellow Citizens, as *they* have the Power to *act*, tho' they are punishable for their *Misconduct*; so ought *he* not to be under the Restraint of an *Imprimatur*; for then his Right of *private Judgment* would be suppressed, and his *Actions* rest on the Will of another. But if he abuses this *Independence*, to the Hurt of Society, or of Individuals, he ought not to be defended, for this would place him above *the Law*, which intends a general Security; and not to give to any, a *Dispensation* to be mischievous with Impunity. If there was no Check to Malice and Falsehood, Government must soon sink into Contempt, and the subject be stript of Protection. Political Writers have justly observed that the Principle of *Honour*, is not less the Strength of an *absolute* Throne, than *publick* Virtue, the Support of a *free State*, like that under which we live; often has it been predicted, that when the Body of the People, become tainted by Error and Corruption, a Dissolution of the Establishment will be unavoidable. What then can have a more fatal Influence, to debauch our Principals, and estrange our Affections, than an *unrestrainted Licence*, to inculcate every wild and pernicious Tenet? To traduce and vilify those in Authority, to misrepresent their Conduct, to expose them to Odium and Contempt, and to excite a general Spirit of Jealousy and Distrust, must it not infallably lead to Faction, to revolt, and open Sedition?[49]

Notwithstanding Gaine's policy, the McDougall case as managed by the Sons of Liberty became America's equivalent of Wilkes's case in England. Indeed, McDougall himself consciously posed as the American Wilkes and turned his imprisonment into a theatrical triumph, while his supporters used the free press issue as an anti-administration weapon. Forty-five, the number of the *North Briton* that had earned Wilkes his conviction for seditious libel, became the talismanic symbol of libertarianism and of the American cause against England. On the forty-fifth day of the year, for example, forty-five Liberty Boys dined in honor of McDougall on forty-five pounds of beef from a forty-five-month-old bull, drank forty-five toasts to liberty of the press and its defenders, and after dinner marched to the city jail to salute McDougall with forty-five cheers. On one particularly festive liberty day, forty-five songs were sung to him by forty-five virgins, every one of whom, reported a damned Tory, was forty-five years old.[50]

At the end of April McDougall, attended by a mob of his partisans on the way from prison to court, finally appeared before the grand jury, which indicted him as the author of a seditious libel against the Assembly. The common-law indictment, the only one of its kind against a popular leader during the revolutionary controversy, was the first of its kind in twenty-five years. Yet the unique fact that every branch of the government, including the Assembly, supported the prosecution made the indictment understandable. So did the fact that the sheriff carefully picked the grand jurors, the "most . . . opulent & substantial gentlemen of the city." The court fixed the date of the trial for its next session in July, and McDougall, this time paying the huge bail assessed against him, quit prison. On July 2, just before the trial, James Parker, the star witness of the prosecution and the only one who could testify from personal knowledge that McDougall had written the seditious broadside, suddenly died. With his death the case against the defendant vanished. The trial was postponed till October and then again indefinitely. If McDougall gloated over the turn of events that promised him a discharge from the indictment, he failed to consider the power of a revengeful Assembly.[51]

With the collapse of the common-law prosecution, the Assembly resolved to punish McDougall on its own authority. Late in 1770 the speaker of the House ordered his arrest; after McDougall spent a week in jail the sergeant-at-arms brought him before the bar of the House. Speaker Henry Cruger then informed McDougall that he stood charged with having libeled the House and asked how he pleaded. McDougall refused to plead to the charge until, he declared, he learned of the identity of his accusers and the evidence against him. Cruger interrupted to threaten that he would be held in contempt for addressing the House without its prior leave, but George Clinton interceded on the prisoner's behalf, so that McDougall received permission to give his reasons for not pleading. He explained that he had no counsel, that the case still pended in the courts, and that the Assembly itself had already declared the broadside to be a seditious libel and its author guilty—in other words that he feared incriminating himself. Moreover, he added, the Assembly, having initiated the prosecution against him, now acted as his judge and jury which it had no power to do, particularly when it would be placing him under double jeopardy because he remained answerable at common law. For these reasons, McDougall declared, he would not answer the question whether he was guilty. Representative de Noyelles interjected that the House had the power to extort his answer and threatened infliction of *peine forte et dure*, a form of torture recognized in English law to force a suspect to plead one way or the other just so the trial might then proceed. One who stood mute, as McDougall, would be spread-eagled on the ground and have heavy metal weights placed upon his body; each day more weights would be added, while the prisoner was fed stale bread and stagnant water on alternate days. The "punishment hard and strong" continued until he either died or pleaded guilty or not guilty.[52] McDougall braved de Noyelle's barbaric threat obstinately refusing to plead to the charge, thereby stymying the proceedings.

The members fell to arguing among themselves whether they might coerce a prisoner to answer an incriminating question or even take jurisdiction of a case still pending in the courts. George Clinton, though he originally voted for the resolution to prosecute McDougall's seditious libel, now supported McDougall on technical grounds. Clinton admitted that if the Assembly were not a party to the common-law indictment it would have full power over him and, if necessary, to make him plead might even throw him out of the window. The Assembly finally agreed to investigate the extent of its own powers in the case and ordered McDougall to state in writing his objections against entering a plea. His statement provoked Speaker Cruger to announce that he had reflected on the honor and dignity of the House. The members then voted that his fresh libels contemned their parliamentary privilege and demanded that he beg for pardon. His refusal prompted another vote sentencing him to an indeterminate period in prison. Only five members of the Assembly, including Clinton, opposed the sentence. As in Pennsylvania's Smith-Moore case, the Assembly ordered the sheriff not to honor a writ of habeas corpus. McDougall obtained a writ without avail, because the sheriff notified the court that the matter did not lie within its jurisdiction: the prisoner had been committed for breach of privilege. The court submitted to the legislature, and McDougall remained in jail. In the meantime the Assembly accepted a committee report, based on precedents of the House of Commons, supporting the lawfulness of its authority and actions in the case. Once more an American legislature endorsed the principle that it possessed an unbounded prerogative even in cases involving personal liberty and freedom of expression. After serving nearly three months in jail, McDougall finally got out when the legislative session ended. The common-law charge against him was dismissed, and America's Wilkes won his freedom.[53]

No cause was more honored by rhetorical declamation and dishonored in practice than that of freedom of expression during the revolutionary period, from the 1760's through the War for Independence. The irony of the period might best be portrayed by a cartoon depicting the tarring and feathering of a Tory speaker or printer under a banner run up by the patriots inscribed, "In

Liberty's Cause." Yankee Doodle's Liberty Boys vociferously claimed for themselves the right to freedom of expression which they denied their opponents, revealing an extraordinarily narrow understanding of the liberty of the press. But there was nothing in their heritage or experience which fitted them for a broader understanding. It is not surprising, even if ironical, that when the New York Sons of Liberty rode out to smash Tory presses, they were led by Alexander McDougall who in 1770 had been jailed for criticizing the provincial assembly.

5

Constitutional History, 1776–1789

ON JULY 4, 1776, KING GEORGE III wrote in his diary, "Nothing of importance this day." When the news of the Declaration of Independence reached him, he still could not know how wrong he had been. The political philosophy of social compact, natural rights, and limited government that generated the Declaration of Independence also spurred the most important, creative, and dynamic constitutional achievements in history; the Declaration itself was merely the beginning. Within a mere thirteen years Americans invented or first institutionalized a bill of rights against all branches of government, the written constitution, the constitutional convention, federalism, judicial review, and a solution to the colonial problem (admitting territories to the Union as states fully equal to the original thirteen). Religious liberty, the separation of church and state, political parties, separation of powers, an acceptance of the principle of equality, and the conscious creation of a new nation were also among American institutional "firsts," although not all these initially appeared between 1776 and 1789. In that brief span of time, Americans created what are today the oldest major republic, political democracy, state constitution, and national constitution. These unparalleled American achievements derived not from originality in speculative theory but from the constructive application of old ideas, which Americans took so seriously that they constitutionally based their institutions of government on them.

From thirteen separate colonies the Second Continental Congress "brought forth a new nation," as Abraham Lincoln said. In May 1776, Congress urged all the colonies to suppress royal authority and adopt permanent governments. On that advice and in the midst of a war the colonies began to frame the world's first written constitutions. When Congress triggered the drafting of those constitutions, Virginia instructed its delegates to Congress to propose that Congress should declare "the United Colonies free and independent states." Neither Virginia nor Congress advocated state sovereignty. Congress's advice implied the erection of state governments with sovereign powers over domestic matters or "internal police."

On June 7, 1776, Congressman Richard Henry Lee of Virginia introduced the resolution as instructed, and Congress appointed two committees, one to frame the document that became the Declaration of Independence and the other to frame a plan of confederation—a constitution for a continental government. When Lincoln declared, "The Union is older than the States, and in fact created them as States," he meant that the Union (Congress) preexisted the states. The Declaration of Independence, which stated that the colonies had become states, asserted the authority of the "United States of America, in General Congress, Assembled."

The "spirit of '76" tended to be strongly nationalistic. The members of Congress represented the states, of course, and acted on their instructions, but they acted for the new nation, and the form of government they thought proper in 1776 was a centralized one. As a matter of fact Benjamin Franklin had proposed such a government on July 21, 1775, when he presented to Congress "Articles of Confederation and perpetual Union." Franklin urged a congressional government with an executive committee that would manage "general continental Business and Interests," conduct diplomacy, and administer finances. His plan empowered Congress to determine war and peace, exchange ambassadors, make foreign alliances, settle all disputes between the colonies, plant new colonies, and, in a sweeping omnibus clause, make laws for "the General Welfare" concerning matters on which individual colonies "cannot be competent," such as "our general Commerce," "general Currency," the establishment of a post office, and governance of "our Common Forces." Costs were to be paid from a common treasury supplied by each colony in proportion to its male inhabitants, but each colony would raise its share by taxing its inhabitants. Franklin provided for an easy amendment process: Congress recommended amendments that would become part of the Articles when approved by a majority of colonial assemblies. Franklin's plan of union seemed much too radical in July 1775, when independence was a year away and reconciliation with Britain on American terms was the object of the war. Congress simply tabled the Franklin plan.

As the war continued into 1776, nationalist sentiment strengthened. Thomas Paine's *Common Sense* called for American independence and "a Continental form of Government." Nationalism and centralism were twin causes. John Langdon of New Hampshire favored independence and "an American Constitution" that provided for appeals from every colony to a national congress "in everything of moment relative to governmental matters." Proposals for a centralized union became common by the spring of 1776, and those proposals, as the following representative samples suggest, tended to show democratic impulses. Nationalism and mitigated democracy, not nationalism and conservatism, were related. A New York newspaper urged the popular election of a national congress with a "superintending power" over the individual colonies as to "all commercial and Continental affairs," leaving to each colony control over its "internal policy." A populistic plan in a Connecticut newspaper recommended that the congress be empowered to govern "all matters of general concernment" and "every other thing proper and necessary" for the benefit of the whole, allowing the individual colonies only that which fell "within the territorial jurisdiction of a particular assembly." The "Spartacus" essays, which newspapers in New York, Philadelphia, and Portsmouth printed, left the state "cantons" their own legislatures but united all in a national congress with powers similar to those enumerated by Franklin, including a paramount power to "interfere" with a colony's "provincial affairs" whenever required by "the good of the continent." "Essex" reminded his readers that "the strength and happiness of America must be Continental, not Provincial, and that whatever appears to be for the good of the whole, must be submitted to by every Part." He advocated dividing the colonies into many smaller equal parts that would have equal representation in a powerful national congress chosen directly by the people, including taxpaying widows. Carter Braxton, a conservative Virginian, favored aristocratic controls over a congress that could not "interfere with the internal police or domestic concerns of any Colony . . ."

Given the prevalence of such views in the first half of 1776, a representative committee of the Continental Congress probably mirrored public opinion when it framed a nationalist plan for confederation. On July 12, one month after the appointment of a thirteen-member committee (one from each state) to write a draft, John Dickinson of Pennsylvania, the committee chairman, presented to Congress a plan that borrowed heavily from Franklin's. The Committee of the Whole of Congress debated the Dickinson draft and adopted it on August 20 with few changes. Only one was significant. Dickinson had proposed that Congress be empowered to fix the western boundaries of states claiming territory to the Pacific coast and to form new states in the west. The Committee of the Whole, bending to the wishes of eight states with extensive western claims, omitted that provision from its revision of the Dickinson draft. That omission became a stumbling block.

On August 20 the Committee of the Whole reported the revised plan of union to Congress. The plan was similar to Franklin's, except that Congress had no power over "general commerce." But Congress, acting for the United States, was clearly paramount to the individual states. They were not even referred to as "states." Collectively they were "the United States of America"; otherwise they were styled "colonies" or "colony," terms not compatible with sovereignty, to which no reference was made. Indeed, the draft merely reserved to each colony "sole and exclusive Regulation and Government of its internal police, in all matters that shall not interfere with the Articles of this Confederation." That crucial provision, Article III, making even "internal police" subordinate to congressional powers, highlighted the nationalist character of the proposed confederation.

The array of congressional powers included exclusive authority over war and peace, land and naval forces, treaties and alliances, prize cases, crimes on the high seas and navigable rivers, all disputes between states, coining money, borrowing on national credit, Indian affairs, post offices, weights and measures, and "the Defence and Welfare" of the United States. Congress also had power to appoint a Council of State and civil officers "necessary for managing the general

Affairs of the United States." The Council of State, consisting of one member from each of the thirteen, was empowered to administer the United States government and execute its measures. Notwithstanding this embryonic executive branch, the government of the United States was congressional in character, consisting of a single house whose members were to be elected annually by the legislatures of the colonies. Each colony cast one vote, making each politically equal in Congress. On all important matters, the approval of nine colonies was required to pass legislation. Amendments to the Articles needed the unanimous approval of the legislatures of the various colonies, a provision that later proved to be crippling.

The Articles reported by the Committee of the Whole provoked dissension. States without western land claims opposed the omission of the provision in the Dickinson draft that gave Congress control over western lands. Large states opposed the principle of one vote for each state, preferring instead proportionate representation with each delegate voting. Sharp differences also emerged concerning the rule by which each state was to pay its quota to defray common expenses. Finally some congressmen feared the centralizing nature of the new government. As Edward Rutledge of South Carolina said, "The Idea of destroying all Provincial Distinctions and making every thing of the most minute kind bend to what they call the good of the whole. . . ." Rutledge resolved "to vest the Congress with no more Power than what is absolutely necessary." James Wilson of Pennsylvania could declare that Congress represented "all the individuals of the states" rather than the states, but Roger Sherman of Connecticut answered, "We are representatives of states, not individuals." That attitude would undo the nationalist "spirit of '76."

Because of disagreements and the urgency of prosecuting the war, Congress was unable to settle on a plan of union in 1776. By the spring of 1777 the nationalist momentum was spent. By then most of the states had adopted constitutions and had legitimate governments. Previously, provisional governments of local "congresses," "conventions," and committees had controlled the states and looked to the Continental Congress for leadership and approval. But the creation of legitimate state governments reinvigorated old provincial loyalties. Local politicians, whose careers were provincially oriented, feared a strong central government as a rival institution. Loyalists no longer participated in politics, local or national, depleting support for central control. By late April of 1777, when state sovereignty triumphed, only seventeen of the forty-eight congressmen who had been members of the Committee of the Whole that adopted the Dickinson draft remained in Congress. Most of the new congressmen opposed centralized government.

James Wilson, who was a congressman in 1776 and 1777, recalled what happened when he addressed the Constitutional Convention on June 8, 1787:

> Among the first sentiments expressed in the first Congs. one was that Virga. is no more. That Massts. is no more, that Pa. is no more &c. We are now one nation of brethren. We must bury all local interests and distinctions. This language continued for some time. The tables at length began to turn. No

sooner were the State Govts. formed than their jealousy & ambition began to display themselves. Each endeavored to cut a slice from the common loaf, to add to its own morsel, till at length the confederation became frittered down to the impotent condition in which it now stands. Review the progress of the articles of Confederation thro' Congress & compare the first and last draught of it. [Farrand, ed., *Records*, I, 166–67]

The turning point occurred in late April 1777, when Thomas Burke of North Carolina turned his formidable localist opinions against the report of the Committee of the Whole. Its Article III, in his words, "expressed only a reservation (to the states) of the power of regulating the internal police, and consequently resigned every other power (to Congress)." Congress, he declared, sought even to interfere with the states' internal police and make its own powers "unlimited." Burke accordingly moved the following substitute for Article III, which became Article II of the Articles as finally adopted: "Each State retains its sovereignty, freedom and independence, and every power, jurisdiction and right, which is not by this confederation expressly delegated to the United States in Congress assembled." Burke's motion carried by the votes of eleven states, vitiating the powers of the national government recommended by the Committee of the Whole.

In the autumn of 1777 a Congress dominated by state-sovereignty advocates completed the plan of confederation. Those who favored proportionate representation in Congress with every member entitled to vote lost badly to those who favored voting by states with each state having one vote. Thereafter the populous wealthy states had no stake in supporting a strong national government that could be controlled by the votes of lesser states. The power of Congress to negotiate commercial treaties effectively died when Congress agreed that under the Articles no treaty should violate the power of the states to impose tariff duties or prohibit imports and exports. The power of Congress to settle all disputes between states became merely a power to make recommendations. The permanent executive branch became a temporary committee with no powers except as delegated by the votes of nine states, the number required to adopt any major measure. Congress also agreed that it should not have power to fix the western boundaries of states claiming lands to the Pacific.

After the nationalist spurt of 1776 proved insufficient to produce the Articles, the states made the Confederation feckless. Even as colonies the states had been particularistic, jealous, and uncooperative. Centrifugal forces originating in diversity—of economics, geography, religion, class structure, and race—produced sectional, provincial, and local loyalties that could not be overcome during a war against the centralized powers claimed by Parliament. The controversy with Britain had produced passions and principles that made the Franklin and Dickinson drafts unviable. Not even those nationalist drafts empowered Congress to tax, although the principle of no taxation without representation had become irelevant as to Congress. Similarly, Congress as late as 1774 had "cheerfully" acknowledged Parliament's legitimate "regulation of our external commerce," but in 1776 Congress denied that Parliament had any authority over America, and by 1777 Americans were unwilling to grant their own central legislature powers they preferred their provincial assemblies to wield. Above all, most states refused to repose their trust in any central authority that a few large states might dominate, absent a constitutionally based principle of state equality.

Unanimous consent for amendments to the Articles proved to be too high a price to pay for acknowledging the "sovereignty" of each state, although that acknowledgement made Maryland capable of winning for the United States the creation of a national domain held in common for the benefit of all. Maryland also won the promise that new states would be admitted to the union on a principle of state equality. That prevented the development of a colonial problem from Atlantic to Pacific and with the Northwest Ordinance of 1787 was the Confederation's finest and most enduring achievement.

The Constitution of 1787 was unthinkable in 1776, impossible in 1781 or at any time before it was framed. The Articles were an indispensable transitional stage in the development of the Constitution. Not even the Constitution would have been ratified if its framers had submitted it for approval to the state legislatures that kept Congress paralyzed in the 1780s. Congress, representing the United States, authorized the creation of the states and ended up, as it had begun, as their creature. It possessed expressly delegated powers with no means of enforcing them. That Congress lacked commerce and tax powers was a serious deficiency, but not nearly so crippling as its lack of sanctions and the failure of the states to abide by the Articles. Congress simply could not make anyone, except soldiers, do anything. It acted on the states, not on people. Only a national government that could execute its laws independently of the states could have survived.

The states flouted their constitutional obligations. The Articles obliged the states to "abide by the determinations of the United States, in Congress assembled," but there was no way to force the states to comply. The states were not sovereign, except as to their internal police and tax powers; rather, they behaved unconstitutionally. No foreign nation recognized the states as sovereign, because Congress possessed the external attributes of sovereignty especially as to foreign affairs and war powers.

One of the extraordinary achievements of the Articles was the creation of a rudimentary federal system. It failed because its central government did not operate directly on individuals within its sphere of authority. The Confederation had no independent executive and judicial branches, because the need for them scarcely existed when Congress addressed its acts mainly to the states. The framers of the Articles distributed the powers of government with remarkable acumen, committing to Congress about all that belonged to a central government except, of course, taxation and commercial regulation, the two powers that Americans of the Revolutionary War believed to be part of state sovereignty. Even Alexander Hamilton, who in 1780 advocated that Congress should have "complete sovereignty," excepted "raising money by internal taxes."

Congress could requisition money from the states, but they did not pay their quotas. In 1781 Congress requisitioned $8,000,000 for the next year, but the states paid less than half a million. While the Articles lasted the cumulative amount paid by all the states hardly exceeded what was required to pay the interest on the public debt for just one year.

Nationalists vainly sought to make the Articles more effective by both interpretation and amendment. Madison devised a theory of implied powers by which he squeezed out of the Articles congressional authority to use force if necessary against states that failed to fulfill their obligations. Congress refused to attempt coercion just as it refused to recommend an amendment authorizing its use. Congress did, however, charter a bank to control currency, but the opposition to the exercise of a power not expressly delegated remained so intense that the bank had to be rechartered by a state. Congress vainly sought unanimous state consent for various amendments that would empower it to raise money from customs duties and to regulate commerce, foreign and domestic. In 1781 every state but Rhode Island approved an amendment empowering Congress to impose a five percent duty on all foreign imports; never again did an amendment to the Articles come so close to adoption. Only four states ratified an amendment authorizing a congressional embargo against the vessels of any nation with whom the United States had no treaty of commerce. Congress simply had no power to negotiate commercial treaties with nations such as Britain that discriminated against American shipping. Nor had Congress the power to prevent states from violating treaties with foreign nations. In 1786 John Jay, Congress's Secretary of Foreign Affairs, declared that not a day had passed since ratification of the 1783 treaty of peace without its violation by at least one state. Some states also discriminated against the trade of others. Madison likened New Jersey, caught between the ports of Philadelphia and New York, "to a cask tapped at both ends." More important, Congress failed even to recommend needed amendments. As early as 1784 Congress was so divided it defeated an amendment that would enable it to regulate commerce, foreign and domestic, and to levy duties on imports and exports. Often Congress could not function for lack of a quorum. The requisite number of states was present for only three days between October 1785 and April 1786. In 1786 Congress was unable to agree on any amendments for submission to the states.

The political condition of the United States during the 1780s stagnated partly because of the constitutional impotence of Congress and the unconstitutional conduct of the states. The controversy with Britain had taught that liberty and localism were congruent. The 1780s taught that excessive localism was incompatible with nationhood. The Confederation was a necessary point of midpassage. It bequeathed to the United States the fundamentals of a federal system, a national domain, and a solution to the colonial problem. Moreover the Articles contained several provisions that were antecedents of their counterparts in the Constitution of 1787: a free speech clause for congressmen and legislative immunity, a privileges and immunities clause, a clause on the extradition of fugitives from justice, a full faith and credit clause, and a clause validating

United States debts. The Confederation also started an effective government bureaucracy when the Congress in 1781 created secretaries for foreign affairs, war, marine, and finance—precursors of an executive branch. When the new departments of that branch began to function in 1789, a corps of experienced administrators, trained under the Articles, staffed them. The courts established by Congress to decide prize and admiralty cases as well as boundary disputes foreshadowed a national judiciary. Except for enactment of the great Northwest Ordinance, however, the Congress of the Confederation was moribund by 1787. It had successfully prosecuted the war, made foreign alliances, established the national credit, framed the first constitution of the United States, negotiated a favorable treaty of peace, and created a national domain. Congress's accomplishments were monumental, especially during wartime, yet in the end it failed.

By contrast, state government flourished. Excepting Rhode Island and Connecticut, all the states adopted written constitutions during the war, eight in 1776. Madison exultantly wrote, "Nothing has excited more admiration in the world than the manner in which free governments have been established in America, for it was the first instance, from the creation of the world that free inhabitants have been seen deliberating on a form of government, and selection of such of their citizens as possessed their confidence to determine upon and give effect to it."

The Virginia Constitution of 1776, the first permanent state constitution, began with a Declaration of Rights adopted three weeks before the Declaration of Independence. No previous bill of rights had restrained all branches of government. Virginia's reflected the widespread belief that Americans had been thrown back into a state of nature from which they emerged by framing a social compact for their governance, reserving to themselves certain inherent or natural rights, including life, liberty, the enjoyment of property, and the pursuit of happiness. Virginia's declaration explicitly declared that as all power derived from the people, for whose benefit government existed, the people could reform or abolish government when it failed them. On the basis of this philosophy Virginia framed a constitution providing for a bicameral legislature, a governor, and a judicial system. The legislature elected a governor, who held office for one year, had no veto power, and was encumbered by an executive council. The legislature chose many important officials, including judges.

Some states followed the more democratic model of the Pennsylvania Constitution of 1776, others the ultraconservative one of Maryland, but all state constitutions prior to the Massachusetts Constitution of 1780 were framed by legislatures, which in some states called themselves "conventions" or assemblies. Massachusetts deserves credit for having originated a new institution of government, a specially elected constitutional convention whose sole function was to frame the constitution and submit it for popular ratification. That procedure became the standard. Massachusetts's constitution, which is still operative, became the model American state constitution. The democratic procedure for making it fit the emerging theory that the sovereign people should be the source of the constitution and authorize its framing by a constitutional convention, rather than the legislature to which the constitution is paramount. Massachusetts was also the first state to give more than lip service to the principle of separation of powers. Everywhere else, excepting perhaps New York, unbalanced government and legislative supremacy prevailed. Massachusetts established the precedent for a strong, popularly elected executive with a veto power; elsewhere the governor tended to be a ceremonial head who depended for his existence on the legislature.

The first state constitutions and related legislation introduced significant reforms. Most states expanded voting rights by reducing property qualifications, and a few, including Vermont (an independent state from 1777 to 1791), experimented with universal manhood suffrage. Many state constitutions provided for fairer apportionment of representation in the legislature. Every southern state either abolished its establishment of religion or took major steps to achieve separation of church and state. Northern states either abolished slavery or provided for its gradual ending. Criminal codes were made more humane. The confiscation of Loyalist estates and of crown lands, like the opening of a national domain westward to the Mississippi, led to a democratization of land holding, as did the abolition of feudal relics like the law of primogeniture and entail. The pace of democratic change varied from state to state, and in some states was nearly imperceptible, but the Revolution without doubt occasioned constitutional and political developments that had long been dammed up under the colonial system.

The theory that a constitution is supreme law encouraged the development of judicial review. Written constitutions with bills of rights and the emerging principle of separation of powers contributed to the same end. Before the Revolution appellate judges tended to be dependents of the executive branch; the Revolution promoted judicial independence. Most state constitutions provided for judicial tenure during good behavior rather than for a fixed term or the pleasure of the appointing power. Inevitably when Americans believed that a legislature had exceeded its authority they argued that it had acted unconstitutionally, and they turned to courts to enforce the supreme law as law. The dominant view, however, was that for a court to hold a statute unconstitutional insulted the sovereignty of the legislature, as the reactions to *Holmes v. Walton* (1780) and *Trevett v. Weeden* (1786) showed. *Commonwealth v. Caton* (1782) was probably the first case in which a state judge declared that a court had power to hold a statute unconstitutional, though the court in that case sustained the act before it. In *Rutgers v. Waddington* (1784), Hamilton as counsel argued that a state act violating a treaty was unconstitutional, but the court declared that the judicial power advocated by counsel was "subversive of all government." Counsel in *Trevett* also contended that the court should void a state act. Arguments of counsel do not create precedents but can reveal the emergence of a new idea. Any American would have agreed that an act against a constitution was void; although few would have agreed that courts have the final power to decide matters of constitutionality, that idea was spreading. The *Ten Pound Act Cases* (1786) were the first in which an American court held a state enactment void, and that New Hampshire precedent was succeeded by a similar decision in the North Carolina case of *Bayard v. Singleton* (1787). The principle of *Marbury v. Madison* (1803) thus originated at a state level before the framing of the federal Constitution.

The Constitution originated in the drive for a strong national government that preceded the framing of the Articles of Confederation. The "critical period" of 1781–87 intensified that drive, but it began well before the defects of the Articles expanded the ranks of the nationalists. The weaknesses of the United States in international affairs, its inability to enforce the peace treaty, its financial crisis, its helplessness during Shays's Rebellion, and its general incapacity to govern resulted in many proposals—in Congress, in the press, and even in some states—for national powers to negotiate commercial treaties, regulate the nation's commerce, and check state policies that adversely affected creditor interests and impeded economic growth. Five states met at the Annapolis Convention in 1786, ostensibly to discuss a "uniform system" of regulating commerce, but those who masterminded the meeting had a much larger agenda in mind—as Madison put it, a "plenipotentiary Convention for amending the Confederation."

Hamilton had called for a "convention of all the states" as early as 1780, before the Articles were ratified, to form a government worthy of the nation. Even men who defended state sovereignty conceded the necessity of a convention by 1787. William Grayson admitted the "the present Confederation is utterly inefficient and that if it remains much longer in its present State of imbecility we shall be one of the most contemptible Nations on the face of the earth. . . ." Luther Martin admitted that Congress was "weak, contemptibly weak," and Richard Henry Lee believed that no government "short of force, will answer." "Do you not think," he asked George Mason, "that it ought to be declared . . . that any State act of legislation that shall contravene, or oppose, the authorized acts of Congress, or interfere with the expressed rights of that body, shall be *ipso facto* void, and of no force whatsoever?" Many leaders, like Thomas Jefferson, advocated executive and judicial branches for the national government with "an appeal from state judicatures to a federal court in all cases where the act of Confederation controlled the question. . . ." Rufus King, who also promoted a "vigorous Executive," thought that the needed power of Congress to regulate all commerce "can never be well exercised without a Federal Judicial." A consensus was developing.

The Annapolis Convention exploited and nurtured that consensus when it recommended to all the states and to Congress that a constitutional convention "meet at Philadelphia on the second Monday in May next (1787), to take into consideration the situation of the United States, to devise such further provisions as shall appear to them necessary to render the constitution of the federal government adequate to the exigencies of the Union. . . ." Several states, including powerful Virginia and Pennsylvania, chose delegates for the Philadelphia convention, forcing Congress to save face on February 21, 1787, by adopting a motion in accord with the Annapolis recommendation, although

Congress declared that the "sole and express purpose" of the convention was "revising the articles of confederation."

The Constitutional Convention of 1787, which formally organized itself on May 25, lasted almost four months, yet reached its most crucial decision almost at the outset. The first order of business was the nationalistic Virginia Plan (May 29), and the first vote of the Convention, acting as a Committee of the Whole, was the adoption of a resolution "that a *national* Government ought to be established consisting of a *supreme* legislative, Executive and Judiciary" (May 30). Thus the Convention immediately agreed on abandoning, rather than amending, the Articles; on writing a new Constitution; on creating a national government that would be supreme; and on having it consist of three branches.

The radical character of this early decision may be best understood by comparing it with the Articles. The Articles failed mainly because there was no way to force the states to fulfill their obligations or to obey the exercise of such powers as Congress did possess. "The great and radical vice in the construction of the existing Confederation," said Alexander Hamilton, "is the principle of legislation for states or governments, in their corporate capacities, and as contradistinguished from the individuals of which they consist." The Convention remedied that vital defect in the Articles, as George Mason pointed out (May 30), by agreeing on a government that "could directly operate on individuals." Thus the framers solved the critical problem of sanctions by establishing a national government that was independent of the states.

On the next day, May 31, the Committee of the Whole made other crucial decisions with little or no debate. One, reflecting the nationalist bias of the Convention, was the decision to establish a bicameral system whose larger house was to be elected directly by the people rather than by the state legislatures. Mason, no less, explained, "Under the existing confederacy, Congress represent the States not the people of the States; their acts operate on the States, not on the individuals. The case will be changed in the new plan of Government. The people will be represented; they ought therefore to choose the Representatives." Another decision of May 31 was to vest in the Congress the sweeping and undefined power, recommended by the Virginia Plan, "to legislate in all cases to which the separate States are incompetent; or in which the harmony of the U.S. may be interrupted by the exercise of individual (state) legislation; to negative all laws passed by the several States contravening in the opinion of the National Legislature the articles of Union, or any treaties subsisting under the authority of the Union." Not a state voted "nay" to this exceptionally nationalistic proposition. Nor did any state oppose the decision of the next day to create a national executive with similarly broad, undefined powers.

After deliberating for two weeks, the Committee of the Whole presented the Convention with its recommendations, essentially the adoption of the Virginia Plan. Not surprisingly, several of the delegates had second thoughts about the hasty decisions that had been made. Gerry reiterated "that it was necessary to consider what the people would approve." Scrapping the Articles contrary to instructions and failing to provide for state equality in the system of representation provoked a reconsideration along lines described by William Paterson of New Jersey as "federal" in contradistinction to "national." Yet injured state pride was a greater cause of dissension than were the powers proposed for the national government. Some delegates were alarmed, not because of an excessive centralization of powers in the national government, but because of the excessive advantages given to the largest states at the expense of the others. Three states—Virginia, Massachusetts, and Pennsylvania—had forty-five percent of the white population in the country. Under the proposed scheme of proportionate representation, the small states feared that the large ones would dominate the others by controlling the national government.

On June 15, therefore, Paterson of New Jersey submitted for the Convention's consideration a substitute plan. It was a small states plan rather than a states' rights one, for it too had a strong nationalist orientation. Contemplating a revision, rather than a scrapping, of the Articles, it retained the unicameral Congress with its equality of state representation, thus appeasing the small states. But the plan vested in Congress one of the two critical powers previously lacking: "to pass Acts for the regulation of trade and commerce," foreign and interstate. The other, the power of taxation, appeared only in a stunted form; Congress was to be authorized to levy duties on imports and to pass stamp tax acts. Except for its failure to grant full tax powers, the Paterson Plan proposed the same powers for the national legislature as the finished Constitution. The Plan also contained the germ of the national supremacy clause of the Constitution, Article Six, by providing that acts of Congress and United States treaties "shall be the supreme law of the respective States . . . and that the Judiciary of the several States shall be bound thereby in their decisions, any thing in the respective laws of the Individual States to the contrary notwithstanding." The clause also provided for a federal judiciary with extensive jurisdiction and for an executive who could muster the military of the states to compel state obedience to the supreme law. Compulsion of states was unrealistic and unnecessary. Paterson himself declared that the creation of a distinct executive and judiciary meant that the government of the Union could "be exerted on individuals."

Despite its nationalist features, the Paterson Plan retained a unicameral legislature, in which the states remained equal, and the requisition system of rising a revenue, which had failed. "You see the consequence of pushing things too far," said John Dickinson of Delaware to Madison. "Some of the members from the small States wish for two branches in the General Legislature and are friends to a good National Government; but we would sooner submit to a foreign power than submit to be deprived of an equality of suffrage in both branches of the Legislature, and thereby be thrown under the domination of the large states." Only a very few dissidents were irreconcilably opposed to "a good National Government." Most of the dissidents were men like Dickinson and Paterson, "friends to a good National Government" if it preserved a wider scope for small state authority and influence.

When Paterson submitted his plan on June 15, the Convention agreed that to give it "a fair deliberation," it should be referred to the Committee of the Whole and that "in order to place the two plans in due comparison, the other should be recommitted." After debating the two plans, the Committee of the Whole voted in favor of reaffirming the original recommendations based on the Virginia Plan "as preferable to those of Mr. Paterson." Only three weeks after their deliberations, had begun the framers decisively agreed, for the second time, on a strong, independent national government that would operate directly on individuals without the involvement of states.

But the objections of the small states had not yet been satisfied. On the next day, Connecticut, which had voted against the Paterson Plan, proposed the famous Great Compromise: proportionate representation in one house, "provided each State had an equal voice in the other." On that latter point the Convention nearly broke up, so intense was the conflict and deep the division. The irreconcilables in this instance were the leaders of the large-state nationalist faction, otherwise the most constructive and influential members of the Convention: Madison and James Wilson. After several weeks of debate and deadlock, on July 16 the Convention narrowly voted for the compromise. With ten states present, five supported the compromise, four opposed (including Virginia and Pennsylvania), and Massachusetts, was divided. The compromise saved small-state prestige and saved the Convention from failure.

Thereafter consensus on fundamentals was restored, with Connecticut, New Jersey, and Delaware becoming fervent supporters of Madison and Wilson. A week later, for example, there was a motion that each state should be represented by two senators who would "vote per capita," that is, as individuals. Luther Martin of Maryland protested that per capita voting conflicted with the very idea of "the States being represented," yet the motion carried, with no further debate, 9–1.

On many matters of structure, mechanics, and detail there were angry disagreements, but agreement prevailed on the essentials. The office of the presidency is a good illustration. That there should be a powerful chief executive provoked no great debate, but the Convention almost broke up, for the second time, on the method of electing him. Some matters of detail occasioned practically no disagreement and revealed the nationalist consensus. Mason, of all people, made the motion that one qualification of Congressmen should be "citizenship of the United States," and no one disagreed. Under the Articles of Confederation, there was only state citizenship; that there should be a concept of national citizenship seemed natural to men framing a constitution for a nation. Even more a revelation of the nationalist consensus was the fact that three of the most crucial provisions of the Constitution—the taxing power, the necessary-and-proper clause, and the supremacy clause—were casually and unanimously accepted without debate.

Until midway during its sessions, the Convention did not take the trouble to define with care the distribution of power between the national government and the states, although the very nature of the "federal" system depended on that distribution. Consensus on fundamentals once again provides the explanation.

There would be no difficulty in making that distribution; and, the framers had taken out insurance, because at the very outset, they had endorsed the provision of the Virginia Plan vesting broad, undefined powers in a national legislature that would act on individuals. Some byplay of July 17 is illuminating. Roger Sherman of Connecticut thought that the line drawn between the powers of Congress and those left to the states was so vague that national legislation might "interfere . . . in any matters of internal police which respect the Government of such States only, and wherein the general welfare of the United States is not concerned." His motion to protect the "internal police" of the states brought no debaters to his side and was summarily defeated; only Maryland supported Connecticut. Immediately after, another small-state delegate, Gunning Bedford of Delaware, shocked even Edmund Randolph of Virginia, who had presented the Virginia Plan, by a motion to extend the powers of Congress by vesting authority "to legislate in all cases for the general interest of the Union." Randolph observed, "This is a formidable idea indeed. It involves the power of violating all the laws and constitution of the States, of intermeddling with their police." Yet the motion passed.

On July 26 the Convention adjourned until August 6 to allow a Committee on Detail to frame a "constitution conformable to the Resolutions passed by the Convention." Generously construing its charge, the committee acted as a miniature convention and introduced a number of significant changes. One was the explicit enumeration of the powers of Congress to replace the vague, omnibus provisions adopted previously by the Convention. Although enumerated, those powers were liberally expressed and formidable in their array. The committee made specific the spirit and intent of the Convention. Significantly the first enumerated power was that of taxation and the second that of regulating commerce among the states and with foreign nations: the two principal powers that had been withheld from Congress by the Articles. When the Convention voted on the provision that Congress "shall have the power to lay and collect taxes, duties, imposts and excises," the states were unanimous and only one delegate, Gerry, was opposed. When the Convention next turned to the commerce power, there was no discussion and even Gerry voted affirmatively.

Notwithstanding its enumeration of the legislative powers, all of which the Convention accepted, the Committee on Detail added an omnibus clause that has served as an ever-expanding source of national authority: "And to make all laws that shall be necessary and proper for carrying into execution the foregoing powers." The Convention agreed to that clause without a single dissenting vote by any state or delegate. The history of the great supremacy clause, Article Six, shows a similar consensus. Without debate the Convention adopted the supremacy clause, and not a single state or delegate voted nay. Finally, Article One, Section 10, imposing restrictions on the economic powers of the states with respect to paper money, *ex post facto* laws, bills of credit, and contracts, also reflected a consensus in the Convention. In sum, consensus, rather than compromise, was the most significant feature of the convention, outweighing in importance the various compromises that occupied most of the time of the delegates.

But why was there such a consensus? The obvious answer (apart from the fact that opponents either stayed away or walked out) is the best: experience had proved that the nationalist constitutional position was right. If the United States was to survive and flourish, a strong national government had to be established. The framers of the Constitution were accountable to public opinion; the Convention was a representative body. That its members were prosperous, well-educated political leaders made them no less representative than Congress. The state legislatures, which elected the members of the Convention, were the most unlikely instruments for thwarting the popular will. The framers, far from being able to do as they pleased, were not free to promulgate the Constitution. Although they adroitly arranged for its ratification by nine state ratifying conventions rather than by all state legislatures, they could not present a plan that the people of the states would not tolerate. They could not control the membership of those state ratifying conventions. They could not even be sure that the existing Congress would submit the Constitution to the states for ratification, let alone for ratification by state conventions that had to be specially elected. If the Framers got too far astray from public opinion, their work would have been wasted. The consensus in the Convention coincided with an emerging consensus in the country that recaptured the nationalist spirit of '76. That the Union had to be strengthened was an almost universal American belief.

For its time the Constitution was a remarkably democratic document framed by democratic methods. Some historians have contended that the Convention's scrapping of the Articles and the ratification process were revolutionary acts which if performed by a Napoleon would be pronounced a coup d'etat. But the procedure of the Articles for constitutional amendment was not democratic, because it allowed Rhode Island, with one-sixtieth of the nation's population, to exercise a veto power. The Convention sent its Constitution to the lawfully existing government, the Congress of the Confederation, for submission to the states, and Congress, which could have censured the Convention for exceeding its authority, freely complied—and thereby exceeded its own authority under the Articles. A coup d'etat ordinarily lacks the deliberation and consent that marked the making of the Constitution and is characterized by a military element that was wholly lacking in 1787. A Convention elected by the state legislatures and consisting of many of the foremost leaders of their time deliberated for almost four months. Its members included many opponents of the finished scheme. The nation knew the Convention was considering changes in the government. The proposed Constitution was made public, and voters in every state were asked to choose delegates to vote for or against it after open debate. The use of state ratifying conventions fit the theory that a new fundamental law was being adopted and, therefore, conventions were proper for the task.

The Constitution guaranteed to each state a republican or representative form of government and fixed no property or religious qualifications on the right to vote or hold office, at a time when such qualifications were common in the states. By leaving voting qualifications to the states the Constitution implicitly accepted such qualifications but imposed none. The Convention, like the Albany Congress of 1754, the Stamp Act Congress, the Continental Congresses, and the Congresses of the Confederation, had been chosen by state (or colonial) legislatures, but the Constitution created a Congress whose lower house was popularly elected. When only three states directly elected their chief executive officer, the Constitution provided for the indirect election of the President by an Electoral College that originated in the people and is still operative. The Constitution's system of separation of powers and elaborate checks and balances was not intended to refine out popular influence on government but to protect liberty; the framers divided, distributed, and limited powers to prevent one branch, faction, interest, or section from becoming too powerful. Checks and balances were not undemocratic, and the Federalists were hard pressed not to apologize for checks and balances but to convince the Anti-Federalists, who wanted far more checks and balances, that the Constitution had enough. Although the Framers were not democrats in a modern sense, their opponents were even less democratic. Those opponents sought to capitalize on the lack of a Bill of Rights, and ratification of the Constitution became possible only because leading Federalists committed themselves to amendments as soon as the new government went into operation. At that time, however, Anti-Federalists opposed a Bill of Rights, because it would allay popular fears of the new government, ending the chance for state sovereignty amendments.

Although the Framers self-consciously refrained from referring to slavery in the Constitution, it recognized slavery, the most undemocratic of all institutions. That recognition was a grudging but necessary price of Union. The three-fifths clause of Article I provided for counting three-fifths of the total number of slaves as part of the population of a state in the apportionment of representation and direct taxation. Artice IV, section 2, provided for rendition of fugitive slaves to the slaveholder upon his claim. On the other hand, Article I, section 9, permitted Congress to abolish the slave trade in twenty years. Most delegates, including many from slaveholding states, would have preferred a Constitution untainted by slavery; but Southern votes for ratification required recognition of slavery. By choosing a Union with slavery, the Convention deferred the day of reckoning.

The Constitution is basically a political document. Modern scholarship has completely discredited the once popular view, associated with Charles Beard, that the Constitution was undemocratically made to advance the economic interests of personality groups, chiefly creditors. The largest public creditor at the Convention was Elbridge Gerry, who refused to sign the Constitution and opposed its ratification, and the largest private creditor was George Mason who did likewise. Indeed, seven men who either quit the Convention in disgust or refused to sign the Constitution held public securities that were worth over twice the holdings of the thirty-nine men who signed the Constitution. The most influential framers, among them Madison, Wilson, Paterson, Dickinson, and

Gouverneur Morris, owned no securities. Others, like Washington, who acted out of patriotism, not profit, held trifling amounts. Eighteen members of the Convention were either debtors or held property that depreciated after the new government became operative. On crucial issues at the Convention, as in the state ratifying conventions, the dividing line between groups for and against the Constitution was not economic, not between realty and personalty, or debtors and creditors, or town and frontier. The restrictions of Article I, section 10 on the economic powers of the states were calculated to protect creditor interests and promote business stability, but those restrictions were not undemocratic; if impairing the obligations of contracts or emitting bills of credit and paper money were democratic hallmarks, the Constitution left Congress free to be democratic. The interest groups for and against the Constitution were substantially similar. Economic interests did influence the voting on ratification, but no simple explanation that ignores differences between states and even within states will suffice, and many non-economic influences were also at work. In the end the Constitution was framed and ratified because most voters came to share the vision held by Franklin in 1775 and Dickinson in 1776; those two, although antagonists in Pennsylvania politics, understood for quite different reasons that a strong central government was indispensable for nationhood.

6

The Bill of Rights

THE BILL OF RIGHTS consists of the first ten amendments to the Constitution of the United States. Congress submitted those amendments to the states for ratification on September 25, 1789, and the requisite number of state legislatures ratified them by December 15, 1791. The triumph of individual liberty against government power is one of our history's noblest and most enduringly important themes, epitomized by the Bill of Rights. Yet James Madison, justly remembered as the "father" of the Bill of Rights, privately referred on August 19, 1789, to the "nauseous project of amendments." He had proposed the Bill of Rights, in part, because, "It will kill the opposition everywhere . . ."—a suggestion that party politics saturated the making of the first ten amendments. Thomas Jefferson, who must have been profoundly gratified by the ratification of the amendments, which he had urged, was the Secretary of State who officially notified the governors of the states that ratification was an accomplished fact: he had the honor, he wrote, of enclosing copies of an act "concerning certain fisheries," another establishing the post office, and "the ratifications by three fourths of the . . . States, of certain articles in addition and amendment of the Constitution. . . ." The history of the Bill of Rights from its rejection by the Philadelphia Constitutional Convention to its belated ratification is not as passionless, because the omission of a bill of rights in the original Constitution had been the most important obstacle in the way of its adoption by the states.

The omission of a bill of rights was a deliberate act of the Constitutional Convention. The Convention's work was almost done when it received from the Committee on Style copies of the proposed Constitution and the letter by which the Convention would submit it to Congress. The major task that remained was to adopt, engross, and sign the finished document. The weary delegates, after a hot summer's work in Philadelphia, were eager to return home. At that point, on September 12, 1787, George Mason of Virginia remarked that he "wished the plan had been prefaced by a Bill of Rights," because it would "give great quiet" to the people. Mason thought that with the aid of state bills of rights as models, "a bill might be prepared in a few hours." He made no stirring speech for civil liberties in general or any rights in particular. He did not even argue the need for a bill of rights or move the adoption of one, though he offered to second a motion if one were made. Elbridge Gerry of Massachusetts then moved for a committee to prepare a bill of rights, and Mason seconded the motion. Roger Sherman of Connecticut observed that the rights of the people should be secured if necessary, but because the Constitution did not repeal the state bills of rights, the Convention need not do anything. Without further debate the delegates, voting by states, defeated the motion 10–0. Two days later, after the states unanimously defeated a motion by Mason to delete from the Constitution a ban on *ex post facto* laws by Congress, Charles Pinckney of South Carolina, seconded by Gerry, moved to insert a declaration "that the liberty of the Press should be inviolably observed." Sherman laconically replied, "It is unnecessary. The power of Congress does not extend to the Press," and the motion lost 7–4. Three days later the Convention adjourned.

In the Congress of the Confederation, Richard Henry Lee of Virginia moved that a bill of rights, which he had adapted from his own state's constitution, be added to the Constitution. Lee was less interested in the adoption of a bill of rights than in defeating the Constitution. Amendments recommended by Congress required ratification by all the state legislatures, not just nine state ratifying conventions. Lee's motion was defeated, but it showed that, from the start of the ratification controversy, the omission of a bill of rights became an Anti-Federalist mace with which to smash the Constitution. Its opponents sought to prevent ratification and exaggerated the bill of rights issue because it was one with which they could enlist public support. Their prime loyalty belonged to states' rights, not civil rights.

Mason, the author of the celebrated Virginia Declaration of Rights of 1776, soon wrote his influential "Objections to the Constitution," which began, "There is no Declaration of Rights. . . ." The sincerity of Mason's desire for a bill of rights is beyond question, but he had many others reasons for opposing the Constitution. Almost two weeks before he raised the issue of a bill of rights on September 12, he had declared "that he would sooner chop off his right hand than put it to the Constitution as it now stands." A bill of rights might protect individuals against the national government, but it would not protect the states. He believed that the new government would diminish state powers and by the exercise of its commerce power could "ruin" the Southern states; the control of commerce by a mere majority vote of Congress was, to Mason, "an insuperable objection." But the lack of a bill of rights proved to be the most powerful argument against ratification of the Constitution in the Anti-Federalist armory.

Why did the Constitutional Convention omit a bill of rights? No delegate opposed one in principle. As George Washington informed Lafayette, "there was not a member of the Convention, I believe, who had the least objection to what is contended for by the advocates for a Bill of Rights. . . ." All the framers were civil libertarians as well as experienced politicians who had the confidence of their constituents and the state legislatures that elected them. Even the foremost opponents of ratification praised the make-up of the Convention.

Mason himself, for example, wrote that "America has certainly upon this occasion drawn forth her first characters . . . of the purest intentions," and Patrick Henry, who led the Anti-Federalists in Virginia, conceded that the states had trusted the "object of revising the Confederation to the greatest, the best, and most enlightened of our citizens." Their liberality of spirit is suggested by the fact that many—Protestants all and including the entire Virginia delegation—made a point of attending divine service at St. Mary's Chapel. As Washington recorded in his diary, "Went to the Romish church to high mass." How could such an "assembly of demigods," as Jefferson called them, neglect the liberties of the people?

On July 26 the Convention had adjourned until August 6 to permit a Committee of Detail to frame a "constitution conformable to the Resolutions passed by the Convention." The committee, consisting of six men including Edmund Randolph of Virginia, James Wilson of Pennsylvania, and Oliver Ellsworth of Connecticut, generously construed its charge by acting as a miniature convention. Introducing a number of significant changes, such as the explicit enumeration of the powers of Congress, the committee, without recommendations from the Convention, decided on a preamble. Randolph left a fragmentary record of the committee's decision that the preamble did not seem a proper place for a philosophic statement of the ends of government because "we are not working on the natural rights of men not yet gathered into society" but upon rights "modified by society and interwoven with what we call . . . the rights of states." According to American revolutionary theory, the natural rights to which Randolph referred were possessed by individuals in the state of nature, which existed before they voluntarily contracted with each other to establish a government whose purpose was to secure their rights. In the state of nature, when only the law of nature governed, the theory posited that—as the first section of the Virginia Declaration of Rights stated—"all men are by nature equally free and independent, and have certain inherent rights, of which, when they enter into a state of society, they cannot, by any compact, deprive or divest their posterity; namely, the enjoyment of life and liberty, with the means of acquiring and possessing property, and pursuing and obtaining happiness and safety." The adoption of the state constitutions having ended the state of nature, there was no need to enumerate the rights reserved to the people—or so the farmers of the Constitution reasoned.

On the other hand they recognized that the existence of organized society and government required the affirmation of certain rights that did not exist in the state of nature but which served to protect natural rights. Trial by jury, for example, was unknown in the state of nature but necessary for the protection of one's life, liberty, and property. Accordingly the framers recognized a class of rights "modified by society," just as they recognized that the legitimate powers of government that did not belong to the central government of the Union could be called "the rights of the states." The principal task of the Convention was to provide for an effective national government by redistributing the powers of government. Thus the Committee of Detail, when enumerating the powers of

Congress, began with the power to tax and the power to regulate commerce among the states and with foreign nations (the two great powers which the Articles of Confederation had withheld from Congress) and ended with an omnibus clause that granted implied powers: "And to make all laws that shall be necessary and proper for carrying into execution the foregoing powers, and all other powers vested, by this Constitution, in the government of the United States, or in any department thereof." That "necessary and proper" clause was the most formidable in the array of national powers, therefore the most controversial, and the one most responsible, later, for the demand for a bill of rights to ensure that the United States did not violate the rights of the people or of the states.

The Committee of Detail, again on its own initiative, recommended some rights ("modified by society"), among them trial by jury in criminal cases, a tight definition of treason to prevent improper convictions, a ban on titles of nobility (a way of guaranteeing against a privileged class), freedom of speech and debate for members of the legislature, and a guarantee that the citizens of each state should have the same privileges and immunities of citizens in other states. In addition the committee introduced the clause guaranteeing to each state a republican form of government. In the minds of the framers, many provisions of the Constitution had a libertarian character—the election of public officials, the representative system, the separation of powers among three branches of government, and the requirement that revenue and appropriation measures originate in the House of Representatives—a protection of the natural right to property and a bar against taxation without representation. During the controversy over the ratification of the Constitution, when the omission of a bill of rights was the major issue, many framers argued, as did Hamilton in *The Federalist* #84, "that the Constitution is itself, in every rational sense, and to every useful purpose, a Bill of Rights."

All the rights recommended by the Committee of Detail eventually found their way into the Constitution, but Charles Pinckney believed that the committee had neglected several others that also deserved constitutional recognition. On August 20 he recommended "sundry propositions," including a guarantee of the writ of *habeas corpus*, which protected citizens from arbitrary arrest; an injunction that the liberty of the press should be "inviolably preserved"; a ban on maintaining an army in time of peace except with the consent of Congress; an explicit subordination of the military to the civil power; a prohibition on the quartering of troops in private homes during peacetime; and a ban on religious tests as a qualification for any United States office.

None of these provisions secured what theoreticians regarded as natural rights. The freedoms of speech and conscience were natural rights, but the liberty of the press was probably distinguishable as a right that did not exist in the state of nature. If liberty of the press was a natural right the convention acted consistently when voting that its protection was unnecessary. Similarly the ban on religious tests, though protecting the right of conscience, was another example of what Randolph had called a right "modified by society," not preexisting it. Significantly Pinckney had not recommended a protection of freedom of religion or of speech. Without debate or consideration the Convention referred his proposals to the Committee of Detail, but it made no recommendations on any of them.

On the floor of the Convention Gerry moved that Congress should be denied the power to pass bills of attainder and *ex post facto* laws. The motion passed with hardly any discussion. Bills of attainder were legislative declarations of the guilt of individuals and legislative imposition of criminal penalties, without the usual judicial proceedings. No instrument of the criminal law was more dreaded or violative of the fair procedures associated with trial by jury than a bill of attainder, the most expeditious way of condemning political opponents. *Ex post facto* laws in the field of criminal law were nearly as notorious and as unfair, for they were legislative acts that made criminal any conduct that was not a crime at the time committed, or acts that retroactively increased the penalty for a crime or changed the rules of evidence in order to obtain a conviction. With little debate the Convention also placed prohibitions on the power of the states to enact bills of attainder and *ex post facto* laws. Some delegates, including George Mason, opposed the ban on the latter because they did not wish to limit the power of the states to enact retroactive legislation in civil cases, and they insisted, against the authority of Sir William Blackstone's *Commentaries*, that *ex post facto* laws included civil legislation as well as criminal. The Supreme Court in 1798 would settle the matter in favor of the Blackstonian interpretation.

Bills of attainder and *ex post facto* laws, being legislative enactments, came into existence after the people had compacted to form a government. Banning such enactments, therefore, constituted means for the protection of natural rights, but the bans did not protect natural rights as such. The same may be said of protecting the cherished writ of *habeas corpus* as a device for insuring the personal liberty of an individual wrongfully imprisoned. After the Convention unanimously adopted the Committee of Detail's recommendation for a clause on trial by jury in criminal cases, Pinckney urged the Convention to secure the benefit of the writ as well, and by a vote of 7–3 a *habeas corpus* clause was adopted. Pinckney also moved a prohibition on religious tests, which the Convention summarily adopted by unanimous vote. In so doing the Convention demonstrated a rare liberality of spirit, because all the framers but those who represented New York and Virginia came from states whose constitutions discriminated against some religious denominations by imposing as a qualification for public office some religious test. In Pennsylvania, for example, a state whose constitution contained the broadest guarantee of religious freedom and a provision that no man acknowledging God should be deprived of any civil right on account of his religion, the oath of office required an acknowledgment of the divine inspiration of the New Testament. A Jew from Philadelphia petitioned the Constitution Convention not to frame a similar oath of office imposing a civil disability upon him. Unitarians, Deists, and Catholics suffered from various religious disabilities in many states. By prohibiting religious tests the

Convention showed a greater regard for religious liberty than most states; yet the Convention did not protect religious liberty itself.

Thus, all the protections written into the Constitution were means of vindicating natural rights but no natural rights were constitutionally protected. The overwhelming majority of the Convention believed, as Sherman succinctly declared, "It is unnecessary." Why was it unnecessary given the fact that the Convention recommended a new and powerful national government that could operate directly on individuals? The framers believed that the national government could exercise only enumerated powers or powers necessary to carry out those enumerated, and no provision of the Constitution authorized the government to act on any natural rights. A bill of rights would restrict national powers, but, as Hamilton declared, such a bill would be "dangerous" as well as unnecessary, because it "would contain various exceptions to powers not granted; and, on this very account, would afford a colorable pretext to claim more than were granted. For why declare that things shall not be done which there is no power to do? Why, for instance, should it be said that the liberty of the press shall not be restrained, when no power is given by which restrictions may be imposed?"

Hamilton expressed a standard Federalist position, echoing other framers and advocates of ratification. Excluding a bill of rights from the Constitution was fundamental to the constitutional theory of the framers. James Wilson, whose influence at the Convention had been second only to that of Madison, led the ratificationist forces in Pennsylvania and several times sought to explain the omission of a bill of rights. The people of the states, he declared, had vested in their governments all powers and rights "which they did not in explicit terms reserve," but the case was different as to a federal government whose authority rested on positive grants of power expressed in the Constitution. For the federal government, "the reverse of the proposition prevails, and everything which is not given, is reserved" to the people or the states. That distinction, Wilson argued, answered those who believed that the omission of a bill of rights was a defect. Its inclusion would have been "absurd," because a bill of rights stipulated the reserved rights of the people, while the function of the Constitution was to provide for the existence of the federal government rather than enumerate rights not divested. Like Hamilton and other Federalists, Wilson believed that a formal declaration on freedom of the press or religion, over which Congress had no powers whatsoever, could "imply" that some degree of power had been granted because of the attempt to define its extent. Wilson also insisted on the impossibility of enumerating and reserving all the rights of the people. "A bill of rights annexed to a constitution," he added, "is an enumeration of the powers reserved. If we attempt an enumeration, everything that is not enumerated is presumed to be given. the consequence is, that an imperfect enumeration would throw all implied powers into the scale of the government; and the rights of the people would be rendered incomplete."

Civil liberties, the supporters of the Constitution believed, faced real dangers from the possibility of repressive state action, but that was a matter to be guarded against by state bills of rights. They also argued, inconsistently, that some states had no bills of rights but were as free as those with bills of rights. They were as free because personal liberty, to Federalist theoreticians, depended not on "parchment provisions," which Hamilton called inadequate in "a struggle with public necessity," but on public opinion, an extended republic, a pluralistic society of competing interests, and a free and limited government structured to prevent any interest from becoming an overbearing majority.

The fact that six states had no bill of rights and that none had a comprehensive list of guarantees provided the supporters of ratification with the argument, made by Wilson among others, that an imperfect bills of rights was worse than none at all because the omission of some rights might justify their infringement by implying an unintended grant of government power. The record was not reassuring: the states had very imperfect bills of rights, which proved to be ineffective when confronted by "public necessity," and the state governments did in fact abridge rights that had not been explicitly reserved.

Virginia's Declaration of Rights, for example, did not ban bills of attainder. In 1778 the Virginia assembly adopted a bill of attainder and outlawry, drafted by Jefferson at the instigation of Governor Patrick Henry, against a reputed cutthroat Tory, one Josiah Philips, and some fifty unnamed "associates." By legislative enactment they were condemned for treason and murder, and on failure to surrender were subject to being killed by anyone. At the Virginia ratifying convention, Edmund Randolph, irked beyond endurance by Henry's assaults on the Constitution as dangerous to personal liberties, recalled with "horror" the "shocking" attainder. When Henry defended the attainder, John Marshall, who supported ratification without a bill of rights, declared, "Can we pretend to the enjoyment of political freedom or security, when we are told that a man has been, by an act of Assembly, struck out of existence without a trial by jury, without examination, without being confronted with his accusers and witnesses, without the benefits of the law of the land?"

The framers of the Constitution tended to be skeptical about the value of "parchment barriers" against "overbearing majorities," as Madison said. He had seen repeated violations of bills of rights in every state. Experience proved the "inefficacy of a bill of rights to those occasions when its control is most needed," he said. In Virginia, for example, despite an explicit protection of the rights of conscience, the legislature had favored an establishment of religion, which was averted only because Madison turned the tide of opinion against the bill. As realists the framers believed that constitutional protections of rights meant little during times of popular hysteria; any member of the Constitutional Convention could have cited examples of gross abridgments of civil liberties in states that had bills of rights.

Virginia's bill was imperfect not just because it lacked a ban on bills of attainder. The much vaunted Declaration of Rights of Virginia also omitted the freedoms of speech, assembly, and petition; the right to the writ of *habeas corpus*; the right to grand jury proceedings; the right to counsel; separation of church and state; and freedom from double jeopardy and from *ex post facto* laws. The rights omitted were as numerous and important as those included. Twelve states, including Vermont, had framed constitutions, and the only right secured by all was trial by jury in criminal cases. Although all protected religious liberty too, five either permitted or provided for establishments of religion. Two states passed over a free press guarantee. Four neglected to ban excessive fines, excessive bail, compulsory self-incrimination, and general search warrants. Five ignored protections for the rights of assembly, petition, counsel, and trial by jury in civil cases. Seven omitted a prohibition of *ex post facto* laws. Nine failed to provide for grand jury proceedings, and nine failed to condemn bills of attainder. Ten said nothing about freedom of speech, while eleven were silent on double jeopardy. Whether omissions implied a power to violate, omissions seemed, in Federalist minds, to raised dangers that could be prevented by avoiding an unnecessary problem entirely: omit a bill of rights when forming a federal government of limited powers.

That the framers of the Constitution actually believed their own arguments purporting to justify the omission of a bill of rights is difficult to credit. Some of the points they made were patently absurd, like the insistence that the inclusion of a bill or rights would be dangerous and, on historical grounds, unsuitable. The last point most commonly turned up in the claim that bills of rights were appropriate in England but not America. Magna Carta, the Petition of Right of 1628, and the Bill of Rights of 1689 had been grants wrested from kings to secure royal assent to certain liberties, and therefore had "no application to constitutions . . . founded upon the power of the people" who surrendered nothing and retained everything. That argument, made in *Federalist #84* and by leading ratificationists as sophisticated as Wilson and Oliver Ellsworth of Connecticut, was so porous that it could persuade no one. Excepting Rhode Island and Connecticut, the two corporate colonies which retained their charters (with all royal references deleted), eleven states had framed written constitutions during the Revolution, and seven drew up bills of rights; even the four without such bills inserted in their constitutions provisions normally found in a bill of rights.

To imply that bills of rights were un-American or unnecessary merely because in America the people were the source of all power was unhistorical. Over a period of a century and a half America had become accustomed to the idea that government existed by consent of the governed, that people created government, that they did it by written compact, that the compact constituted fundamental law, that the government must be subject to such limitations which are necessary for the security of the rights of the people and, usually, that the reserved rights of the people were enumerated in bills of rights. Counting Vermont (an independent republic from 1777 until its admission to the Union in 1791), eight states had bills of rights—notwithstanding any opinion that such bills properly belonged only in a compact between a king and his subjects. The dominant theory in the United States from the time of the Revolution was that the fundamental law limited all branches of the government, not just the crown as in England where the great liberty documents did not limit the legislative power.

When Randolph for the Committee of Detail alluded to the fact that "we are not working on the natural rights of men not yet gathered into society," he was thinking of the framing of the state constitutions. The constitution of Wilson's state began with an elaborate preamble followed by as comprehensive a "Declaration of the Rights of the Inhabitants" as existed in any state. Yet Wilson repeatedly informed Pennsylvania's ratifying convention that rights and liberties could be claimed only in a contract between king and subjects, not when "the fee simple of freedom and government is declared to be in the people." Governor Randolph at the Virginia ratifying convention merely exaggerated when claiming that the Virginia Declaration of Rights "has never secured us against any danger; it has been repeatedly disregarded and violated." But Randolph's rhetoric became unpardonable when he declared that although a bill of rights made sense in England to limit the king's prerogative, "Our situation is radically different from that of the people of England. What have we to do with bills of rights? . . . A bill of rights, therefore, accurately speaking, is quite useless, if not dangerous to a republic." At the Constitutional Convention, however, Randolph had been able to distinguish natural rights from some rights modified by society.

That supporters of the Constitution could ask, "What have we to do with a bill of rights?" suggests that they had made a colossal error of judgment, which they compounded by refusing to admit it. Their single-minded purpose of creating an effective national government had exhausted their energies and good sense, and when they found themselves on the defensive, accused of threatening the liberties of the people, their frayed nerves led them into indefensible positions. Any Anti-Federalist could have answered Randolph's question, Wilson's speeches, or Hamilton's #84, and many capably did so without resorting to Patrick Henry's grating hysteria. "Centinel," who answered Wilson in a Philadelphia newspaper, declared that the explanation for the omission of a bill of rights "is an insult on the understanding of the people."

Abroad, two wise Americans serving their country in diplomatic missions, coolly appraised the proposed Constitution without the obligation of having to support a party line. John Adams, in London, having received a copy of the document, wrote a short letter to Jefferson in Paris. The Constitution seemed "admirably calculated to preserve the Union," Adams thought, and he hoped it would be ratified with amendments adopted later. "What think you," he asked, "of a Declaration of Rights? Should not such a Thing have preceded the Model?" Jefferson, in his first letter to Madison on the subject of the Constitution, began with praise but ended with what he did not like: "First the omission of a bill of rights. . . ." After listing rights he thought deserved special protection, starting with freedom of religion and of the press, Jefferson dismissed as campaign rhetoric Wilson's justification for the omission of a bill of rights and concluded: "Let me add that a bill of rights is what the people are entitled to against every government on earth, general or particular, and what no just government should refuse, or rest on inference."

Adams and Jefferson in Europe were much closer to popular opinion that the framers of the Constitution who had worked secretly for almost four months and, with their supporters, became locked into a position that defied logic and experience. During the ratification controversy, some Federalists argued that the Constitution protected basic rights, exposing them to the reply that they had omitted the liberty of the press, religious freedom, security against general warrants, trial by jury in civil cases, and other basic rights. If the framers intended to protect only the rights arising from the existence of society and government and unknown in a state of nature, they were inconsistent. In the first place they protected only some of the non-natural rights; the first ten amendments are crowded with such rights which the framers neglected. Second, any reader of John Locke would realize that the clause in Article 1, section 10, prohibiting the states from impairing the obligation of contracts, protected a natural right. At the close of chapter two of *The Second Treatise on Government*, Locke wrote that the "promises and bargains" between two men on a desert island or between a Swiss and an Indian in the woods of America "are binding to them, though they are perfectly in a state of nature to one another. . . ." Oddly, the Convention had failed to adopt the contract clause when it was proposed; the Committee on Style inserted it into the Constitution, and the Convention, without discussion, agreed to the clause in its closing days. The inclusion of one natural right raises the question why all others were excluded. The contract clause, of course, operates only against state infringement, raising the additional question why the Convention failed to include a comparable prohibition on the United States.

Natural rights, in accordance with American theory and experience, required protection in any government made by compact. At the Convention Madison declared that the delegates had assembled to frame "a compact by which an authority was created paramount to the parties, and making laws for the government of them." Some of the states, when formally ratifying the Constitution, considered themselves to be "entering into an explicit and solemn compact," as Massachusetts declared. During the ratification controversy, publicists on both sides referred to the Constitution as a compact. Chief Justice John Jay, who had been one of the authors of *The Federalist*, observed in *Chisholm v. Georgia* (1793) that "the Constitution of the United States is . . . a compact made by the people of the United States in order to govern themselves."

The new compact created a government whose powers seemed intimidating. Article VI, declaring the Constitution, laws made in its pursuance, and treaties of the United States to be the supreme law of the land, anything in the state constitutions to the contrary notwithstanding, seemed to many Anti-Federalists as superseding their state bills of rights and authorizing laws "repugnant to every article of your rights," as "The Impartial Examiner" wrote. Most believed that enumerated powers could be abused at the expense of fundamental liberties. Congress's power to tax for example, might be aimed at the press and was thus, in the words of Richard Henry Lee, "a power to destroy or restrain the freedom of it." Others feared that taxes might be exacted from the people for the support of a religious denomination. Tax collectors, unrestrained by a ban on general warrants, Patrick Henry argued, might invade homes "and search, ransack, and measure, every thing you eat, drink, and wear."

The necessary and proper clause particularly enraged advocates of a bill of rights. They saw that clause as the source of undefined and unlimited powers to aggrandize the national government and victimize the people, unless as "An Old Whig" declared, we had a bill of rights to which we might appeal." "A Democratic Federalist" wrote: "I lay it down as a general rule that wherever the powers of government extend to the lives, the persons, and properties of the subject, all their rights ought to be clearly and expressly defined, otherwise they have but a poor security for their liberties." Henry warned that Congress might "extort a confession by the use of torture," in order to convict a violator of federal law. Numerous opponents of ratification contended that Congress could define as crimes the violation of any laws it might legitimately enact, and in the absence of a bill of rights, accused persons might be deprived of the rights to counsel, to indictment, to cross-examine witnesses against them, to produce evidence in their own behalf, to be free from compulsory self-incrimination, to be protected against double jeopardy or excessive bail, to be exempt from excessive fines or cruel and unusual punishments, and to enjoy other rights traditionally belonging to accused persons. Such an argument was invariably advanced as one among many refuting the Federalist claim that a bill of rights was unnecessary.

If it was unnecessary, Anti-Federalists asked, why did the Constitution protect some rights? The protection of some opened the Federalists to devastating rebuttal. They claimed that because no bill of rights could be complete, the omission of any particular right might imply a power to abridge it as unworthy of respect by the government. That argument, in effect that to include some would exclude all others, boomeranged. The protection of trial by jury in criminal cases, the bans on religious tests, *ex post facto* laws, and bills of attainder, the narrow definition of treason, and the provision for the writ of *habeas corpus*, by the Federalists' own reasoning was turned against them. Robert Whitehall, answering Wilson on the floor of the Pennsylvania ratifying convention, noted that the writ of *habeas corpus* and trial by jury had been expressly reserved and in vain called on Wilson to reconcile the reservation with his "favorite proposition." "For, if there was danger in the attempt to enumerate the liberties of the people," Whitehall explained, "lest it should prove imperfect and defective, how happens it, that in the instances I have mentioned, that danger has been incurred? Have the people no other rights worth their attention, or is it to be inferred, agreeable to the maxim of our opponents, that every other right is abandoned?" Stipulating a right, he concluded, destroyed the "argument of danger." Surely, Anti-Federalists said, their opponents might think of some rights in addition to those protected. The ban on religious tests could have reminded them of freedom of religion. Did not its omission, by their reasoning, necessarily mean that the government could attack freedom of religion?

Henry cleverly observed that the "fair implication" of the Federalist argument against a bill of rights was that the government could do anything not forbidden by the Constitution. Since the provision on the writ of *habeas corpus* allowed its suspension when the public safety required, Henry reasoned, "It results clearly that, if it had not said so, they could suspend it in all cases whatsoever. It reverses the position of the friends of this Constitution, that every thing is retained which is not given up; for, instead of this, every thing is given up which is not expressly reserved." In his influential *Letters of a Federal Farmer*, Lee observed that a clause of the Constitution prohibited Congress from granting titles of nobility. If the clause had been omitted, he wondered whether Congress would have the power to grant such titles and concluded that it would not under any provision of the Constitution. "Why then by a negative clause, restrain congress from doing what it had no power to do? This clause, then, must have no meaning, or imply, that were it omitted, congress would have the power in question . . . on the principle that congress possess the powers not expressly reserved." Lee objected to leaving the rights of the people to "logical inferences," because Federalist principles led to the implication that all the rights not mentioned in the Constitution were intended to be relinquished.

Far from being dangerous, a bill of rights, as "A Federal Republican" stated in answer to Wilson, "could do no harm, but might do much good." Lee, discoursing on the good it might do, observed that having a bill of rights assisted popular "education," because it taught "truths" upon which freedom depends and which the people must believe as "sacred." James Winthrop of Massachusetts, writing as "Agrippa," explained another positive value of a bill of rights. It "serves to secure the minority against the usurpations and tyranny of the majority." History, he wrote, proved the "prevalence of a disposition to use power wantonly. It [a bill of rights] is therefore as necessary to defend an individual against the majority in a republick as against the king in a monarchy."

In sum, the usually masterful politicians who had dominated the Convention had blundered by botching constitutional theory and making a serious political error. Their arguments justifying the omission of a bill of rights were impolitic and unconvincing. Mason's point that a bill of rights would quiet the fears of the people was unanswerable. Alienating him and the many who agreed with him was bad politics and handed to the opposition a stirring cause around which they could muster sentiment against ratification. The single issue that united Anti-Federalists throughout the country was the lack of a bill of rights. No rational argument—and the lack of a bill of rights created an intensely emotional issue because people believed that their liberties were at stake—could possible allay the fears generated by demagogues like Henry and principled opponents of ratification like Mason. Washington believed that even Mason's "Objections" were meant "to alarm the people." And, when Anti-Federalists in New York demanded a bill of rights, Hamilton alleged, "It is the plan of men of this stamp to frighten the people with ideal bugbears, in order to mould them to their own purposes. The unceasing cry of these designing croakers is, My friends, your liberty is invaded!" The Anti-Federalists capitalized on the

Federalist blunder, hoping to defeat the Constitution or get a second convention that would revise it in order to hamstring the national government.

In Pennsylvania, the second state to ratify, the minority demanded a comprehensive bill of rights similar to that in their state constitution. Massachusetts, the sixth state to ratify, was the first to do so with recommended amendments. Only two of the recommended amendments, dealing with jury trial in civil suits and grand jury indictment, belonged in a bill of rights. Supporters of the Constitution in Massachusetts had withdrawn a proposed bill of rights on the supposition that Anti-Federalists would use it as proof that the Constitution endangered liberty. Maryland too would have recommended a bill of rights, but the Federalist majority jettisoned it when the Anti-Federalists tried to insert curbs on national powers to tax and regulate commerce. Nevertheless, Federalists grudgingly accepted ratification with recommended amendments to ward off conditional ratification or the defeat of the Constitution. New Hampshire, whose approval as the ninth state made ratification an accomplished fact, urged a comprehensive bill of rights for adoption by amendments after the new government went into operation. Virginia and New York, whose ratification was politically indispensable, followed suit. North Carolina was the fourth state to ratify with a model bill of rights among its recommendations. But the states also recommended crippling restrictions on delegated powers.

Thus, the Constitution was ratified only because crucial states, where ratification had been in doubt, were willing to accept the promise of a bill of rights in the form of subsequent amendments to the Constitution. State recommendations for amendments, including those of the Pennsylvania minority, received nationwide publicity, adding to the clamor for a bill of rights. Every right that became part of the first ten amendments was included in state recommendations except the clause in the Fifth Amendment requiring just compensation for private property taken for public use.

James Madison was one of the Federalists who finally realized that statecraft and political expediency dictated a switch in position. At the Virginia ratifying convention in June 1788 Madison had upheld the usual Federalist arguments for the omission of a bill of rights but finally voted to recommend such a bill in order to avoid previous amendments. He later conceded that the Constitution would have been defeated without a pledge from its supporters to back subsequent amendments. In Virginia, Madison's own political position deteriorated because he had opposed a bill of rights. The Anti-Federalists, who controlled the state legislature, elected two of their own, Richard Henry Lee and William Grayson, as the state's first United States Senators. Madison faced a tough contest for election to the House of Representatives, and he feared that the Anti-Federalists might succeed in their call for a second constitutional convention. He needed to clarify his position on a bill of rights.

Although Madison had periodically apprised Jefferson, in Paris, on ratification developments, he had not answered Jefferson's letter of December 1787 supporting a bill of rights. On October 17, 1788, the eve of his campaign for a House seat, Madison faced the issue. He favored a bill of rights, he wrote, but had "never thought the omission a material defect" and was not "anxious to supply it even by subsequent amendments"; he did not even think the matter important. Still agreeing with Wilson that the delegated powers did not extend to reserved rights, Madison also worried about the difficulty of adequately protecting the most important rights; experience proved that a bill of rights was a mere parchment barrier when most needed. Government, after all, was the instrument of the majority, which could endanger liberty. "What use then . . . can a bill of rights serve in popular Governments?" Its political truths, he conceded, by way of answer, could educate the people, thereby inhibiting majority impulses.

Jefferson's reply of March 15, 1789, had a profound influence on Madison, as Madison's great speech of June 8 would show. An argument for a bill of rights that Madison had omitted, wrote Jefferson, was "the legal check which it puts into the hands of the judiciary." Jefferson believed that an independent court could withstand oppressive majority impulses by holding unconstitutional any acts violating a bill of rights. The point was not new to Madison, for he himself, when defending a ban on ex post facto laws at the Constitutional Convention, had declared that it would "oblige the Judges to declare [retrospective] interferences null and void." As for the point that the delegated powers did not reach the reserved rights of the people, Jefferson answered that because the Constitution protected some rights but ignored others, it raised implications against them, making a bill or rights "necessary by way of supplement." Moreover, he added, the Constitution "forms us into one state as to certain objects," requiring a bill of rights to guard against abuses of power. As for the point that a bill of rights could not be perfect, Jefferson replied with the adage that half a loaf is better than none; even if all rights could not be secured, "let us secure what we can." Madison had also argued that the limited powers of the federal government and the jealousy of the states afforded enough security, to which Jefferson answered that a bill of rights "will be the text whereby to try all the acts of the federal government." That a bill of rights was inconvenient and not always efficacious did not impress Jefferson. Sometimes, he replied, it was effective, and if it inconveniently cramped the government, the effect was short-lived and remediable, while the inconveniences of not having a bill of rights could be "permanent, afflicting, and irreparable." Legislative tyranny, Jefferson explained, would be a formidable dread for a long time, and executive tyranny would likely follow.

Jefferson's arguments, however persuasive, would have been unproductive but for the dangerous political situation, which Madison meant to ameliorate. Four states, including his own and New York, had called for a second convention, whose purpose, Madison feared, would be to "mutilate the system," especially as to the power to tax. Omitting it "will be fatal" to the new federal government. Madison correctly believed that many Anti-Federalists favored an effective Union on condition that a bill of rights bridled the new government. His strategy was to win them over by persuading the first Congress to adopt protections of civil liberties, thereby alleviating the public's anxieties, providing popularity and stability for the government, and isolating those Anti-Federalists whose foremost objective was "subverting the fabric . . . if not the Union itself."

In the first Congress, Representative Madison sought to fulfill his pledge of subsequent amendments. His accomplishment in the face of opposition and apathy entitles him to be remembered as "father of the Bill of Rights" even more than as "father of the Constitution." Many Federalists thought that the House had more important tasks, like the passage of tonnage duties and a judiciary bill. The opposition party, which had previously exploited the lack of a bill of rights in the Constitution, realized that its adoption would sink the movement for a second convention and make unlikely any additional amendments that would cripple the substantive powers of the government. They had used the bill of rights issue as a smokescreen for objections to the Constitution that could not be dramatically popularized, and now they sought to scuttle Madison's proposals. They began by stalling, then tried to annex amendments aggrandizing state powers, and finally depreciated the importance of the very protections of individual liberty that they had formerly demanded as a guarantee against impending tyranny. Madison meant to prove that the new government was a friend of liberty; he also understood that his amendments, if adopted, would thwart the passage of proposals aggrandizing state powers and diminishing national ones. He would not be put off; he was insistent, compelling, unyielding, and, finally, triumphant.

On June 8, 1789, he made his long memorable speech before an apathetic House, introducing amendments culled mainly from state constitutions and state ratifying convention proposals, especially Virginia's. All power, he argued, is subject to abuse and should be guarded against by constitutionally securing "the great rights of mankind." The government had only limited powers, but it might, unless prohibited, abuse its discretion as to its choice of means under the necessary and proper clause; it might, for example, use general warrants in the enforcement of its revenue laws. In Britain, bills of rights merely erected barriers against the powers of the crown, leaving the powers of Parliament "altogether indefinite," and the British constitution left unguarded the "choicest" rights of the press and of conscience. The great objective he had in mind, Madison declared, was to limit the powers of government, thus preventing legislative as well as executive abuse, and above all preventing abuses of power by "the body of the people, operating by the majority against the minority." Mere "paper barriers" might fail, but they raised a standard that might educate the majority against acts to which they might be inclined.

To the argument that a bill of rights was not necessary because the states constitutionally protected freedom, Madison had two responses. One was that some states had no bills of rights, others "very defective ones," and the states constituted a greater danger to liberty than the new national government. The other was that the Constitution should, therefore, include an amendment, that "No State shall violate the equal rights of conscience, or the freedom of the press, or the trial by jury in criminal cases." This, Madison declared, was "the most valuable amendment in the whole list." To the contention that an enumeration of rights would disparage those not protected, Madison replied that the danger could be guarded against by adopting a proposal of his composition that became the Ninth Amendment. If his amendments were "incorporated" into the Constitution, Madison said, using another argument borrowed from Jefferson, "independent tribunals of justice will consider themselves in a peculiar manner the guardians of those rights; they will be an impenetrable bulwark against every assumption of power in the legislative or executive; they will be naturally led to resist every encroachment upon rights expressly stipulated for in the constitution . . ."

Although many Federalists preferred to give the new government time to operate before amending the Constitution, supporters of Madison exulted, largely for political reasons. Hugh Williamson of North Carolina, a signer of the Constitution, informed Madison that the Anti-Federalists of that state did not really want a bill of rights; William R. Davie, who had been Williamson's colleague in the convention, gleefully reported to Madison that his amendments had "confounded the Anties exceedingly. . . ." Edmund Pendleton of Virginia wrote of Madison's amendments that "nothing was further from the wish of some, who covered their Opposition to the Government under the masque of incommon zeal for amendments. . . ." Tench Coxe of Pennsylvania praised Madison for having stripped the Constitution's opponents of every rationale "and most of the popular arguments they have heretofore used."

Notwithstanding the support of correspondents, Madison's speech stirred no immediate support in Congress. Indeed, every speaker who followed him, regardless of party affiliation, either opposed a bill of rights or believed that the House should attend to far more important duties. Six weeks later Madison "begged" for a consideration of his amendments, but the House assigned them to a special committee instead of debating them. That committee, which included Madison, reported in a week. It added freedom of speech to the rights protected against state abridgment, deleted Madison's reference to no "unreasonable searches and seizures," made some stylistic revisions, but otherwise recommended the amendments substantially as he had proposed them. The committee's report was tabled, impelling Madison on August 3 to implore its consideration.

On August 13 the House finally began to consider the reported amendments, and in the course of debate it made some significant changes. Madison had proposed to "incorporate" the amendments within the text of the Constitution at appropriate points. He did not recommend their adoption as a separate "bill of rights," although he had referred to them collectively by that phrase. Members objected, however, that to incorporate the amendments would give the impression that the framers of the Constitution had signed a document that included provisons not of their composition. Another argument for lumping the amendments together was that the matter of form was so "trifling" that the House should not squander its time debating the placement of the various amendments. Ironically, Roger Sherman, who still believed that the amendments were unnecessary, deserves the credit for insistently arguing that they should be appended as a supplement to the Constitution instead of being interspersed within it. Thus, what became the "Bill of Rights" achieved its significant collective form over the objections of its foremost proponent, Madison, and because of the desire of its opponents in both parties to downgrade its importance.

The House recast the free exercise of religion clause and its allied clause banning establishments of religion, improving Madison's original language. The House also confined to criminal cases Madison's broad phrasing that no person should be compelled to give evidence against himself. On the other hand the House restored the extremely important principle against unreasonable searches and seizures, dropped by the committee. In another major decision the House decisively defeated Gerry's motion, for the Anti-Federalists, to consider not just the committee's report but all amendments that the several states had proposed; the Anti-Federalist thus failed to intrude crippling political amendments. Finally the House added "or to the people" in the recommendation by Madison that the powers not delegated to the United States be reserved to the states. On the whole the House adopted Madison's amendments with few significant alterations during the course of its ten day debate on the Bill of Rights.

In the midst of that debate Madison wrote a letter to a fellow Federalist explaining why he was so committed to "the nauseous project of amendments" which some of the party supported reluctantly. Protecting essential rights was "not improper," he coolly explained, and could be of some influence for good. He also felt honor bound to redeem a campaign pledge to his constituents, mindful that the Constitution "would have been *certainly* rejected" by Virginia without assurances from its supporters to seek subsequent amendments. Politics, moreover, made proposing the amendments a necessity to beat the Anti-Federalists at their own game. If Federalists did not support the amendments, Anti-Federalists would claim that they had been right all along and gain support for a second convention. And, Madison wrote, the amendments "will kill the opposition everywhere, and by putting an end to disaffection to the Government itself, enable the administration to venture on measures not otherwise safe."

Madison had, in fact, upstaged and defeated the Anti-Federalists. That is why Congressman Aedanus Burke of South Carolina, cried sour grapes. During the debate on what became our First Amendment, he argued that the proposals before the House were "not those solid and substantial amendments which the people expect; they are little better than whip-syllabub, frothy and full of wind . . . Upon the whole, I think . . . we have done nothing but lose our time, and that it will be better to drop the subject now, and proceed to the organization of the Government." The private correspondence of Senators Lee and Grayson of Virginia reveals the explanation for the attitude of their party toward a bill of rights. A few days after Madison had introduced his amendments, Grayson complained to his mentor, Patrick Henry, that the Federalists meant to enact "amendments which shall effect [sic] personal liberty alone, leaving the great points of the Judiciary, direct taxation, &c, to stand as they are." Lee and Grayson had failed in their effort to have the Senate amend the House's proposals by adopting the Virginia ratifying convention's recommendations on direct taxation and the treaty and the commerce powers. Lee then regretted the original Anti-Federalist strategy of opposing the Constitution unless revised by the addition of a bill of rights and other amendments. He sorrowfully informed Henry that "the idea of subsequent amendments, was little better than putting oneself to death first, in expectation that the doctor, who wished our destruction, would afterwards restore us to life." Later, after the Senate had approved of the amendments that became the Bill of Rights, Grayson reported, "they are good for nothing, and I believe, as many others do, that they will do more harm than benefit."

The Senate, which kept no record of its debates, had deliberated on seventeen amendments submitted by the House. One the Senate killed, the proposal Madison thought "the most valuable": protection against state infringement of speech, press, religion, or trial by jury. The motion to adopt failed to receive the necessary two-thirds vote, though by what margin is unknown. The Senate also weakened the House's ban on establishments of religion. Otherwise the Senate accepted the House proposals, although the Senate combined several, reducing the total number from seventeen to twelve. The first of the twelve dealt with the relation of population to the number of representatives from each state, and the then second would have preventing any law going into effect increasing the salaries of members of Congress until after the next election.

The House adamantly refused to accept the Senate's version of its ban on establishments. A conference committee of both houses met to resolve differences. The committee, which included Madison, accepted the House's ban on establishments but otherwise accepted the Senate's version. On September 24, 1789, the House voted for the committee report; on the following day the Senate concurred, and the twelve amendments were submitted to the states for ratification.

Within six months nine states ratified the Bill of Rights, although of the twelve amendments submitted for approval, the first and second were rejected. The four recalcitrant states by mid-1790 were Virginia, Massachusetts, Connecticut, and Georgia. The admission of Vermont to the Union made necessary the ratification by eleven states. Connecticut and Georgia refused to ratify. Georgia's position was that amendments were superfluous until experience under the Constitution proved a need. Connecticut believed that any suggestion that the Constitution was not perfect would add to the strength of Anti-Federalism.

In Massachusetts Federalist apathy to the Bill of Rights was grounded on a satisfaction with the Constitution as it was, and the Anti-Federalists were more interested in amendments that would strengthen the states at the expense of the national government. Nevertheless the Massachusetts lower house adopted all but the first, second, and twelfth amendments, and the upper house adopted all but the first, second, and tenth. Thus both houses of the Massachusetts legislature actually approved what became our First through Seventh Amendments and the Ninth, but a special committee, dominated by Anti-Federalists, urged that all amendments recommended by Massachusetts should be adopted before the state concurred in any amendments. As a result the two houses never passed a bill promulgating ratification of eight amendments. Jefferson, the Secretary of State, believed that Massachusetts, "having been the 10th state which has ratified, makes up the threefourth [*sic*] of the legislatures whose ratification was to suffice." He wrote to a Massachusetts official, asking for clarification. The reply was, "It does not appear that the Committee ever reported any bill." In 1939 Massachusetts joined Connecticut and Georgia when they belatedly ratified on the sesquicentennial anniversary of the Constitution.

Ratification of the Bill of Rights by Vermont, in November 1789, left Virginia the last state to act. Its ratification as the eleventh state was indispensable, although the hostility of its Anti-Federalist leaders presaged a doubtful outcome. Senators Grayson and Lee reported to the Virginia legislature that they transmitted the recommended amendments "with grief." They still hoped for a new constitutional convention that would devise "real and substantial Amendments" to "secure against the annihilation of the state governments. . . ." Patrick Henry vainly moved to postpone consideration of the Bill of Rights. The victims of a dilemma of their own making, the Anti-Federalists then sought to sabotage the Bill of Rights and finally, after delaying ratification for nearly two years, irresolutely acquiesced. The Federalists of Virginia, however, eagerly supported the Bill of Rights in the knowledge that its adoption would appease public fears and stymie the amendments supported by the Anti-Federalists. Virginia's lower house, controlled by the Federalists, acted quickly, but the opposition dominated the state senate. Not all Anti-Federalists, were implacably opposed. Some respected George Mason's opinion. When he had first heard of Madison's amendments he called them "Milk and Water Propositions," not "important & substantial Amendments"; but Mason changed his mind, saying that they gave "much satisfaction," though he still wanted other amendments, including one that prevented commercial regulations by mere majority vote of Congress. Virginia's senate, as Edmund Randolph reported to Washington, postponed consideration of the amendments, "for a majority is unfriendly to the government." As a member of the lower house reported to Madison, the senate inclined to reject the Bill of Rights, not because of opposition to its guarantees, but from an apprehension "that the adoption of them at this time will be an obstacle to the chief object of their pursuit, the amendment on the subject of direct taxation." For that reason, Randolph reported to Washington, the Federalists meant to "push" the Bill of Rights; passage would "discountenance any future importunities for amendments."

Virginia's senate at the close of 1789 rejected what became the First, Sixth, Ninth, and Tenth Amendments, at least until the next session, thereby allowing time for the electorate to express itself. The Anti-Federalists still hoped to drum up support for "radical" amendments, as Lee called them. The senators in the majority also issued a statement grossly misrepresenting the First Amendment (then the third). Madison confidently expected that this Anti-Federalist tactic would backfire, and it did. For the senators' statement was not only inaccurate on its face; it came from men who with a single exception did not go before the electorate with clean hands. Like Henry and Lee who planned the senators' statement, the senators had records of having voted against religious liberty and in favor of compulsory taxes for the support of religion. By contrast Madison had led the fight in Virginia against a state establishment of religion and for religious liberty, and his supporters in the Virginia senate had aided him. In the end Madison's confidence proved justified. Jefferson made his influence felt on behalf of the Bill of Rights, and the Anti-Federalists grudgingly gave ground before public opinion. On December 15, 1791, after two years of procrastination, the senate finally ratified without record vote, thereby completing the process of state ratification and making the Bill of Rights part of the Constitution.

The history of the framing and ratification of the Bill of Rights indicates slight passion on the part of anyone to enshrine personal liberties in the fundamental law of the land. We know almost nothing about what the state legislatures thought concerning the meanings of the various amendments, and the press was perfunctory in its reports, if not altogether silent. But for Madison's persistence the amendments would have died in Congress. Our precious Bill of Rights, at least in its immediate background, resulted from the reluctant necessity of certain Federalists to capitalize on a cause that had been originated, in vain, by the Anti-Federalists for ulterior purposes. The party that had first opposed the Bill of Rights inadvertently wound up with the responsibility for its framing and ratification, while the party that had at first professedly wanted it discovered too late that it not only was embarrassing but disastrous for those ulterior purposes. The Bill of Rights had a great healing effect, however; it did, as Mason originally proposed, "give great quiet" to people. The opposition to the Constitution, Jefferson informed LaFayette, "almost totally disappeared," as Anti-Federalist leaders lost "almost all their followers." The people of the United States had had the good sense, nourished by traditions of freedom, to support the Constitution and the Bill of Rights.

The traditions that gave shape and substance to the Bill of Rights had English roots, but a unique American experience colored that shape and substance. "We began with freedom," as Emerson wrote in "The Fortune of the Republic." The first charter of Virginia contained a provision that the colonists and their descendants "shall have and enjoy all "Liberties, Franchises, and Immunities . . . as if they had been abiding and born, within this our Realm of England. . . ." Later charters of Virginia contained similar clauses, which extended to legal rights of land tenure and inheritance, trial by jury, and little else; but the vague language, which was repeated in numerous other charters for colonies from New England to the South, allowed Americans to believe they were entitled to all the rights of Englishmen, their constitutional system, and common law. American experience with and interpretations of charters eased the way to written constitutions of fundamental law that contained bills of rights.

Freedom was mainly the product of new world conditions, the English legal inheritance, and skipping a feudal stage. Because of America's post-feudal beginnings, it was unencumbered by oppressions associated with an *ancien régime*—a rigid class system dominated by a reactionary and hereditary aristocracy, arbitrary government by despotic kings, and a single established church extirpating dissent. Americans were the freest people, therefore the first colonials to rebel. A free people, as Edmund Burke said, can sniff tyranny in a far-off breeze—even if non-existent. American "radicals" actually believed that the Stamp Act reduced Americans to slavery. They resorted to arms in 1775, the Continental Congress declared, "not to establish new liberties but to defend old ones." In fact they established many new liberties but convinced themselves that those liberties were old. That was an English custom: marching forward into the future facing backwards to the past, while adapting old law to changing values. Thus Magna Carta had come to mean indictment by grand jury, trial by jury, and a cluster of related rights of the criminally accused, and Englishmen believed, or made believe, that it was ever so. That habit crossed the Atlantic.

So did the hyperbolic style of expression by a free people outraged by injustice. Thus, James Madison exclaimed that the "diabolical Hell conceived principle of persecution rages," because some Baptist ministers were jailed briefly for unlicensed preaching. By European standards, however, persecution hardly existed in America, not even in the seventeenth century except on a local and sporadic basis. America never experienced anything like the Inquisition, the fires of Smithfield, the St. Bartholomew's Day Massacre, or the deaths of over 5 000 nonconformist ministers in the jails of Restoration England. Draconian colonial statutes existed but were rarely enforced. Broad libertarian practices were the rule, not the exception.

On any comparative basis civil liberty flourished in America, a fact that intensified the notoriety of exceptional abridgments, such as the hanging of four Quakers in Massachusetts or the 1735 prosecution of John Peter Zenger for seditious libel. Although a stunted concept of the meaning and scope of freedom of the press existed in America until the Jeffersonian reaction to the Sedition Act of 1798, an extraordinary degree of freedom of the press existed in practice, in America as in England. Criticism of the government, however, especially of the popular assemblies was dangerous. If Zenger, the printer of the *New-York Weekly Journal*, had attacked the assembly instead of the royal governor, he would have been summarily convicted at the bar of the house, jailed, and forgotten. But Zenger was an instrument of the popular party against a detested administration, and so the jury, stirred by an eloquent lawyer, returned a popular verdict of not guilty, against the instructions of the court. The law, as laid down by the court, incidentally, was correct and remained the law, despite the verdict. Zenger's case was one of only a very few prosecutions by "royal judges" for seditious libel, and almost the last of its kind; prosecutions by governor and council or by the assemblies were a greater threat to a free press. When Alexander McDougall, a "Son of Liberty," assailed the New York assembly, it instigated a prosecution against him for seditious libel, jailed him when he refused to post excessive bail, and when the case against him collapsed because of the death of the star witness for the prosecution, arrested and convicted him for libeling the house. Despite that 1770 case, the American press remained extraordinarily free except for the suppression of Tory opinion during the Revolution.

The predominance of the social compact theory in American thought reflected a condition of freedom and, like the experience with charters, contributed to the belief in written bills of rights. The social compact theory hypothesized a pre-political state of nature in which people were governed only by the laws of nature, free of human restraints. From the premise that man was born free, the deduction followed that he came into the world with God-given or natural rights. Born without the restraint of human laws, he had a right to possess liberty and to work for his own property. Born naked and stationless, he had a right to equality. Born with certain instincts and needs, he had a right to satisfy them—a right to the pursuit of happiness. These natural rights, as John Dickinson declared in 1766, "are created in us by the decrees of Providence, which establish the laws of our nature. They are born with us; exist with us; and cannot be taken from us by any human power without taking our lives." When people left the state of nature and compacted for government, the need to secure their rights motivated them. A half-century before John Locke's *Second Treatise on Government*, Thomas Hooker of Connecticut expounded the social compact theory. Over a period of a century and a half, America became accustomed to the idea that government existed by consent of the governed, that the people created the government, that they did it by a written compact, that the compact reserved their natural rights, and that it constituted a fundamental law to which the government was subordinate. Constitutionalism, or the theory of limited government, was in part an outgrowth of the social compact.

In America, political theory and law, as well as religion, taught that government was limited. But Americans took their views on such matters from a highly selective and romanticized image of seventeenth-century England, and they perpetuated it in America even as that England changed. Seventeenth-century England was the England of the great struggle for constitutional liberty by the common law courts and Puritan parliaments against Stuart kings. Seventeenth-century England was the England of Edward Coke, John Lilburne, and Locke. It was an England in which religion, law, and politics converged to produce limited monarchy and, ironically, parliamentary supremacy. To Americans, however, Parliament had irrevocably limited itself by reaffirmations of Magna Carta and passage of the Petition of Right of 1628, the Habeas Corpus Act of 1679, the Bill of Rights of 1689, and the Toleration Act of 1689. Americans learned that a free people are those who live under a government so constitutionally checked and controlled that its powers must be reasonably exercised without abridging individual rights.

In fact, Americans had progressed far beyond the English in securing their rights. The English constitutional documents limited only the crown and protected few rights. The Petition of Right reconfirmed Magna Carta's provision that no freeman could be imprisoned but by lawful judgment of his peers or "by the law of the land"; it also reconfirmed a 1354 version of the great charter which first used the phrase "by due process of law" instead of "by the law of the land." The Petition invigorated the liberty of the subject by condemning the military trial of civilians as well as imprisonment without cause or on mere executive authority. Other sections provided that no one could be taxed without parliament's consent or be imprisoned or forced to incriminate himself by having to answer for refusing an exaction not authorized by parliament. The Habeas Corpus Act safeguarded personal liberty, without which other liberties cannot be exercised. The act secured an old right for the first time by making the writ of habeas corpus an effective remedy for illegal imprisonment. The only loophole in the act, the possibility of excessive bail, was plugged by the Bill of Rights ten years later. That enactment, its exalted name notwithstanding, had a narrow range of protections, including the freedoms of petition and assembly, free speech for members of Parliament, and, in language closely followed by the American Eighth Amendment, bans on excessive bail, excessive fines, and cruel and unusual punishments. As an antecedent of the American Bill of Rights, the English one was a skimpy affair, though important as a symbol of the rule of law and of fundamental law. The Toleration Act was actually "A Bill of Indulgence," exempting most nonconformists from the penalties of persecutory laws of the Restoration, leaving those laws in force but inapplicable to persons qualifying for indulgence. England maintained an establishment of the Anglican Church, merely tolerating the existence of non-Anglican trinitarians, who were still obligated to pay tithes and endure many civil disabilities.

In America, England promoted Anglicanism in New York and in the southern colonies but wisely prevented its establishments in America from obstructing religious peace, because immigrants were an economic asset, regardless of religion. England granted charters to colonial proprietors on a nondiscriminatory basis—to Cecil Calvert, a Catholic, for Maryland; to Roger Williams, a Baptist, for Rhode Island; and to William Penn, a Quaker, for Pennsylvania and Delaware. The promise of life in America drew people from all of western Christendom and exposed them to a greater degree of liberty and religious differences than previously known. James Madison, whose practical achievements in the cause of freedom of religion were unsurpassed, said that it arose from "that multiplicity of sects which pervades America."

But a principled commitment to religious liberty came first in some colonies. Maryland's Toleration Act of 1649 was far more liberal than England's Toleration Act of forty years later. Until 1776 only Rhode Island, Pennsylvania, Delaware, and New Jersey guaranteed fuller freedom than Maryland by its act of 1649, which was the first to use the phrase, "the free exercise of religion," later embodied in the First Amendment. The act also symbolized the extraordinary fact that for most of the seventeenth century in Maryland, Catholics and Protestants openly worshipped as they chose and lived in peace, if not amity. The act applied to all trinitarian Christians but punished others as well as the reproachful use of divisive terms such as heretic, puritan, papist, anabaptist, or antinomian. The Maryland act was a statute, but the Charter of Rhode Island, which remained its constitution until 1842, made the guarantee of religious liberty a part of the fundamental law. It secured for all inhabitants "the free exercise and enjoyment of their civil and religious rights" by providing that every peaceable person might "freely and fullye hav and enjoye his and theire owne judgments and consciences, in matters of religious concernments . . ." Thus, the principle that the state has no legitimate authority over religion was institutionalized in some American colonies, including those under Quaker influence.

Massachusetts, the colony that least respected private judgment in religious matters, was the first to safeguard many other rights. Its Body of Liberties, adopted in 1641, was meant to limit the magistrates in whom all power had been concentrated. As John Winthrop observed, the objective was to frame limitations "in remarkable resemblance to Magna Charta, which . . . should be received for fundamental laws." The Body of Liberties was, in effect, a comprehensive bill of rights compared with which the later English Bill of Rights was rudimentary and the liberties of Englishmen few in number Among the guarantees first protected in writing by Massachusetts were freedom of assembly and of speech at least in public meetings, the equal protection of the laws, just compensation for private property taken for public use, freedom to emigrate, the right to bail, the right to employ counsel, trial by jury in civil cases, the right to challenge jurors, restrictions on imprisonment for debt, speedy trial, no double jeopardy, and no cruel or excessive punishments. In addition to traditional liberties, like trial by jury in criminal cases, and Magna Carta's principle of the rule of law, the Body of Liberties also protected some rights of women: widows received a portion of the estate of husbands even if cut off by will; physical punishment of women by their husbands was prohibited; and daughters received a right to inherit if parents died intestate and without male heirs. Servants, slaves, foreigners, and even animals received humane consideration too.

The Body of Liberties was a statute but the (1677) Charter or Fundamental Laws of West New Jersey, the work probably of William Penn, functioned as a written constitution because it began with the provision that the "common law or fundamental rights" of the colony should be "the foundation of government, which is not to be altered by the Legislative authority . . ." The liberty documents of England limited only the crown, not the legislature. The principle of limiting all governmental authority was written into Penn's Frame of Government for Pennsylvania in 1682, a document which extensively enumerated rights that were to last "for ever," including, for the first time, a ban on excessive fines, a guarantee of indictment by grand jury in capital cases, delivery to the accused of a copy of the charges against him, and assurance that a jury's verdict of not guilty was final. Penn's charter carefully particularized the rights of the criminally accused. Americans were learning that charters of liberty must assure fair and regularized procedures, without which there could be no liberty. Vicious and ad hoc procedures had been used to victimize religious and political minorities. One's home could not be his castle or his property be his own, nor could his right to express his opinion or to worship his God be secure, if he could be searched, arrested, tried, and imprisoned in some arbitrary way.

The case of Sir Thomas Lawrence in 1693 illustrates. Secretary of Maryland, a judge, and a member of the governor's council, Lawrence broke politically with the government and denounced it. Summoned by the council for examination, he was accused of having a treasonable letter. On his refusal to produce it, the council had him searched against his protests, found the letter, and convicted him of unspecified crimes, deprived him of his offices, and jailed him without bail. Lawrence appealed his conviction to the Assembly on the grounds of having been forced to incriminate himself by an illegal search, of having been convicted without trial by jury, without knowing the charges against him or the names of his accusers, and of having been denied bail and habeas corpus "which is the great security of the lives & Libertyes of every English Subject." The Assembly vindicated English liberties by supporting Lawrence on every point, found all the proceedings against him illegal, and freed and restored him.

The American colonial experience, climaxed by the controversy with England leading to the Revolution, honed American sensitivity to the need for written constitutions that protected rights grounded in "the immutable laws of nature" as well as in the British constitution and colonial charters. An English nobleman told Benjamin Franklin that Americans had the wrong ideas about the constitution. English and American ideas did differ, radically, because the Americans had a novel concept of "constitution." The word signified to them a supreme law creating government, limiting it, unalterable by it, and paramount to it. A town orator of Boston announced that Independence offered the people a chance of reclaiming rights "attendant upon the original state of nature, with the opportunity of establishing a government for ourselves . . ." "To secure these rights," Jefferson declared, "governments are instituted among men."

The Virginia constitution of 1776, the first permanent state constitution, began with a Declaration of Rights that restrained all branches of government. As the first such document it contained many constitutional "firsts," such as the statements that "all men" are equally free and have inherent rights which cannot be divested even by compact; that among these rights are the enjoyment of life, liberty, property, and the pursuit of happiness; and that all power derives from the people who retain a right to change the government if it fails to secure its objectives. The declaration recognized "the free exercise of religion" and freedom of the press, and included clauses that were precursors, sometimes in rudimentary form, of the Fourth through the Eighth Amendments of the Constitution of the United States. Inexplicably the convention voted down a ban on bills of attainder and on *ex post facto* laws and omitted the freedoms of speech, assembly, and petition, the right to the writ of *habeas corpus*, grand jury proceedings, the right to compulsory process to secure evidence in one's own behalf, the right to counsel, and freedom from double jeopardy. Although religious liberty was guaranteed, the ban on an establishment of religion awaited enactment of the Virginia Statute of Religious Freedom in 1786.

Pennsylvania's bill of rights was more comprehensive than Virginia's. Pennsylvania omitted bans on excessive fines and cruel punishments as well as the right to bail but added freedom of speech, assembly, and petition; separated church and state; recognized the right of conscientious objection; protected the right to counsel in all criminal cases; secured the right to keep arms; and guaranteed the right to travel or emigrate—all constitutional "firsts." Pennsylvania also recognized that "the people have a right to hold themselves, their houses, papers, and possessions free from search and seizure," in contrast to Virginia's prohibition of general warrants. Delaware's bill of rights was the first to ban ex post facto laws and the quartering of troops in homes during peacetime; Maryland added a prohibition on bills of attainder. Vermont's contribution was the first outlawing of slavery and the first constitutional provision for just compensation in cases of eminent domain. Connecticut and Rhode Island retained their charters as their constitutions, while New Jersey, Georgia, New York, and South Carolina protected some rights in their constitutional texts but had no separate bills of rights and no noteworthy innovations.

Massachusetts, the last of the original states to adopt a constitution (1780), contributed the most to the concept of a bill of rights. It had the most comprehensive bill of rights and was the first to secure citizens against "all unreasonable searches and seizures," the formulation closest to that of the later Fourth Amendment. Massachusetts was also the first state to replace the weak "ought not" found in all previous bills of rights (e.g., "the liberty of the press ought not be restrained") with the injunction "shall not," which Madison later followed. Most important, Massachusetts was the first state which framed its fundamental law by a specially elected constitutional convention, which exercised no legislative authority and submitted the document for popular ratification. In every other state before 1780, legislatures, sometimes calling themselves conventions, wrote the fundamental law and promulgated it. Theoretically a bill of rights framed by a legislature could be changed by ordinary legislation, a fact deplored by Jefferson as a capital defect in Virginia's model. The procedure first adopted by Massachusetts was copied by New Hampshire when it revised its constitution in 1784, with the first guarantee against double jeopardy; thereafter the Massachusetts procedure prevailed.

The framing of the first constitutions with bills of rights ranks among America's foremost achievements, the more remarkable both because unprecedented and realized during wartime. Nevertheless, the phrasing of various rights and the inclusion or omission of particular ones in any given state constitution seem careless. Why so few states protected the rights against double jeopardy and bills of attainder, and why so many omitted habeas corpus and freedom of speech, among others, is inexplicable except in terms of shoddy craftsmanship. Even so, the existence of eight state bills of rights with constitutional status invigorated Anti-Federalist arguments that a bill of rights should be appended to the Constitution of 1787. The state ratifying conventions produced about seventy-five recommendations for amendments, providing Madison with an invaluable list from which to create the proposals that he submitted to Congress.

Congress itself supplied a final precedent, the Northwest Ordinance of 1787, which planned the evolution of territories to statehood. The ordinance was the first federal document to contain a bill of rights. To extend "the fundamental principles of civil and religious liberty," Congress included articles that were to remain "forever ... unalterable," guaranteeing to territorial inhabitants habeas corpus, trial by jury, representative government, judicial proceedings "according to the course of the common law," and, as an additional assurance of due process, an encapsulated provision from Magna Carta protecting liberty and property from being deprived except "by the judgment of ... peers, or the law of the land." The ordinance also included articles protecting the right to bail except in capital cases, enjoined that all fines should be "moderate," and prohibited "cruel or unusual punishment." Another article provided a federal precedent for still another provision of the Bill of Rights: just compensation for property taken for public purposes. The ordinance also protected the sanctity of private contracts, outlawed sex discrimination in land ownership, banned slavery, and provided for religious liberty. Thus the federal as well as colonial and state experience with written instruments to safeguard rights enhanced the claim that a bill of rights should bridle the new national government.

The Bill of Rights did just that: it was a bill of restraints. The First Amendment begins with the clause, "Congress shall make no law respecting an establishment of religion. ..." What is an establishment of religion? The debates of the Congress that proposed the amendment provide inadequate support for either a broad or narrow interpretation, although Congress rejected various phrasings that embraced the narrow one, namely that Congress could not establish a state church or prefer one religion over others. Madison doubtlessly believed that government aid to religion generally or on a nonpreferential basis to all religions constituted an establishment. But the "great object" of the Bill of Rights, he declared, was to "limit and qualify the powers of Government" by making certain that none of its granted powers could be used in forbidden fields, such as religion. A narrow interpretation of the clause leads to the impossible conclusion that the First Amendment added to Congress's powers. Except, perhaps, in the District of Columbia and the territories. Congress was bereft of power to control or support religion even in the *absence* of the amendment. An express prohibition could not vest power to aid religion generally. Madison observed that the Bill of Rights was not framed "to imply powers not meant to be included in the enumeration." When Congress framed the First Amendment six states maintained or authorized establishments. The amendment was meant to prevent congressional legislation concerning those establishments and to ensure that Congress could not do what those states were doing. In each of the six an establishment of religion was not restricted to a single state church or public support of one denomination; in all an establishment meant public support to all denominations and sects on a nonpreferential basis, not just public support of one over others. History explains the meaning of the text. Similarly the seemingly specific injunctions of the remainder of the Bill of Rights are not self-defining and do not necessarily exclude exceptions.

Freedom of speech and press may not be abridged, but what is an abridgment, and what is the "freedom of speech" that is protected? Libels, obscenity, and pornography, whatever they might mean, as well as direct and successful incitements to crime, were not intended to be constitutionally protected. The guarantee of freedom of religion is that it may not be "prohibited"; may it be abridged or regulated in some way short of a prohibition? The injunction against laws respecting an establishment of religion does not literally apply to speech or press; can Congress pass laws respecting freedom of the press if not abridging it? What are the "arms" that may be kept and borne? When is the militia "well-regulated"? What is an "unreasonable" search or seizure? No warrants shall issue "but on probable cause." What is a "probable cause," and may there be searches without warrants? They existed in 1791. What is an "infamous" crime? What is the meaning of compulsion in the safeguard that no personal shall be "compelled" to be a witness against himself in a criminal case? What is the process of law that is "due" to anyone who might be deprived of life, liberty, or property? What is "public use" or "just" compensation? Do the many rights of the Sixth Amendment really extend to "all" criminal prosecutions? Trial by jury did not extend to persons facing less than six months' imprisonment. When does a criminal prosecution or case begin and does it include legislative or grand jury investigations? Does the "assistance of counsel" or the right not to be a witness against oneself apply to such investigations? What is a "speedy" trial or an "impartial" jury? Does trial by jury mean only a jury of twelve and a unanimous verdict? Does the ban against double jeopardy mean that an acquittal in federal court bars a state trial for the same act? What is "excessive" bail or a punishment that is "cruel and unusual"? There were probably no constitutional absolutes in 1791, and no guarantees that were clear and precise in meaning. Ambiguities cannot be strictly construed.

"Congress shall make no law . . . abridging the freedom of speech, or of the press" seems clear enough, in one sense. The intent was to prevent any congressional enactments regulating speech or press, as by means of a licensing act, a tax act, or a seditious libel act. The framers meant Congress to be totally without power to enact legislation respecting the press, although the First Amendment does not say so. At the time of its adoption, the English common law definition of freedom of the press was the only one known and no other definition existed in America: the press was free in the absence of previous restraints. One could speak or publish as he pleased without censorship, but he was not exempt from punishment for libelous utterances, whether scandalizing public morals, religion, or government. Jefferson, for example, when writing his great bill for religious liberty provided that "opinions in matters of religion" should never be punished unless they incited "overt acts against peace and good order." But he never applied the same principle to political opinions. When drafting a constitution for Virginia in 1776 he included a provision that religious freedom "shall not be held to justify any seditious preaching or conversation against the authority of the civil government." Everyone favored unrestricted public discussion of issues, but "unrestricted" meant merely the absence of censorship prior to publication; people were accountable under the criminal law for licentious use of freedom.

Before 1798 the avant-garde among American libertarians staked everything on the principles of the Zenger case, which they thought beyond improvement. They believed that no greater liberty could be conceived than a right to publish unrestricted, if only a person being prosecuted could plead truth as a defense and if a jury had authority to determine the criminality of his words. Libertarians never rejected the substance of the law of criminal libels—not until the Sedition Act of 1798 embodied Zengerian principles and the prosecutions revealed those principles to be virtually worthless. The Sedition Act of 1798 was unconstitutional not because it abridged the freedom of the press but because it was an exercise of power in a forbidden field; the First Amendment in that regard left prosecutions for criminal libel exclusively to the states. The Sedition Act would have been unconstitutional even in the absence of the First Amendment.

The Fourth Amendment consists of two parts, one embodying the rule that searches and seizures shall not be "unreasonable," the other requiring specific warrants. The principle of the rule originated in England, although the English limitations on the search process were few and slight. The English used general warrants on a massive basis in everyday law enforcement as well as to search for evidence of political crimes like seditious libel. Colonial governments also made widespread use of general warrants, but in Massachusetts the intense opposition to them led to their displacement by specific warrants, beginning in the 1750s. England's reliance on writs of assistance, a form of general warrant, to uproot colonial customs violations in the 1760s led to American arguments supporting specific warrants. In 1774 the Continental Congress censured general warrants as unreasonable violations of privacy, and eight of the early state constitutions repudiated them. The Massachusetts constitution of 1780 contained the model that Madison relied upon when writing what became the Fourth Amendment.

The Fifth Amendment, the most varied of all, guarantees grand jury proceedings before one can be put to trial for a serious offense; bans double jeopardy; safeguards against compulsory self-incrimination; requires due process of law before deprivation of life, liberty, or property; and assures just compensation for public takings of private property. The Sixth Amendment clusters many rights of the criminally accused. The Eighth proscribes excessive bail, fines, or punishment. Of these amendments, the self-incrimination and due process clauses of the Fifth pose special problems. The self-incrimination clause, though controversial, embodies a fundamental principle of liberty and justice that inheres in the very idea of a free government. It protects a right, which developed before most others, to ward off inquisitions; it is the central feature of our accusatory system of criminal justice. While the framers were committed to perpetuating a system that minimized the possibilities of convicting the innocent, they were not less concerned about the humanity that the supreme law should show even to offenders. Protection of the right reflected their judgment that the determination of guilt or innocence by just procedures, in which the accused made no unwilling contribution to his conviction, was more important than punishing the guilty.

As for due process of law, which was to become the most influential concept in American constitutional law, it had developed as a rough equivalent to the more commonly used "law of the land" clause of Magna Carta. Due process had no single or fixed meaning in England or America. Still evolving in meaning, it referred narrowly to specific common law writs, broadly to regularized courses of legal proceeding in civil and criminal cases, and still more broadly to the very concept of fundamental law. The first American constitution to include a due process clause was the federal Constitution, thanks to Madison's preference for that phrasing instead of "the law of the land." But the inclusion of the clause raised problems. Due process signified customary or appropriate procedures but also connoted protection of the substantive rights of life, liberty, and property. The same clause necessarily safeguarded both procedural and substantive rights but thereby invited confusion in interpretation. Moreover the clause was a redundant because every clause of the Constitution supposedly has an independent meaning. Due process was constitutional shorthand and for many particular rights that other clauses of the Fifth and Sixth Amendments explicitly protected, most obviously grand jury proceedings and trial by jury. Inclusion of the clause showed conventional deference to Magna Carta and enhanced assurances that the new national government would treat citizens in accustomed ways, especially in matters of criminal justice.

By completing the Constitution with the Bill of Rights the framers sounded a tocsin against the dangers of government oppression of the individual. They were endorsing the principle that liberty of expression in matters of private conscience and public opinion are basic to a free society; so too, the rights of the criminally accused are legitimate defenses of the individual against government, because the enduring interests of that society require justice to be done as fairly as possible. The Bill of Rights symbolized a new system of public morality based on the premise that government is but an instrument of man, its sovereignty held in subordination to his rights. As amended, the Constitution became permanent reminder of its framers' view that the citizen is the master of his government, not its subject. Americans understood that the individual may be free only if the government is not.

7

The Original Meaning of
the Establishment Clause

THE FIRST AMENDMENT BEGINS with the clause against an establishment of religion: "Congress shall make no law respecting an establishment of religion." There are two basic interpretations of what the framers meant by this clause.

The Supreme Court advanced the broad interpretation most authoritatively in *Everson v. Board of Education* in 1947. Justice Black, speaking for the majority, declared:

> The "establishment of religion" clause of the First Amendment means at least this: Neither a state nor the Federal Government can set up a church. Neither can pass laws which aid one religion, aid all religions, or prefer one religion over another. Neither can force nor influence a person to go to or to remain away from church against his will or force him to profess a belief or disbelief in any religion. No person can be punished for entertaining or professing religious beliefs or disbeliefs, for church attendance or non-attendance. No tax in any amount, large or small, can be levied to support any religious activities or institutions, whatever they may be called, or whatever form they may adopt to teach or practice religion. Neither a state nor the Federal Government can, openly or secretly, participate in the affairs of any religious organizations or groups and vice versa. In the words of Jefferson, the clause against establishment of religion by laws was intended to erect "a wall of separation between Church and State."[1]

The dissenting justices in the Everson case, while disagreeing with the majority on the question of whether the "wall of separation" had in fact been breached by the practice at issue, concurred with the majority on the historical question of the intention of the framers. Justice Rutledge's opinion, endorsed by all the dissenting justices, declared: "The Amendment's purpose was not to strike merely at the establishment of a single sect, creed or religion, outlawing only a formal relation such as had prevailed in England and some of the colonies. Necessarily it was to uproot all such relationships. But the object was broader than separating church and state in this narrow sense. It was to create a complete and permanent separation of the spheres of religious activity and civil authority by comprehensively forbidding every form of public aid or support for religion."[2] Thus the heart of this broad interpretation is that the First Amendment prohibits even government aid impartially and equitably administered to all religious groups.

The second or narrow interpretation of the establishment clause holds that it was intended to prevent government recognition of a single state church that would have preferences of any sort over other churches. According to this interpretation, the members of the First Congress understood "establishment of religion" as "a formal, legal union of a single church or religion with government, giving the one church or religion an exclusive position of power and favor over all other churches or denominations."[3] Advocates of this view reject Justice Rutledge's contention that every form of public aid or support for religion is prohibited; they also reject Justice Black's opinion that government cannot aid all religions. In their view, the wall of separation was intended merely to keep the government from abridging religious liberty by discriminatory practices against religion generally or against any particular sects or denominations. The wall was not intended, however, to create a sharp division between government and religion or to enjoin the government from fostering religion in general.

These two interpretations of the no-establishment clause are patently irreconcilable, yet almost every writer who has explored the evidence has concluded that the interpretation of his choice is historically "right." The subject, apparently because of its implications for current public policy in the field of education, seems to transform into partisans all who approach it. But the issue is certainly more debatable than partisans on either side would have us believe, and historical investigation is hampered by the fact that the sources are often unclear and always disappointingly incomplete. A preponderance of the evidence, however, indicates that the Supreme Court's interpretation is historically the more accurate one.

THE BACKGROUND: THE CONSTITUTIONAL CONVENTION

The Constitutional Convention of 1787 gave only slight attention to the subject of a Bill of Rights and even less to the subject of religion. In contrast to the Declaration of Independence and to many acts of the Continental Congress, the Constitution contained no references to God; the Convention did not even invoke divine guidance for its deliberations. Its only reference to religion banned religious qualifications for federal officeholders.[4] On August 20 Charles Pinckney proposed that "no religious test or qualification shall ever be annexed to any oath of office under the authority of the U.S."[5] The proposal was referred to the Committee on Detail without debate or consideration by the Convention. When the committee reported ten days later, it ignored Pinckney's proposal. From the floor of the convention, he moved it again. The chairman of the committee, Roger Sherman of Connecticut, stated that such a provision was "unnecessary, the prevailing liberality being a sufficient security against such tests."[6] However, two delegates, in unreported speeches, "approved the motion" by Pinckney, and when put to a vote without further debate it passed.[7] Rephrased by the Committee on Style, it was incorporated into Article VI, clause 3 of the Constitution: "No religious test shall ever be required as a qualification to any office or public trust under the United States."

This clause "went far," according to one scholar, "in thwarting any State Church" in the United States.[8] The reasoning behind this thought is that in the absence of the clause, Congress might have had the power to require subscription to the articles of faith of some particular church,[9] or to Protestantism, or to Christianity generally. But the scope of the protection was not defined by anyone at the time; that is, the implied ban against an establishment of religion is of slight aid in explaining the meaning of such an establishment.

No other references to the subject of religion occurred at the Constitutional Convention. When George Mason of Virginia expressed a wish that the new Constitution "had been prefaced with a Bill of Rights," he offered no suggestions as to the contents of such a bill. Nor did Elbridge Gerry of Massachusetts who, agreeing with Mason, moved for a committee to prepare a Bill of Rights. This motion aroused opposition on the ground that the state bills of rights "being in force are sufficient." Mason rejoined, "The Laws of the U.S. are to be paramount to State Bills of Rights," but without further debate the motion that a Bill of Rights be prepared was defeated ten to zero, the delegates voting as state units.[10] Thus, on its face, the record of the Constitutional Convention is no guide to discerning the understanding of the framers as to establishments of religion.

On the other hand, the failure of the convention to provide for a Bill of Rights should not be misunderstood. The members of the convention did not oppose personal liberties; in the main they simply regarded a Bill of Rights as superfluous. The new national government possessed only limited powers; no power had been granted to legislate on any of the subjects that would be the concern of a Bill of Rights. Because no such power existed, none could be exercised or abused, and therefore all provisions against that possibility were unnecessary. Of the many statements of this argument,[11] the most widely publicized was that of Alexander Hamilton in *The Federalist* where he concluded, simply: "For why declare that things shall not be done which there is no power to do? Why, for instance, should it be said that the liberty of the press shall not be restrained, when no power is given by which restrictions may be imposed?"[12]

The framers of the Constitution have left abundant evidence of their belief that Congress was bereft of any authority over the subject of religion.[13] Congress was powerless, therefore, even in the absence of the First Amendment, to enact laws which benefited one religion or church in particular or all of them equally and impartially. Although it is important to try to understand the no-establishment clause of the First Amendment, this effort must be viewed within the larger framework of the Constitution.

THE RATIFICATION CONTROVERSY

From late 1787 through the following year, the proposed Constitution submitted to state conventions for ratification engrossed the political attention of the country. A torrent of speeches, essays, articles, and pamphlets poured forth from partisans on both sides. Opponents of ratification feared most of all that the centralizing tendencies of a consolidated national government would extinguish the rights of states and individuals. They objected most particularly to the failure of the instrument to provide for a Bill of Rights, and the Constitution probably would not have received the requisite number of state votes for ratification had not James Madison and other Federalist leaders pledged themselves to seek amendments constituting a Bill of Rights as soon as the new government went into operation. Indeed, six of the thirteen original states accompanied their instruments of ratification with recommendations for amendments that would secure specific personal liberties.[14]

In the light of these facts, it is astonishing to discover that the debate on a Bill of Rights was conducted on a level of abstraction so vague as to convey the impression that Americans of 1787–88 had only the most nebulous conception of the meanings of the particular rights they sought to insure. The insistent demands for the "rights of conscience" or "trial by jury" or "liberty of the press" by the principal advocates of a Bill of Rights were unaccompanied by a reasoned analysis of what these rights meant, how far they extended, and in what circumstances they might be limited. In addition many opponents of ratification had discovered that denouncing the omission of a Bill of Rights provided a useful mask for less elevating, perhaps even sordid, objections relating to such matters as taxation and commerce.

One cannot assume that the existence of widely known and agreed upon definitions of specific rights precluded the necessity for discussion of their meanings. They did not. Even trial by jury, which was protected by more state constitutions than any other right, differed in meaning and scope from state to state.[15] Moreover, the states differed substantially in the character and number of the rights they guaranteed.[16] Several state conventions in ratifying the Constitution even recommended amendments to protect rights not known in their own constitutions.[17] Whatever the explanation, the tens of thousands of words exchanged on the subject of a Bill of Rights during the ratification controversy do not illuminate the understanding and content attached at that time to particular rights.

This generalization applies to the subject of establishments of religion. An awareness of the need for precision and analysis in discussing the subject might be expected, considering the variety of historical experiences with establishments before and after independence and considering the diversity of relevant state constitutions and statutory provisions. At the very least, one would expect frequent expressions of fear and concern on the subject. Amazingly, however, it received rare and then only brief mention. One searches in vain for a definition in the rhetorical effusions of leading advocates of a Bill of Rights.

The debates of the state ratifying conventions offer no help either.[18] The perfunctory reports of the ratifying conventions of Delaware, New Jersey, and Georgia reveal nothing of value. Moreover, each ratified unconditionally and without proposing any amendments. Nothing, therefore, can be said of opinion in those states.

In Connecticut, which also ratified without recommendations for amendments, the fragmentary record of the debates shows only that Oliver Wolcott, briefly mentioning the value of the clause against test oaths, said: "Knowledge and liberty are so prevalent in this country, that I do not believe that the United States would ever be disposed to establish one religious sect, and lay all others under legal disabilities."[19] Similarly, Oliver Ellsworth referred in a tract to the fact that religious tests for office were always found in European nations where one church was established as the state church.[20] Neither Ellsworth nor Wolcott, both Federalists, believed that Congress could legislate on the subject of religion.

In Pennsylvania the state convention ratified unconditionally, after voting against a series of amendments constituting a Bill of Rights proposed by the minority. These defeated amendments, while protecting the "rights of conscience," contained no provision respecting an establishment of religion,[21] which Pennsylvania never experienced. Anti-ratificationists from the town of Carlisle proposed that "none should be compelled contrary to his principles or inclination to hear or support the clergy of any one established religion."[22] "Centinel," who also recommended a Bill of Rights, proposed more broadly in the language of the state constitution that "no man ought, or of right can be compelled to attend any religious worship, or erect or support any place of worship, or maintain any ministry, contrary to or against his own free will and consent. . . ."[23]

Massachusetts, which maintained an establishment of religion at the time of ratification, was the first state to ratify with proposed amendments, but the only rights mentioned were those of the criminally accused.[24] Isaac Backus, agent for the New England Baptists and a delegate to the Massachusetts ratifying convention, described the Constitution as a door "opened for the establishment of righteous government, and for securing of equal liberty, as never before opened to any people upon earth."[25] Backus, and Baptists generally, passionately opposed the Massachusetts Church-State system, by which the state mandated support for all Protestant churches. Clearly he had not the slightest suspicion that the federal government could do likewise. No person in the state convention believed that the new government would have any power in religious matters.[26]

Maryland ratified without amendments, although fifteen had been recommended, including a proposal "that there be no national religion established by law; but that all persons be equally entitled to protection in their religious liberty." Maryland's constitution permitted an establishment of religion, though none existed. All fifteen defeated amendments were designed chiefly to protect state governments from infringement by the national.[27] They failed not because the Federalist-dominated convention of Maryland disagreed with them, but because it wished to ratify unconditionally for the purpose of demonstrating confidence in the new system of government.[28] The same may be said of Pennsylvania and all the other states that ratified without recommending amendments.

In South Carolina the Reverend Francis Cummins made the only reference to an establishment of religion when he condemned "religious establishments; or the states giving preference to any religious denomination."[29] The convention's recommendations for amendments, however, mentioned nothing about a Bill of Rights.[30] At the time, South Carolina proclaimed the "Christian Protestant . . . religion to be the established religion of this state." No churches received public financial support, but those that subscribed to a stated set of beliefs were "considered as established."[31]

New Hampshire's debates are nonexistent. Though the state maintained an establishment, its instrument of ratification included among recommendations for amendments the following: "Congress shall make no laws touching Religion, or to infringe the rights of Conscience."[32]

In Virginia, where the most crucial struggle against establishments of religion had ended in victory just three years before the state ratifying convention met, only two speakers during the course of the lengthy debates alluded to an establishment. Edmund Randolph, defending the Constitution against Patrick Henry's allegation that it endangered religious liberty, pointed out that Congress had no power over religion and that the exclusion of religious tests for federal officeholders meant "they are not bound to support one mode of worship, or to adhere to one particular sect." He added that there were so many different sects in the United States "that they will prevent the establishment of any one sect, in prejudice to the rest, and forever oppose all attempts to infringe religious liberty."[33] James Madison, also addressing himself to Henry's general and unsupported accusation, argued at this time that a "multiplicity of sects" would secure freedom of religion, but that a Bill of Rights would not. He pointed out that the Virginia Declaration of Rights (which guaranteed "the free exercise of religion, according to the dictates of conscience") would not have exempted people "from paying to the support of one particular sect, if such sect were exclusively established by law." If a majority were of one sect, liberty would be poorly protected by a Bill of Rights. "Fortunately for this commonwealth," he added, "a majority of the people are decidedly against any exclusive establishment. I believe it to be so in the other states. There is not a shadow of right in the general government to intermeddle with religion. Its least interference with it would be a most flagrant usurpation. . . . A particular state might concur in one religious project. But the United States abound in such a variety of sects, that it is a strong security against religious persecution; and it is sufficient to authorize a conclusion that no one sect will ever be able to outnumber or depress the rest."[34]

Nonetheless, Madison and his party could not muster sufficient votes to secure Virginia's ratification of the Constitution without accepting a recommendation for amendments, which were first submitted by Patrick Henry. Henry's amendments, including a Declaration of Rights, were read before the convention, but not recorded in its record of proceedings; the reporter stated that they "were nearly the same as those ultimately proposed by the Convention"[35] after perfunctory endorsement by a committee on amendments. Among the recommended amendments was a provision that "no particular religious sect or society ought to be favored or established, by law, in preference to others."[36]

In New York Thomas Tredwell, an Anti-Ratificationist, in his speech favoring a bill of rights, made the only reported reference to an establishment: "I could have wished also that sufficient caution had been used to secure to us our religious liberties, and to have prevented the general government from tyrannizing over our consciences by a religious establishment—a tyranny of all others most dreadful, and which will assuredly be exercised whenever it shall be thought necessary for the promotion and support of their political measures."[37] The New York debates were fully reported until the closing days of the convention, when John Lansing, an Anti-Ratificationist leader, introduced a bill of rights to be prefixed to the Constitution. Although debate on this subject began on July 19, 1788, and continued intermittently through July 25, when Lansing's bill of rights was adopted, not a single word of the debate is reported.[38] Accordingly, the convention members left no explanation of what they understood by their recommendation "that no Religious Sect or Society ought to be favored or established by Law in preference of others."[39] This wording matched that used in the state constitution of 1777, which abolished establishments of religion in New York.

North Carolina, which had abolished its establishment in 1776, recommended an amendment like that of Virginia and New York.[40] The subject first arose in the convention when Henry Abbot, a delegate expression concern about the possibility of the general government's infringing religious liberty, asserted that "some people" feared that a treaty might be made with foreign powers to adopt the Roman Catholic religion in the United States. "Many wish to know what religion shall be established," he added. He was "against any exclusive establishment; but if there were any, I would prefer the Episcopal." In the next breath, he expressed a belief that the exclusion of religious tests was "dangerous," because Congressmen "might all be pagans."[41]

James Iredell responded to Abbot's fears by pointing out that the exclusion of a religious test indicated an intent to establish religious liberty. Congress was powerless to enact "the establishment of any religion whatsoever; and I am astonished that any gentleman should conceive they have. Is there any power given to Congress in matters of religion? . . . If any future Congress should pass an act concerning the religion of the country, it would be an act which they are not authorized to pass, by the Constitution, and which the people would not obey."[42] Governor Samuel Johnston agreed with Iredell and concluded: "I hope, therefore, that gentlemen will see there is no cause of fear that any one religion shall be exclusively established."[43] The Reverend David Caldwell, a Presbyterian minister, then spoke in favor of a religious test that would eliminate "Jews and pagans of every kind."[44] Samuel Spencer, the leading Anti-Federalist, took Caldwell's statement as endorsing the establishment of "one particular religion," which Spencer feared would lead to persecution. He believed that religion should stand on its own "without any connection with temporal authority."[45] William Lenoir agreed with Spencer, but warned that federal ecclesiastical courts might be erected, and they "may make any establishment they think proper."[46] Richard Dobbs Spaight, who had been a delegate to the Federal Convention, answered: "As to the subject of religion, I thought what had been said [by Iredell] would fully satisfy that gentleman and every other. No power is given to the general government to interfere with it at all. Any act of Congress on this subject would be a usurpation."[47]

When Rhode Island's convention tardily met to ratify the Constitution, eight states had already ratified the Bill of Rights. Thus Rhode Island's recommendation for an amendment against an establishment,[48] modeled after those of New York, Virginia, and North Carolina was a superfluous flourish that had no effect on the framing of the First Amendment.

SCANTY AS THEY ARE, the relevant data drawn from the period of the ratification controversy have been described in full. What conclusions do they yield?

1) No state or person favored an establishment of religion by Congress. On those few occasions when a convention delegate or a contemporary writer mentioned an establishment of religion, he spoke either against its desirability and/or against the likelihood that there would be one.

2) The evidence does not permit a generalization as to what was meant by an establishment of religion. To be sure, most of the few references to an establishment expressly or in context referred to the preference of one church or sect or religion above others. Clearly, however, this fact taken by itself proves little. Madison, for example, was simply saying to those who believed that religious liberty was endangered by the proposed national government, "Not even your least fears shall come to pass." As for the recommendations for amendments by Virginia, New York, North Carolina, and Rhode Island, they are not clarifying. They do not even necessarily indicate that preference of one sect over others was all that was comprehended by an establishment of religion. They do indicate that preference of one sect over others was something so feared that to assuage that fear by specifically making it groundless became a political necessity.

3) The members of the Constitutional Convention and Americans throughout the states shared a widespread understanding that the new central government would have no power whatever to legislate on the subject of religion either to aid one sect exclusively or to aid all equally. Many contemporaries, especially in New England, believed that governments could and should foster religion, or at least Protestant Christianity. All agreed, however, that the matter pertained to the realm of state government and that the federal government possessed no authority to meddle in religious matters.

DRAFTING AND RATIFICATION OF THE NO-ESTABLISHMENT CLAUSE

In the first United States Congress, Madison championed a Bill of Rights. Only after considerable prodding, however, did he succeed in getting a house preoccupied with what it considered the more important subject of getting the government organized to turn its attention to this matter.[49] Madison's determination represented a change of heart on his part. Originally he opposed a Bill of Rights on several grounds. He thought it unnecessary because the Constitution gave the national government no power to interfere in matters touching personal freedoms; he believed that liberty would be best protected not by "paper barriers," but by competition and a multiplicity of interests in society and sects in religion. In addition he feared that a Bill of Rights might even endanger liberty by implying that the federal government possessed powers not specifically denied it.[50]

A number of factors combined to change his mind. He realized that acceding to the demand for a Bill of Rights would deflate the movement for a new convention and assist in the ratification of the Constitution.[51] Moreover, his friend Thomas Jefferson, as well as the Virginia Baptists, whose support he needed to be elected to Congress, insisted on the need for a Bill of Rights. Jefferson, then American minister to France, sent back to Madison a steady stream of commentary on the need for a Bill of Rights, including a statement to ensure that "Religious faith shall go unpunished."[52] Jefferson has left ample evidence of his understanding of the proper relationship between Church and State, especially in his *Act for Establishing Religious Freedom*. Considered by Jefferson himself as one of the three crowning achievements of his life, the Act forbade Virginia's government to meddle in religion in any way. None could be "compelled to frequent or support any religious worship, place or ministry whatsoever." Nor could the government even demand that a citizen support a minister of his own choice.[53]

The First Amendment as passed perfectly satisfied Jefferson's desire for the protection of religious liberty on the national level, as demonstrated by his famous statement to the Danbury (Connecticut) Baptist Association in 1802: "I contemplate with sovereign reverence the act of the whole American people which declared that their legislature should 'make no law respecting an establishment of religion, or prohibiting the free exercise thereof,' thus building a wall of separation between church and state."[54]

Virginia's Baptists, too, insisted vehemently that religion be supported only by voluntary, not by tax, contributions. They reasoned that if "the State provide a Support for Preachers of the gospel, and they receive it in Consideration of their Services, they must certainly when they Preach act as officers of the State."[55] Alarmed by Anti-Federalist propaganda, they feared that Madison had reneged on his former position and that religious liberty was in danger. When John Leland, one of their most influential ministers, represented Baptists' fears to Madison personally, he assured them of his constancy and promised to work for a Bill of Rights including a protection for religious liberty.[56] Consequently,

Madison felt himself "bound in honor" to secure amendments; hence his persistence in doing so.[57] That the amendment in its final form "completely satisfied" both Jefferson and the Baptists[58] lends strong support to the argument that the parties most interested in its passage saw it as prohibiting the government from interfering in religious matters in order to aid either one or many sects or religions.

On June 8, 1789, at the first session of the first United States Congress, Representative Madison proposed for House approval a series of amendments to the Constitution.[59] He accompanied his presentation with a lengthy speech explaining his action and defending the value of a Bill of Rights, but he did not discuss the proposal relating to an establishment of religion. The section on religion read: "The civil rights of none shall be abridged on account of religious belief or worship, nor shall any national religion be established, nor shall the full and equal rights of conscience be in any manner, or on any pretext, infringed."[60]

Proponents of the narrow interpretation of the no-establishment clause see in the word "national" proof of their contention that Madison intended nothing more than a prohibition against the preference for one church or religion over others.

This argument presumes a drastic change of opinion on Madison's part for which no evidence exists. He had been one of the principal leaders in the fight against a general assessment in Virginia in 1785. Although that plan proposed tax support not for one religion exclusively but for all Christian religions, Madison, in his famous *Memorial and Remonstrance*, referred to it repeatedly as an "establishment of religion."[61] That same year the Continental Congress attempted unsuccessfully to set aside a section of land for the "support of religion" in the western territories. Madison described this non-preferential aid to religion as "unjust in itself, so foreign to the authority of Congress, . . . and smelling so strongly of antiquated bigotry."[62]

His subsequent actions show that he became if anything even more scrupulous on Church-State separation. As President he vetoed a land-grant bill intended to remedy the peculiar situation of a Baptist church that had, through a surveying error, been built on public land. Congress sought to rectify the error by permitting the church to have the land rather than buy it or be dispossessed. Here was no making of broad public policy, yet President Madison saw a dangerous precedent, and he vetoed the bill on the ground that it "comprises a principle and precedent for the appropriation of funds of the United States for the use and support of religious societies, contrary to the article of the Constitution which declares that 'Congress shall make no law respecting a religious establishment.' "[63] He also vetoed a bill that would have incorporated a church in the District of Columbia.

In his "Detached Memoranda," written after he had retired from the Presidency, Madison expressed his disapproval of Presidential proclamations of days of thanksgiving, and of tax-supported chaplains for Congress and the armed services. Significantly, he described these as "establishments" or "the establishment of a national religion." He commented: "If religion consists in voluntary acts of individuals, singly, or voluntarily associated, and it be proper that public functionaries, as well as their Constituents should discharge their religious duties, let them like their Constituents, do so at their own expense."[64] Years earlier, at the Virginia ratifying convention, Madison had cited his "uniform conduct" on the subject of religious liberty.[65] Clearly he remained constant on this subject all his life. The evidence points to the conclusion that in 1789 as later he used the phrase "national establishment" to signify not a preference for a single religion, but national action on behalf of one or all religions. Indeed, the fact that he followed his statement limiting the national government in religion with one that read, "No state shall violate the equal rights of conscience"[66] adds further weight to this interpretation.

Without debate Madison's recommendations for amendments were referred for consideration to a select committee of the House, composed of one member from each state, including Madison himself.[67] Although we know nothing of the committee's week-long deliberations, its report to the House shows that Madison was the dominating figure, because his amendments were kept intact with but slight changes in phraseology in the interests of brevity. From the proposal on religion, the committee deleted the clause on "civil rights" and the word "national." The proposed amendment then read: "No religion shall be established by law, nor shall the equal rights of conscience be infringed."[68] The report of the select committee to the House was merely a redrafting of the original proposals; no explanation of changes was included.

Sitting as a Committee of the Whole, the House began and ended its debate on the amendment on August 15. Our only account of the debate, in the *ANNALS OF CONGRESS*, is probably more in the nature of a condensed and paraphrased version than it is a verbatim report. The account, dated Saturday, August 15, is brief enough to be given here in full:

AMENDMENT TO THE CONSTITUTION

The House again went into a Committee of the Whole on the proposed amendments to the constitution, Mr. Boudinot in the chair.

The fourth proposition being under consideration, as follows:

Article 1. Section 9. Between paragraphs two and three insert "no religion shall be established by law, nor shall the equal rights of conscience be infringed."

Mr. Sylvester had some doubts of the propriety of the mode of expression used in this paragraph. He apprehended that it was liable to a construction different from what had been made by the committee. He feared it might be thought to have a tendency to abolish religion altogether.

Mr. Vining suggested the propriety of transposing the two members of the sentence.

Mr. Gerry said it would read better if it was, that no religious doctrine shall be established by law.

Mr. Sherman thought the amendment altogether unnecessary, inasmuch as Congress had no authority whatever delegated to them by the constitution to make religious establishments; he would, therefore, move to have it struck out.

Mr. Carroll.—As the rights of conscience are, in their nature, of peculiar delicacy, and will little bear the gentlest touch of governmental hand; and as many sects have concurred in opinion that they are not well secured under the present constitution, he said he was much in favor of adopting the words. He thought it would tend more towards conciliating the minds of the people to the Government than almost any other amendment he had heard proposed. He would not contend with gentlemen about the phraseology, his object was to secure the substance in such a manner as to satisfy the wishes of the honest part of the community.

Mr. Madison said, he apprehended the meaning of the words to be, that Congress should not establish a religion, and enforce the legal observation of it by law, nor compel men to worship God in any manner contrary to their conscience. Whether the words are necessary or not, he did not mean to say, but they had been required by some of the State Conventions, who seemed to entertain an opinion that under the clause of the constitution, which gave power to Congress to make all laws necessary and proper to carry into execution the constitution, and the laws made under it, enabled them to make laws of such a nature as might infringe the rights of conscience, and establish a national religion; to prevent these effects he presumed the amendment was intended, and he thought it as well expressed as the nature of the language would admit.

Mr. Huntington said that he feared, with the gentleman first up on this subject, that the words might be taken in such latitude as to be extremely hurtful to the cause of religion. He understood the amendment to mean what had been expressed by the gentleman from Virginia; but others might find it convenient to put another construction upon it. The ministers of their congregations to the Eastward were maintained by the contributions of those who belonged to their society; the expense of building meeting-houses was contributed in the same manner. These things were regulated by by-laws. If an action was brought before a Federal Court on any of these cases, the person who had neglected to perform his engagements could not be compelled to do it; for a support of ministers, or building places of worship might be construed into a religious establishment.

By the charter of Rhode Island, no religion could be established by law; he could give a history of the effects of such a regulation; indeed the people were now enjoying the blessed fruits of it. [Intended as irony.] He hoped, therefore, the amendment would be made in such a way as to secure the rights of conscience, and a free exercise of the rights of religion, but not to patronize those who professed no religion at all.

Mr. Madison thought, if the word national was inserted before religion, it would satisfy the minds of honorable gentlemen. He believed that the people feared one sect might obtain a pre-eminence, or two combine together, and establish a religion to which they would compel others to conform. He thought if the word national was introduced, it would point the amendment directly to the object it was intended to prevent.

Mr. Livermore was not satisfied with that amendment; but he did not wish them to dwell long on the subject. He thought it would be better if it was altered, and made to read in this manner, that Congress shall make no laws touching religion, or infringing the rights of conscience.

Mr. Gerry did not like the term national, proposed by the gentleman from

Virginia, and he hoped it would not be adopted by the House. It brought to his mind some observations that had taken place in the conventions at the time they were considering the present constitution. It had been insisted upon by those who were called anti-federalists, that this form of Government consolidated the Union; the honorable gentleman's motion shows that he considers it in the same light. Those who were called antifederalists at that time complained that they had injustice done them by the title, because they were in favor of a Federal Government, and the others were in favor of a national one; the federalists were for ratifying the constitution as it stood, and the others not until amendments were made. Their names then ought not to have been distinguished by federalists and antifederalists, but rats and antirats.

Mr. Madison withdrew his motion, but observed that the words "no national religion shall be established by law," did not imply that the Government was a national one; the question was then taken on Mr. Livermore's motion, and passed in the affirmative, thirty-one for, and twenty against it.[69]

Present-day proponents of both the narrow and the broad interpretations of the no-establishment clause are quick to see in this House debate conclusive proof for their respective points of view. But in fact it proves nothing conclusively. It was apathetic and unclear: ambiguity, brevity, and imprecision in thought and expression characterized the comments of the few members who spoke. That the House understood the debate, cared deeply about its outcome, or shared a common understanding of the finished amendment is doubtful.

Not even Madison himself, dutifully carrying out his pledge to secure amendments, seems to have troubled to do more than was necessary to get something adopted in order to satisfy popular clamor and deflate Anti-Federalist charges. Indeed, he agreed with Sherman's statement that the amendment was "altogether unnecessary, in as much as Congress had no authority whatever delegated to them by the constitution to make religious establishments." The difficulty, however, lies in the fact that neither Sherman, Madison, nor anyone else took the trouble to define what "religious establishments" were. And what did the select committee on amendments intend by recommending that "no religion shall be established by law"? Madison's statement that the words meant "that Congress should not establish a religion" hardly showed the clarity for which we might have hoped. Livermore's motion for a change of wording apparently expressed what Madison meant by his use of the word "national" and satisfied the Committee of the Whole. The proposed amendment, adopted by a vote of thirty-one to twenty, then read: "Congress shall make no laws touching religion, or infringing the rights of conscience." But a few days later, on August 20, when the House took up the report of the Committee of the Whole and voted clause by clause on the proposed amendments, an additional change was made. Fisher Ames of Massachusetts moved that the amendment read: "Congress shall make no law establishing religion, or to prevent the free exercise thereof, or to infringe the rights of conscience"[70] Without debate this was adopted by the necessary two-thirds of the House. Apparently there was a feeling that the draft of the clause based on Livermore's motion might not satisfy the demand of those who wanted something said specifically against establishments of religion. The amendment as submitted to the Senate reflected a stylistic change that gave it the following reading: "Congress shall make no law establishing religion, or prohibiting the free exercise thereof, nor shall the rights of conscience be infringed."

The Senate began debate on the House amendments on September 3 and continued through September 9. The debate was conducted in secrecy and no record of it exists except for the bare account of motions and votes in the *Senate Journal*. According to the record of September 3, three motions of special interest here were defeated on that day.[71] These motions were clearly intended to restrict the ban in the proposed amendment to establishments preferring one sect above others. The first motion would have made the clause in the amendment read: "Congress shall make no law establishing one religious sect or society in preference to others." After the failure of a motion to kill the amendment, a motion was made to change it to read: "Congress shall not make any law infringing the rights of conscience, or establishing any religious sect or society." The last defeated motion restated the same thought differently: "Congress shall make no law establishing any particular denomination of religion in preference to another."

The failure of these three motions, each of which clearly expressed a narrow intent, would seem to show that the Senate intended something broader than merely a ban on preference to one sect. Yet, if anything is really clear about this problem of "meaning" and "intent," it is that nothing is clear; when the Senate returned to the clause six days later, the House amendment was changed to read: "Congress shall make no law establishing articles of faith or a mode of worship, or prohibiting the free exercise of religion."[72] Like the three previously defeated motions, this has the unmistakable meaning of limiting the ban to acts that prefer one sect over.

We are indebted to the Senate's wording for provoking the House to action that would make *its* intent clear, as the next step in the drafting of the amendment reveals. In voting on the Senate's proposed amendments, the House accepted some and rejected others. Among those rejected was the Senate's article on religion. To resolve the disagreement between the two branches, the House proposed a joint conference committee. The Senate refused to recede from its position, but agreed to the proposal. The committee, a strong and distinguished one, consisted of Madison as chairman of the House conferees, joined by Sherman and Vining, and of Ellsworth as chairman of the Senate conferees, joined by Paterson and Carroll. Four of the six men had been influential members of the Constitutional Convention. The House members of the conference committee flatly refused to accept the Senate's version of the amendment on religion, indicating that the House would not be satisfied with merely a ban on preference of one sect or religion over others. The Senate conferees abandoned the Senate version, and the amendment was redrafted to give it its present phraseology. On September 24 Ellsworth reported to the Senate that the House would accept the Senate's version of the other amendments provided that the amendment on religion "shall read as follows: 'Congress shall make no laws respecting an establishment of religion, or prohibiting the free exercise thereof.'" On the same day, the House sent a message to the Senate verifying Ellsworth's report. On the next day, September 25, the Senate by a two-thirds vote accepted the condition laid down by the House. Congress had passed the no-establishment clause.[73]

The outstanding fact that emerges from this review of the drafting of the amendment is that Congress very carefully considered and rejected the phraseology spelling out the narrow interpretation. Through its rejection of the Senate's version of the amendment, rather than through its own ambiguous and imprecise debates, the House showed its intent *not* to frame an amendment that banned only Congressional support to one sect, church, denomination, or religion. The amendment was definitely intended to mean something broader than the narrow interpretation some scholars have given it. At bottom the amendment was an expression of the fact that the framers of the Constitution had not intended to empower Congress to act in the field of religion. The "great object" of the Bill of Rights, as Madison explicitly said when introducing his draft of amendments to the House, was to "limit and qualify the powers of Government"[74] for the purpose of making certain that the powers granted could not be exercised in forbidden fields, such as religion.

The history of the drafting of the no-establishment clause does not provide us with an understanding of what was meant by "an establishment of religion." To argue, however, as proponents of the narrow interpretation do, that the amendment permits Congressional aid and support to religion in general or to all churches without discrimination leads to the impossible conclusion that the First Amendment added to Congress' power. Nothing supports such a conclusion. Every bit of evidence goes to prove that the First Amendment, like the others, was intended to restrict Congress to its enumerated powers. Since the Constitutional Convention gave Congress no power to legislate on matters concerning religion, Congress had no such power even in the absence of the First Amendment. It is therefore unreasonable to believe that an express prohibition of power—"Congress shall make no law respecting an establishment of religion"—creates the power, previously nonexistent, of supporting religion by aid to one or all religious groups. The Bill of Rights, as Madison said, was not framed "to imply powers not meant to be included in the enumeration."[75]

RATIFICATION OF THE FIRST AMENDMENT

The deliberations of the state legislatures to which the amendments to the Constitution were submitted for ratification shed little light on the meaning of the no-establishment clause. Records of state debates are nonexistent; private correspondence, newspapers, and tracts are no help.

By mid-June of 1790, nine states had summarily approved the Bill of Rights.[76] Georgia, Connecticut, Massachusetts, and Virginia, had not yet taken action; indeed, the first three states did not ratify the Bill of Rights until 1939, on the sesquicentennial anniversary of the Constitution.

Of these states, Georgia took the position that amendments were unnecessary until experience under the Constitution demonstrated the need for them.[77] Connecticut's lower house voted to ratify in 1789 and again the following year, but the state senate, apparently in the belief that a Bill of Rights was superfluous, adamantly refused to do so. Yankee Federalists in Connecticut seem to have thought any suggestion that the Constitution was not perfect would add to the strength of the Anti-Federalists. The same sentiment was prevalent in Massachusetts. There Federalist apathy to the Bill was grounded on satisfaction with the Constitution as it was, unamended, while Anti-Federalists were more interested in amendments that would weaken the national government and strengthen the states than in efforts to protect personal liberties. With the Bill of Rights thus caught between conflicting party interests, Massachusetts failed to act on the proposed amendments.

The circumstances surrounding ratification in Virginia are of particular interest. Ratification there was held up for nearly two years while the amendment was attacked as inadequate. The eight state senators who opposed it explained their vote publicly in these words: "The 3d amendment [our First Amendment] recommended by Congress does not prohibit the rights of conscience from being violated or infringed: and although it goes to restrain Congress from passing laws establishing any national religion, they might, notwithstanding, levy taxes to any amount, for the support of religion or its preachers; and any particular denomination of christians might be so favored and supported by the General Government, as to give it a decided advantage over others, and in process of time render it as powerful and dangerous as if it was established as the national religion of the country. . . . This amendment then, when considered as it relates to any of the rights it is pretended to secure, will be found totally inadequate."[78]

Taken out of context and used uncritically, this statement by the eight Virginia state senators has been offered as proof that the no-establishment clause carried only the narrowest intent, that the Virginia legislators so understood it, and that the state ultimately approved it only in that narrow sense. Because the eight senators who favored a broader ban were ultimately defeated, the conclusion is drawn that the amendment did not purport to ban government aid to religion generally or to all sects without discrimination. However, examination of the intricate party maneuverings and complex motives in the Virginia ratification dispute sheds a different light on the senators' statement.

Virginia's Anti-Federalists, led by Patrick Henry and United States Senators Richard Henry Lee and William Grayson, had opposed the ratification of the Constitution for a variety of reasons. Chief among these was the belief that it established too strong a central government at the expense of the states. For example, the Anti-Federalists wanted amendments to the Constitution that would restrict Congress' commerce and tax powers. It is true enough that they were also in the forefront of the movement for amendments that would protect personal liberties, but there is considerable reason to suspect that many deplored the absence of a Bill of Rights primarily for the purpose of defeating the

Constitution itself. Anti-Federalists in the first session of Congress sought to secure amendments which would aggrandize state powers, but they failed in this effort. Then, in order to force Congress to reconsider the whole subject of amendments, Virginia's Anti-Federalists attempted to defeat the proposed Bill of Rights. Virginia's Federalists, on the other hand, eagerly supported the Bill of Rights in order to prevent additional amendments that might hamstring the national government.

On November 30, 1789 Virginia's lower house, dominated by the Federalists, "and without debate of any consequence," quickly passed all the amendments proposed by Congress. But the opposition party controlled the state senate. "That body," reported Randolph to Washington, "will attempt to postpone them [the amendments]; for a majority is unfriendly to the government."[79] As a member of the Virginia lower house reported to Madison, the state senate was inclined to reject the amendments not from dissatisfaction with them, but from apprehension "that the adoption of them at this time will be an obstacle to the chief object of their pursuit, the amendment on the subject of direct taxation."[80] As Randolph had predicted, the state senate, by a vote of eight to seven, did decide to postpone final action on what are now the First, Sixth, Ninth, and Tenth Amendments until the next session of the legislature, thereby allowing time for the electorate to express itself. It was on this occasion that the eight senators in question made their statement on the alleged inadequacy of the First Amendment, bidding for electoral support against an allegedly weak Bill of Rights by presenting themselves as champions of religious liberty and advocates of separation between government and religion.

Madison remained unworried by this tactic, confidently predicting that the action of the senators would boomerang. "The miscarriage of the third article [the First Amendment], particularly, will have this effect," he wrote to Washington.[81] His confidence is explainable on several counts.

First, Madison knew that the First Amendment had the support of the Baptists, the one group most insistent upon the voluntary support of religion.[82] Second, he knew that the eight senators did not come before the electorate with clean hands. Like Henry and Lee, who laid out their strategy for them, they had consistently voted against religious liberty and in favor of taxes for religion. Their legislative record on this score was well known. By contrast, the seven senators who favored ratification of the First Amendment had stood with Jefferson and Madison in the first from 1784 to 1786 against a state establishment of religion and for religious liberty.[83] Finally, Madison reasoned that the statement by the eight senators was an inept piece of propaganda with little chance of convincing anyone, because it was obviously misleading and inaccurate. The eight senators alleged that "any particular denomination of Christians might be so favored and supported by the general government, as to give it a decided advantage over others,"—a construction of the First Amendment that not even proponents of the narrow interpretation would accept—and the same senators also asserted that the amendment "does not prohibit the rights of conscience from being violated or infringed,"—whereas anyone might read for himself the amendment's positive statement that Congress shall not abridge the free exercise of religion.

In the end, Madison's confidence proved justified. On December 15, 1791, after a session of inaction on the Bill of Rights, the state senate finally ratified without a record vote. In the context of Anti-Federalist maneuverings, there is every reason to believe that Virginia supported the First Amendment with the understanding that it had been misrepresented by the eight senators. There is no reason to believe that Virginia ratified with the understanding that the amendment permitted any government aid to religion.

What conclusions can one come to, then, in connection with ratification of the First Amendment by the states? In Virginia, the one state for which there is some evidence, we can arrive only at a negative conclusion: The evidence does not support the narrow interpretation of the no-establishment clause. In nine other states there was perfunctory ratification, with no record of the debates, and in the remaining three states there was inaction. In the absence of other evidence, therefore, it is impossible to determine solely on the basis of ratification just what the general understanding of the no-establishment clause actually was.

MEANING OF THE CLAUSE

By now the difficulty of trying to explain exactly what was intended by the no-establishment clause should be obvious. What was meant by an establishment of religion? Was the prohibition in the First Amendment intended only to ban preference for one church? Or was it designed to ban nondiscriminatory government support to all religious bodies and to religion generally? Here an examination of the American experience with establishments of religion is essential.

This experience was in many respects unique, for it did not always follow the pattern of European precedent. Some scholars have arbitrarily assigned to the phrase "an establishment of religion" its European meaning only. James O'Neill, one of the first advocates of the narrow interpretation, without examining establishments of religion in colonial America or the establishments that existed after the Revolution and at the time of the framing of the First Amendment, concluded in capital letters that an establishment of religion has always and everywhere meant "A SINGLE CHURCH OR RELIGION ENJOYING FORMAL, LEGAL, OFFICIAL, MONOPOLISTIC PRIVILEGE THROUGH A UNION WITH THE GOVERNMENT OF THE STATE."[84]

Other scholars[85] who insist that the First Amendment only banned a single privileged state church also fail to deal with the history of colonial and revolutionary periods, which provides repeated examples demonstrating that establishment of religion in America commonly meant something different than it did in Europe. Indeed, at the time of the framing of the Bill of Rights all state establishments that still existed in America were *multiple* establishments of *several* churches, something unknown in European experience.

THE COLONIAL EXPERIENCE

On the eve of the Revolution, establishments of religion in the European sense existed only in the Southern colonies of Virginia, Maryland, North Carolina, South Carolina, and Georgia, where the Church of England or Episcopalian Church was the state church. All persons, regardless of belief or affiliation, were taxed for its support as the official church of these colonies. Taxes so collected were spent to build and maintain church buildings and pay salaries of Episcopalian clergy. These Southern establishments were therefore comparable to European counterparts.

The record in Rhode Island, Pennsylvania, Delaware, and New Jersey is equally clear: these four colonies never experienced any establishment of religion. In the colonies of New York, Massachusetts, Connecticut, and New Hampshire, however, the pattern of establishment was diversified and uniquely American.

New York. New York's colonial history of Church–State relationships provides the first example of an establishment of religion radically different from the European type, an establishment of religion in general—or at least of Protestantism in general—and without preference to one church over others. When the English conquered New Netherlands in 1664, renaming it New York in honor of its new proprietor, the Duke of York (James II), they found that the Dutch Reformed Church (Calvinist) was exclusively established as the state church; but after the colony passed to English control, this church lost its government support. In 1665 the people of Long Island agreed to what came to be known as the "Duke's Laws," which made provisions for the regulation of churches in that area. Any church of the Protestant religion could become an established church. In a sense, of course, this was an exclusive establishment of one religion, Protestantism; but the system involved a multiple establishment of several different Protestant churches, in sharp contrast to European precedents, which provided for the establishment of one church only.

Under the "Duke's Laws," every township was obliged publicly to support some Protestant church and a minister. The denomination of the church did not matter. Costs were to be met by a public tax: "Every inhabitant shall contribute to all charges both in Church and State."[86] A local option system prevailed. On producing evidence of ordination "from some Protestant bishop or minister,"[87] the minister selected by a town was inducted into his pastorate by the governor representing the state. In other words, this was an establishment of religion in which there was a formal, legal, official union between government and religion on a nonpreferential basis and without the establishment of any individual church. In 1683 the New York Assembly enacted a "Charter of Liberties" that adopted the Long Island system of multiple establishments and extended it to the whole colony.

Following the Glorious Revolution of 1688, the English government expected and instructed its governors of New York to implement an establishment of Anglicanism there.[88] In 1693 Governor Benjamin Fletcher managed to have a recalcitrant legislature, composed almost entirely of non-Anglicans, pass "An Act for Settling a Ministry & raising a Maintenance for them" in the four counties of New York, Richmond, Queens, and Westchester. The law called only for "a good and sufficient Protestant Minister" and nowhere mentioned the Church of England.[89] The royal governors, together with most Anglicans, asserted that the Act had established their church; but many Non-Anglican New Yorkers disagreed. Thus, in 1695, the legislature agreed with the New York City vestry that according to the terms of the 1693 act, it was entitled to select a "Dissenting Protestant Minister," i.e., a non-Anglican one, although the governor refused to permit this.[90] A few years after, in 1699, Lewis Morris, a staunch Anglican and later Chief Justice of the province, wrote: "The People were generally dissenters [and] fancied they had made an effectual provision for Ministers of their own persuasion by this Act."[91]

In 1703 and 1704 Anglicans, with the assistance of Lord Cornbury, the highhanded governor of the colony, managed to gain possession of the church and parsonage in the town of Jamaica, Long Island. These buildings had been erected at public expense, and the town had chosen a Presbyterian minister. The Anglicans' action set off a long and bitter controversy. The Presbyterians refused to pay the salary of the Anglican minister because, as the Church of England townspeople reported, "they [the Presbyterians] stick not to call themselves the Established Church."[92] In 1710 the Presbyterians managed to seize and retain the parsonage, and in 1727 they brought suit for the recovery of the church, which the provincial court, in an unreported decision, awarded them.[93] For much of the remainder of the colonial period, Anglicans managed to pry a minister's salary out of the reluctant inhabitants, but not without constant complaints and a further attempt, defeated by the courts in 1768, to withhold the minister's salary.[94]

Elsewhere on Long Island, the inhabitants supported the non-Anglican town ministers chosen by the majority. Brookhaven certainly supported such a minister, and given the scarcity of Anglicans and Anglican ministers in the colony, most towns probably reached their own accommodations with the minister of their choice.[95]

In the 1750s the organization of King's (later Columbia) College provoked a fierce controversy over the nature of New York's establishment. Anglicans demanded that they control the new school because they enjoyed "a preference by the Constitution of the province."[96] Non-Anglicans rejected both claims. A young lawyer, William Livingston, and two associates, William Smith Jr., and John Morin Scott, organized the opposition. The Triumvirate, as the three came to be known, specifically denied that the Anglican Church was exclusively established in the colony. They publicized this refutation in their paper *The Independent Reflector* and Smith devoted a section to it in his *History*.[97] The Triumvirate insisted that the establishment "restricted no particular Protestant Denomination whatsoever," and that the people were to choose which ministers to establish.[98] Here again is evidence that the concept of a multiple establishment of religion was not only understood by but also engaged the attention of the inhabitants of colonial New York.

Although New York Anglicans claimed an exclusive establishment of their church, a large number of the colony's population understood the establishment set up by the Act of 1693 not simply as a state preference for one religion or sect over others, but as allowing public support for many different churches to be determined by popular vote. Thus, in 1775, Alexander Hamilton, New York's leading citizen, was able to define "an established religion" as "a religion which the civil authority engaged, not only to protect, but to support."[99]

New England

Massachusetts, the major and archetypal New England colony, proclaimed no establishment of the Congregational church by name after 1692. That year the General Court provided for an establishment of religion on a town basis by simply requiring every town to maintain an "able, learned and orthodox" minister, to be chosen by the voters of the town and supported by a tax levied on all taxpayers.[100] By law several different denominations could benefit from the establishment. In fact because Congregationalists constituted the overwhelming majority in nearly every town, they reaped the benefits of the establishment of religion. Except in Boston, where all congregations were supported voluntarily, the law operated to make the Congregational church the privileged one, which unquestionably was the purpose of the statute, and non-Congregationalists, chiefly Episcopalians, Baptists, and Quakers, were for a long time taxed for the support of Congregationalism.

The growing number of dissenters, however, forced Congregationalists to retreat and make concessions. The retreat began in 1727, when the Episcopalians won the statutory right of having their religious taxes applied to the support of their own churches.[101] By coincidence the Connecticut legislature passed a similar act on behalf of the Episcopalian churches in the same year.[102] In 1728 Massachusetts exempted Quakers and Baptists from taxes for the payment of ministerial salaries. Then, in 1731 and 1735, each denomination was respectively exempted from sharing the taxes for building new town churches.[103] After those dates tax exemption statutes on behalf of Quakers and Baptists were periodically renewed, so that members of these denominations were not supposed to pay religious taxes for the benefit of either Congregational churches or of their own.

As a result of a variety of complicated legal technicalities, as well as outright illegal action, frequent abuses occurred under the system of tax exemption, which also prevailed in Connecticut. In both colonies many Quakers and Baptists were unconscionably forced to pay for the support of Congregational churches, and even Episcopalians who lived too far from a church of their own denomination to attend its services were taxed for support of Congregational ones. But these abuses of both the letter and spirit of the law do not alter the basic fact that after 1728 the establishments of religion in both colonies meant government support of two churches, Congregationalist and Episcopalian, without specified preference to either.

These injustices arose out of the overwhelming numerical superiority of Congregationalists. However, although Congregationalists in fact made up the establishment in New England, prominent spokesmen among them understood that they did not constitute an exclusive establishment. Cotton Mather wrote that "the Person elected by the Majority of the Inhabitants . . . is . . . the King's Minister," and he went on to state that the minister elected by each town was the official minister and as such entitled to the taxes of the place.[104] Benjamin Colman declared: "If any Town will chuse a Gentleman of the Church of England for their Pastor . . . he is their Minister by the Laws of our Province as much as any Congregational Minister."[105] Near the end of the colonial period, Johnathan Mayhew made the most explicit statement of all on this subject. Massachusetts, he explained, did not establish a single church, but rather "protestant churches of various denominations." He understood that "an hundred churches, all of different denominations . . . might all be established in the same . . . colony, as well as one, two, or three."[106] Thus did three of the most prominent New England ministers of the eighteenth century specify their understanding that the Massachusetts establishment was something other than an exclusive preference for one church. In fact two groups, Congregationalists and Episcopalians, received tax support for their churches, and all agreed that were it not for the fact that Congregationalists constituted a majority in the towns, ministers of other churches could be elected and be established according to the laws of the colony. Massachusetts, and Connecticut to a lesser extent, clearly proclaimed not an exclusive but a dual or plural establishment of religion.

The situation did not substantially differ in New Hampshire. Down to the middle of the eighteenth century, the town system of establishment operated to benefit the Congregational church exclusively. New Hampshire, however, did not systematically require the payment of rates by dissenters nor concern itself with the support of their ministers. Quakers, Episcopalians, Presbyterians, and Baptists were exempt from supporting the local established church, which was usually Congregationalist. In some towns, however, Episcopalians and Presbyterians were authorized to establish their own parishes and to use town authority to collect taxes for their churches. By the eve of the Revolution, the pattern of establishment had become bewilderingly diverse. Some towns maintained dual establishments, others multiple establishments, with free exercise for dissenters.[107]

No New England colony maintained a single provincial establishment supported by all, or even by the taxes of its own members alone. In Massachusetts, Connecticut, and New Hampshire, other groups apart from Congregationalists were eligible for and received public tax support for religion. Clearly, New Englanders understood that an individual town could decide which denomination would be established within its precincts.

EARLY STATE CONSTITUTIONS

In the wake of the American Revolution and its attendant atmosphere of liberty, those exclusive establishments of religion inherited from the colonial period collapsed. States that had never had establishments renewed their barriers against them, except for Rhode Island, which did not adopt a new state constitution.

New Jersey provided by its constitution of 1776 that no person should "ever be obliged to pay tithes, taxes, or any other rates, for the purpose of building or repairing any other church or churches, place or places of worship, or for the maintenance of any minister or ministry, contrary to what he believes to be right, or has deliberately or voluntarily engaged himself to perform."[108] Delaware adopted a similar article.[109] Both states, however, banned an establishment of "one sect in preference to others."[110] Pennsylvania's provision in its constitution of 1776 was equally broad: "No man ought or of right can be compelled to attend any religious worship, or erect or support any place of worship, or maintain any ministry, contrary to, or against, his own free will and consent."[111]

In New York, where a multiple establishment had been maintained in New York City and three adjoining counties, the long history of an insistence by the Church of England that it was rightfully the only established church influenced the writing of the clause against establishments in the constitution of 1777. The system of multiple establishments of religion was ended by the following words, reflecting the stubborn determination of non-Episcopalians never to admit, even by implication, that there had ever been an exclusive or preferential establishment of the Church of England: "That all such parts of the said common law, and all such of the said statutes and acts aforesaid, or parts thereof, *as may be construed to establish or maintain any particular denomination of Christians or their ministers . . . be, and they hereby are, abrogated and rejected.*"[112]

Nowhere in America after 1776 did an establishment of religion restrict itself to a state church or to a system of public support of one sect alone; instead, an establishment of religion meant public support of several or all churches, with preference to none. The six states that continued to provide for public support of religion were careful to make concessions to the spirit of the times by extending their establishments to embrace many different sects.

Three of these six states were in New England. Massachusetts adopted its constitution in 1780. Article III of its Declaration of Rights commanded the legislature to authorize the "several towns, parishes, precincts, and other bodies politic, or religious societies, to make suitable provision, at their own expense, for the institution of the public worship of God, and for the support and maintenance of public Protestant teachers of piety, religion, and morality." Clause two of Article III empowered the legislature to make church attendance compulsory. Clause three provided that the towns and parishes were to have the right of electing their ministers. Clause four was the principal one relevant to the problem under inquiry. It stated: "And all moneys paid by the subject to the support of public worship, and all the public teachers aforesaid, shall, if he require it, be uniformly applied to the support of the public teacher or teachers of his own religious sect or denomination, provided there be any on whose instructions he attends; otherwise it may be paid towards the support of the teacher or teachers of the parish or precinct in which the said moneys are raised." A fifth clause even provided that "no subordination of any one sect or denomination to the other shall ever be established by law."[113] In the context of Article III, the fifth clause, against preference, proves that constitutionally speaking the several churches of the establishment were on a non-preferential basis. Clearly establishment in Massachusetts meant government support of religion and of several different churches in an equitable manner. As in colonial days, the Congregationalists were the chief beneficiaries of the establishment, primarily because they were by far the most numerous and because they resorted to various tricks to fleece non-Congregationalists out of their share of religious taxes. But the fact remains that Baptist, Episcopalian, Methodist, Unitarian, and even Universalist churches were publicly supported under the establishment after 1780.[114] The establishment in Massachusetts lasted until 1833.

In New Hampshire the state constitution of 1784, by Article VI of its Declaration of Rights, created a statewide multiple establishment with the guarantee that no sect or denomination should be subordinated to another.[115] As in Massachusetts all Protestant churches benefited. The multiple establishment in New Hampshire ended in 1819.

Connecticut's story is also like that of Massachusetts. Like Rhode Island, the state adopted no constitution at this time; its establishment was regulated by the "Act of Toleration" of 1784, which was in force when the Bill of Rights was framed. By this statute each town was to choose which minister to support, and no sect was to be subordinated to any other. Those who did not belong to the majority established church were exempted from paying towards its support as long as they contributed to their own congregation. The establishment lasted until 1818.[116]

In Maryland, Georgia, and South Carolina, "an establishment of religion" meant very much what it did in the three New England states that maintained multiple establishments. In Maryland, where the Church of England had been exclusively established, the constitution of 1776 provided that no person could be compelled "to maintain any particular place of worship, or any particular ministry," thus disestablishing the Episcopalian church. But the same constitution provided for a new establishment of religion: "Yet the Legislature may, in their discretion, lay a general and *equal tax*, for the support of the Christian religion; leaving to each individual the power of appointing the payment over of the money, collected from him, to the support of any particular place of worship or minister."[117] "Christian" rather than "Protestant" was used in Maryland because of the presence of a large Catholic population, thus insuring non-preferential support of all churches existing in the state. In 1785 the Maryland legislature sought to exercise its discretionary power to institute non-preferential support, but "a huge uproar arose against the measure," and it was denounced as a new establishment and decisively beaten.[118] In 1810 the power to enact a multiple establishment was taken from the legislature by a constitutional amendment providing that "an *equal* and *general* tax or any other tax . . . for the support of *any religion*" was not lawful.[119]

Georgia's constitution of 1777 tersely effected the disestablishment of the Church of England while permitting a multiple establishment of all churches without exception: "All persons whatever shall have the free exercise of their religion; . . . and shall not, unless by consent, support any teacher or teachers except those of their own profession."[120] "This, of course, left the way open for taxation for the support of one's own religion," says the historian of eighteenth-century Church-State relationships in Georgia, "and such a law was passed in 1785,"[121] although similar bills had failed in 1782 and 1784. According to the 1785 law, all Christian sects and denominations were to receive tax support in proportion to the amount of property owned by their respective church members, but it is not clear whether this measure even went into operation. What is clear is that an establishment of religion meant government tax support to all churches, with preference to none. The constitution in effect at the time of the framing of the Bill of Rights was adopted in 1789. Its relevant provision declared that no persons should be obliged "to contribute to the support of any religious profession but their own," thereby permitting a multiple establishment as before. In the state constitution adopted in 1798, however, Georgia separated Church and State by a guarantee against any religious taxes and by placing the support of religion on a purely voluntary basis.[122]

South Carolina's constitution of 1778 was the sixth state constitution providing for a multiple establishment of religion. Article XXVIII most elaborately spelled out the details for the maintenance of the "Christian Protestant religion" as "the established religion of this State." Adult males forming themselves into any religious society of a Protestant denomination were declared to be "a church of the established religion of this State," on condition of subscribing to a belief in God, promising to worship him publicly, a belief in Christianity as "the true religion", and a belief in the divine inspiration of the Scriptures. Pursuant to this law, Baptists, Independents, Methodists, and Anglicans qualified as "Established" churches. The state also specifically guaranteed that "no person shall, by law, be obliged to pay towards the maintenance and support of a religious worship that he does not freely join in, or has not voluntarily engaged to support."[123] In 1790 South Carolina, reflecting the influence of the federal Bill of Rights, adopted a new constitution with no provisions whatever for public support of religion.[124]

The constitutions of North Carolina and Virginia did not provide for an establishment of religion of any kind. In 1776 North Carolina banned state support for religion and disestablished the Church of England.[125] By contrast Virginia's constitution of 1776 was noncommittal on the subject of an establishment.

At the close of 1776, the Church of England was for all practical purposes disestablished in Virginia by a statute which 1) forever exempted all nonmembers from taxes for its support, and 2) suspended for one year the collection of any taxes from Church of England members. The suspension of religious taxes for members was renewed in 1777 and 1778; in 1779 the old colonial statute levying those taxes was repealed. Thus the Church of England received no government support after 1776. But the statute of 1776 that initiated the end of the exclusive establishment expressly reserved for future decision the question whether religion ought to be placed on a private, voluntary basis or be supported on a non-preferential basis by a new "general" assessment.[126]

In 1779 a general assessment bill for support on a non-preferential basis was introduced; at the same time, however, Jefferson's "Bill for Religious Freedom" was introduced, providing, in part, "that no man shall be compelled to frequent or support any religious worship, place, or ministry whatsoever."[127] The principle underlying this provision was Jefferson's belief that religion was a personal matter between the individual and God and not rightfully a subject under the jurisdiction of the civil government. By contrast the "General Assessment Bill" was predicated on the supposition, expressed in its preamble, that the state must encourage religion. This bill stipulated that the Christian religion should be "the established religion," that societies of Christians organized for the purpose of religious worship should in law be regarded as churches of the established religion, each to have its own "name or denomination" and each to share the tax proceeds assessed on tithable personal property and collected by county sheriffs. Every person was to designate the church of his membership, and that church alone would receive his taxes; money collected from persons not disignating membership was to be divided proportionately among all churches of his county.[128]

Confronted by two diametrically opposed bills, the Virginia legislature deadlocked, and neither bill could muster a majority. In 1784 Patrick Henry reintroduced a general assessment plan under the title "A Bill Establishing a Provision for the Teachers of the Christian Religion," in which the stated purpose was to require "a moderate tax or contribution annually for the support of the Christian religion, or of some Christian church, denomination or communion of Christians, or for some form of Christian worship."[129] A resolution in favor of the bill was passed against the opposition of a minority led by Madison.

Only the notes of Madison's speech against the measure remain. These show that he argued that religion is a matter of private rather than civil concern, and that taxes in support of religion violated religious liberty. The true question, he declared, was not "Is religion necessary?", but rather "Are religious establishments necessary for religion?", to which he argued in the negative.[130] Through masterly political maneuvering, Madison got Henry out of the legislature by supporting his election as governor and then managed to get a final vote on the bill postponed until the next session of the legislature, nearly a year later, in November of 1785. In the meantime, he brought his case to the people by writing his famous "Memorial and Remonstrance Against Religious Assessments." This widely distributed pamphlet acted as a catalyst for the opposition to the assessment bill and resulted in the election of a legislature with an overwhelming majority against it. The new legislature let the bill die unnoticed, and by a vote of sixty-seven to twenty enacted instead Jefferson's bill for religious freedom with its provision against government support of religion.

The struggle in Virginia is usually featured in accounts of the history of separation of Church and State in America. No doubt historians focus their attention on the Virginia story because the sources are uniquely ample,[131] the struggle was important and dramatic, and the opinions of Madison, the principal framer of the Bill of Rights, not to mention those of Jefferson, were fully elicited. As a result, the details of no other state controversy over Church-State relationships are so familiar. If, however, one is concerned with attempting to understand what was meant by "an establishment of religion" at the time of the framing of the Bill of Rights, the histories of the other states are equally important. Indeed, the abortive effort in Virginia to enact Patrick Henry's assessment bill is less important than the fact that five states actually had constitutional provisions authorizing general assessments for religion, and a sixth (Connecticut) provided for the same by statute. Had the assessment bill in Virginia been enacted, it would simply have increased the number of states maintaining multiple establishments from six to seven.

Clearly the provisions of these six states show that to understand the American meaning of "an establishment of religion" one cannot arbitrarily adopt a definition based on European experience. In every European precedent of an establishment, the religion established was that of a single church. Many different churches, or the religion held in common by all of them, i.e., Christianity or Protestantism, were never simultaneously established by any European nation. Establishments in America, on the other hand, both in the colonial and early state periods, were not limited in nature or in meaning to state support of one church. *An establishment of religion in America at the time of the framing of the Bill of Rights meant government aid and sponsorship of religion, principally by impartial tax support of the institutions of religion, the churches.*

In no state or colony, of course, was there ever an establishment of religion that included every religion without exception. Neither Judaism, Buddhism, Mohammedanism, nor any but a Christian religion was ever established in America. In half of the six multiple establishments existing in 1789, Protestantism was the established religion; in the other half, Christianity was. No member of the First Congress came from a state that supported an exclusive establishment of religion; no such example could have been found in the America of 1789. Of those states that provided public support for religion, half of them had provided for such at least theoretically since the early eighteenth century; the remainder did so from the time of the American Revolution. Their experience told the legislators in 1789 that an establishment of religion meant not state preference for one religion but non-preferential support for many.

8

Liberty and the First Amendment:
1790–1800

IN 1798 THERE WAS a sudden break-through in American libertarian thought on Freedom of speech and press—sudden, radical, and transforming, like an underwater volcano erupting its lava upward from the ocean floor to form a new island. The Sedition Act, which was a thrust in the direction of a single-party press and a monolithic party system, triggered the Republican surge. The result was the emergence of a new promontory of libertarian thought jutting out of a stagnant Blackstonian sea.

To appreciate the Republican achievement requires an understanding of American libertarian[1] thought on the meaning and scope of freedom of political discourse. Contrary to the accepted view,[2] neither the Revolution nor the First Amendment superseded the common law by repudiating the Blackstonian concept that freedom of the press meant merely freedom from prior restraint. There had been no rejection of the concept that government may be criminally assaulted, that is, seditiously libeled, simply by the expression of critical opinions that tended to lower it in the public's esteem.

To be sure, the principle of a free press, like flag, home, and mother, had no enemies. Only seditious libels, licentious opinions, and malicious falsehoods were condemned. The question, therefore, is not whether freedom of the press was favored but what it meant and whether its advocates would extend it to a political opponent whose criticism cut to the bone on issues that counted. Jefferson once remarked that he did not care whether his neighbor said that there are twenty gods or no God, because "It neither picks my pocket nor breaks my leg."[3] But in drafting a constitution for Virginia in 1776 he proposed that freedom of religion "shall not be held to justify any seditious preaching or conversation against the authority of the civil government."[4] And in the same year he helped frame a statute on treasonable crimes, punishing anyone who "by any word" or deed defended the cause of Great Britain.[5] Apparently political opinions could break his leg or pick his pocket, thus raising the question of what he meant by freedom of the press. We can say that he and his contemporaries supported an unrestricted public discussion of issues if we understand that "unrestricted" meant merely the absence of censorship in advance of publication: no one needed a government license to express himself, but he was accountable under the criminal law for abuse of his right to speak or publish freely.[6]

Before 1798 the *avant-garde* among American libertarians staked everything on the principles of the Zenger case,[7] which they thought beyond improvement. No greater liberty could be conceived than the right to publish without restriction if only the defendant might plead truth as a defense in a criminal prosecution for seditious, blasphemous, obscene, or personal libel, and if the criminality of his words might be determined by a jury of his peers rather than by a judge. The substantive law of criminal libels was unquestioned.

Zengerian principles, however, were a frail prop for a broad freedom of the press. Granted, a defendant representing a popular cause against the administration in power might be acquitted, but if his views were unpopular, God help him—for a jury would not, nor would his plea of truth as a defense. A jury, then as today, was essentially a court of public opinion, often synonymous with public prejudice. Moreover, the opinions of men notoriously differ: one man's truth is another's falsehood. Indeed political opinions may be neither true nor false and are usually not capable of being proved by the rules of evidence, even if true. An indictment for seditious libel, based on a defendant's accusation of bribery or corruption by a public official, can be judged by a jury. But the history of sedition trials indicates that indictments are founded on accusations of a different order, namely, that the government, or one of its measures or officials, is unjust, tyrannical, or contrary to the public interest. Libertarians who accepted Zengerian principles painted themselves into a corner. If a jury returned a verdict of guilty despite a defense of truth, due process had been accorded, and protests were groundless, for the substance of the law that made the trial possible had not been challenged.

American acquiescence in the British or common-law definition of a free press was so widespread that even the frail Zengerian principles seemed daring, novel, and had few adherents. It was not until 1790, after the framing, but before the ratification, of the First Amendment, that the first state, Pennsylvania, took the then radical step of adopting the Zengerian principles[8] which left the common law of seditious libel intact. The Pennsylvania provision was drafted by James Wilson, who (in the state convention that ratified the Constitution) declared, without challenge by any of the ardent proponents of a bill of rights: "what is meant by the liberty of the press is that there should be no antecedent restraint upon it; but that every author is responsible when he attacks the security or welfare of the government. . . ." The mode of proceeding, Wilson added, should be by prosecution.[9] The state constitutional provision of 1790 reflected this proposition, as did state trials before and after 1790.[10]

Delaware and Kentucky followed Pennsylvania's lead in 1792,[11] but elsewhere the *status quo* prevailed. In 1789 William Cushing and John Adams worried about whether the guarantee of a free press in Massachusetts ought to mean that truth was a good defense to a charge of criminal libel, but they agreed that false publications against the government were punishable.[12] In 1791, when a Massachusetts editor was prosecuted for a criminal libel against a state official, the Supreme Judicial Court divided on the question of truth as a defense, but, like the Pennsylvania judges,[13] agreed that the state constitutional guarantee of a free press was merely declaratory of the common law in simply prohibiting a licensing system.[14]

The opinions of Jefferson, the acknowledged libertarian leader in America, and of Madison, the father of the Bill of Rights, are especially significant. Jefferson, in 1783, when proposing a new constitution for Virginia, exempted the press from prior restraints, but carefully provided for prosecution—a state criminal trial—in cases of false publication.[15] In 1788, when urging Madison to support a bill of rights to the new federal Constitution, Jefferson made the same recommendation.[16] Madison construed it in its most favorable light, observing: "The Exemption of the press from liability in every case for *true facts* is . . . an innovation and as such ought to be well considered."[17] On consideration, however, he did not add truth as a defense to the amendment that he offered on the press when proposing a bill of rights to Congress.[18] Yet his phrasing appeared too broad for Jefferson who stated that he would be pleased if the press provision were altered to exclude freedom to publish "false facts . . . affecting the peace of the confederacy with foreign nations,"[19] a clause whose suppressive possibilities can be imagined in the context of a foreign policy controversy such as the one on Jay's Treaty.

Madison fortunately ignored Jefferson's proposal but there is no evidence warranting the belief that he dissented from the universal American acceptance of the Blackstonian definition of a free press. At the Virginia ratifying convention in 1788 Madison remained silent when George Nicholas, one of his closest supporters, declared that the liberty of the press was secure because there was no power to license the press.[20] Again Madison was silent when John Marshall rose to say that Congress would never make a law punishing men of different political opinions "unless it be such a case as much satisfy the people at large."[21] In October 1788, when replying to Jefferson's argument that powers of the national government should be restricted by a bill of rights,[22] Madison declared: "absolute restrictions in cases that are doubtful, or where emergencies may overrule them, ought to be avoided."[23] When Madison proposed an amendment in Congress guaranteeing freedom of the press, he did not employ the emphatic language of the Virginia ratifying convention's recommendation that the press cannot be abridged "by any authority of the United States."[24] The amendment, in the form in which Madison introduced it, omitted the important clause "by any authority of the United States,"[25] which would have covered the executive and the judiciary as well as Congress. The omitted clause would have prohibited the federal courts from exercising any common-law jurisdiction over criminal libels. As ratified, the First Amendment declared only that Congress should make no law abridging the freedom of speech or press.

What did the amendment mean at the time of its adoption? More complex than it appears, it meant several things, and it did not necessarily mean what it said or say what it was intended to mean. First, as is shown by an examination of the phrase "the freedom of the press," the amendment was merely an assurance that Congress was powerless to authorize restraints in advance of publication. On this point the evidence for the period from 1787 to 1791 is uniform and nonpartisan. For example, Hugh Williamson of North Carolina, a Federalist signatory of the Constitution, used freedom of the press in Blackstonian or common-law terms,[26] as did Melancthon Smith of New York, an Antifederalist. Demanding a free press guarantee in the new federal Constitution, despite the fact that New York's constitution lacked that guarantee, Smith argued that freedom of the press was "fully defined and secured" in New York by "the common and statute law of England" and that a state constitutional provision was therefore unnecessary.[27] No other definition of freedom of the press by anyone anywhere in America before 1798 has been discovered. Apparently there was, before that time, no dissent from the proposition that the punishment of a seditious libeler did not abridge the proper or lawful freedom of the press.[28]

That freedom was so narrowly understood that its constitutional protection did not, per se, preclude the enactment of a sedition law. The security of the state against libelous attack was always and everywhere regarded as outweighing any social interest in completely unfettered discussion. The thought and experience of a lifetime, indeed the taught traditions of law and politics extending back many generations, supplied an unquestioned assumption that freedom of political discourse, however broadly conceived, stopped short of seditious libel.

The injunction of the First Amendment, nevertheless, was not intended to imply that a sedition act might be enacted without abridging "the freedom of the press." A sedition act would not be an abridgment, but that was not the point of the amendment. To understand its framers' intentions, the amendment should not be read with the focus on the meaning of "the freedom of the press." It should not, in other words, be read merely to mean that Congress could impose no prior restraints. It should be read, rather, with the stress on the opening clause: "Congress shall make no law. . . ." The injunction was intended and understood to prohibit any congressional regulation of the press, whether by means of a licensing law, a tax, or a sedition act. The framers meant Congress to be totally without power to enact legislation respecting the press. They intended a federal system in which the central government could exercise only such powers as were specifically enumerated or were necessary and proper to carry out the enumerated ones. Thus James Wilson declared that, because the national government had "no power whatsoever" concerning the press, "no law . . . can possibly be enacted" against it. Thus Hamilton, referring to the demand for a free press guarantee, asked, "why declare that things shall not be done which there is no power to do?"[29] The illustrations may be multiplied fiftyfold. In other words, no matter what was meant or understood by freedom of speech and press, the national government, *even in the absence of the First Amendment,* could not make speech or press a legitimate subject of restrictive legislation. The amendment itself was superfluous. To quiet public apprehension, it offered an added assurance that Congress would be limited to the exercise of its delegated powers. The phrasing was intended to prohibit the possibility that those powers might be used to abridge speech and press. From this viewpoint, the Sedition Act of 1798 was unconstitutional.

That act was also unnecessary as a matter of law, however necessary as a matter of Federalist party policy. It was unnecessary because the federal courts exercised jurisdiction over nonstatutory or common-law crimes against the United States. At the Pennsylvania ratifying convention James Wilson declared that, while Congress could enact no law against the press, a libel against the United States might be prosecuted in the state where the offense was committed, under Article III, Section 2, of the Constitution which refers to the judicial power of the United States.[30] A variety of common-law crimes against the United States were, in fact, tried in the federal courts during the first decade of their existence.[31] There were, in the federal courts, even a couple of common-law indictments for the crime of seditious libel.[32] All the early Supreme Court judges, including several who had been influential in the Philadelphia Convention, or in the state ratifying conventions, or in the Congress that passed the Judiciary Act of 1789, assumed the existence of a federal common law of crimes.[33] Ironically, it was a case originating as a federal prosecution of Connecticut editors for seditious libels against President Jefferson that finally resulted in a ruling by a divided Supreme Court in 1812 that there was no federal common law of crimes.[34]

There was unquestionably a federal common law of crimes at the time of the Sedition Act. Why then was the act passed if it was not legally needed? Even in England, where the criminal courts exercised an unquestioned jurisdiction over seditious libels, it was politically advisable in the 1790's to declare public policy in unmistakable terms by the enactment of sedition statutes.[35] Legislation helped ensure effective enforcement of the law and stirred public opinion against its intended victims. The Federalists, hoping to control public opinion and elections, emulated the British model. A federal statute was expedient also because the Republicans insisted that libels against the United States might be tried only by the state courts.

This suggests another original purpose of the First Amendment. It has been said that a constitutional guarantee of a free press did not, in itself, preclude a sedition act, but that the prohibition on Congress did, though leaving the federal courts free to try cases of seditious libel. It now appears that the prohibition on Congress was motivated far less by a desire to give immunity to political expression that by a solicitude for states' rights and the federal principle. The primary purpose of the First Amendment was to reserve to the states an exclusive legislative authority in the field of speech and press.

This is clear enough from the countless states' rights arguments advanced by the Antifederalists during the ratification controversy, and it is explicit in the Republican arguments during the controversy over the Sedition Act. In the House debates on the bill, Albert Gallatin, Edward Livingston, John Nicholas, and Nathaniel Macon all agreed—to quote Macon on the subject of liberty of the press: "The States have complete power on the subject. . . ."[36] Jefferson's Kentucky Resolutions of 1798 expressed the same proposition,[37] as did Madison's "Address of the General Assembly to the People of the Commonwealth of Virginia" in 1799.[38]

It is possible that the opponents of the Sedition Act did not want or believe in state prosecutions, but argued for an exclusive state power over political libels because such an argument was tactically useful as a means of denying national jurisdiction, judicial or legislative. If so, how shall we explain the Republican prosecution in New York in 1803 against Harry Croswell, a Federalist editor, for a seditious libel against President Jefferson?[39] How shall we explain the Blackstonian opinions of the Republican judges in that case?[40] How shall we explain Jefferson's letter to the governor of Pennsylvania in the same year? The President, enclosing a newspaper piece that unmercifully attacked him, urged a "few prosecutions" because they "would have a wholesome effect in restoring the integrity of the presses."[41] How shall we explain Jefferson's letter to Abigail Adams in 1804 in which he said: "While we deny that Congress have a right to controul the freedom of the press, we have ever asserted the right of the states, and their exclusive right to do so."[42] And if exclusive state power was advanced not as a principle but as a tactic for denying federal jurisdiction, how shall we explain what Jefferson's opponents called his "reign of terror":[43] the common-law indictments in 1806 in the United States Circuit Court in Connecticut against six men charged with seditious libel of the President?[44] How shall we explain his letter of 1807 in which he said of the "prosecutions in the Court of the U S" that they could "not lessen the useful freedom of the press," if truth were admitted as a defense?[45]

Earlier, in 1798, the Federalists had also felt that the true freedom of the press would benefit if truth—their truth—were the measure of freedom. Their infamous Sedition Act, in the phrase of Gilbert and Sullivan, was the true embodiment of everything excellent. It was, that is, the very epitome of libertarian thought since the time of Zenger's case, proving that American libertarianism went from Zengerian principles to the Sedition Act in a single degeneration. Everything that the libertarians had ever demanded was, however, incorporated in the Sedition Act: a requirement that criminal intent be shown; the power of the jury to decide whether the accused's statement was libelous as a matter of law as well as of fact; and truth as a defense—an innovation not accepted in England until 1843.[46] By every standard the Sedition Act was a great victory for libertarian principles of freedom of the press—except that libertarian standards abruptly changed because the Republicans immediately recognized a Pyrrhic victory.

The Sedition Act provoked them to develop a new libertarian theory. It began to emerge when Congressmen Albert Gallatin, John Nicholas, Nathaniel Macon, and Edward Livingston argued against the enactment of the sedition bill.[47] It was further developed by defense counsel, most notably George Blake, in Sedition Act prosecutions.[48] It reached its most reflective and systematic expression in tracts and books which are now unfortunately rare and little known even by historians. The main body of original Republican thought on the scope, meaning, and rationale of the First Amendment is to be found in George Hay's tract, *An Essay on the Liberty of the Press;*[49] in Madison's *Report* on the Virginia Resolutions for the Virginia House of Delegates;[50] in the book *A Treatise Concerning Political Enquiry, and the Liberty of the Press,* by Tunis Wortman of New York;[51] in John Thomson's book *An Enquiry, Concerning the Liberty, and Licentiousness of the Press;*[52] and in St. George Tucker's appendix to his edition of Blackstone's *Commentaries,*[53] a most significant place for the repudiation of Blackstone on the liberty of the press. Of these works, Wortman's philosophical book is pre-eminent; it is an American masterpiece, the only equivalent on this side of the Atlantic to Milton and Mill.

The new libertarians abandoned the strait-jacketing doctrines of Blackstone and the common law, including the recent concept of a federal common law of crimes. They scornfully denounced the no prior restraints definition. Said Madison: "this idea of the freedom of the press can never be admitted to be the American idea of it" because a law inflicting penalties would have the same effect as a law authorizing a prior restraint. "It would seem a mockery to say that no laws shall be passed preventing publications from being made, but that laws might be passed for punishing them in case they should be made."[54] As Hay put it, the "British definition" meant that a man might be jailed or even put to death for what he published provided that no notice was taken of him before he published.[55]

The old calculus for measuring the scope of freedom was also rejected by the new libertarians. "Liberty" of the press, for example, had always been differentiated from "licentiousness," which was the object of the criminal law's sanctions. "Truth" and "facts" had always divided the realm of lawfulness from "falsehoods," and a similar distinction had been made between "good motives" and "criminal intent." All such distinctions were now discarded on grounds that they did not distinguish and, therefore, were not meaningful standards that might guide a jury or a court in judging an alleged verbal crime. The term "licentiousness," said Thomson, "is destitute of any meaning" and is used by those who wish "nobody to enjoy the liberty of the Press but such as were of their own opinion."[56] The term "malice," Wortman wrote, is invariably confused with mistaken zeal or prejudice.[57] It is merely an inference drawn from the supposed evil tendency of the publication itself, just a further means of punishing the excitement of unfavorable sentiments against the government even when the people's contempt of it was richly deserved. Punishment of "malice" or intent to defame the government, concluded Madison, necessarily strikes at the right of free discussion, because critics intend to excite unfavorable sentiments.[58] Finding criminality in the tendency of words was merely an attempt to erect public "tranquility . . . upon the ruins of Civil Liberty," said Wortman.[59]

Wholesale abandonment of the common law's limitations on the press was accompanied by a withering onslaught against the constrictions and subjectivity of Zengerian principles. The Sedition Act, Hay charged, "appears to be directed against falsehood and malice only; in fact . . . there are many truths, important to society, which are not susceptible of that full, direct, and positive evidence, which alone can be exhibited before a court and a jury."[60] If, argued Gallatin, the administration prosecuted a citizen for his opinion that the Sedition Act itself was unconstitutional, would not a jury, composed of the friends of that administration, find the opinion "ungrounded, or, in other words, false and scandalous, and its publication malicious? And by what kind of argument or evidence, in the present temper of parties, could the accused convince them that his opinions were true?"[61] The truth of opinions, the new libertarians concluded, could not be proved. Allowing "truth" as a defense and thinking it to be a protection for freedom, Thomson declared, made as much sense as letting a jury decide which was "the most palatable food, agreeable drink, or beautiful color."[62] A jury, he asserted, cannot give an impartial verdict in political trials. The result, agreed Madison, is that the "baleful tendency" of prosecutions for seditious libel "is little diminished by the privilege of giving in evidence the truth of the matter contained in political writings."[63]

The renunciation of traditional concepts reached its climax in the assault on the very idea that there was a crime of seditious libel. That crime, Wortman concluded, could "never be reconciled to the genius and constitution of a Representative Commonwealth."[64] He and the others constructed a new libertarianism that was genuinely radical because it broke sharply with the past and advocated an absolute freedom of political expression. One of their major tenets was that a free government cannot be criminally attacked by the opinions of its citizens. Hay, for example, insisted that freedom of the press, like chastity, was either "absolute"[65] or did not exist. Abhorring the idea of verbal political crimes, he declared that a citizen should have a right to "say everything which his passions suggest; he may employ all his time, and all his talents, if he is wicked enough to do so, in speaking against the government matters that are false, scandalous and malicious."[66] He should be "safe within the sanctuary of the press" even if he "condemns the principle of republican institutions. . . . If he censures the measures of our government, and every department and officer thereof, and ascribes the measures of the former, however salutary, and the conduct of the latter, however upright, to the basest motives; even if he ascribes to them measures and acts, which never had existence; thus violating at once, every principle of decency and truth."[67]

In brief the new libertarians advocated that only "injurious conduct," as manifested by "overt acts" or deeds, rather than words, might be criminally redressable.[68] They did not refine this proposition except to recognize that the law of libel should continue to protect private reputations against malicious falsehoods. They did not even recognize that under certain circumstances words may immediately and directly incite criminal acts.

This absolutist interpretation of the First Amendment was based on the now familiar but then novel and democratic theory that free government depends for its existence and security on freedom of political discourse. According to this theory, the scope of the amendment is determined by the nature of the government and its relationship to the people. Since the government is their servant, exists by their consent and for their benefit, and is constitutionally limited, responsible, and elective, it cannot, said Thomson, tell the citizen, "You shall not think this, or that upon certain subjects; or if you do, it is at your peril."[69] The concept of seditiousness, it was argued, could exist only in a relationship based on inferiority, when people are subjects rather than sovereigns and their criticism implies contempt of their master. "In the United States," Madison declared, "the case is altogether different."[70] Coercion or abridgment of unlimited political opinion, Wortman explained, would violate the very "principles of the social state," by which he meant a government of the people.[71] Because such a government depended upon popular elections, all the new libertarians agreed that the widest possible latitude must be maintained to keep the electorate free, informed, and capable of making intelligent choices. The citizen's freedom of political expression had the same scope as the legislator's, and for the same reasons.[72] That freedom might be dangerously abused, but the people would decide men and measures wisely if exposed to every opinion.

This brief summary of the new libertarianism scarcely does justice to its complexity, but suggests its boldness, originality, and democratic character.[73] It developed, to be sure, as an expediency of self-defense on the part of a besieged political minority struggling to maintain its existence and right to function unfettered. But it established virtually all at once and in nearly perfect form a theory justifying the rights of individual expression and of opposition parties. That the Jeffersonians in power did not always adhere to their new principles does not diminish the enduring nobility and rightness of those principles. It proves only that the Jeffersonians set the highest standards of freedom for themselves and posterity to be measured against. Their legacy was the idea that there is an indispensable condition for the development of free men in a free society: the state must be bitted and bridled by a bill of rights which is to be construed in the most generous terms and whose protections are not to be the playthings of momentary majorities.

9

Jefferson As a Civil Libertarian

THERE IS A STORY about two Roman soothsayers whose job was to edify the populace with prophecies that were intended to sustain the ancient faith. While solemnly examining the entrails of an ox for signs and portents, they winked at each other. Historians who perpetuate an idealized image of Jefferson should be no less realistic about their own craft. William James once wrote that the notion of God's omnipotence must be relinquished if God is to be kept as a religious object, because the only God worthy of the name must be finite. Similarly the notion of Jefferson's perfection as a libertarian must be relinquished if he is to be kept as a model of values to which we aspire as a nation. The only worthy Jefferson must also be finite. Yet the Jefferson who has seized the American historical imagination is the Jefferson of nearly infinite wisdom on questions of personal freedom.

Although history can be quoted to support any cause, just as scripture can be quoted by the devil, no wrenching of the past can alter a transcending fact about Thomas Jefferson: he believed in the right and capacity of the ordinary man to live responsibly in freedom. Lincoln testified for the ages that the principles of Jefferson were "the definitions and axioms of free society." It is Jefferson, if not Lincoln himself, who is the central figure in the history of American democracy. He fervently believed that the will and welfare of the people were the only prop and purpose of government. Others pitted liberty and equality against each other as if a tension, even a contradiction, existed between them. To Jefferson liberty and equality were complementary qualities of the condition to which man had a moral right. He suffused the Declaration of Independence with an ethical philosophy—not merely a political or legal one— that permanently nourished the American spirit.

Jefferson's principles sprang from the deepest aspirations of the people. A communion of sentiment tied him to them, despite his tendency to shrink from too close a personal contact. He expressed himself in literary utterance that was a model of clarity and beauty—understandable, appealing, and almost unfailingly humane. With crisp eloquence he memorably voiced the noblest hopes for human fortune on earth. In so doing, he somehow illuminated the lives of his compatriots—their needs, their best values, their ambitions. His deepest sympathies belonged to the disadvantaged and downtrodden; his deepest trust was in the power of his fellow men to do justice and to fulfil themselves on their own terms, self-reliant and self-governing, as long as they had the opportunity to make informed, unfettered choices; his deepest faith was in the emancipating effect of education and freedom on the human personality. His confidence in popular government, bounded only by respect for minority rights, was anchored in a belief that counting heads was a much better way to rule than breaking them. It secured sounder policies, more beneficial to the general welfare, than those determined by the privileged few.

Jefferson "still survives," to quote the famous deathbed words of John Adams, because a free people still cherishes the spirit of liberty and its foremost exponent among the founders of the Republic. Jefferson hated tyranny and war, poverty and privilege, bigotry and ignorance; he hated whatever crippled man's spirit or body. His influence was zealously devoted to securing the conditions of freedom that would make possible the "pursuit of happiness" by all. He championed free public education and attacked the aristocratic system of entail and primogeniture. He condemned slavery and recommended its gradual abolition. He saved untold thousands from bondage by championing the end of the foreign slave trade. He reformed the criminal code of his state, and he tightened the constitutional definition of treason to prevent the use of the criminal law as an instrument of political oppression. He advocated freedom of the press and resisted the noxious Alien and Sedition Acts. He insisted on subordination of the military to the civil authority. He converted Madison to the cause of adding the Bill of Rights to the new federal Constitution. He supported a broadening of the base of popular government by public-land grants that would enable every citizen to meet the property qualifications on the right to vote. Almost always Jefferson's impulses were generous and liberating. And on some matters, like religious liberty, he displayed a principled consistency.

When religious persecution still menaced Virginia, thanks to the legal establishment of the Church of England, Jefferson, in a magnificent collaboration with Madison, led a ten-year battle—the severest, said Jefferson, in which he had ever engaged—culminating in a victory for the free exercise of religion and separation of church and state. He believed, as had Roger Williams, that "compulsion stincks in God's nostrils." Toleration, a mere concession from the state, was only less repugnant; at its best it implied no enforced tithes or civil disabilities. Jefferson believed that religion was a private duty which free men owed their Creator. The manner of discharging that duty was none of the state's business. It was, rather, an unquestionable and illimitable natural right to be exercised freely according to the dictates of conscience.

Although the Virginia Declaration of Rights of 1776 recognized the principle of religious liberty rather than toleration, Jefferson lost on the main issue of the relation of church to state. The legislature reserved for future decision the question of whether religion ought to be supported on a nonpreferential basis by a new establishment in which all denominations would proportionally share tax proceeds. When Patrick Henry, with the backing of Washington, Randolph, and Lee, introduced a measure to create a multiple establishment benefiting all churches, Jefferson countered with his Bill for Establishing Religious Freedom. It was a classic expression of the American creed on intellectual as well as religious liberty, although Jefferson never applied its "overt acts" test to the expression of political opinion. The test, which insured the widest possible latitude for the expression of religious opinion, was "that it is time enough for the rightful purposes of civil government for its officers to interfere when principles break out into overt acts against peace and good order." The bill provided also that no man should be compelled to frequent or support any worship whatever, nor be restrained in any way on account of his religious opinions. The bill became law in 1786. Jefferson's pride of authorship was so great that he ranked the bill with the Declaration of Independence as contributions for which he most wanted to be remembered.

He faithfully adhered to the principles of his bill throughout his life. As President he departed from the precedents of Washington and Adams by refusing to recommend or designate any day for national prayer, fasting, or thanksgiving. For the President to recommend exercises of a religious character would, in his opinion, constitute an establishment of religion in violation of the First Amendment. Only a totally principled commitment to the privacy and voluntary nature of religious belief explained so exquisite a constitutional conscience.

Jefferson's consistency in applying the principle of the separation of church and state was also evident in the field of education. He was the complete secularist, opposed to the use of public funds for the teaching of religion in schools. His various proposals for establishing a system of public education in Virginia omitted religious instruction at a time when it was a prominent feature in the schools everywhere else. He was instrumental in the abolition of the school of divinity at the College of William and Mary, and when he founded the University of Virginia, neither the professorships nor the curriculum related to religion. Everywhere else in the colleges and universities of the country, ministers were commonly presidents and members of the boards, daily chapel attendance was compulsory, courses in religion were required, and professors of divinity had a prominent place on the faculties.

Jefferson cared very deeply about religious liberty. Diligent study and thought had given him a systematic theory, the most advanced of his age, and he put it into practice. His position was clearly defined, publicly stated, and vigorously defended. Although it exposed him to abusive criticism he carried on his fight for separation of church and state, and for the free exercise of religion, throughout his long public career without significant contradictions. In sum his thought on religious liberty was profoundly libertarian, and his actions suited his thought.

However, Jefferson's ideas on many other issues were not always libertarian; and when they were, his practice did not always match his professions. Between his words and deeds on religious liberty there was an almost perfect congruence, but it was not one that was characteristic of Jefferson as a civil libertarian. Historians and biographers have fixed a libertarian halo around his brow as if he were a plaster saint or a demigod in the pantheon of freedom. He has been depicted as a noble figure caught in a mythic stance: swearing eternal hostility to every form of tyranny over the mind of man. But Jefferson had his darker side: it should be recognized and understood.

His baffling complexity on all matters other than religious liberty has been the subject of critical analysis from his own time to the present. Historians have been fascinated with him as a figure of contradictions and ambiguities. The incandescent advocate of natural rights was a slaveholder; the strict constructionist of constitutional powers purchased Louisiana and adopted the Embargo; the philosopher wrote the *Manual of Parliamentary Practice*; the aristocrat championed democracy; and the democrat never introduced a proposal for universal manhood suffrage. A chiaroscuro of Jefferson would fill a huge canvas. But one image has remained relatively pure and undisputed, if not indisputable: Jefferson as the apostle of liberty. Occasional inconsistencies between his actions and libertarian values have been regarded as momentary aberrations, the exceptions that proved the rule. Even unsympathetic historians have endorsed the traditional image that lays claim to our devotion and admiration, without ever sugggesting more than the possibility that the democratic idol had a toe of clay. Sympathetic historians, including Commager, Malone, and Peterson, who are represented in the pages of this book, have written of Jefferson as wholly committed to the rights of man.

Freedom's apostle was not its apostate. Yet Jefferson's thoughts and actions on a variety of occasions and issues over an extended period followed a pattern that does not easily square with the conventional image. The familiar Jefferson is the one who, in his *Notes on the State of Virginia*, condemned temporary dictatorships even in time of war and impending invasion. The unfamiliar Jefferson, who requires our attention, is the one who wrote the following letter shortly after the acquittal of Burr and his fellow conspirators:

> I did wish to see these people get what they deserved; and under the maxim of the law itself, that *inter arma silent leges*, that in an encampment expecting daily attack from a powerful enemy, self-preservation is paramount to all law, I expected that instead of invoking the forms of the law to cover traitors, all good citizens would have concurred in securing them. Should we have ever gained our Revolution, if we had bound our hands by manacles of the law, not only in the beginning, but in any part of the revolutionary conflict? There are extreme cases where the laws become inadequate even to their own preservation, and where the universal resources is a dictator, or martial law.

The unfamiliar Jefferson at one time or another supported loyalty oaths; countenanced internment camps for political suspects; drafted a bill of attainder; urged prosecutions for seditious libel; trampled on the Fourth Amendment's protection against unreasonable searches and seizures; condoned military despotism; used the army to enforce laws in time of peace; censored reading; chose professors for their political opinions; and endorsed the doctrine that the means, however odious, were justified by the ends.

The conventional image of Jefferson has been partially fashioned from a national impulse to have a libertarian hero larger than life. When the American people honor Jefferson as freedom's foremost exponent, they reflect their own ideals and aspirations more, perhaps, than they reflect history. The darker side of both Jefferson and of the American experience is not venerated, but its existence is undeniable. American history yields more than one tradition. Abridgements of civil liberty are as old a story as the nation itself; Jefferson embodied and reflected both traditions.

From the standpoint of civil liberties Jefferson's conduct during the revolutionary war conformed with the maxim that the laws are silent in time of war. The benefits of another maxim, more congenial to the spirit of liberty, let justice be done though the heavens fall, were denied to citizens suspected of Tory thoughts and sympathies. The imperatives of victory and political survival superseded the moral and legal values that normally claimed the respect of humane, libertarian leaders. Jefferson, like the others, believed that there could be no toleration for serious differences of opinion on the issue of independence, no acceptable alternative to complete submission to the patriot cause. Everywhere there was unlimited liberty to praise it, none to criticize it. Jefferson, as a member of Congress, a leader of the Virginia legislature, and a wartime governor, declared himself to be an enemy to traitorous views. He and John Adams drafted the first American Articles of War, punishing "traitorous or disrespectful words" against the United States. In 1806 President Jefferson signed into law the bill that altered this provision by punishing any "contemptuous or disrespectful words" against the President or Congress. This clause, adopted in time of peace and under a Constitution protecting freedom of speech—and passed after the Sedition Act of 1798 which it resembled—showed a Jeffersonian insensitivity to the First Amendment.

During the Revolution, Virginia's civilian counterpart of the military code against traitorous opinions consisted of a vicious loyalty oath and an act against crimes injurious to independence but less than treason. Jefferson supported both and had a hand in writing the loose prohibition against any "word" or attempt to "persuade" in behalf of British authority. This act passed the abyss between defensible war measures such as the punishment of incitement to seditious conduct, and the repression of opinion such as punishment of a toast to the king's health. The same statute, which was broadened when Jefferson was Governor, was used as a dragnet against persons suspected of treason or disaffection but against whom proof was lacking.

The loyalty oath, which in Jefferson's phrase was aimed at "traitors in thought, but not in deed," stripped non-jurors of their civil rights. They could not vote, sue, or sell property; Jefferson himself wrote the amendment subjecting them to triple taxation. He also helped write the act retroactively legalizing the internment of political suspects in time of danger, and when Governor he supported a similar bill authorizing him to jail or intern in places of security persons suspected of political disaffection. Many who were jailed languished without a hearing and without even learning of the charges against them.

The most striking departure from standards of due process of law was undoubtedly the Bill of Attainder and Outlawry, drafted by Jefferson in 1778, against the Tory officer Josiah Philips and unnamed members of his gang of reputed traitors and murderers. An attainder is a legislative declaration of guilt and punishment, devoid of judicial and procedural safeguards. Outlawry, which had been in bad odor since Magna Carta, was controlled in England by an elaborate common-law process; Jefferson's bill declared an open hunting season on Philips and the unnamed men whose guilt was legislatively assumed. Anyone might be killed with impunity on the mere supposition that he was an associate of Philips. Although Edmund Randolph and others connected with the attainder-and-outlawry subsequently regretted it and expressed their horror at what had been done, Jefferson continued long after to defend his attainder and to insist that an outlaw had no right to the privileges of citizenship or to ordinary legal process. He also sought to exclude from an historical account of the case opinions to the contrary. In 1815, when musing on the bill of 1778, he wrote: "I was then thoroughly persuaded of the correctness of the proceeding, and am more and more convinced by reflection. If I am in error, it is an error of principle." The libertarian standard was the one proposed by Jefferson himself in 1783 when he prepared a new draft constitution for Virginia, explicitly denying to the legislature any power "to pass any bill of attainder (or other law declaring any person guilty) of treason or felony."

Jefferson's reputation as a libertarian derived in part from his habitual repetition of inspired reveries about freedom, expressed in memorable aphorisms. On countless occasions, for example, he testified to his belief in liberty of the press; his maxims on the subject earned him a place with Milton and Mill. However, there were significant inconsistencies between his deeds and his words. In the long run his pen was mightier than his practice, for his rhetoric helped to create an American creed and to shape the standards by which even he must be measured. There was, for example, that imperishable remark in his first Inaugural Address in which he said, "If there be any among us who would wish to dissolve this Union or to change its republican form, let them stand undisturbed as monuments of the safety with which error of opinion may be tolerated where reason is left free to combat it." Yet his views on the scope of permissible freedom of political expression were very narrow and did not change even after Madison, Gallatin, and others in his camp had developed a very broad theory of free speech and press.

In 1776 Jefferson proposed a constitution for Virginia without a clause on either speech or press. He also, incidentally, omitted guarantees against exclusive privileges, excessive bail, general search warrants, compulsory self-incrimination, and most of the positive rights of the criminally accused which the Virginia Declaration of Rights included. The restrictiveness of his thinking on political expression is suggested by a trial clause on religious liberty: "This [the liberty of religious opinions] shall not be held to justify any seditious preaching or conversation against the authority of the civil government." He was groping for a formula to ensure the unfettered right to propagate religious opinions without relinquishing the power of the state to curb dangerous political opinions. He finally settled on the "overt acts" test for religious opinions, but, significantly, he never applied that test to political opinions and never questioned the conventional doctrine that the government can be criminally assaulted by seditious words. In a draft constitution for Virginia in 1783 and again in a letter to Madison in 1788, he proposed that the presses be subject to prosecution for falsity, especially for false facts affecting the peace of the country. This was a particularly dangerous standard or test, because in political matters, one man's falsity is another's truth. Had Jefferson's test prevailed and been taken seriously, its suppressive possibilities can well be imagined in the midst of a foreign policy controversy like the ones provoked by Jay's treaty, or the Louisiana Purchase, or the Embargo. Noteworthy too is the fact that Jefferson did not propose that in trials for seditious libel the jury, rather than the judge, should be empowered to return a verdict on the alleged criminality of the defendant's words.

Jefferson's celebrated opposition to the Sedition Act of 1798, which he did not publicly attack, was primarily based on a states' rights doctrine. His concept of federalism, rather than a theory of free speech, dominated his thinking. Far from assaulting the concept of seditious libel, he contended that the Sedition Act was unconstitutional because the First Amendment intended that the states alone might wield the power of abridging the freedom of the press. On half a dozen instances when he was President, in both his correspondence and public statements, he continued to endorse the exclusive power of the states to prosecute criminal libels against the government. On one occasion he urged a specific state prosecution and hoped that it would be emulated in other states. On another occasion, which his Federalist enemies exaggerated as Jefferson's "reign of terror," he permitted common-law prosecutions of his critics in a federal court during his Presidency.

Jefferson was a thin-skinned, fierce political partisan. He once remarked that whether his neighbor said that there were twenty gods or none "neither picks my pocket nor breaks my leg." But political opinions could pick his pocket or break his leg. His threshold of tolerance for hateful political ideas was less than generous. Eloquently and felicitously he declared himself in favor of freedom of speech and press, but invariably either in favor of the liberty of his own political allies or merely in abstract propositions. Under concrete circumstances he found it easy to make exceptions when the freedom of his opponents was at stake. To Madison the test of free speech or press was whether a man could with impunity express himself openly even in times of stress and on matters that counted deeply. Freedom for the other fellow was the test, not freedom for the friendly opponent, but for the one with the detested, scurrilous, and outrageous views who challenged on fundamentals and whose criticism cut to the bone. Jefferson simply did not concern himself about such freedom. He cared deeply for the intellectual liberty of religious, scientific, or philosophical heretics but not for the freedom of political heretics—unless political heresies of his own adherence were involved.

During the Burr case he betrayed an insensibility to standards of criminal justice and behaved as if he were prosecutor, judge, and jury. He wanted convictions on the treason charge and was not particularly scrupulous as to how he got them. After Burr had been freed by a federal grand jury in the West, the President mobilized public opinion against him by declaring him to be guilty beyond question, although there were at the time nothing but rumors and suspicions on which to base a judgement—and in any case it was the business of a jury, not of the President, to declare Burr guilty. To secure a conviction, Jefferson accepted the word of a real traitor, General Wilkinson, and praised him as a loyal and honorable patriot. Jefferson found it necessary also to betray a witness by violating a pledge not to reveal or use against him his self-incriminatory statements. The President was also prepared to sign a bill that would have suspended the writ of habeas corpus in order to keep in military custody Wilkinson's illegally held prisoners. Jefferson assaulted the integrity and loyalty of the federal courts which ensured due process in Burr's case, and he accused them of protecting traitors. He supported a constitutional amendment that would have made the judges removable from office by vote of Congress. He favored committing a prisoner to trial on probable suspicion rather than on prima facie evidence of guilt. He yearned for a packed jury in Burr's case. He flirted with doctrines of constructive treason when citing as proof of Burr's guilt the "universal belief" of his guilt, the "rumors" of his guilt, newspaper stories, and Burr's flight from arrest. Yet Jefferson admitted that he did not know what overt acts of treason would be proved by the government three months after he had publicly declared Burr guilty and three weeks after the indictment. He suspected critics of the government's case as being associates in Burr's treason.

Jefferson also condoned Wilkinson's despotic acts in new Orleans. The General defied both the civil authorities and judicial writs of habeas corpus; he arrested men without warrants—including a judge and an editor; he transported his prisoners in chains out of the territory, denying them trial by jury of the vicinage. He rifled the mails in an illegal search for evidence, generally terrified the city, and subordinated the civil to the military, acting as if he were ruling by martial law—and to all this Jefferson applauded and merely cautioned Wilkinson against arresting on suspicion only for fear that he might lose public support. The President judged his general not by legal or moral standards, but by the extent to which his actions might be supported by public opinion. An officer must risk going beyond the law when the public preservation requires, wrote Jefferson. He informed Governor Claiborne that the political opposition "will try to make something of the infringement of liberty by the military arrest and deportation of citizens, but if it does not go beyond such offenders as Swartwout, Bollman, Burr, Blennerhassett, etc., they will be supported by public approbation." As in the Philips attainder case, Jefferson's position was that bad men do not deserve the benefit of the usual forms of the law. His position was reprehensible on both constitutional and libertarian grounds. His final view on

Wilkinson's actions—that there were only two opinions: one held by "the guilty" and the other "by all honest men"—betrayed an impulse to stamp all opposition and criticism as illegitimate.

That same impulse, so dangerous to democratic procedure, was revealed abundantly during the Embargo era, when a national policy of passive resistance was enforced at home by bayonets. Jefferson can not be faulted for the Embargo itself as an experiment in the avoidance of war, but for the manner of its adoption, its execution, and its abridgements of public and private liberty, as well as its failure, he bears the greatest responsibility. The failure was the failure of responsible democratic leadership. The task of the President was to enlist bipartisan support by educating the nation on the need for complying with laws that required a free people to suffer loss of some liberty and acute economic privation for the sake of a national goal. But Jefferson never explained, never gave the facts, and never sought understanding, and he treated Congress as he did the nation, expecting blind, dutiful obedience. His sphinx-like silence during fifteen months of agonizing national trial contributed to the subversion of principles of self-government.

The first four Embargo acts—the last of which was a severe force act—were rammed through Congress almost without debate. Jefferson showed no concern whatever about constitutional questions, not even in regard to the force act which carried the administration to the precipice of unlimited and arbitrary powers as measured by any known American standards. There was an unprecedented concentration of powers in the executive: he could detain vessels on his authority, employ the navy for enforcement purposes, and search and seize on mere suspicion without warrant in disregard of the Fourth Amendment. The President was unable, however, to get from Congress the power that he wanted: to search and seize without court process any goods, any time, any place, and this would have been a power far more despotic than the writs of assistance which the patriot party condemned in the years before the Revolution.

As civil disobedience spread Jefferson was increasingly tempted to more severe measures to force compliance. The Embargo, begun as a means of coercing European powers into respect for American rights, became an instrument of coercion against American citizens, abridging their rights. Gallatin, in the summer of 1808, apprised Jefferson that the Embargo was failing and probably could not be enforced under any circumstances, but that if the attempt were made, "arbitrary powers" that were "equally dangerous and odious" would have to be employed, including enforcement by the regular army. Jefferson, who two months later expressed the opinion that in extreme cases "the universal resource is a dictator, or martial law," replied decisively: "Congress," he instructed, "must legalize all means which may be necessary to obtain its end." The standing peacetime army, formerly the *bête noire* of republicanism, had already been tripled; now it was used (on a prolonged and systematic basis) to enforce the Embargo at home, without lawful authority in numerous instances. In accord with the dangerous theory that the ends justify the means, Jefferson also permitted his Attorney-General to experiment with a treason prosecution as another means of enforcement, and he deliberately and lawlessly ordered his collectors of the customs to ignore a federal court ruling that he had exercised his detention power illegally. However, he resisted his temptation to adopt the guilt-by-association principle by attaining and blockading entire towns because some of their citizens showed "a general spirit of resistance." Still, he recommended a new and terrible enforcement measure, the Fifth Embargo Act.

In the detention case, it was Justice William Johnson, a Republican of Jefferson's own choosing, who declared that even the President was subject to legal restraints and should not attempt an unsanctioned encroachment upon individual liberty. Jefferson, defying Johnson's ruling, issued orders that it be ignored—a subversion of the concept of the independent judiciary which Jefferson had once valued as a bulwark of liberty against zealous rulers. In the treason case, growing out of a violation of the Embargo, Justice Brockholst Livingston, another Republican appointee of the President, thwarted him by delivering a scorching attack on the theory of the prosecution. Pointing out that the crime at hand was merely a riot and trespass, Livingston declared that the court would not permit the establishment of so dangerous a precedent that would destroy the constitutional protection against constructive treason.

The Fifth Embargo Act, which like its predecessors was framed by Jefferson and Gallatin, disclosed an ugly spirit. It contained unbelievable violations of many provisions of the Bill of Rights, including the right to be free from compulsory self-incrimination, from unreasonable searches and seizures, and from unfair trial. The statute also authorized the regular army, at the President's discretion and without procedural safeguards, to enforce the Embargo laws. The Federalists were not so wrong in denouncing the act as a step toward military despotism.

In retirement, during his declining years, the fires of Jefferson's faith in his fellow men flickered as if dampened by the ashes of disillusion. Although he still claimed that men would choose wisely if given the facts, his doubts revealed themselves even in the area of intellectual liberty and academic freedom. Afflicted with that occupational vanity of intellectuals, the notion that reading can profoundly influence a man's ideas, he began to worry about dangerous books. Although he wanted citizens to think freely, he wanted them to think Republican thoughts. Blackstone and Hume, he believed, stood in the way, particularly Hume, whose widely read *History of England* was filled with pernicious political heresies. Reading Hume, Jefferson thought, made Americans Tories. For years, therefore, he tried to secure publication of a "republicanised" version of Hume edited by an English radical, John Baxter. What attracted Jefferson to Baxter's edition was its intellectual deception. Baxter had hit upon the "only remedy" for reading Hume: he "gives you the text of Hume, purely and verbally, till he comes to some misrepresentation or omission . . . then he alters the text silently, makes it what truth and candor say it should be, and resumes the original text again, as soon as it becomes innocent, without having warned you of your rescue from misguidance." For years Jefferson tried to switch American readers from Hume to Baxter, apparently in the belief that truth could not best error in a fair encounter. Eager to influence young minds, future political leaders, Jefferson did not want them exposed to wrong opinions.

His career as a censor continued as founder and rector of the University of Virginia. By that time Jefferson had become a narrow localist, a strict construc-tionist, a southern advocate. "In the selection of our law professor," he wrote, "we must be rigorously attentive to his political principles." Denouncing northern principles of "consolidation," he proclaimed it a duty to "guard against such principles being disseminated among our youth, and the diffusion of that poison, by a previous prescription of texts to be followed in their discourses." The law school, which taught the principles of government, became a training ground for the propagation of the Virginia creed of 1798.

That creed made room for human slavery. It was originally a states' rights creed whose purpose was to defend freedom; it remained a states' rights creed but its purpose changed to a defense of slavery. Yet Jefferson abhorred slavery with the same passion that he reserved for any form of tyranny. Anyone

> nursed, educated, and daily exercised in tyranny [he said of the slave system] cannot but be stamped by it with odious peculiarities. . . . And with what execration should the statesman be loaded, who permitting one half the citizens thus to trample on the rights of the other, transforms those into despots, and these into enemies, destroys the morals of the one part, and the amor patriae of the other.

Jefferson himself was nursed, educated, and daily exercised in tyranny. The system made him a despot—a benevolent one, to be sure, but a despot nevertheless, and it corrupted his political morals. He loathed slavery. It filled him with a sense of shame, guilt, and sin: "this evil thing," he called it. Above all it filled him with a sense of despair; he felt helpless to bring about its end. Yet he did little to try, however much he believed in emancipation.

To describe him as one of the foremost racists of his time, as several historians have in recent years, or to say, as Winthrop Jordan has, that his derogation of the Negro "constituted, for all its qualifications, the most intense, extensive, and extreme formulation of anti-Negro 'thought' offered by any American in the thirty years after the Revolution," is unbelievably present-minded, ununderstanding, misleading, and inaccurate. If Jefferson was a racist, as was every other white man in the South, and perhaps in the North too, he could be no other. He was born white in eighteenth-century Virginia. He was a plantation aristocrat, the master of 10,000 acres, and when he wrote that all men are created equal, he owned 180 slaves (the number had increased to over 260 by the time of his death). He depended upon his slaves for his livelihood and his elegant style of life. The slave system conditioned him. He knew that blacks were human beings and were entitled to the same God-given inalienable rights as whites, yet he could write that he used potatoes and clover "to feed every animal on the farm except my negroes. . . ." But he could also write to the black scientist, Benjamin Banneker, "Nobody wishes more than I to see such proofs as you exhibit, that nature has given to our black brethren, talents equal to those of the other colors of men, and that the appearance of a want of them is owing merely to the degraded condition of their existence, both in Africa and America." If Jefferson was a racist in his own time, a South Carolina Senator would not have condemned him for "fraternizing with negroes, writing them complimentary epistles, stiling them his black brethren, congratulating them on the evidence of their genius, and assuring them of his good wishes for the speedy emancipation."

The description of Jefferson as a racist depends mainly upon his discussion of slavery and blacks in his *Notes on the State of Virginia* (1787). His views never changed throughout his life. Significantly he began his discussion with a reference to his bill to emancipate all slaves born after its adoption. It did not pass, like similar measures that he recommended. His plan was to free the slaves and to colonize them out of the country, for he did not believe that the two races could live together in peace and equality. "Deep rooted prejudices entertained by the whites," the bitter memories of the blacks, and racial differences would, he believed, result in race wars. He also suspected that blacks were not the equals of whites, especially not intellectually. The remarkable fact is that he only suspected it to be so; he did not hold it as a fixed conviction. It was a "conjecture," an opinion "hazarded with great diffidence," "a suspicion only." His plan to remove the emancipated slaves "beyond the reach of mixture" reflected the white supremacist views of his time. By contrast Jefferson believed that an "amalgamation" between Indians and whites would be beneficial to both races.

Although his opinion on blacks was on balance uncomplimentary, he was in the forefront of Virginia's anti-slavery sentiment. It remained little more than sentiment. After 1784 Jefferson no longer spoke out publicly against slavery. Thereafter he reserved for his private correspondence his denunciation of slavery and his various plans of emancipation and expatriation. Still, no other prominent Virginian did more than he to abolish slavery, and, paradoxically, no other did more than he to confine it and to extend it. He sought to exclude slavery from the West by his abortive Ordinance of 1784, yet when he was President, he did nothing to exclude it from the vast reaches of the Louisiana Purchase and he agreed to its protection there where it already existed. By the time of the Missouri Compromise he had become a bitter and frantic southern apologist. After Congress outlawed slavery in the northern half of the Louisiana territories, Jefferson wrote despairingly that he was about to die in the belief that the sacrifices made by "the generation of 1776" were to be wasted.

His record on the greatest of all civil libertarian issues, the abolition of slavery and equality for blacks, was thus mixed. It too had its darker side. But on one related issue of almost equal importance he did as much or more than any man of his time to make this a free nation. He condemned the importation of slaves from Africa even before the American Revolution, and he consistently urged the end of the foreign slave trade. Virginia, in 1778, enacted his bill to close that trade. The Constitution of the United States permitted a continuance of it until 1808, authorizing Congress thereafter to abolish it, but not making it mandatory to do so. Jefferson was President when that critical year approached. He asked Congress "to withdraw the citizens of the United States from all further paticipation in those violations of human rights which have been so long continued on the unoffending inhabitants of Africa, and which morality, the reputation, and the best interests of our country, have long been eager to proscribe." Congress responded as the President wished. As a result, tens of thousands, perhaps hundreds of thousands of blacks were saved from slavery. Moreover, by keeping so many from bondage, a scarcity in numbers increased the value of those enslaved in America, thereby preventing their masters from working them to death as if they were cheap, expendable beasts of burden. The practical results of ending the slave trade more than compensated for any belief on Jefferson's part in the inferiority of blacks.

Still, the evidence taken as a whole discloses an anti-libertarian pattern in Jefferson's thought and action extending throughout his long career. How are we to understand it?

A few years after Jefferson's death, John Quincy Adams, upon reading Jefferson's *Autobiography*, yielded to his censorious and cantankerous nature. Jefferson, confided Adams to his diary, told nothing that was not creditable to him, as if he had always been right. Yet he had a "pliability of principle," a "treacherous" memory, a "double dealing character," and was so filled with "deep duplicity" and "insincerity" that in deceiving others, "he seems to have begun by deceiving himself." The curious thing about this massive indictment, which was founded on just enough shreds of truth not to be utterly ridiculous, was that Adams spiced it with a dash of credit and a pinch of praise. Even from his jaundiced view, Jefferson was a great patriot with an "ardent passion for liberty and the rights of man." Thus the image of Jefferson as the apostle of freedom had formed even in his own time.

Unlike the Liberty Bell, that image never tarnished or cracked in any serious way. After all, nations live by symbols and have a need for vital illusions. Thomas Jefferson was by no means ill-suited for the symbolic role in which he has been cast by American history. It was a role that he had cast for himself when he left instructions for the epitaph bearing testimony to the three achievements by which he wished "most to be remembered:"

> Here was buried
> Thomas Jefferson
> Author of the Declaration of American Independence
> of the Statute of Virginia for Religious Freedom
> & Father of the University of Virginia

The words chosen for inscription on the Jefferson Memorial: "I have sworn upon the altar of God, eternal hostility against every form of tyranny over the mind of man," reflect his enduring spirit and will speak to mankind as long as liberty is cherished on earth. At the dedication of the shrine built by a grateful nation, President Franklin Roosevelt in 1943 quite naturally discoursed on

"Thomas Jefferson, Apostle of Freedom." "We judge him," declared Roosevelt, "by the application of his philosophy to the circumstances of his life. But in such applying we come to understand that his life was given for those deeper values that persist throughout all time." The sentiment was a noble one, poetically true. But it was not the whole historical truth.

When judged by his application of "his philosophy to the circumstances of his life," a fair enough test, the saintly vapors that veil the real Jefferson clear away. He himself hated hagiolatry. Posterity, about which he cared so much, had a greater need for a realistic understanding of their heritage than for historical fictions paraded as "images." Jefferson was not larger than life; he was human and held great power. His mistaken judgments were many, his failings plentiful. Much of Jefferson that passed for wisdom has passed out of date. He was, to be sure, a libertarian, and American civil liberties were deeply in his debt. But he was scarcely the constantly faithful libertarian and rarely, if ever, the courageous one.

The finest moments of American liberty occurred when men defied popular prejudices and defended right and justice at the risk of destroying their own careers. Thus John Adams, at a peak of passionate opposition to the British, defended the hated redcoats against a charge of murder growing out of the Boston Massacre. By contrast Thomas Jefferson never once risked career or reputation to champion free speech, fair trial, or any other libertarian value. On many occasions he was on the wrong side. On others he trimmed his sails and remained silent.

As Secretary of State Jefferson signed the proclamation against the Whiskey Rebels; as Vice President and presiding officer of the Senate, he signed the warrant of arrest for the journalist William Duane for a seditious contempt of that august body. Jefferson chose the easy path of lawful performance of his duties instead of conscientious opposition on the ground that liberty and justice were being victimized. In neither case did he speak out *publicly*. He signed in silence and characteristically complained in his private correspondence about the government's abridgements of freedom. His opposition to the Alien and Sedition Acts is famous: what is not so well known is that he never publicly declared his opposition during the period of hysteria. He kept his participation in the Kentucky Resolutions of 1798–9 a secret. In the winter of liberty's danger there was the greatest need for the heated and undisguised voice of dissent to be heard in the land.

Any depiction of Jefferson as the nearly faultless civil libertarian, the oracle of freedom's encyclicals and model of its virtues, should provoke a critical reader who is reasonably aware of human frailties—from which political figures are not notably exempt—to react with skepticism. Jefferson was no demigod. That he was a party to many abridgements of personal and public liberty should neither shock nor surprise. It would have been surprising had he not on occasion during his long career taken his hatchet in hand and cut down a few libertarian cherry trees. He said himself that he had been bent like a long bow by irresistible circumstances, his public life being a war against his natural feelings and desires.

The compulsions of politics, the exigencies of office, and the responsibilities of leadership sometimes conspired to anesthetize his sensitivity to libertarian values. Nor did his own drives have an opposite effect. He yearned for the contemplative intellectual life but he could not resist the temptations of power. He had as great a need for the means of carrying out policies in the national interest, as he understood it, as he did for the quiet life of scholarship.

He was capable of ruthlessness in the exercise of power. As President he behaved as if compensating for his notorious weakness as wartime Governor of Virginia, when constitutional scruples and an inclination to shrink from the harsher aspects of politics had made him incapable of bold leadership. Thereafter he acted as if he had disciplined himself to serve in office with energy and decisiveness, at whatever cost. A hard resolution to lead and triumph certainly characterized his Presidency.

Often the master politician, he was not averse to the most devious and harsh tactics to achieve his ends. Usually gentle and amiable in his personal relationships, he possessed a streak of wilfulness that sometimes expressed itself in flaring temper, violence, and toughness. His grandson portrayed him as a "bold and fearless" horseman who loved to ride booted, with whip in hand. "The only impatience of temper he ever exhibited," recalled Thomas Jefferson Randolph, "was with his horse, which he subdued to his will by a fearless application of the whip, on the slightest manifestation of restiveness." He rode the nation in the same way, booted and spurred during the Embargo days, notwithstanding the fact that one of his most memorable utterances announced his belief that mankind had not been born with saddles on their backs to be ridden booted and spurred by those in power over them.

It is revealing that Jefferson arrogated to himself the power to decide personally how much bread, and with what degree of whiteness, the American people could eat during the Embargo. He regulated the nation down to its table fare, despite an aversion to centralized government and a dedication to the belief that domestic concerns were a matter of personal or local government. The eye of President Jefferson was so prying, his enemies bitterly joked, that a baby couldn't be born without clearance from a government customs house.

Practices once reprehended by Jefferson as shocking betrayals of natural and constitutional rights suddenly seemed innocent, even necessary and salutary, when the government was in his hands. His accession to power seemed to stimulate a fresh understanding of the existence of public dangers requiring forceful measures that often did not result in a union of principle and practice. When, for example, the party faithful were victims of the Sedition Act, unchecked tyranny was abroad in the land with frightening consequences for the future of liberty. When he was in power the uncontrolled licentiousness and malice of the opposition press took on the hideous features of sedition, deserving of a few exemplary prosecutions to protect the public. Jefferson's Presidency, particularly the second term which witnessed the federal sedition prosecutions in Connecticut, the Wilkinson–Burr imbroglio and trials, and the five Embargo acts, was an obligato on the arts of political manipulation and severity.

Some of his anti-libertarianism can be explained by the ironic fact that he was, in the words of a clear-eyed admirer, a "terrifying idealist, tinged with fanaticism." What other sort of man would impersonally applaud a little bloodletting now and then to fertilize the tree of liberty? Jefferson held his convictions with a fierceness that admitted little room for compromise—if he was in a position of power to deny it—and no room for self-doubt. Unduly sensitive to criticism by others, he wore a hair shirt—often a dangerous attire for a politician—which covered a spirit rarely capable of objective disinterestedness.

Jefferson had the mentality and passion of a true believer, certain that he was absolutely right, a marked contrast to the skepticism of modern libertarians such as Justice Oliver Wendell Holmes or Judge Learned Hand. Holmes believed that the first mark of a civilized man was the capacity to doubt his own first principles, while Hand remarked that the spirit of liberty was the spirit which was not too sure that it was right. Jefferson was a product of the eighteenth century which regarded truths as immutable and self-evident. Yet philosophic truths concerning the nature of man or the first principles of government were not on a footing with practical legislation or executive policies. Jefferson had read Locke and the British empiricists as well as the Deists, scientists, and French *philosophes*. He might reasonably have been somewhat more skeptical of the rightness of his own favorite theories that he translated into national policy; he might have been less cocksure, less ready to subscribe to the proposition that certitude was the test of certainty.

In politics, particularly, where the art of the possible is often the highest value, making compromise a necessity, the capacity to doubt one's own convictions is indispensable. The poorest compromise is almost invariably better than the best dictation which leaves little if any scope of freedom to the losing side and corrupts the spirit of those in power. In his old age Jefferson observed wisely:

> A government held together by the bands of reason only, requires much compromise of opinion; that things even salutary should not be crammed down the throats of dissenting brethren, especially when they may be put into a form to be willingly swallowed, and that a good deal of indulgence is necessary to strengthen habits of harmony and fraternity.

The observation was not an abstract one. Jefferson was arguing at the time in behalf of a constitutional amendment that would authorize the national government (which by then he was denominating the "foreign" department in contrast to the states that composed the "domestic" department) to build roads and canals. He had an utterly exquisite constitutional conscience when he was not in power.

Jefferson's only constitutional qualms during his Presidency concerned what he believed to be his questionable authority to purchase Louisiana. He never doubted for a moment the rightness of his behavior during the Burr and Embargo episodes. The intensity of his convictions and his incapacity for self-criticism propelled him onward, more resolute than ever in the face of outside criticism. The certainty that he was right, combined with his terrifying idealism, led him to risk the fate of the nation on the chance that an experiment in commercial sanctions might prove a substitute for war. Opposition only goaded him to redouble his efforts to prove himself right. He behaved as if a prisoner of his ideas, or, to put the thought less charitably, as a doctrinaire "tinged with fanaticism."

The self-skeptic, the practical politician, and the democrat conduct themselves otherwise. Any one of them in a position of power tends to operate with an understanding of the necessity of compromise and the obnoxiousness, not to mention the immorality or political stupidity, of cramming legislation "down the throats of dissenting brethren." Legislation, as William James once observed about democracy generally, is a business in which something is done, followed by a pause to see who hollers; then the hollering is relieved as best it can be until someone else hollers. Jefferson, however, was faintly doctrinaire. Exhilarated by the experience of putting an idea in motion and backing it by force, he could not back down or admit that he had been wrong. What counted most was the attainment of his objective, the validation of his conviction, not its impact on those who, failing to appreciate his idealism or personal stake, hollered long and loud. He reacted not by relieving their hollering but by a stretch of the rack that increased their protests and his own power to override them.

Jefferson tended to stretch his political powers as he stretched his mind in intellectual matters, leaving his conscience behind—and something his good sense. His voluminous correspondence showed no hint that he suffered from uncertainty or was tormented by his conscience when he so readily used the army to enforce the Embargo and recklessly disregarded the injunctions of the Fourth Amendment. Lincoln, in the greatest of all crises in American history, had a supreme moral objective as well as a political one to sustain him; but he was constantly racked by self-doubt. The exercise of power, not always constitutionally justifiably, exacted of him a price that included melancholy and an agonized soul. In moments of despair he could doubt that Providence was with him and even that his position was indeed the morally superior one.

The contrast with Jefferson was towering. Thwarted by the courts in Burr's case, Jefferson doubted not himself but the loyalty of the judges. Evasions of the Embargo filled him with astonishment not that his policy could have such a result but that the people could be so rankly fraudulent and corrupt. Rumors of resistance were matched by his impulse to crush it by force. There was no inner struggle in Jefferson; the tragedy of his anti-libertarianism lacked poignancy. He was oblivious of the tragedy itself, symbolized by that moment of enormity when he approved of the use of any means, even if odious and arbitrary, to achieve his end.

Vanity, the enemy of self-doubt, also played its role in fashioning his darker side. His *amour-propre* prevented him from checking an illiberal act once begun or from admitting his error after the event. Witness his conduct of the Burr prosecutions and the way in which he was driven to defend Wilkinson. His persistent defense of his role in the case of Josiah Philips bears testimony to the same trait. When caught in a flagrancy, as when it was revealed that he had hired the journalistic prostitute Callendar to poison the reputations of political opponents, or when he was accused of permitting sedition prosecutions in a federal court, he denied the truth. In deceiving others, as John Quincy Adams said, he deceived himself. In deceiving himself he denied himself insight into his abridgements of liberty, though he was acutely perceptive of abridgements by others.

Perhaps the chief explanation of his darker side was his conviction that the great American experiment in self-government and liberty was in nearly constant danger. He completely identified with that experiment, to the point that an attack on him or on the wisdom of his policies quickly became transmuted in his mind as a threat to the security of the tender democratic plant.

During the Revolution, coercive loyalty oaths and proscription of Tory opinions seemed a cheap price to pay when independence was the goal and the outcome was in doubt. The Alien and Sedition Acts, following the enactment of Hamilton's economic policies, forever convinced Jefferson that his political opponents were unalterably committed to the destruction of public liberty in America. In the flush of victory, at that splendid moment of the First Inaugural, he admitted the Federalists into the camp of loyal Americans, but not for long. If the scurrilousness of the Federalist press did not convince him that his magnanimous judgment had been mistaken, opposition to the purchase of Louisiana, coupled to threats of secession, proved his belief that popular government in America was imperiled. Burr's conspiracy brought the ugly menace to a head, justifying drastic countermeasures.

Open defiance of the Embargo once again threw the Union's future into grave doubt. That defiance seemed to sabotage majority rule and the only hope of avoiding a war that might end the democratic experiment. In time of such acute crisis, when insurrection existed on a widespread basis and treason itself again loomed, the methods of Dracon were tempting. The behavior of the Essex Junto during the War of 1812 reconfirmed Jefferson's worst fears. In the postwar period, from his hilltop at Monticello, he imagined that a monarchistic, clerical cabal had re-formed under a new party guise, employing doctrines of nationalistic consolidation to destroy public liberty.

Over the years he constantly sensed a conspiracy against republicanism. He had a feeling of being besieged by the enemies of freedom who would use it to subvert it. The face of the enemy changed: now that of a Tory; later that of a monarchist, a political priest, an Essex Juntoman, a Quid, or a Burrite; still later that of a judicial sapper-and-miner, an American-system consolidationist, or a Richmond lawyer. The face of the enemy or his name might change, but not his Tory principles nor his subversive goal.

To the experiment of democracy in America, as Jefferson called it, he was committed heart, mind, and soul. Believing that experiment to be in grave jeopardy throughout most of his public life, he was capable of ruthlessness in defeating its enemies. His own goal was free men in a free society, but he did not always use freedom's instruments to attain it. He sometimes confused the goal with self-vindication or the triumph of his party. On other occasions instability and a lack of faith were revealed by his doubts of the opposition's loyalty. They were prone, he believed, to betray the principles of the Revolution as expressed in the Declaration of Independence. On still other occasions his eagerness to make America safe for democracy made him forgetful of Franklin's wise aphorism that they who seek safety at the expense of liberty deserve neither liberty nor safety.

The terrible complexities of any major issue, such as Burr's conspiracy or the Embargo, particularly as seen from the White House, also help to explain Jefferson's conduct. The strain and responsibilities of the highest office did not stimulate the taking of bold risks on the side of liberty when it seemed to be pitted against national security. Moreover, problems had a way of presenting themselves in a form that mixed conflicting political considerations and obscured clearcut decisions on libertarian merits. To a mind that was keenly alerted against the conspiracies of Federalist bogeymen and sensed a union between self, party, and nation, the virtue of an independent judiciary became the vice of judicial interference with majority rule; fair trial and a strict interpretation of treason became obstacles to the preservation of the Union; academic freedom became a guise for the dissemination of pernicious doctrines.

Jefferson's darker side derived in part, too, from the fact that he had no systematic and consistent philosophy of freedom. He was neither a seminal nor a profound thinker. Part of his genius consisted of his ability to give imperishable expression to old principles and to the deepest yearnings of his fellow citizens. Style, as much as substance, accounted for his staying power. He once defended himself against the accusation that there was not a single fresh idea in the Declaration of Independence by replying that the objective was not to find new principles or arguments never before thought of. It was, rather,

> to place before mankind the common sense of the subject, in terms so plain and firm as to command their assent. . . . Neither aiming at originality of principle or sentiment, nor yet copied from any particular and previous writing, it was intended to be an expression of the American mind, and to give to that expression the proper tone and spirit called for by the occasion. All its authority rests then on the harmonizing sentiments of the day.

As a distinguished admirer has written, "Jefferson's seminal achievement was to institutionalize familiar eighteenth-century ideas. He made abstract notions about freedom a dominating faith and thereby the dynamic element in the strivings of men." Moreover he had the superlative talent of organizing a party that might realize his ideals by infusing the new nation with a sense of its special democratic destiny. But his failure to develop a theory of liberty existed and more than likely influenced his anti-libertarian thought and action.

In the thousands of pages of his published works there is a notable scarcity of extended treatments on a single subject. Insatiably curious, he knew a little about nearly everything under the sun and a great deal more about law and politics than any man of his time. But in all his writings, over a period of fifty years of high productivity, there is not a single sustained analysis of liberty. He was pithy, felicitous, repetitive, and ever absorbed by the subject, but never wrote a book or even a tract on the meaning of liberty, its dimensions, limitations, and history.

That he made no contribution of this kind is not *per se* a criticism, for the brief preambles to the Declaration of Independence and the Virginia Statute of Religious Freedom are worth all the books that have been written on liberty. He had not, however, thought through the tough and perplexing problems posed by liberty: the conditions for its survival and promotion; the types of liberty and conflicts between them; the validity of various legal tests for measuring the scope of liberty or its permissible area of operation; and the competing claims of other values.

Jefferson contented himself with a dedication to the general principle, apparently without realizing that general principles do not satisfactorily decide hard, concrete cases. Only in the area of religious liberty did he have a well-developed philosophy, replete with a usable and rationalized test for application to specific cases. There his contribution was pre-eminent, even if derived from English sources. It is significant, however, that he did not apply the "overt acts" test outside of the realm of the free exercise of religion. It is even more significant that his literary remains show no evidence that he ever tried to work out a usable test for cases of verbal political crimes.

A philosopher of freedom without a philosophy of freedom, Jefferson was ill-equipped, by his ritualistic affirmations of nebulous and transcendental truths, to confront the problem posed by General Wilkinson's conduct in New Orleans, or the circulation of Hume's *History of England* in the colleges, or the savage distortions of the opposition press. He reacted expediently on an *ad hoc* basis and too often hastily. Then his *amour-propre* prevented his candid acknowledgement of a mistaken judgment that demeaned the libertarian values he symbolized to the nation.

Regret and remorse are conspicuously absent from Jefferson's writings, as is reflective reconsideration of a problem. Something in his make-up, more than likely a stupendous ego, inhibited second thoughts. Whether he would deny the plain facts or stubbornly reiterate his original position, he failed to work out fresh guide lines for future conduct. Restatement, not re-evaluation, marked his thinking, and beneath an eloquently turned phrase there lurked a weary, problem-begging cliché. That it was commonplace rarely deprived it of its profundity as a libertarian principle. The "self-evident truths" of the Declaration of Independence will continue to survive all scorn of being "glittering generalities." They tend, however, to overarch real cases.

Jefferson, for example, might declare in his first Inaugural Address that enemies of the Republic should be free to express themselves, but the principle was so broad that it failed to have pertinence for him when he learned that a few "political Priests" and "Federal printers," who have been confident that no federal court would take cognizance of their seditious calumnies, were being criminally prosecuted for their libels against him and his administration. His awareness of the general distinction between preparation and attempt, or between conspiracy to commit treason and overt acts of treason, escaped application in the case of the Burrites, though not in the case of the Whiskey Rebels. A commitment to the large principle of intellectual liberty had no carry-over when the possibility arose that a "Richmond lawyer" might be appointed professor of law at the University of Virginia.

Maxims of liberty—"glittering generalities"—were frail props for a sound, realistic libertarianism. A mind filled with maxims will falter when put to the test of experience. A mind filled with maxims contents itself with the resonant quality of a noble utterance. Such a mind, although libertarian, cannot produce a libertarian analysis such as Madison's *Report* of 1799–1800 on the Alien and Sedition Acts, or Wortman's *Treatise Concerning Political Enquiry.* Jefferson's only tracts and books were *A Summary View of the Rights of British America* which was a protest against British encroachments on colonial freedom at the eve of the Revolution; *Notes on the State of Virginia*, a guidebook and utilitarian history; the *Manual of Parliamentary Practice*; his *Autobiography* and *The Anas*, which comprise his memoirs; *The Life and Morals of Jesus of Nazareth*; and the philological work, *Essay on Anglo-Saxon.* Despite his interest in freedom, its meaning did not interest him as a subject for even an essay.

A plausible but not wholly convincing explanation of Jefferson's darker side may be founded on the argument that he lived at a time when the understanding of civil liberties was quite different from that of our own. Libertarian standards were also quite new and inchoate, making modern yardsticks of judgment anachronistic as well as unfair and ununderstanding. The first bill of rights did not come into existence until 1776; the national Bill of Rights not until 1791. The meanings of their provisions were not always clear; their restraints in that formative era constituted an experiment in government. Deviations, inconsistencies, and even gross abridgements were to be expected when experience provided few guides. It was a time of testing, of groping and growth, of trial and error, out of which issued the improved wisdom of subsequent generations. In any case, counsels of perfection and hindsight come rather cheap when aimed by those not on the firing line or of a later time.

This explanation is certainly a plausible one. Yet it is like the theory that was spoiled by the facts. During the revolutionary war, only Tory voices—and they were not necessarily wrong—could be found in opposition to loyalty tests, bills of attainder, and suppression of "traitorous" speech. Thereafter there were always respectable, instructive voices, even if heard only in dissent, to sound the alarm against abridgements of liberty. Jefferson needed only to hear or read in order to know that a particular measure could be seriously construed as a threat to the Bill of Rights or the undermining of a libertarian value. For every example of his darker side that has been mentioned in this essay, a congressional speech, a popular tract, a letter, a newspaper editorial, a judicial opinion, or, more likely than not, a pronouncement by Jefferson himself can be adduced to show a judgment of his own time placing his action in an anti-libertarian light. By 1800 or thereabouts the standards of his own time did not noticeably differ from those of ours on the kind of civil-liberty questions that he confronted.

Though contributing little to any breakthrough in libertarian thought, except in the important realm of freedom of religion, Jefferson more than any other man was responsible for the public sensitivity to libertarian considerations. If the quality of the new nation was measured by the ideals and aspirations that animated it, Jefferson had erred only slightly in confusing his own reputation with that of the democratic experiment. Notwithstanding the reciprocal scurrilities and suspicions of the opposed parties, or more importantly their conflicting interests, Americans were indeed all Federalists, all Republicans. They were equally attached to the "experiment in freedom" and the "empire of liberty." Anyone who depreciates the national commitment to libertarian values, which were based on an extraordinary legal and political sophistication, deprives himself of an understanding of the times—and of the impact of Thomas Jefferson upon it.

That Jefferson's libertarianism was considerably less than perfect or that his practice flagged behind his faith, does not one whit diminish the achievements by which he is and should be best remembered. That he did not always adhere to his libertarian principles does not erode their enduring rightness. It proves only that Jefferson often set the highest standard of freedom for himself and posterity to be measured against. His legacy was the idea that as an indispensable condition for the development of free men in a free society, the state must be bitted and bridled by a bill of rights which should be construed in the most generous terms, its protections not to be the playthings of momentary majorities or of those in power.

10

History and Judicial History: The Case of the Fifth Amendment

BY NOW WE ALL KNOW the notorious fact: The Supreme Court has flunked history. The justices stand censured for abusing historical evidence in a way that reflects adversely on their intellectual rectitude as well as on their historical competence. They frequently use "law office history," which is a function of advocacy. The Court artfully selects historical facts from one side only, ignoring contrary data, in order to give the appearance of respectability to judgments resting on other grounds. Alfred H. Kelly showed that the Court's historical scholarship is simplistic, manipulative, and devoid of impartiality. He referred to the Court's "historical felony," "mangled constitutional history," and the confusion of the writing of briefs with the writing of history.

Ever since Charles Fairman demolished Justice Black's 1947 opinion in *Adamson v. California* on the question whether the Fourteenth Amendment was intended to incorporate the Bill of Rights, scholars have criticized the Court's use of history. Alexander Bickel negated the Court's reading of the history of the Fourteenth Amendment on the question of racial segregation. I disproved the Court's assertion that the First Amendment was intended to supersede the common law of seditious libel. The Court's use of history in cases on the Fifth Amendment's self-incrimination clause also fits a pattern of historical incompetence and law-office history.

The most historically minded opinion on the Fifth Amendment was Justice Moody's in *Twining v. New Jersey*, decided in 1908. *Twining*, which the Court abandoned in 1964, runs counter to the general trend of decisions favoring a liberal construction of the Fifth Amendment. But the Court's use of history in *Twining* is representative of its historical knowledge. The question was whether the right against self-incrimination was "a fundamental principle of liberty and justice which inheres in the very idea of free government" and therefore ought to be included within the concept of due process of law safeguarded from state abridgment. Relying on its version of history, the Court decided against the right. Justice Moody said that he had resorted to "every historical test by which the meaning of the phrase [of the Fifth Amendment] can be tried." The 1637 trial of Anne Hutchinson proved, he alleged, that the Massachusetts authorities were "not aware of any privilege against self-incrimination or any duty to respect it." Justice Black, in his famous *Adamson* dissent, in effect exclaimed, "Of course not," because the court that tried Anne Hutchinson for heresy, believing that its religious convictions must be forced upon others, could not believe that dissenters had any rights worth respecting. But, incriminating interrogation was routine in 1637 on both sides of the Atlantic in criminal cases. Nevertheless the Hutchinson case could not reveal whether the judges were aware of the right against self-incrimination or of a duty to respect, because she did not claim it. She welcomed incriminating questions as an opportunity to reveal God's word as she saw it; she freely and voluntarily incriminated herself. Justice Moody did not know that in 1637 the same Massachusetts court, when put on the defensive by objections to its procedure and questioning, explained that it did not seek to examine the defendant by compulsory means, by using an incriminating oath, nor seek to "draw matter from him whereupon to proceed against him." The maxim *nemo tenetur seipsum prodere*—no one is bound to accuse himself—was widely known among the Massachusetts Puritans.

Moody said in *Twining* that the right was not in Magna Carta and that the practice of self-incriminatory examinations had continued for more than four centuries after 1215. That was short of the whole truth. As early as 1246, when the church introduced its inquisitorial oath-procedure into England, a procedure that required self-incrimination, Henry III condemned it as "repugnant to the ancient Customs of his Realm" and to "his peoples Liberties." In the fourteenth century Parliament outlawed the church's incriminatory oath-procedure, and when the King's Council emulated that procedure, Parliament protested and reenacted section 29 of Magna Carta. One such reenactment, in 1354, for the first time used the phrase "by due process of law," and seen in its context that great statute condemned incriminating examinations, when conducted outside the common-law courts, as violations of Magna Carta or denials of due process. In *Twining* the Supreme Court failed to recognize that Magna Carta grew in meaning and became the symbol and source of the expanding liberties of the subject. Thus, in 1590 Robert Beale, the clerk of the Privy Council, declared that "by the Statute of Magna Carta and the olde lawes of this realme, this oathe for a man to accuse himself was and is utterlie inhibited." This became the view of other common-lawyers, of Chief Justice Edward Coke, and of Parliament. To allege that Magna Carta did not outlaw compulsory self-incrimination was to rest on its meaning in 1215, not on what it came to mean. The *Twining* Court was wrong too when declaring that the Petition of Right of 1628 did not address itself to the evil of compulsory self-incrimination. It did, in the passage censuring "an oath . . . not warrantable by the laws or statutes of this realm. . . ." That oath, which preceded interrogation, operated to coerce confessions.

The Court in *Twining* also found significance in the fact that compulsory self-incrimination was not condemned by the Stamp Act Congress, the Continental Congress, or the Northwest Ordinance. But the Stamp Act Congress mentioned only trial by jury among the many well-established rights of the criminally accused; failure to enumerate them all proved nothing. The Court failed to note that the Continental Congress did claim that the colonists were "entitled to the common law of England," which had long protected the right against self-incrimination, nor did the Court note, or know, that Congress in 1778, in an investigation of its own, did respect that right when a witness claimed it. The Northwest Ordinance did contain a guarantee of "judicial proceedings according to the course of the common law." Indeed, the Supreme Court itself said in *Twining* that by 1776 courts recognized the right even in the states whose constitutions did not protect it. Justice Moody mentioned six states whose constitutions did provide such protection, but there were eight. What Moody did not recognize was that every state that had a separate bill of rights protected the right against self-incrimination. He noted that only four of the original thirteen states insisted that the right be incorporated in the new United States Constitution, but he failed to note that these were the only states which ratified the Constitution with recommendations for a national bill of rights. Using Moody's yardstick, one could argue that the fundamental concept of due process of law was not fundamental at all because it did not appear in any of the thirteen state constitutions and was recommended by only one state ratifying convention. Moody remarked that the principle that no person could be compelled to be a witness against himself "distinguished the common law from all other systems of jurisprudence." Since the principle was first elevated to constitutional status in America, and since it was safeguarded by every state having a bill of rights, and since it fit the several definitions of due process that Moody offered, there is no explaining the Court's finding that the right came into existence as a mere rule of evidence that was not "an essential part of due process." *Twining* was founded on inaccurate and insufficient data. Contrary to the Court's assertion, the right against self-incrimination did evolve as an essential part of due process and as a fundamental principle of liberty and justice. Thus, Ben Franklin in 1735 called it a natural right ("the common Right of Mankind"), and Baron Geoffrey Gilbert, the foremost English authority on evidence at the time, called it part of the "Law of Nature."

Other cases reveal the justices to be equally inept as historians even when conscripting the past into service for the defense and expansion of the Fifth Amendment. The most historically minded opinion of this kind was Justice Douglas's dissent in *Ullmann v. United States*, decided in 1956. The seven-man majority, speaking through Justice Frankfurter, sustained the constitutionality of Congress's Immunity Act of 1954. That act required that in certain cases involving national security, a federal court might require a witness to testify or produce records that might incriminate him, on condition that his revelations could not be used as evidence against him in any criminal proceeding. Frankfurter's opinion for the majority stressed the importance of history in interpreting the Fifth. History, he said, showed that it should be construed broadly, though he construed it narrowly. Frankfurter observed that, "the privilege against self-incrimination is a specific provision of which it is peculiarly true that 'a page of history is worth a volume of logic.' " But Frankfurter did not provide that page of history. He offered only the brief platitude that the Fifth was aimed against a recurrence of the Inquisition and of the Star Chamber. Though Frankfurter was the most historically minded scholar on the Court, he was apparently unaware of the several colonial precedents in support of his argument that the right cannot be claimed if the legal peril, which is the reason for its existence, ceases.

Douglas's dissent, in which Black joined, is a splendid specimen of law-office history; most of his history was not even relevant to his conclusion that the Immunity Act violated the Fifth Amendment. Douglas's relevant history, which dealt with the concept of infamy, was unsound. He claimed that the act was unconstitutional because it was not broad enough: it did not protect against infamy or public disgrace. In support of this proposition he had to prove that the framers of the Fifth meant it to protect against disclosures resulting in public disgrace. Such evidence as history provided to support his proposition was unknown to Douglas. His evidence was far-fetched, for he based his argument on the fact that protection against infamy is found in the ideas of Beccaria and the *Encyclopedistes* whom Jefferson read. But the Fifth Amendment was exclusively the product of English history and American colonial experience. The influence of Continental theorists was nonexistent. As for Jefferson, he had nothing to do with the making of the Fifth. Indeed, he omitted protections against self-incrimination in the two model constitutions that he proposed for Virginia.

Douglas's other evidence dealt not with the issue in question, immunity, but with the general origins of the Fifth. He referred to the Puritan hatred of the self-incriminatory oath ex officio used by the Star Chamber and its ecclesiastical counterpart, the High Commission. The hatred existed, but there were significant differences between the Star Chamber's use of the oath and the High Commission's. The High Commission required the suspect to take that oath to tell the truth as the first step of the examination, and then interrogated him orally without telling him the charges against him or the identity of his accusers. By contrast, the Star Chamber normally provided a bill of complaint, as specific as common-law indictment, and permitted the accused to have plenty of time to answer the charges in writing and with the advice of counsel; only then did the accused have to take the oath and be orally interrogated. The maxim *nemo tenetur seipsum prodere*, from which the right against self-incrimination derived, did not operate in the High Commission, but the Star Chamber respected the maxim. Accordingly the common lawyers who supported that maxim and assaulted the oath ex officio, did not attack the use of the oath by the Star Chamber. Too often the Star Chamber is identified as the symbol of inquisitional procedure, the opposition to which gave rise to the right against self-incrimination. Thus Justice Black in his *Adamson* dissent spoke loosely of the Star Chamber practice of compelling people to testify against themselves, and the same thought is in Chief Justice Warren's opinion for the Court in the

Miranda case which extended the right against self-incrimination to the police station.

Black in *Adamson*, Douglas in *Ullmann*, and Warren in *Miranda* referred to John Lilburne's Star Chamber trial of 1637 and his refusal to take the oath. As these justices imply, Lilburne was more responsible than any other single individual for the recognition by the common-law courts of the right against self-incrimination, but not because of Lilburne's opposition to the oath in 1637. In that case the Star Chamber had abandoned its normal procedure by demanding the oath first instead of providing the written complaint first; so, Lilburne refused the oath, the first—he said—ever to have done so before the Star Chamber—proof that its procedure in 1637 was exceptional. Justice Douglas should have quoted later statements by Lilburne when tried by common-law courts in the 1640s that even in the absence of the oath and after common-law indictment, Magna Carta and the Petition of Right protected a man from being examined on interrogatories concerning himself—"concerning," which is far broader than "incriminating." At his treason trial in 1649 Lilburne placed the right against self-incrimination squarely in the context of what he called "fair play," "fair trial," "the due process of the law," and "the good old laws of England." Justice Douglas gave to John Lilburne a page of his opinion in *Ullmann*, straining the evidence and never knowing that history provided him with stronger facts with which to construct his one-sided argument.

Douglas's *Ullmann* opinion distorted the evidence concerning an important episode in the colonial history of the right against self-incrimination. He mentioned that Governor Bradford of Plymouth sought the advice of his ministers on the question, "How farr a magistrate may extracte a confession from a delinquente, to acuse himselfe of a capitall crime, seeing *Nemo tenetur prodere seipsum*." Inexplicably, Douglas omitted the Latin phrase that both supported his argument and invalidated the generalization in *Twining*, based on the Anne Hutchinson case, that the right against self-incrimination was then unknown. Three Plymouth ministers, Douglas said, were unanimous in concluding that the oath was illegal, and he quoted as "typical" only the answer of Ralph Patrich that the magistrate might not extract a confession "by any violent means," whether by oath or "punishment." Douglas concealed the answer of Charles Chauncy who said, "But now, if the question be mente of inflicting bodly torments to extract a confession from a mallefactor, I conceive that in matters of highest consequence, such as doe conceirne the saftie or runie magistrates may proceede so farr to bodily torments, as racks and hote-irons to extracte a confession, espetially wher presumptions are strounge; but otherwise by no means."

Chauncy would not force self-incrimination by oath, but he would employ torture to coerce confessions in matters such as sedition or treason and perhaps heresy. Douglas's account omitted Chauncy and omitted the fact that Governor Winthrop, who received the opinions of the elders and magistrates of Massachusetts Bay, New Haven, and Connecticut, as well as of Plymouth, recorded that "most" answered that in a capital case if one witness or "strong presumptions" pointed to the suspect, the judge could examine him "strictly," and "he is bound to answer directly, though to the peril of this life." History is not a judicial strong point, but judges must look at the text as well as at history.

What illumination is available from the face of the Fifth? Its words include more than merely a right against self-incrimination, which is a phrase of modern origin. Yet, the Fifth Amendment is virtually synonymous with the right against self-incrimination. One who "pleads the Fifth" is not insisting on grand jury indictment, freedom from double jeopardy, or just compensation for property taken by the government—all safeguarded in the same amendment. He is saying that he will not reply to an official query because his truthful answer might expose him to criminal jeopardy. He seems to be saying that he has something to hide, making the Fifth appear to be a protection of the guilty; it is, but probably no more so than other rights of the criminally accused. The right against self-incrimination is the most misunderstood, unrespected, and controversial of all constitutional rights.

Its very name is a problem. It is customarily referred to as "the privilege" against self-incrimination, following the usage of lawyers in discussing evidentiary privileges (e.g., the husband–wife privilege, the attorney–client privilege). Popular usage, however, contrasts "privilege" with "rights," and the Fifth Amendment's clause on self-incrimination creates a constitutional right with the same status as other rights. Its "name" is unknown to the Constitution, whose words cover more than merely a right or privilege against self-incrimination: "no person . . . shall be compelled in any criminal case to be a witness against himself." What does the text mean?

The protection of the clause extends only to natural persons, not organizations like corporations or unions. A member of an organization cannot claim its benefits if the inquiry would incriminate the organization but not him personally. He can claim its benefits only for himself, not for others. The text also suggests that a prime purpose of the clause is to protect against government coercion; one may voluntarily answer any incriminating question or confess to any crime—subject to the requirements for waiver of constitutional rights. In some respects the text is broad, because a person can be a witness against himself in ways that do not incriminate him. He can, in a criminal case, injure his civil interests or disgrace himself in the public mind. Thus the Fifth can be construed on its face to protect against disclosures that expose one to either civil liability or infamy. The Fifth can also be construed to apply to an ordinary witness as well as the criminal defendant himself. In Virginia, where the right against self-incrimination first received constitutional status, it appeared in a paragraph relating to the accused only. The Fifth Amendment is not similarly restrictive, unlike the Sixth Amendment which explicitly refers to the accused, protecting him alone. The location of the clause in the Fifth, rather than in the Sixth, and its reference to "no person" makes it applicable to witnesses as well as to the accused.

On the other hand, the clause has a distinctively limiting factor: it is restricted on its face to criminal cases. The phrase "criminal case" seems to exclude civil cases. Some judges have argued that no criminal case exists until a formal charge has been made against the accused. Under such an interpretation the right would have no existence until the accused is put on trial; before that, when he is taken into custody, interrogated by the police, or examined by a grand jury, he would not have the benefit of the right. Nor would he have its benefit in a nonjudicial proceeding such as legislative investigation or an administrative hearing. The Supreme Court has given the impression that the clause, if taken literally, would be so restricted; but the Court refuses to take the clause literally. Thus, in *Counselman v. Hitchcock* (1892), the Court held that the Fifth does protect ordinary witnesses, even in federal grand jury proceedings. Unanimously the Court declared, "It is impossible that the meaning of the constitutional provision can only be that a person shall not be compelled to be a witness against himself in a criminal prosecution against himself." Although the Court did not explain why it was "impossible," the Court was right. Had the framers of the Fifth intended the literal, restrictive meaning, their constitutional provision would have been a meaningless gesture. There was no need to protect the accused at his trial; he was not permitted to give testimony, whether for or against himself, at the time of the framing of the Fifth. Making the criminal defendant competent to be a witness in his own case was a reform of the later nineteenth century, beginning the state courts with Maine in 1864, in the federal courts by an act of Congress in 1878. Illumination from the face of a text that does not mean what it says is necessarily faint.

The American origins of the right derive largely from the inherited English common law system of criminal justice. But the English origins, so much more complex, spill over legal boundaries and reflect the many-sided religious, political, and constitutional issues that racked England during the sixteenth and seventeenth centuries: the struggles between Anglicanism and Puritanism, between Parliament and king, between limited government and arbitrary rule, and between freedom of conscience and suppression of heresy and sedition. Even within the more immediate confines of law, the history of the right against self-incrimination is enmeshed in broad issues: the contests for supremacy between the accusatory and the inquisitional systems of procedure, the common law and the royal prerogative, and the common law and its canon and civil law rivals. Against this broad background the origins of the concept that "no man is bound to accuse himself" (*nemo tenetur seipsum accusare*) must be understood and the concept's legal development traced.

The right against self-incrimination originated as an indirect product of the common law's accusatory system and of its opposition to rival systems which employed inquisitorial procedures. Toward the close of the sixteenth century, just before the concept first appeared in England on a sustained basis, all courts of criminal jurisdiction habitually sought to exact self-incriminatory admissions from persons suspected of or charged with crime. Although defendants in crown cases suffered from this and many other harsh procedures, even in common law courts, the accusatory system afforded a degree of fair play not available under the inquisitional system. Moreover, torture was never sanctioned by the common law, although it was employed as an instrument of royal prerogative until 1641.

By contrast, torture for the purpose of detecting crime and inducing confession was regularly authorized by the Roman codes of the canon and civil law. "Abandon all hope, ye who enter here" well describes the changes of an accused person under inquisitorial procedures characterized by presentment based on mere rumor or suspicion, indefiniteness of accusation, the oath *ex officio*, secrecy, lack of confrontation, coerced confessions, and magistrates acting as accusers and prosecutors as well as "judges." This system of procedure, by which heresy was most efficiently combated, was introduced into England by ecclesiastical courts.

The use of the oath *ex officio* by prerogative courts, particularly by the ecclesiastical Court of High Commission, which Elizabeth I reconstituted, resulted in the defensive claim that "no man is bound to accuse himself." The High Commission, an instrument of the Crown for maintaining religious uniformity under the Anglican establishment, used the canon law inquisitorial process, but made the oath *ex officio*, rather than torture, the crux of its procedure. Men suspected of "heretical opinions," "seditious books," or "conspiracies" were summoned before the High Commission without being informed of the accusation against them or the identity of their accusers. Denied due process of law by common law standards, suspects were required to take an oath to answer truthfully to interrogatories which sought to establish guilt for crimes neither charged nor disclosed.

A nonconformist victim of the High Commission found himself thrust between hammer and anvil: refusal to take the oath or, having taken it, refusal to answer the interrogatories meant a sentence for contempt and invited Star Chamber proceedings; to take the oath and respond truthfully to questioning often meant to convict oneself of religious or political crimes and, moreover, to supply evidence against nonconformist accomplices; to take the oath and then lie meant to sin against the Scriptures and risk conviction for perjury. Common lawyers of the Puritan party developed the daring argument that the oath, although sanctioned by the Crown, was unconstitutional because it violated Magna Carta, which limited even the royal prerogative.

The argument had myth-making qualities, for it was one of the earliest to exalt Magna Carta as the symbol and source of English constitutional liberty. As yet there was no contention that one need not answer incriminating questions after accusation by due process according to common law. But a later generation would use substantially the same argument—"that by the Statutes of Magna Carta . . . for a man to accuse himself was and is utterlie inhibited"—on behalf of the contention that one need not involuntarily answer questions even after one had been properly accused.

Under Chief Justice Edward Coke the common law courts, with the sympathy of Commons, vindicated the Puritan tactic of litigious opposition to the High Commission. The deep hostility between the canon and common law systems expressed itself in a series of writs of prohibition issued by Coke and his colleagues, staying the Commission's proceedings. Coke, adept at creating legal fictions which he clothed with the authority of resurrected "precedents" and inferences from Magna Carta, grounded twenty of these prohibitions on the allegedly ancient common law rule that no man is bound to accuse himself criminally.

In the 1630s the High Commission and the Star Chamber, which employed similar procedures, reached the zenith of their powers. But in 1637 that flinty Puritan agitator, John Lilburne, refused the oath. His well-publicized opposition to incriminatory questioning focused England's attention upon the injustice and illegality of such practices. In 1641 the Long Parliament, dominated by the Puritan party and common lawyers, condemned the sentences against Lilburne and others, abolished the Star Chamber and the High Commission, and prohibited ecclesiastical authorities from administering any oath obliging one "to confess or to accuse himself or herself of any crime."

Common law courts, however, continued to ask incriminating questions and to bully witnesses into answering them. The rudimentary idea of a right against self-incrimination was nevertheless lodged in the imperishable opinions of Coke, publicized by Lilburne and the Levellers, and firmly associated with Magna Carta. The idea was beginning to take hold of men's minds. Lilburne was again the catalytic agent. At his various trials for his life, in his testimony before investigating committees of Parliament, and in his ceaseless tracts, he dramatically popularized the demand that a right against self-incrimination be accorded general legal recognition. His career illustrates how the right against self-incrimination developed not only in conjunction with a whole gamut of fair procedures associated with "due process of law" but also with demands for freedom of conscience and expression. After Lilburne's time the right became entrenched in English jurisprudence, even under the judicial tyrants of the Restoration. As the state became more secure and as fairer treatment of the criminally accused became possible, the old practice of bullying the prisoner for answers gradually died out. By the early eighteenth century the accused was no longer put on the stand at all; he could not give evidence in his own behalf even if he wished to, although he was permitted to tell his story, unsworn. The prisoner was regarded as incompetent to be a witness for himself.

After the first quarter of the eighteenth century, the English history of the right centered primarily upon the preliminary examination of the suspect and the legality of placing in evidence various types of involuntary confessions. Incriminating statements made by suspects at the preliminary examination could be used against them at their trials; a confession, even though not made under oath, sufficed to convict. Yet suspects could not be interrogated under oath. One might be ensnared into a confession by the sharp and intimidating tactics of the examining magistrates; but there was no legal obligation to answer an incriminating question—nor, until 1848, to notify the suspect or prisoner of his right to refuse answer. One's answers, given in ignorance of his right, might be used against him. However, the courts excluded confessions that had been made under duress. Only involuntary confessions were seen as a violation of the right. Lord Chief Baron Geoffrey Gilbert in his *Law of Evidence* (1756) declared that although a confession was the best evidence of guilt, "this Confession must be voluntary and without compulsion; for our Law . . . will not force any Man to accuse himself; and in this we do certainly follow that Law of Nature" that commands self-preservation.

Thus, opposition to the oath *ex officio* ended in the common law right to refuse to furnish incriminating evidence against oneself even when all formalities of common law accusation had first been fulfilled. The prisoner demanded that the state prove its case against him, and he confronted the witnesses who testified against him. The Levellers, led by Lilburne, even claimed a right not to answer any questions concerning themselves, if life, liberty, or property might be jeopardized, regardless of the tribunal or government agents directing the examination, be it judicial, legislative, or executive. The Leveller claim to a right against self-incrimination raised the generic problem of the nature of sovereignty in England and spurred the transmutation of Magna Carta from a feudal relic of baronial reaction into a modern bulwark of the rule of law and regularized restraints upon government power.

The claim to this right also emerged in the context of a cluster of criminal procedures whose object was to ensure fair play for the criminally accused. It harmonized with the principles that the accused was innocent until proved guilty and that the burden of proof was on the prosecution. It was related to the idea that a man's home should not be promiscuously broken into and rifled for evidence of his reading and writing. It was intimately connected to the belief that torture or any cruelty in forcing a man to expose his guilt was unfair and illegal. It was indirectly associated with the right to counsel and the right to have witnesses on behalf of the defendant, so that his lips could remain sealed against the government's questions or accusations. It was at first a privilege of the guilty, given the nature of the substantive law of religious and political crimes. But the right became neither a privilege of the guilty nor a protection of the innocent. It became merely one of the ways of fairly determining guilt or innocence, like trial by jury itself; it became part of due process of the law, a fundamental principle of the accusatorial system. It reflected the view that society benefited by seeking the defendant's conviction without the aid of his involuntary admissions. Forcing self-incrimination was thought to brutalize the system of criminal justice and to produce untrustworthy evidence.

Above all, the right was closely linked to freedom of speech and religious liberty. It was, in its origins, unquestionably the invention of those who were guilty of religious crimes such as heresy, schism, and nonconformity, and later, of political crimes such as treason, seditious libel, and breach of parliamentary privilege. More often than not, the offense was merely criticism of the government, its policies, or its officers. The right was associated, then, with guilt for crimes of conscience, of belief, and of association. In the broadest sense it was not so much a protection of the guilty, or even the innocent, but a protection of freedom of expression, of political liberty, and of the right to worship as one pleased. The symbolic importance and practical function of the right certainly settled matters, taken for granted, in the eighteenth century. And it was part of the heritage of liberty that the common law bequeathed to the English settlers in America.

Yet, the right had to be won in every colony, invariably under conditions similar to those that generated it in England. The first glimmer of the right in America was evident in the heresy case of John Wheelwright, tried in 1637 in Massachusetts. In colony after colony, people exposed to the inquisitorial tactics of the prerogative court of the governor and council refused to answer to incriminating interrogatories in cases heavy with political implications. By the end of the seventeenth century the right was unevenly recognized in the colonies. As the English common law increasingly became American law and the legal profession grew in size, competence, and influence, Americans developed a greater familiarity with the right. English law books and English criminal procedure provided a model. From Edmond Wingate's *Maxims of Reason* (1658), which included the earliest discussion of the maxim, "*Nemo tenetur accusare seipsum,*" to Gilbert's *Evidence*, law books praised the right. It grew so in popularity that in 1735 Benjamin Franklin, hearing that a church wanted to examine the sermons of an unorthodox minister, could declare: "It was contrary to the common Rights of Mankind, no Man being obliged to furnish Matter of Accusation against himself." In 1754 a witness parried a Massachusetts legislative investigation into seditious libel by quoting the well-known Latin maxim, which he freely translated as "A Right of Silence as the Priviledge of every Englishman." In 1770 the attorney general of Pennsylvania ruled that an admiralty court could not oblige people to answer interrogatories "which may have a tendency to criminate themselves, or subject them to a penalty, it being contrary to any principle of Reason and the Laws of England." When, in 1770, New York's legislature jailed Alexander McDougall, a popular patriot leader who refused answer to incriminating queries about a seditious broadside, the public associated the right with the patriot cause, and the press printed the toast, "No Answer to Interrogatories, when tending to accuse the Person interrogated." Thereafter the New York legislature granted absolute immunity to recalcitrant malefactors whose testimony was required in trials or investigations.

In 1776 the Virginia Constitution and Declaration of Rights provided that in criminal prosecutions the accused party cannot "be compelled to give evidence against himself." Every state (eight including Vermont) that prefaced its constitution with a bill of rights imitated Virginia's phrasing, although two, by placing the clause in a section apart from the rights of the accused, extended the right to third parties or witnesses. Whether the right was constitutionally secured or was protected by common law made little difference, because the early decisions, even in states that constitutionally secured the right, followed the common law rather than the narrower phrasing of their constitutions. For example, the Pennsylvania Constitution of 1776 had a self-incrimination clause that referred to "no man," which the 1790 constitution narrowed to "the accused." Nevertheless, in the first case on this clause the state supreme court applied it to the production of papers in civil cases and to questions involving exposure to "shame or reproach."

During the controversy over the ratification of the Constitution of 1787, only four states recommended that a comprehensive bill of rights should be added to the new document, but those four demanded a self-incrimination clause modeled on the conventional phrasing that no person should be compelled to give evidence against himself. James Madison, in framing what became the Fifth Amendment, urged in sweeping language that no person should be "compelled to be a witness against himself." That phrasing was amended to apply only to criminal cases, thereby permitting courts to compel a civil defendant to produce documents against himself, injuring his civil interest without infringing his traditional rights not to produce them if they could harm him criminally. Whether the framers of the clause in the Fifth meant it to be fully coextensive with the still expanding common law principle is unknown. The language of the clause and it framers' understanding may not have been synonymous, especially because a criminal defendant could not testify under oath even in the absence of the self-incrimination clause. It was intended as a ban on torture, but it also represented the opinion of the framers that the right against self-incrimination was a legitimate defense possessed by every individual against government. The framers were tough-minded revolutionaries who risked everything in support of their belief that legitimate government exercises its powers in subordination to personal rights. The framers were not soft, naive, or disregardful of the claims of law and order. They were mindful that the enduring interests of the community required justice to be done as fairly as possible: that no one should have to be a witness against himself in a criminal case was a central feature of the accusatory system of criminal justice, which the framers identified with fairness. Deeply committed to a system of criminal justice that minimized the possibilities of convicting the innocent, they were not less concerned about the humanity that the law should show even to the offender. The Fifth Amendment reflected their judgment that in a society based on respect for the individual, the government shouldered the entire burden of proving guilt and the accused need make no unwilling contribution to his conviction.

What is the present scope of the right and how have the Supreme Court's interpretations compared with the history of the right? Generally the Court has construed the clause of the Fifth as if the letter killeth. Seeking the spirit and policies of the clause, the Court has tended to give it an ever widening meaning, on the principle that "it is as broad as the mischief against which it seeks to guard," as the Court said in *Counselman*. In effect the Court has taken the position that the Fifth embodied the still evolving common law of the matter rather than a rule of fixed meaning. Often the Court has had history on its side without knowing it, with the result that many apparent innovations could have rested on old practices and precedents.

History supported the decision in *Boyd v. United States* (1886) connecting the Fifth and Fourth Amendments and holding that the seizure of one's records for use as evidence against him compels him to be a witness against himself. Beginning in the early eighteenth century the English courts had widened the right against self-incrimination to include protection against the compulsory production of books and papers that might incriminate the accused. In a 1744 case a rule emerged that to compel a defendant to turn over the records of his corporation would be forcing him to "furnish evidence against himself." In the 1760s in *Wilkes's Cases*, the English courts extended the right to prevent the use of general warrants to seize private papers in seditious libel cases. Thus the right against self-incrimination and freedom of the press, closely allied in their origins, were linked to freedom from unreasonable searches and seizures. In *Entick v. Carrington* (1765), Lord Camden (Charles Pratt) declared that the law obliged no one to give evidence against himself "because the necessary means of compelling self-accusation, falling upon the innocent as well as the guilty, would be both cruel and unjust; and it should seem that search for evidence is disallowed upon the same principle." American colonists made similar arguments against writs of assistance, linking the right against unreasonable search to the right against self-incrimination. *United States v. White* (1944), which required the production of an organization's records even if they incriminated the witness who held them as custodian, was a departure from history.

That the right extends to witnesses as well as the accused is the command of the text of the Fifth. Protection of witnesses, which can be traced to English cases of the mid-seventeenth century, was invariably accepted in American manuals of practice as well as in leading English treatises throughout the eighteenth century. The Supreme Court's decision in *McCarthy v. Arndstein* (1924) extending the right to witnesses even in civil cases if a truthful answer might result in a forfeiture, penalty, or criminal prosecution, rested on dozens of English decisions going back to 1658 and to American precedents beginning in 1767. In a little known aspect of *Marbury v. Madison* (1803), Chief Justice John Marshall asked Attorney General Levi Lincoln what he had done with Marbury's missing commission. Lincoln, who probably had burned the commission, refused to incriminate himself by answering, and Marshall conceded that he need not reply, though he was a witness in a civil suit.

Many early state decisions held that neither witnesses nor parties were required to answer against themselves if to do so would expose them to public disgrace or infamy. The origins of so broad a right of silence can be traced as far back as sixteenth-century claims by Protestant reformers such as William Tyndale and Thomas Cartwright in connection with their argument that no one should be compelled to accuse himself. The idea passed to the common lawyers and Coke, was completely accepted in English case law, and found expression in William Blackstone's *Commentaries* as well as American manuals of practice. Yet the Supreme Court in *Brown v. Walker* (1896) restricted the scope of the historical right when ruling that the Fifth did not protect against compulsory self-infamy. Its decision was oblivious to history as was its reaffirmation of that decision in *Ullmann v. United States* (1956).

From the standpoint of history that 1896 holding and its 1956 reaffirmation correctly decided the main question whether a grant of full immunity supersedes the witness's right to refuse answer on Fifth Amendment grounds. Colonial precedents support absolute or transactional immunity, as did the immunity grant decisions in 1896 and 1956. The Court departed from its own precedents and history when ruling in *Kastigar v. United States* (1972) that limiting the right to use and derived-use immunity does not violate the right not to be a witness against oneself.

History supports the decisions made by the Court for the first time in *Quinn v. United States* (1955) and *Watkins v. United States* (1957) that the right extends to legislative investigations. As early as 1645 John Lilburne, relying on his own reading of Magna Carta and the Petition of Right, claimed the right, unsuccessfully, before a parliamentary committee. In 1688 the Pennsylvania legislature recognized an uncooperative witness's right against self-incrimination. Other colonial assemblies followed suit though New York's did not do so until forced by public opinion after McDougall's case. That Parliament also altered its practice is clear from the debates in 1742 following the refusal of a witness to answer incriminatory questions before an investigating committee. The Commons immunized his testimony against prosecution, but the bill failed in the Lords in part because it violated one of the "first principles of English law," that no person is obliged to accuse himself or answer any questions that tend to reveal what the nature of his defense requires to be concealed. In 1778 the Continental Congress investigated the corrupt schemes of Silas Deane, who invoked his right against self-incrimination, and Congress, it seems, voted that it was lawful for him to do so.

History belies the two-sovereignties rule, a stunting restriction upon the Fifth introduced by the Court in 1931 but abandoned in *Murphy v. Waterfront Commission* (1964). The rule was that a person could not refuse to testify on the grounds that his disclosures would expose him to prosecution in another jurisdiction. The Court mistakenly claimed that the rule had the support of historical precedents; history clearly contradicted that rule as the Court belatedly confessed in 1964.

History supports the rule of *Bram v. United States* (1897) that in criminal cases in the federal courts—this was extended by *Malloy v. Hogan* (1964) to the state courts, too—whenever a question arises whether a confession is incompetent because it is involuntary or coerced, the issue is controlled by the self-incrimination clause of the Fifth. Partly because of John H. Wigmore's intimidating influence and partly because of the rule of *Twining* denying that the Fourteenth Amendment extended the Fifth to the states, the Court until 1964 held that the coercion of a confession by state or local authorities violated due process of law rather than the right against self-incrimination. Wigmore, the master of evidence, claimed that the rule against coerced confessions and the right against self-incrimination had "no connection," the two being different in history, time or origin, principle, and practice.

Wigmore was wrong. From the fact that a separate rule against coerced confessions emerged in English decisions of the eighteenth century, nearly a century after the right against self-incrimination had become established, he concluded that the two rules had *no* connection. That the two operated differently in some respects and had differing rationales in other respects led him to the same conclusion. But he focused on their differences only and so exaggerated those differences that he fell into numerous errors and inconsistencies of statement. The relationship of the two rules is apparent from the fact that the shadow of the rack was part of the background from which each rule emerged. The disappearance of torture and the recognition of the right against compulsory self-incrimination were victories in the same political struggle. The connections among torture, *compulsory* self-incrimination, and *coerced* confessions was a historical fact as well as a physical and psychological one. In the sixteenth and seventeenth centuries, the argument against the three, resulting in the rules that Wigmore said had no connection, overlapped. Compulsory self-incrimination was always regarded by its opponents as a species of torture. An act of 1696 regulating treason trials required that confessions be made willingly, without violence, and in open court. The quotation above from Geoffrey Gilbert disproves Wigmore's position. When the separate rule against coerced confessions emerged, its rationale was that a coerced confession is untrustworthy evidence. There remained, however, an indissoluble and crucial nexus with the right against self-incrimination because both rules involved coercion or the involuntary acknowledgment of guilt. Significantly the few references to the right against self-incrimination, in the debates on the ratification of the Constitution, identified the right with a protection against torture and inquisition, that is, against coerced confessions. Wigmore fell into error by assuming that the right against self-incrimination had a single rationale and a static meaning. In fact it always had several rationales, was an expanding principle of law, and spun off into different directions. One spin-off was the development of a separate rule against coerced confessions. If there was "an historical blunder," it was made by the English courts of the eighteenth century when they divorced the confessions rule from the self-incrimination rule.

History is not clear on the Court's distinction between testimonial compulsion, which the Fifth prohibits, and nontestimonial compulsion, which it does not prohibit. Blood samples, photographs, fingerprints, voice exemplars, and most other forms of nontestimonial compulsion are of modern origin. The fact that the Fifth refers to the right not to be a witness against oneself seems to imply the giving of testimony rather than keeping records or revealing body characteristics for identification purposes. The distinction made by the Court in *Schmerber v. California* (1966) was reasonable. Yet, limiting the Fifth to prohibit only testimonial compulsion poses problems. The accused originally could not testify at all, and the history of the right does not suggest the *Schmerber* limitations. The common law decisions and the wording of the first state bills of rights explicitly protected against compelling anyone to give or furnish "evidence" against himself, not just testimony.

The fact that history does not support some of the modern decisions limiting the scope of the right hardly means that history always substantiates decisions expanding it. Decisions like *Slochower v. Board of Education* (1956) and *Garrity v. New Jersey* (1967) which protect against penalizing the invocation of the right or chilling its use, draw no clear support from the past. Indeed, the decision in *Griffin v. California* (1965) which prohibited comment on the failure of a criminal defendant to testify on ground that such comment "is a remnant of the inquisitorial system" is historically farfetched.

Finally, history is ambiguous on the controversial issue whether the right against self-incrimination extends to the police station. When justices of the peace performed police functions and conducted the preliminary examination of suspects, their interrogation was inquisitorial in character (as it is in the interrogation rooms of modern police stations) and it usually had as its object the incrimination of the suspect. Yet he could not be examined under oath, and he did have a right to withhold the answer to incriminating questions. On the other hand, he had no right to be told that he need not answer or be cautioned that his answers could be used against him. However, the right against self-incrimination grew out of a protest against incriminating interrogation *prior to* formal accusation. That is, the maxim *nemo tenetur seipsum prodere* originally meant that no one was obligated to supply the evidence that could be used to indict him. Thus, from the very inception of the right, a suspect could invoke it at the earliest stages of his interrogation.

In *Miranda v. Arizona* (1966) the Supreme Court expanded the right beyond all precedent, yet not beyond its historical spirit. *Miranda's* purpose was to eliminate the inherently coercive and inquisitional atmosphere of the interrogation room and to guarantee that any incriminating admissions are made voluntarily. That purpose was, historically, the heart of the Fifth, the basis of its policy. Even the guarantee of counsel to effectuate that purpose has precedent in a historical analogy: the development of the right to counsel originally safeguarded the right against self-incrimination at the trial stage of prosecution. When the defendant lacked counsel, he had to conduct his own case, and although he was not put on the stand and did not have to answer incriminating questions, his failure to rebut accusations and insinuations by the prosecution prejudiced the jury, vitiating the right to silence. The right to counsel permitted the defendant's lips to remain sealed; his "mouthpiece" spoke for him. In *Miranda* the Court extended the protection of counsel to the earliest stage of a criminal action, when the need is the greatest because the suspect is most vulnerable.

Nevertheless, the *Miranda* warnings were an invention of the Court, devoid of historical support. Excepting rare occasions when judges intervened to protect a witness against incriminatory interrogatories, the right had to be claimed or invoked by the person seeking its protection. Historically it was a fighting right; unless invoked it offered no protection. It did not bar interrogation or taint an uncoerced confession as improper evidence. Incriminating statements made by a suspect could always be used at his trial. That a person might unwittingly incriminate himself when questioned in no way impaired his legal right to refuse answer. He lacked the right to be warned that he need not answer; he lacked the right to have a lawyer present at his interrogation; and he lacked the protection of the strict waiver requirements that now accompany the *Miranda* rules. From a historical view, the decision in *Brewer v. Williams* (1977) and the limits on interrogation imposed by *Rhode Island v. Innes* (1980) extraordinarily inflate the right. What was once a fighting right has become a pampered one. Law should encourage, not thwart, voluntary confessions. The Fifth should be liberally construed to serve as a check on modern versions of the "third degree" and the spirit of McCarthyism, but the Court should distinguish rapists and murderers from John Lilburne and realize that law enforcement agencies today are light years away from the behavior revealed in *Brown v. Mississippi* (1936) and *Chambers v. Florida* (1940).

The Court said in *Palko v. Connecticut* (1937) that the right against compulsory self-incrimination was not a fundamental right; it might be lost, and justice might still be done if the accused "were subject to a duty to respond to orderly inquiry." Few would endorse that judgment today, but it is a yardstick for measuring how radically different the constitutional law of the Fifth became in half a century.

History surely exalts the right if precedence be our guide. It won acceptance earlier than did the freedoms of speech, press, and religion. It preceded a cluster of procedural rights such as benefit of counsel. It is older, too, than immunities against bills of attainder, *ex post facto* laws, and unreasonable searches and seizures. History also exalts the origins of the right against self-incrimination, for they are related to the development of the accusatorial system of criminal justice and the concept of fair trial; to the principle that fundamental law limits government—the very foundation of constitutionalism; and to the heroic struggles for the freedoms of the First Amendment. History does not, however, exalt the right against the claims of justice.

11

Subversion of *Miranda*

IN *Harris* v. *New York*, the "illegal confessions" case, decided in 1971,[1] the opinion of the Court, given by Chief Justice Warren Burger, was surely one of the most scandalous, extraordinary, and inexplicable in the history of the Court. Compared with most constitutional cases, this one was rather simple and non-controversial. The police, suspecting that Harris was a pusher as well as a dope addict, arranged for an undercover agent to buy heroin from him. The officer later testified that he made the purchase from Harris and that on a subsequent day made another. (If Harris sold him heroin on the first occasion, why should the agent have made the second purchase?) The police arrested Harris and took him into custody for interrogation. They did not tell him his rights to silence and counsel. Though he asked for counsel, they ignored him and continued the interrogation until he incriminated himself.

The arrest took place before the *Miranda* decision,[2] though after the decision in *Escobedo* (1964), which required the presence of counsel, if requested, during a custodial interrogation in order to protect the suspect's right not to be a witness against himself.[3] Moreover, a New York statute required cautioning a suspect before an admissible confession could be taken. Harris made a statement admitting not that he sold heroine to the officer but that he had bought some; he claimed that he had acted as an intermediary for the police, who paid him for his services. His trial took place after the *Miranda* decision, which applied to all subsequent trials. At his trial, Harris took the stand to testify in his own defense and contradicted his earlier statement. Although he denied selling anything to the officer on the first occasion, he claimed that on the second he sold harmless baking powder that appeared to be heroin. On cross-examination the prosecutor used Harris's earlier statement against him for the purpose of discrediting his testimony. Defense counsel, overruled by the trial judge, objected that Harris's statement could not be used against him for any purpose because he had made it involuntarily and contrary to the requirements of *Miranda*. The trial judge ruled that an illegally obtained statement, while inadmissible as proof of defendant's guilt, could be used to impeach his credibility as a witness. After the cross-examination, Harris's counsel restated for the record his objections to using the statement for impeachment purposes.

The jury convicted Harris for having sold heroin on the second occasion only.

After New York's highest court sustained the conviction, Harris appealed to the Supreme Court. In the briefs and oral argument, as well as in the appellate proceedings in the state, the defendant through counsel persistently sought a reversal on ground that his involuntary statement should not have been used against him. During the oral argument, the following colloquy took place:[4]

> Q. Well, then, as to coercion, the involuntariness of this statement, do I understand it to be your submission that because of the attitude the prosecutor took, the ruling of the court was that even assuming it was coerced it could still be used?
> A. Exactly, but I also say—
> Q. We should decide this case therefore on the hypothesis, whatever the facts may be, that this was coerced?
> A. Exactly . . .

Counsel, in response to questions, also asserted that the statement was involuntary even in the pre-*Miranda* sense; in other words, that the statement had been coerced by the police and did not represent Harris's free will, even in the absence of any requirement that he be notified prior to interrogation that he had a right to counsel and to silence and that he could waive his rights only knowingly, voluntarily, and intelligently.[5]

Counsel for New York, acknowledging that defendant claimed the contrary, argued that Harris's statement had been voluntarily made. When asked whether a coerced confession could be used to impeach the defendant's testimony, counsel for the state also acknowledged that if the confession had been coerced it could not be used "for any purpose."[6] The question was further explored in this exchange between Justice Potter Stewart and counsel for the state:[7]

> Q. I didn't mean an untrue confession, I meant simply an involuntary confession, could you use that to impeach him?
> A. No. Mr. Justice Stewart, I don't think we could, for this reason: The point I am trying to make is a voluntary confession, if it is voluntary in the traditional sense [i.e., pre-*Miranda*], can be relied upon to express the truth, whereas an involuntary confession is subject, to take the obvious example, a man will say anything to keep from being beaten and all we have to do is go to some of the countries beyond the Iron Curtain to demonstrate that. There is a point beyond which human endurance can't continue. . . .
> Q. . . . And let's assume further that it is wholly true. Could you have used that to impeach him?
> A. I don't think so, Mr. Justice Stewart, because the thought is that we must define a class of confessions which may be used for these purposes, and I think once you define the class as being a true confession rather than a voluntary confession, then you're getting into extraneous matters that perhaps aren't properly explored in the context of this.
> Q. What you are saying then is that it can't be given any use because it is inherently unreliable as being involuntary?
> A. As being involuntary, yes . . .

Despite his claim that Harris's statement was voluntary, counsel for the state admitted that the confession Harris had made about selling heroin on the second occasion—the only sale for which the jury convicted—was a "false account."[8]

When stating the facts of the case in his opinion for the Court, Burger, in a shocking distortion, declared flatly, "Petitioner makes no claim that the statements made to the police were coerced or involuntary."[9] The trial record, the appellate proceedings in the state, and the briefs and oral arguments before the Supreme Court show that Harris made exactly that claim from start to finish.[10] No one lacking powers of divination or access to candid statements from the members of the Court can explain Burger's misstatement of the record, nor the failure of those joining in the disposition of the case to correct that record in a separate, concurring opinion, nor the failure of even the dissenters to take issue with the Chief Justice's remark. The Court's failure on all sides shakes confidence in its integrity or its craftsmanship. Surely the route traveled by the Court, especially in a majority opinion, must be along the straightest path of intellectual rectitude and professional expertness in stating the facts, not to mention the controlling precedents.

Given the facts of this case, the Court might simply have found that, as the state acknowledged, a statement involuntarily made, whether in the pre- or post-*Miranda* sense, cannot be used in any way against the defendant, not even to discredit his testimony. In this case, given the dispute whether the statement had been voluntarily made, the Court might have ruled on the question of voluntariness, the record permitting, or might have remanded the case to the state courts for a determination whether Harris's statement was voluntary and, if so, whether usable to impeach him in light of *Miranda*. At no point in the state proceedings had there been a hearing to determine whether Harris had made his statement voluntarily, because the trial court had ruled that even an illegally obtained confession could be used to impeach the witness's credibility, and the high court of New York agreed, in a 3-to-2 decision.[11]

By alleging that Harris made no claim that his statement was coerced or involuntary, Burger altered the posture of the question before the Court and put himself into a position to ridicule contentions contrary to those which he asserted. Conceivably, the dissenters did not correct Burger's misstatement because they wanted to settle the question he in effect raised: whether the prosecution may use for the purpose of discrediting the defendant a statement made by him that was not coerced in any physical or psychological sense but was admittedly obtained in violation of the *Miranda* prescription that certain warnings must be made prior to in-custody interrogation. Was *Miranda* controlling? Burger acknowledged that there were "some comments" in warren's opinion in the *Miranda* case that could be read as a bar against the use of any uncounseled statement for any purpose, but Burger dismissed such comments as mere dicta—a discussion of the issue "not at all necessary to the Court's holding and cannot be regarded as controlling."[12] Contrary to Burger, *Miranda* did not bar the use of uncounseled statements for any purpose, because the Court permitted a knowing, intelligent, and voluntary waiver of the right to counsel. More important, Warren in *Miranda* had made much more than merely "some comments" that might be read to decide the question before the Court as defined by Burger in *Harris*. There was nothing remotely equivocal about what Warren had declared. Early in his opinion he announced that the Court's "holding" would be spelled out with specificity, "but briefly stated it is this: The prosecution may not use statements, whether exculpatory or inculpatory, stemming from custodial interrogation of the defendant unless it demonstrates the use of procedural safeguards effective to secure the privilege against self-incrimination." More than thirty pages later, Warren summed up as follows:[13]

> The warnings required and the waiver necessary in accordance with our opinion today are, in the absence of a fully effective equivalent, prerequisites to the admissibility of *any* statement made by a defendant. No distinction can be drawn between statements which are direct confessions and statements which amount to "admissions" or part or all of an offense. The privilege against self-incrimination protects the individual from being compelled to incriminate himself in any manner; it does not distinguish degrees of incrimination. Similarly, for precisely the same reason, no distinction may be drawn between inculpatory statements and statements alleged to be merely "exculpatory." If a statement made were in fact truly exculpatory it would, of course, never be used by the prosecution. In fact, statements merely intended to be exculpatory by the defendant are often used to impeach his testimony at trial or to demonstrate untruths in the statement given under interrogation and thus to prove guilt by implication. These statements are incriminating in any meaningful sense of the word and may not be used without the full warnings and effective waiver required for any other statement. . . . The principles announced today deal with the protection which must be given to the privilege against self-incrimination when the individual is first subjected to police interrogation while in custody at the station or otherwise deprived of his freedom of action in any significant way.

When Harris, after police defiance of the *Escobedo* decision, made an uncounseled statement denying the first sale and alleging that the second was merely of baking soda, he intended, of course, an exculpatory statement of *exactly* the sort described in *Miranda*. Warren's opinion for the Court laid down a general constitutional principle, not just a passing dictum. Six United States Courts of Appeals and the highest courts of fourteen states followed the *Miranda* holding on impeaching the credibility of the defendant; New York was one of four states whose appellate court found to the contrary. With good reason, Brennan, in his dissenting opinion in *Harris*, quoted Warren to support an assertion that, "We settled this proposition in *Miranda*. . . ."[14]

Burger, nevertheless, declared that *Miranda* did not establish that evidence clearly inadmissible against the defendant to prove the offense charged is barred for all purposes, "provided of course that the trustworthiness of the evidence satisfies legal standards."[15] If Warren had gone out of his way to decide too much, Burger did not even bother to explain himself. The only legal standard that he mentioned anywhere in his opinion was voluntariness. But if *Miranda* had any meaning at all it was that in the absence of notice and waiver of one's constitutional rights, custodial interrogation is so inherently coercive that no statement can be voluntary. Moreover, a statement may be voluntarily given and still be untrustworthy. Men under police examination, even innocent men, have been known to volunteer outright lies, false information, and, indeed, fabricated confessions. Some speak freely yet unreliably out of fear, others out of a desire for notoriety. Motivation is complex, but voluntariness is not alone a sure standard of the trustworthiness of evidence. In the *Harris* case even the state admitted that the confession that had been illegally obtained was false.

Burger himself made much of the point that men might give untrustworthy evidence even under oath, but he did so with verbal trickery that was calculated to disparage the right against self-incrimination. Every defendant, he pointed out, is "privileged to testify in his own defense, or to refuse to do so. But that privilege cannot be construed to include the right to commit perjury."[16] Nor can it be construed to include the right to be Chief Justice of the United States, to rocket to the moon, or to play the violin. No one claimed that the Fifth Amendment vested a right to perjure, but Burger went on to declare, redundantly, that *Miranda*'s shield "cannot be perverted into a license to use perjury by way of a defense, free from the risk of confrontation with prior inconsistent utterances."

In a footnote he gave as an example the hypothetical case of a man who, under circumstances making his confession inadmissible as evidence, admitted to a homicide and led the policy to the body. Harris's argument, Burger continued, would have the Court believe that the murderer could take the stand, deny every fact disclosed to the police or discovered from his confession, and be "free from confrontation with his prior statements and acts. The voluntariness of the confession would, on this thesis, be totally irrelevant. We reject such an extravagant extension of the Constitution."[18] In this example Burger once again took for granted that an illegally obtained confession could be voluntary. It would surely be trustworthy if leading to the discovery of the body, but if involuntary its use would as surely compel the man to be a witness against himself, as was the case, even more surely, in *Harris*. But there is a crucial distinction between the cases. In the hypothetical one posed by Burger the evidence was hard and irrefutable—the fact that the man led the police to the grave and the body itself. In Harris's case the evidence was soft, consisting of utterances made under an illegal interrogation. Burger failed to distinguish between "statements and acts." In the hypothetical case the police could testify as eyewitnesses to the man's taking them to the body, and there would be no need to impeach the defendant by using his otherwise inadmissible confession. In either case, once the defendant took the stand he in effect waived his right under the Fifth Amendment not to be a witness against himself; he could be cross-examined. But in neither, because the prior confession had been made under circumstances that rendered it inadmissible, could the defendant justly be said to have waived his right to let it speak against him, not even for impeachment purposes. The cases are otherwise dissimilar.

Burger's failure to distinguish between hard and soft evidence led him to a flagrant misuse of a roughly analogous 1954 decision that he treated as if it were controlling. He rode booted and spurred over *Miranda*, but in *Walder* v. *United States* he found a convincing precedent.[19] *Walder* was a sideshoot of the exclusionary rule developed by the Court in the *Weeks* case of 1914.[20] Evidence seized in violation of the Fourth Amendment's injunction against unreasonable searches and seizures may not be introduced as evidence at the trial. The purpose of the exclusionary rule is to deter the government and the police from engaging in unconstitutional searches and seizures. Presumably, if they cannot use the fruits of their unconstitutional behavior they will be deterred from continuing it. In *Walder* the Court permitted physical evidence, otherwise inadmissible to prove guilt, to be introduced to discredit the defendant. The Court distinguished between excluding the evidence to prove the crime charged and the defendant's use for his own advantage of the fact that the seizure was illegal; he sought to make its illegality a shield against contradiction of his own lies. Burger, having quoted the Court's exact words in making this point in *Walder*, continued the quotation without ellipsis marks as follows, giving the impression that the next words of the *Walder* opinion were:

> [T]here is hardly justification for letting the defendant affirmatively resort to perjurious testimony in reliance on the Government's disability to challenge his credibility.[21]

But for the bracketed capital letter that begins the quote, one would not know that Burger had emasculated the *Walder* opinion, omitting from it language that altered the impression left by his bowdlerized version.

Walder's case was wholly unlike Harris's. Tainted evidence was not used on cross-examination to impeach Walder's testimony on matters directly relating to the crime charged. In *Walder* the evidence was used to discredit the defendant's testimony on a different and unrelated matter. Indicted for purchasing heroin, he successfully moved to suppress the use of the physical evidence on ground that it had been illegally seized. The government dismissed the prosecution because it could not employ the fruits of an unconstitutional seizure. Two years later Walder was indicted for another narcotics violation unrelated to the earlier one. He took the stand and on direct examination denied that he had ever in his life possessed narcotics. That denial flatly contradicted the affidavit filed by him in the earlier proceeding. Over his objection the prosecution then questioned him about the heroin unlawfully seized on that occasion. When he persisted in his denial, the government did not introduce his affidavit against him. Government agents who had been involved in the illegal search took the stand to impeach his credibility. They could not and did not testify as to the crime for which he then stood indicted. The only issue in *Walder*, said Frankfurter, for the Court, was "whether the defendant's assertion on direct examination that he had never possessed any narcotics opened the door, solely for the purpose of attacking the defendant's credibility, to evidence of the heroin unlawfully seized in connection with the earlier proceeding."[22] By way of answer, Frankfurter declared, in words Burger ignored:

Of his own accord, the defendant went beyond a mere denial of complicity in the crimes of which he was charged and made the sweeping claim that he had never dealt in or possessed any narcotics. Of course, the Constitution guarantees a defendant the fullest opportunity to meet the accusation against him. *He must be free to deny all the elements of the case against him* without thereby giving leave to the Government to introduce by way of rebuttal evidence illegally secured by it, and therefore not available for its case in chief. Beyond that, however . . .[23]

And at that point Burger continued his quotation from the case with the words quoted above that begin with the bracketed capital letter.

Brennan, dissenting in *Harris*, quoted from the omitted language in Frankfurter's opinion and drew from those words the lesson they taught. In *Walder* the Court distinguished the case of an accused whose testimony, as in *Harris*, was a denial of complicity in the crime charged. *Harris* was a case involving the use of illegally obtained evidence to impeach the accused's direct testimony on matters directly related to the case against him. He was free to deny "all the elements of the case against him" without the government's being able to use by way of rebuttal the forbidden evidence. Yet the evidence permitted by Burger for impeachment was a statement concerning the details of the very crime alleged in the indictment against Harris.

Brennan failed to add that *Walder* did not establish a new principle of law, as Burger seemed to suggest; rather, *Walder* was an exception to a principle established in a 1925 case, when the government, having been rebuffed in its effort to introduce tainted evidence to prove the crime charged, sought to smuggle it in by way of cross-examination—precisely the situation in the *Harris* case.[24] *Walder* was a special exception to the principle established by the 1925 precedent, namely that "the contention that the evidence of the search and seizure was admissible in rebuttal is without merit." The reason given for that principle was that the defendant, like Harris, "had done nothing to waive his constitutional protection or to justify cross-examination" in respect to that evidence.[25]

Burger in *Harris* admitted that there was a distinction between that case and *Walder*. "It is true," he said, "that Walder was impeached as to collateral matters included in his direct examination, whereas petitioner here was impeached as to testimony bearing more directly on the crimes charged." He immediately added, however, "We are not persuaded that there is a difference in principle that warrants a result different from that reached by the Court in *Walder*."[26]

The difference in principle that Burger failed to see did in fact exist. It was a substantial and vital, the difference once again between hard evidence and soft as well as between a judicially made constitutional rule and the language of the Constitution itself. The difference, in short, is between the Fourth Amendment and the Fifth's self-incrimination clause. The Fourth, by judicial interpretation, prohibits the admission in evidence of illegal searches and seizures, while the Fifth, which by the force of its own terms is a constitutionally mandated exclusionary rule, prohibits the admission in evidence of statements unwillingly made by a witness against himself.

Judicial exceptions to the Fifth are not as warranted as in cases involving the Fourth. *Miranda* established a judicially made constitutional rule that applied the Fifth's exclusionary principle to custodial interrogation and to pretrial statements made in the absence of the *Miranda* notices of constitutional rights and waiver. *Miranda* was parallel to and had the same force of law as the Fourth Amendment interpretation in *Weeks* that created the exclusion of illegally obtained evidence. But the evidence excluded by *Miranda*, as well as by the Fifth Amendment itself, was testimonial in character and therefore not as trustworthy as the evidence that was the butt of the *Weeks* exclusionary rule. That rule addressed itself to evidence that is real, tangible, and physical, such as bags of heroin. The evidence excludable by the Fifth Amendment is inherently suspect and not on its face reliable, as bags of heroin are. The Fifth applies mainly to the words of the accused—his confession or statements in any degree or manner incriminating, even if they are intended as exculpatory but lend themselves to prosecutorial use as incriminatory. The statements of human beings, human nature being what it is, do not have the evidentiary value of their acts nor of things. Contraband like bags of heroin are mute proof of fact that hardly need the same degree of corroboration as an outright confession, let alone a statement subject to contradiction. The trustworthiness of physical evidence is such that without it a case may not be supported. When the exclusionary rule forced the government to abandon its effort to admit in evidence the heroin illegally seized from Walder, the government was obliged to dismiss its prosecution. An illegally obtained statement, even if necessarily excludable as a violation of the Fifth Amendment, is not as crippling to the prosecution if it has other evidence such as physical proof and the statements of eyewitnesses. Consequently, the government can press its case in the face of violation of the self-incrimination clause without the jeopardy to itself as when it has violated the search-and-seizure clause.

Impeachment on testimony bearing directly on the crime charged is different in principle from impeachment on collateral matters, Burger's statement to the contrary notwithstanding. The differences between Harris's case and Walder's need not again be stated. The point is that the introduction of the evidence in question against Walder did not at all relate to the crime he was indicted for two years later. The jury, if believing that evidence, could only conclude that he was a liar. It could not convict on the basis of that evidence relating to a different crime at an earlier date. Harris's pretrial statement that was being used against him concerned the very crime for which he was then being prosecuted. The trial judge warned the jury that the statement could be used only to attack Harris's credibility as a witness, not as proof of the crime itself. But juries, as fallible as the rest of humanity, are likely to conclude that if the defendant lies on the stand, he is probably guilty of the crime.

The use of Harris's pretrial statement to impeach his testimony necessarily influenced the jurors, perhaps prejudiced them against him. Why else would the prosecution wish to use an otherwise inadmissible statement that had been illegally obtained? Since it had been illegally obtained, its use against him forced him to be an unwilling witness against himself in violation of the Fifth Amendment. Jurors are not notably sympathetic to a defendant who openly invokes that amendment at his trial. Even if he does not take the stand, they tend to wonder whether he has something to hide, raising suspicions of his guilt. If he should risk taking the stand to tell his story, thereby exposing himself to cross-examination and impeachment, the trial judge's instruction to the jury to disregard his pretrial statement is unlikely to alter what they have heard. One authority has written that such an instruction,

> as seems to be generally agreed, is a mere verbal ritual. The distinction is not one that most jurors would understand. If they could understand it, it seems doubtful that they would attempt to follow it. Trial judges seem to consider the instruction a futile gesture. If the prior statement and the present testimony are to be considered and compared, what is the purpose? The intuitive good sense of laymen and lawyers seems to agree that the only rational purpose is not merely to weigh the credibility of the testimony, but to decide *which of the two stories is true*. To do this is ordinarily to decide the substantive issue.[27]

Thus, permitting the use of the defendant's illegally obtained statement intolerably burdens the constitutional right of a person not to be a witness against himself. He has not been a witness against himself of his own free will, least of all in the sense of *Miranda*. And he has been placed between hammer and anvil: If he fails to testify, thereby excluding any use of his pretrial statement, he exposes himself to the jury's suspicions; if he testifies, he exposes that illegal statement and his credibility too, and he stands in jeopardy of conviction. The right protected by the Fifth Amendment is inherently fragile; it cannot withstand the attenuation or the disparagement explicit in Burger's opinion. Nor can the jury in criminal cases be expected to withstand the tension placed upon it by the even more fragile instruction of a trial judge to ignore the evidence obtained in violation of the Fifth Amendment except to test the credibility of the defendant. As the Court said in a 1968 opinion, " . . . there are some contexts in which the risk that the jury will not, or cannot, follow instructions is so great, and the consequences of failure so vital to the defendant, that the practical and human limitations of the jury system cannot be ignored."[28] *Harris* was such a case. Burger cannot be believed when he said that the impeachment process in Harris's case "undoubtedly provided valuable aid to the jury in assessing petitioner's credibility, and," Burger added, "the benefits of the process should not be lost, in our view, because of the speculative possibility that impermissible police conduct will be encouraged thereby."[29]

Burger intended the reference to a "speculative possibility" as a rejoinder to Brennan's dissent. Brennan's outrage flared like a flame fed by a bellows. Deterring improper police conduct, he noted, was only part of the greater objective of protecting the integrity of our adversary system. Its basic mainstay is the right against self-incrimination whose values are jeopardized by the Court's exception to the principle against admitting "tainted" statements. "Moreover," Brennan declared,[30]

> it is monstrous that courts should aid or abet the lawbreaking police officer. It is abiding truth that "nothing can destroy a government more quickly than its failure to observe its own laws, or worse, to disregard the charter of its own existence." Thus even to the extent that *Miranda* was aimed at deterring police practices in disregard of the Constitution, I fear that today's holding will seriously undermine the achievement of that objective. The Court today tells the police that they may freely interrogate an accused incommunicado and without counsel and know that although any statement they obtain in violation of *Miranda* can't be used on the State's direct case, it may be introduced if the defendant has the temerity to testify in his own defense. This goes far toward undoing much of the progress made in conforming police methods to the Constitution.

"Monstrous" was the right word to describe the fundamentally immoral opinion by Burger. It was based on deceit and distortion. It denigrated the Fifth Amendment by allowing in evidence a statement violating the right not to be a witness against oneself, and it ridiculed the same constitutional provision by declaring that it did not extend to a right to commit perjury. It disparaged the Fourth Amendment's exclusionary rule as well as the Fifth's. It was an opinion rendered on the heels of political and police charges that the Warren Court, by decisions like that in *Mapp* and *Miranda*, had coddled criminals, contributed to the crime wave, and handcuffed the cops. In that context the opinion in *Harris* was an apostolic message to the police and prosecutors throughout the land that the courts would cooperate in condoning deliberate misconduct and excesses.

Miranda can have slight deterrent effect in ending illegal police behavior given the incentive provided by *Harris:* The courts will look the other way if the police disregard the *Miranda* requirements of notice of silence, of counsel, and of waiver rights. If the police, in violation of *Miranda*, can get a statement from the accused, they may not be able to use it to prove guilt but they will have something that might contribute to a jury's verdict of guilty if the victim of police misconduct dares to take the stand. The incentive to get the statement, despite *Miranda*, is increased because of the fact that the suspect may unwittingly provide leads to evidence otherwise not obtainable, and that evidence may be introduced at the trial to prove guilt. No exclusionary rule can operate with effective deterrence if it is riddled with loopholes sanctioned by the highest court and that court reveals its hostility to the rationale of such a rule. Justice Brandeis once pointed out that the government is the omnipresent teacher of the people it serves. "For good or for ill, it teaches the whole people by its example. Crime is contagious. If the government becomes a lawbreaker, it breeds contempt for law. . . ."[31] The opinion in *Harris* taught that government may commit crimes in order to secure the conviction of criminals. It taught the odious doctrine that in the administration of the criminal law, the end justifies the means and the Constitution can be circumvented.[32]

Harris did not overrule *Miranda*. *Harris* throttled *Miranda*, circumvented it, excepted it, and invited law-enforcement agencies to do the same; more, it provided them with advantages for doing the same. *Miranda* intended to create more respect for the law and, thus, in the long run, make the job of the police easier. In the short run, *Harris* and opinions like it will make their job easier, but the question is whether the welfare of our nation is secured by judicial opinions that say, in effect, that our legal system is stacked in such a way as to condone, conceal, and encourage criminal conduct on the part of our law-enforcement agencies. Never to be forgotten is that *Harris* plainly denied the truth, that the defendant did claim that his statement was involuntary, and that the Court did permit the use of a statement which it conceded had been illegally obtained. The Court's elephantine misrepresentations and mangling of precedents could not have been deliberately calculated. Incompetence may have some claim to an explanation of *Harris*. But the truth about it, which cannot be known, probably derives from the same sort of zeal that drives the police to become lawless in the act of apprehending and interrogating suspects. "The greatest dangers to liberty," Brandeis once warned, "lurk in insidious encroachment by men of zeal, well-meaning but without understanding."[33]

12

Judicial Activism and
Strict Construction

THE WARREN COURT'S CRIMINAL JUSTICE
"REVOLUTION," LTD.

WHEN EARL WARREN became Chief Justice of the United States in 1953, American constitutional law, like the nation it served, teetered between two worlds. One, which nothing short of lethal could move or remove, deserved a speedy, contemptible death; it was the world of racism, political rotten boroughs, McCarthyism, discriminations against the poor, puritanism in sexual matters, denial of the suffrage, and egregious infringements on the rights of the criminally accused. The other was a world struggling to be born, eager to remedy injustices and make the fundamental law of the land have a liberating and egalitarian impact. The Supreme Court under Warren was a sometime midwife to the newer world. Freedom of expression and association, and, even more important, racial justice, criminal justice, and political justice became the Court's obsession. Never since the early nineteenth century, when the great John Marshall presided, had the Court made our constitutional law so generative, even transforming—indeed there were friends and foes alike who spoke of a "revolution" presided over by judges; and not since Marshall's time had the Court, which periodically suffered withering criticism, been so vilified by its critics and so rapturously acclaimed by its supporters.

The Court operates in the main as a judicial team, every man playing a vital part, rather than as individual stars. The principle of majority rule, based on "one man, one vote," has always prevailed within the Court. It is a collective institution with a perpetual corporate life. The Chief Justice, however, was its symbol, literally its head, figuratively its heart. Like a lightning rod, he drew the kudos as well as the aspersions, even the psychotic hatreds epitomized by the scream "Impeach Earl Warren!" Nervous nellies, who cautiously approved of the law's new direction but worried about the swiftness and exent of change, blamed him for the Court's having overreached itself. Distinguished law-school professors parsed his opinions; their concern for legal *petit point* caused them to lose sight of his grand enterprise and the functional nature of law, and they clucked disapprovingly of Warren when they detected a missing or botched stitch.[1] President Dwight Eisenhower, who had appointed him, grew to regret his choice and is supposed to have said it was the "biggest damnfool mistake I ever made." President Lyndon Johnson handed Warren the accolade "the greatest Chief Justice of them all."[2]

Warren served with able associates—sixteen altogether during the length of his tenure—and they, as much as he, shaped the Court's controversial opinions, even when bickering and dissenting. Still, the public identified the Court with its Chief Justice, and he did in fact associate himself with its trailblazing decisions in every area of constitutional law except on the subject of obscenity. Although Warren was not responsible for the constitutional "revolution," he was responsive to it, and in the crucial areas of civil rights and electoral representation he led it. That revolution might not have taken place without him. He certainly lent it respectability, the public influence of his high position, and above all, perhaps, his universally recognized attributes of "humanity . . . fairness, integrity, dignity," to quote the words of President Nixon, one of the most vociferous critics of the "Warren Court."[3]

Nixon made the Warren Court a major political issue in his 1968 presidential campaign. The politics of law and order, capitalizing on genuine fears about crime in America and deeper racial anxieties, paid off handsomely. In one speech Nixon would allege that the courts should be respected and in the next breath denigrate them. When he accepted the nomination of his party, he expressed a theme that persisted throughout the fall campaign: Judicial decisions, he said, "have gone too far in weakening the peace forces as against the criminal forces in this country. . . . If we are to have respect for law in America we must have laws that deserve respect."[4] In his first campaign speech on crime Nixon left the impression that the courts were to blame for the frightening increase in the crime rate. "Today," he concluded, "all across the land guilty men walk free from hundreds of courtrooms. Something has gone terribly wrong in America."[5] The message was clear: Permissive judges enforced the Warren Court's strained interpretations of the Constitution in favor of the criminal forces. Nixon popularized and gave respectability to that charge that had originated with right-wing groups and many law-enforcement officials. The charge damaged the Supreme Court's moral authority by diminishing public confidence in it. A Gallup Poll revealed that the majority believed that the Court was "too soft" on criminals, protected their rights at the expense of society, and was "making" rather than "interpreting" the laws.[6]

If Nixon had been able to dictate the decisions of the Court in every case dealing with criminal justice during the years when Warren was Chief Justice, the crime rate in America in 1968 would have varied little if at all. Decisions of appellate courts have approximately the same effect upon the causes of crime as gamma rays. The courts rarely set the guilty free. Four years after Warren retired, the Supreme Court unanimously held that when there has been a denial of speedy trial in violation of the Sixth Amendment, the case against the defendant must be altogether dismissed.' That decision was unique. If there has been a denial of any other constitutional right of the criminally accused, the reversal of a conviction does not liberate the criminal (assuming that the defendant is guilty); reversal returns his case to the trial court, which can try him again, on the prosecution's initiative, according to the law as determined by the appellate court.

The Supreme Court is not a supreme jury. It does not decide guilt or innocence. It concerns itself with means, not ends. It decides whether proper procedures have been followed and whether proper evidence has been admitted, not whether the verdict was proper. A lawful end cannot be achieved by means dishonoring the Constitution or by using illegally obtained evidence. To make the law an instrumentality for securing convictions by violating individual rights would in the long run corrupt the integrity of the law and of the courts, brutalize the police and impair methods of detection, and turn the criminal law into a tool of tyranny. Justice Felix Frankfurter once pointed out, "The history of liberty has largely been the history of the observance of procedural safeguards."[8] Justice Robert Jackson declared that he would rather live under Soviet law enforced by American procedures than under American law enforced by Soviet procedures. "Procedural fairness and regularity," said Jackson, "are of the indispensable essence of liberty."[9] That is the reason why most of the provisions of the Bill of Rights are procedural in character. They protect society, as well as the accused, against law-enforcement excesses that taint the government.

The criminal-justice system in this country has been grinding to a halt and is in danger of massive breakdown, but not because of the Bill of Rights or its interpretation by the Warren Court. The fundamental cause is the staggering rise in the number of crimes and the resultant congestion of prosecutorial case loads and court dockets. The Warren Court unquestionably contributed to that congestion by revitalizing old rights and recognizing new ones that prolonged the criminal process from arrest to final appeal. Swift and certain punishment has always been about as effective a deterrent to crime as any our criminal-justice system can provide. The Warren Court, on balance, made a negative contribution in that direction. Its decisions tended to make convictions more difficult to get, verdicts of guilty were difficult to stick, and sentences more difficult to execute. Nevertheless, even punishment that is swift and certain cannot alter the conditions that breed crime, nor can the toughest law-and-order policies like third-degree tactics, the use of evidence that is not subject to suppression, more convictions, severer sentences, and harsher prisons. When the criminal process was summary in form, when pickpocketing was a capital crime, and when executions were public spectacles, pickpockets fleeced the crowds that turned out to watch other pickpockets being hanged after a swift trial. Swift and harsh punishment was not a deterrent to the other criminals: In the 1920s, when the police used rubber truncheons to beat confessions out of suspects and searched and seized virtually at will, they did not reduce the crime rate. Law-and-order advocates always contend that if accused persons receive some right or other, the crime rate will burgeon, the guilty will go free, and the law-abiding will be unsafe. Four years of law-and-order policies of the Nixon Administration and of pro-prosecutorial decisions by the appellate courts did not stem the tide. Crimes of violence are still on the increase.[10]

If the courts did not restrain the police or reverse the convictions of the guilty, and if prosecutors gained convictions of all who are guilty, crime in America would not significantly decrease. The number of people imprisoned would increase. We might be a safer society, but not by much, and we would probably be a less free society. Society is hurt when the criminal escapes punishment because of a "legal technicality," but in the long run a democratic society is hurt still more when lawless conduct by law-enforcement agencies goes unchecked. Further, the men behind bars eventually come out. Our prisons not only fail to rehabilitate but seem to serve as training schools for the production of more criminals and more dangerous ones. Ex-convicts return for the most part to lives in circumstances like those that led them to crime. Rejuvenating our cities, our schools, and our economy would deter crime far more effectively than swift and certain justice, or turning the Supreme Court around, or watering down the Bill of Rights.

The Warren Court did "handcuff the cops," in some respects; its job was to do just that by keeping the police within the law they enforced. The Constitution deliberately provided for this conflict between the courts and the law-enforcement agencies. When a defendant has the benefit of legal counsel or demands trial by jury or invokes any other constitutional right, police power is circumscribed. The Warren Court enlarged the rights of the criminally accused, evoking strenuous protests from responsible as well as hysterical opponents. Every expansion of the rights of the criminally accused in American history has confronted the warning that handicapping the state makes conviction of the guilty more difficult. More than six decades ago, an essay by a prosecutor on "Coddling the Criminal" attributed the failures of law enforcement to judicial observance of the constitutional protections against double jeopardy and compulsory self-incrimination.[11] The presumption of innocence, trial by jury, writ of habeas corpus, and every other procedural safeguard has been blamed at one time or another for causing crime or hampering the police.

The courts would have little reason to reverse convictions if the police did not break the law in order to enforce it. The argument against the Warren Court's strict observance of the Bill of Rights was essentially an argument that the police should be above the law in order to protect society from those who violate it. Our constitutional law is intended to secure all of us from improper, even criminal, police conduct and from prosecutorial shortcuts with the law. The object of the criminal law is to assess guilt or innocence according to canons of fairness and see that justice is done; the object is not simply to convict the guilty by whatever means. "If the exercise of constitutional rights will thwart the effectiveness of a system of law enforcement," as the Warren Court said, "then there is something very wrong with that system."[12] We should not fear if an accused person receives the assistance of a lawyer, if he learns what his rights are and exercises them.

In *Miranda*, his most controversial criminal-justice opinion, Chief Justice Warren quoted these words:

> Law enforcement, however, in defeating the criminal, must maintain inviolate the historic liberties of the individual. To turn back the criminal, yet, by so doing, destroy the dignity of the individual, would be a hollow victory. . . .
>
> We can have the Constitution, the best laws in the land, and the most honest reviews by courts—but unless the law enforcement profession is steeped in the democratic tradition, maintains the highest in ethics, and makes its work a career of honor, civil liberties will continually—and without end—be violated. . . . The best protection of civil liberties is an alert, intelligent and honest law enforcement agency.[13]

The author of that statement, made before Warren joined the Court, was no permissive judge or soft-headed social theorist; he was the director of the FBI, J. Edgar Hoover.

Hoover's statement suggests that Supreme Court decisions are not self-enforcing. The Court has no way of effectively monitoring compliance with its mandates. The opposition of law-enforcement agencies can obstruct change commanded by the Court. The Court cannot even ensure that state trial courts, let alone lower appellate courts, will adhere faithfully to its decisions. The Court has other incapacities. It cannot, by its adjudicatory process, overhaul the criminal-justice system. It can decide only individual cases. It cannot initiate cases; it must wait for a case or controversy to come before it. Thus, the Court is not able to revolutionize the rules of criminal procedure and evidence. It cannot bring about sudden, drastic, or wholesale change. The Warren Court allegedly revolutionized the constitutional law of criminal procedure and evidence, yet the trial courts of the nation still operate substantially as they did before the revolution. Criminal prosecutions still shame the constitutional principles of due process of law and equal justice under the law. In the main, the Warren Court only marginally affected practices, though it changed our idealized picture of the criminal prosecution. Whether the Court was responsible for a "revolution" at any level is, perhaps, a subjective judgment that depends on one's tolerance for the pace and character of change.[14]

Essentially, the revolution took the form of a case-by-case abolition of an old double standard that had prevailed in state and federal criminal cases. The Court simply applied the Bill of Rights to the states, commanding them to follow the same Fourth, Fifth, and Sixth Amendment procedures that previously had applied only to cases arising in the federal courts. The states have always had the responsibility for prosecuting the overwhelming bulk of criminal cases, and in the execution of that responsibility they had an obligation under the United States Constitution to honor only the Fourteenth Amendment. That amendment, which was adopted in 1868, provides that no state—and that includes the local police officer, prosecutor, and trial court—shall deny to any person life, liberty, or property without due process of law, nor deny to any person the equal protection of the laws. Before Warren's time, the Court had kept the federal law-enforcement agencies and federal courts to a fairly strict observance of the Bill of

Rights, but had left the states pretty much alone, allowing them to define due process of law, for all practical purposes, as they pleased in matters of criminal justice.[15]

The Court superintended the state administration of criminal justice only enough to ensure that due process of law meant a respect for the "decencies of civilized conduct" and an avoidance of "conduct that shocks the conscience" or offends the "sense of justice" or of "fair play."[16] The only particular procedural right that the Court regarded as "fundamental," in the sense that to deny it denied due process, was the right to counsel in capital cases.[17] Otherwise, due process was so nebulous a standard that it varied in meaning from case to case and depended on the idiosyncracies of a majority of the Court at any given moment. For example, in a case decided in 1952 the Court ruled that forcing incriminating evidence from a person by means of a stomach pump was equivalent to compelling him to testify against himself criminally and therefore denied due process.[18] A year later the Court had the case of an illiterate black man whom North Carolina sentenced to death on the basis of a confession that he made after having been held on suspicion for five days without being charged with a crime and for eighteen days thereafter without being brought before a magistrate for a preliminary hearing. Nor did he have counsel until the day of his trial. The Court held that because these facts did not prove that he had confessed his guilt involuntarily, the state had not denied due process.[19] Justices Hugo L. Black and William O. Douglas believed that state criminal cases should be decided like federal ones according to the specific requirements of the Bill of Rights. In their view, the Fourteenth Amendment "incorporated" or embodied the Fourth Amendment's protection against unreasonable searches and seizures, the Fifth's safeguard against double jeopardy and compulsory self-incrimination, and the Sixth's battery of rights applicable to "all criminal prosecutions."

Beginning in 1961 the Supreme Court under Warren finally began to accept the views that Black and Douglas had advocated, on the theory that the rights in question, contrary to earlier rulings, were fundamental to the American system of justice. In 1961 the Court incorporated the Fourth Amendment within the Fourteenth, making the fruits of an illegal search and seizure excludable as evidence in a state trial; thereafter, the federal rules on the exclusion of evidence governed state cases.[20] A year later the Court incorporated the Eighth Amendment's ban against cruel and unusual punishments.[21] In 1963 the right to be represented by counsel in all felony cases joined the list of due-process rights, as applicable against the states as against the United States. Thus, the states had to provide counsel for all felony defendants too poor to hire their own.[22] A year later the Court ruled that state denial of the Fifth Amendment's right not to be a witness against oneself in a criminal case was a denial of due process.[23] In 1965 the Court incorporated the right of the defendant to confront the witnesses against him and two years later incorporated other Sixth Amendment safeguards—the right to a speedy trial and the right to compulsory process in securing witnesses in one's behalf.[24] In 1968 the Court added trial by jury to the incorporated rights and in the following year, on the last day of Warren's tenure, the right against double jeopardy.[25] Thus, by a piecemeal process of selective incorporation, the Court extended to the states most of the criminal-justice provisions of the Bill of Rights—indeed, all the essential ones except the right to bail. The Warren Court's criminal-law revolution, then, consisted in nationalizing the Bill of Rights.

The Warren Court was not equally innovative in expanding the meanings of old rights to new situations. A 1956 opinion expressed the truly radical principle that there cannot be equal justice under the law "where the kind of trial a man gets depends on the amount of money he has."[26] However, when Warren retired thirteen years later, the Court had done no more than require that indigent defendants must receive at public expense necessary transcripts, filing costs, and legal services on appeals or postconviction proceedings.[27] In 1963 the Court substantially expanded postconviction remedies by allowing federal courts, on a writ of habeas corpus, to review state convictions allegedly in violation of constitutional rights.[28] That did not expand the scope of the rights at issue. Nor did the Court's extension of various procedural rights to juvenile-delinquency proceedings.[29] Of all constitutional rights, the Court most expanded the least controversial, the right to the assistance of counsel. The Court extended it to indigents wherever it was applicable and applied it to pretrial judicial proceedings, to pretrial custodial police proceedings, to juvenile proceedings, and to appellate proceedings.[30] The Court also expanded the most controversial of all rights, not to be a witness against oneself criminally, by ruling that it applied to custodial interrogations in the police station, where it was most needed.[31]

Consistency, however, has rarely been a virtue of the Supreme Court, and under Warren its record was par for the course. The question of consistency, or rather, the lack of it, does point to a fact about the Warren Court that stressing its affirmations of Bill of Rights freedoms often obscures. On balance, it was liberal activist, but many of its decisions were deplored by libertarians as encroachments on the rights of the criminally accused. Such decisions do not square with the Court's reputation for hostility to the police or with Warren's professed dedication to passing on to future generations a better Bill of Rights, burnished by growing use and imaginatively applied to new situations.[32] The controversial Fifth Amendment right, which the Court kept tightly reined in many cases, is a good example.

Rejecting claims based on the right against self-incrimination, the Court sustained the constitutionality of a congressional immunity act that forced witnesses to testify aginst themselves concerning subversive activities.[33] In three cases the Court upheld the dismissals from public service of persons who refused to answer concerning their alleged Communist affiliations.[34] In still other Fifth Amendment cases not dealing with internal security, the Court denied that the right against self-incrimination protected against blood tests to determine drunkenness. In one case the police had taken blood from an unconscious driver whose vehicle killed others, and in another case from a suspected drunk who protested against the test.[35] The rationale of these decisions narrowly limited the

Fifth Amendment to a safeguard against testimonial compulsion and excluded real or physical evidence that was nontestimonial in character. In related cases, which prosecutorial forces usually depicted as showing that the Warren Court released criminals on constitutional technicalities at the expense of society, the Fifth Amendment also fared badly.[36] The Court broadened the Sixth Amendment right to counsel in these cases, by extending it to police lineups conducted for purposes of identifying suspects; but, the Court rejected the claims that lineups, fingerprinting, photographs, and physical measurements violated the Fifth Amendment. In view of the previous distinction between testimonial and nontestimonial evidence, there was nothing surprising in the lineup cases to this point. However, the Court went beyond the rationale of its precedents when it ruled that the Fifth Amendment does not prevent suspects from being compelled to speak at a lineup or to give samples of handwriting. Speaking and writing seem to be inherently testimonial in character.

In another case the Court rejected the contention that the admission in evidence of criminal revelations unwittingly made to a paid government informer, who posed as a close associate, violated the Fifth Amendment.[37] The Court reasoned that the incriminating statements were not the product of compulsion, and they were not. The significance of the decision is that by construing compulsion so literally, the Court denied the protection of the amendment to confessions obtained by deceit rather than by force. Consequently, the Court legitimated police tactics of considerable value to law enforcement.

The police and prosecutors also received substantial aid from several important search-and-seizure cases that limited the protection of the Fourth Amendment. In one the Court sustained a conviction based on the testimony of an undercover narcotics officer who entered the accused's home under false pretenses to buy marijuana from him.[38] In a related case the Court sustained a conviction in which the evidence consisted of an informer's tape recording of an attempted bribery.[39] The Court sided with the police when it rejected a challenge to a warrantless arrest by a defendant who claimed that unless the officer was compelled to disclose the name of an anonymous informer on whose tip the police acted, there was no way to determine whether probable cause for the arrest existed or whether the informer actually existed.[40] In another case the Court overruled the doctrine that since 1921 had restricted the introduction in evidence of any property seized by the police if it was "mere evidence."[41] They could seize contraband such as narcotics, which a citizen may not lawfully possess; they could seize the fruits of a crime, such as stolen goods, or the instrumentalities of a crime, such as a getaway car or weapons; but, they could not seize private property, such as clothing that identified the criminal, because it was "mere evidence." Overruling that doctrine opened the door to convictions that otherwise might not be possible.

The same result flowed from a decision that civil libertarians applauded. Although the Court overruled a 1927 precedent that excluded wiretapping from the Fourth Amendment's protection, and reversed a conviction obtained by warrantless electronic eavesdropping, it rejected the claims that all wiretapping and eavesdropping necessarily violated the amendment.[42] The Court refused to endorse the argument that there is no way to frame a sufficiently specific search warrant because of the inherently dragnet character of surveillance by tapping and bugging. Thus, the Court opened the door to evidence seized on the authority of valid warrants issued to sanction the use of secret eavesdropping. In another unprecedented decision the Court ruled that even if the police have no probable cause for making an arrest or a search, they may stop a suspicious person and frisk him for a weapon.[43]

The Warren Court did decide many other Fourth Amendment cases against the police; however, the Warren Court had a genuine concern for the needs of law enforcement. Its decisions did not at all show a single pattern of upholding the claims of the criminally accused. Its "revolution" in criminal procedures and evidence was distinctly limited. It often, and in important cases, did not handcuff the cops when civil libertarians thought that it should have.

When Warren retired on June 23, 1969, President Nixon stood before the Court, a representative of the American bar, to give a muted tribute to Warren, a price worth his paying to witness the unique event in the Court's history of the retiring Chief Justice swearing in his successor, Warren E. Burger, Nixon's appointee. The President declared that the sixteen years during which Warren had presided "without doubt, will be described by historians as years of greater change in America than any in our history. . . . Change with continuity," he ventured, "can mean progress," and quite remarkably he added that of the three great branches of the government, none had been more responsible "for that continuity with change than the Supreme Court of the United States."[44] The nation already knew what the President belatedly, if only ceremonially recognized, that the Constitution had triumphantly survived the change and still stood, despite all vicissitudes, but that it most definitely had not stood still: Under Warren it had progressed.

In his extemporaneous response, the retiring Chief Justice stressed the theme of continuity with change. Observing that the Court is a continuing body, he pointed out the stunning fact that the judicial careers of just seven men, including the still-sitting Hugo L. Black, connected without break the 180-year history of the Court. Then Warren added, "We, of course, venerate the past, but our focus is on the problems of the day and of the future as far as we can foresee it." In one sense at least, he declared, the Court's position was similar to that of the President, for it had the awesome responsibility quite often of speaking the last word "in great governmental affairs" and of speaking for the whole American public. "It is a responsibility that is made more difficult in this Court because we have no constituency. We serve no majority. We serve no minority. We serve only the public interest as we see it, guided only by the Constitution and our own consciences. . . ." The Court, he concluded, had applied constitutional principles, so broadly stated in the document, in a manner consistent with the public interest and with the future "so far as it can be discerned."[45]

Warren's candid and simple valedictory in effect endorsed the view, stated by both the Court's admirers and critics, that the Justices seemed to consider themselves as movers and shakers of the country's destiny rather than as impersonal spokesmen of "the law." Warren would surely have agreed with Woodrow Wilson, who declared that the country looked for "statesmanship" in its judges, because the Constitution was not "a mere lawyers' document" but, rather, the "vehicle of a nation's life."[46] Chief Justice Burger quite as clearly professed a far more restrictive view of the Court's role, one more in keeping with the "strict construction" of the Constitution that President Nixon avowed to be the proper standard for members of the high tribunal in the exercise of constitutional adjudication.

By coincidence, both Earl Warren and Warren E. Burger expressed themselves in off-Court, public statements two years after their respective appointments as Chief Justice, and the contrast was both startling and revealing. Warren, in an article on "The Law and the Future" published in *Fortune* magazine in 1955, was characteristically expansive, warm, and idealistic. His prime concern for the law was that it must adapt to changing circumstances by keeping its rules in harmony with the enlightened common sense of the nation. That meant to him that the Supreme Court faced "a single continuous problem: how to apply to ever changing conditions the never changing principles of freedom." The Constitution, existing for the individual as well as the nation, best fulfilled its mission, he asserted, by serving the unchanging cause of human justice. Significantly, he fastened upon "the 462 words of our Bill of Rights" as "the most precious part of our legal heritage," yet he presided over the Court at a time, he said, when the Bill of Rights confronted subtle and pervasive attack. Turning to needed reforms of our constitutional system, he noted that the proud inscription above the portals of the Supreme Court Building—"Equal Justice Under Law"—described a goal by no means secured for all citizens. The rights due to them, particularly to oppressed minorities and the poor, had been infringed, neglected, or unperfected. Focusing on the fact that our system of criminal justice was "pockmarked with . . . procedural flaws and anachronisms," making for unequal access to justice, he observed: "Suspects are sometimes arrested, tried, and convicted without being adequately informed of their right to counsel. Even when he knows of this right, many a citizen cannot afford to exercise it." The remark foreshadowed some of the most disputed reforms inaugurated by the Warren Court.

Freedom, like justice, Warren continued, required constant vigilance. Making no allowance for exceptions, he declared that when the rights of any individual or group were "chipped away, the freedom of all erodes." Warren's statement recognized implicitly that the Supreme Court had a crucial responsibility, one that could not be evaded, for helping to regenerate and fulfill the noblest aspirations for which this nation stood. In effect, he was saying that the law, though remaining constantly rooted in the great ideals of the past, must change in order to realize them. Thus, when posterity receives the Bill of Rights from the present generation, the document will not have the same meaning as it had when we received it from past generations. "We will pass on a better Bill of

Rights," Warren asserted, "or a worse one, tarnished by neglect or burnished by growing use. If these rights are real, they need constant and imaginative applications to new situations." Such "constant and imaginative applications" earned for the Warren Court its reputation for "activism."[47]

On July 4, 1971, *The New York Times* published excerpts from an exclusive interview with Chief Justice Warren E. Burger, headlining the front-page story that accompanied the interview, "Burger Asserts Reform Is Not Role of Courts." Unlike the interventionism that permeated Warren's philosophy, Burger embraced the philosophy of judicial self-restraint. Moreover, he was surprisingly unimaginative, conservative, and even a bit crabbed. Immediately he de-emphasized the influence that the Supreme Court might have for changes in the law. "And changes in the law made by judicial decisions," he added, "ought to be approached with considerable caution. It was never contemplated in our system that judges would make drastic changes by judicial decision. That is what the legislative function and the rule-making function is all about." The Court sat, he declared, merely to decide cases. From its decisions, he acknowledged, "some changes develop, but to try to create or substantially change civil or criminal procedure, for example, by judicial decision is the worst possible way to do it." When asked whether youthful hopes might be justified by "the prospects of accomplishing a change in the system through law," Burger replied: "I sincerely trust that some of their hopes may be justified, but I am beginning to have an uneasy feeling that this may be another one of the situations in this era that we are living in of creating expectations that are beyond fulfillment." He added that young people entering the legal profession "on the theory that they can change the world by litigation in the courts" were bound to be disappointed. They were entering the profession for the wrong reason, because the law "is not the route by which basic changes in a country like ours should be made. That is a legislative and policy process, part of the political process. And there is a very limited role for the courts in this respect."

When asked what he saw as the greatest challenge to the Supreme Court in the next few years, he did not discourse on the Bill of Rights or on reform of any sort; he replied, "I would say the greatest challenge is to try to keep up with the volume of work and maintain the kind of quality that ought to come from this Court." At the conclusion of the interview, Burger summed up his judicial philosophy as follows: "Inherently, the Supreme Court function is one in which nothing ought to happen very rapidly except the disposition of specific cases. In the evolution of legal doctrine, legal principle can't be sound if its growth is too fast."[48] He might have added, though he did not, that legal principle cannot be sound if its growth is too quickly stunted or if the Court overruled, blunted, or distinguished away recent decisions merely because new members of the Court disliked them.

STRICT CONSTRUCTION CONSTRUED

From the beginning of its history the Supreme Court displayed an audacious capacity to manipulate precedents, to reveal its own values and policy choices, and to read the Constitution to mean whatever it wanted. Despite pretenses to the contrary, the Court could do no other, for as beauty exists in the eye of the beholder, so American constitutional law exists in the collective eye of those who happen at any moment in time to dominate the Court. What counts is not what the Constitution says, because it says so very little; what counts, rather, is what the Court has said about the Constitution—in more than four hundred volumes thus far. The Constitution itself necessarily plays a secondary role in American constitutional law. It is too concise and ambiguous to be any more than a point of departure in judicial decisions. As Justice Jackson once observed, when the Court had to construe the First Amendment's injunction against establishments of religion, it was "idle to pretend that this task is one for which we can find in the Constitution one word to help us as judges to decide where the secular ends and the sectarian begins in education."[49] That principle of realism applies with equal force to any case within the field of criminal justice.

Justices who look to the Constitution, its Bill of Rights, or the Fourteenth Amendment for more than a Delphic phrase delude themselves. They might just as well turn to the newest fiction list for all the guidance they will find on how to decide most of the great cases that involve national public policy, whether the question relates to regulation of the economy, racial segregation, reapportionment, abortion, subversive activities, public-school prayers, or pornography. In the field of criminal justice, the Court must decide questions on the presumption of innocence, the death penalty, proof of guilt beyond reasonable doubt, nonunanimous jury verdicts, juries of less than twelve, exclusionary rules, cross-examination, warrantless searches and seizures, electronic eavesdropping, juvenile courts, stop and frisk, police lineups, custodial interrogation, and use immunity, to mention a few. There is surely no clear word in the Constitution on these or most of the subjects of great import with which the Court must deal. The framers of the Constitution had a genius for studied imprecision and calculated ambiguity. Their Constitution, which they expressed in very generalized terms, resembled Martin Chuzzlewit's grandnephew who, Dickens said, had no more than "the first idea and sketchy notion of a face." It thereby permitted, even encouraged—nay, necessitated—continuous reinterpretation and adaptation to changing circumstances and needs. Thus, the commerce clause today applies to Telstar communication, racial discrimination in motels, stolen cars, stock-exchange transactions, and the wages of window washers.

The document itself, with all its amendments, clearly delineates the structure of the American national government but only roughly maps the contours of power and the rights that it guarantees. We know unmistakably that there is to be a President whose term of office is four years; but what is "the executive power" with which he is vested? Chief Justice John Marshall once happily noted that the Constitution has none of the prolixity of a legal code. It has, rather, the virtue of muddy brevity. Very few of its several thousand words have any significance in constitutional law or criminal procedure and evidence. Almost without exception these significant words are the purposely protean or undefined words like general welfare, due process of law, commerce among the states, equal protection, privileges and immunities of citizenship, direct taxes, and necessary and proper. Other words of crucial importance in constitutional law are not even in the Constitution, including clear and present danger, fair trial, equal justice, self-incrimination, presumption of innocence, cross-examination, separate but equal, separation of church and state, the police power, community standards, exigent circumstances, privacy, hearsay, and the war powers. They are all judicial glosses.

Even the seemingly specific injunctions of the Bill of Rights do not always exclude exceptions to their rules, nor are they self-defining. What is an "establishment of religion"? Freedom of speech and press may not be "abridged," but what is an abridgment and what, indeed, is the freedom of speech that is protected? Libels, obscenity, and pornography (whatever they may mean), as well as direct and successful verbal incitements to crime, were not intended to be within the constitutional protection. The guarantee of freedom of religion is that it may not be "prohibited." May freedom of religion be abridged or regulated in some way short of a prohibition? There shall be no laws "respecting" an establishment of religion; can there be laws respecting freedom of speech or press without abridging them? What is an "unreasonable" search or seizure? No warrants shall issue "but on probable cause." What is "probable cause," and may there be searches without warrants? What is an "infamous" crime? What is the meaning of compulsion in the safeguard that no person shall be compelled in any criminal case to be a witness against himself? What is the process of law that is "due" to anyone who might be denied life, liberty, or property? What is "public use" or "just" compensation? Do the many rights of the Sixth Amendment really extend to "all" criminal prosecutions? What, indeed, is a "criminal prosecution"? What is a "speedy" trial or an "impartial" jury, and what does the "assistance of counsel" mean? What is "excessive" bail or a punishment that is "cruel and unusual"?

There are no constitutional absolutes; the words on the parchment do not speak precisely and clearly; and, there is no constitutional question, at least none that has come before the Court, that can be sliced so thin that it has only one side. During Burger's first term as Chief Justice, the Court decided the Alabama preliminary-hearings case.[50] The question was whether there is a right to the assistance of counsel at a preliminary hearing, prior to indictment, even if the state in which the case arose did not require that hearing in every prosecution. Long before, the Court had held that a person accused of crime "requires the guiding hand of counsel at every step in the proceedings against him."[51] In this case, Justice Brennan, for a majority of the Court, enumerated the various reasons that counsel must be furnished at a preliminary hearing, when there is one, in order to protect "the indigent accused against an erroneous or improper prosecution."[52] Justice Black, who was from the state in which the case arose, explained in a concurring opinion why the preliminary hearing was a critical step in that state's prosecution, and he observed that the "plain language" of the Sixth Amendment requires that in "all criminal prosecutions, the accused shall enjoy the right . . . to have the assistance of counsel for his defense."[53] Justice Douglas, also concurring, made Black's point explicit when he declared, rather amazingly, that "a strict construction of the Constitution requires the result reached."[54] Justices White and Harlan agreed that recent decisions of the Court furnished ample ground for holding that the preliminary hearing was a critical event in the progress of a criminal prosecution, warranting the right to counsel. Harlan asserted that had he been free to consider the case "upon a clean slate," he would have voted to affirm the convictions, but that was not a course open to him given his "due regard for the way in which the adjudicatory process of this Court, as I conceive it, should work."[55] Justice Stewart dissented because the trial record did not show that evidence from the preliminary hearing was used against the accused at their trial.

Given this posture of the Court, Burger's dissenting opinion was excessively distempered. He accused the majority of making new law on the basis of their views of "sound policy." He also displayed an egregious contempt for precedents and for the facts of constitutional life, when he declared:

> . . . I do not acquiesce in prior holdings that purportedly, but nonetheless erroneously, are based on the Constitution. That approach simply is an acknowledgment that the Court having previously amended the Sixth Amendment now feels bound by its actions. . . . I am bound to reject categorically Mr. Justice Harlan's and Mr. Justice White's thesis that what the Court said lately controls over the Constitution. While our holdings are entitled to deference I will not join in employing recent cases rather than the Constitution, to bootstrap ourselves into a result, even though I agree with the objective of having counsel at preliminary hearings. By placing a premium on "recent cases" rather than the language of the Constitution, the Court makes it dangerously simple for future Courts, using the technique of interpretation, to operate as a "continuing Constitutional convention."[56]

Reading the Sixth Amendment literally, Burger found that it did not stipulate the right to counsel at a preliminary hearing. He then accused the majority of seeking to "reshape the Constitution in accordance with predilections of what is deemed desirable."[57]

Burger's dissenting opinion had a Lockean quality in at least one sense. The great John Locke, a dreadfully inept constitution maker, believed that written statements of fundamental law must, like the laws of the universe, be immutable in order to be eternal. He once framed for Carolina a constitution expressly providing that "every part thereof, shall be and remain the sacred and unalterable form and rule of government for Carolina forever." As insurance, he added that "all manner of comments and expositions on any part of these fundamental constitutions, or on any part of the common or statute laws of Carolina, are absolutely prohibited."[58] By contrast the framers of the United States Constitution recognized the inevitability of change and the need for plasticity. They therefore provided for an orderly amendment procedure and for a "judicial power of the United States" that "shall extend to all cases, in law and equity, arising under this Constitution, the Laws of the United States, and Treaties made, or which shall be made. . . ." That required courts to engage in what Locke called "all manner of comments and expositions." Burger's literalism or strict construction, had it prevailed, would have enshrined Locke's approach, wiped the slate clean of precedents, and put the Constitution into an eighteenth-century deep-freeze.

Burger to the contrary, the Supreme Court is and must be for all practical purposes a "continuous constitutional convention" in the sense that it must keep updating the original charter by reinterpretation—and in the sense that it simply cannot decide cases on the basis of what the Constitution says. One who used the phrase so repugnant to Burger was a very conservative Solicitor General of the United States who accurately described the duties of the Court as "political in the highest sense of the word as well as judicial."[59] Many scholars and even members of the Supreme Court who had an appreciation of the realities of the situation have used the phrase too. In very much the same sense, many Justices, including such distinguished ones as Brandeis, Frankfurter, and Black, have described the Court, sometimes despairingly, as a superlegislature. It is that in some respects and cannot help but be so. The reason is simply that the Constitution, as Jefferson said in exasperation, is "merely a thing of wax" which the Court "may twist and shape into any form they please."[60] Judge Learned Hand observed that when a judge must pass on a question of constitutional law, "The words he must construe are empty vessels into which he can pour nearly anything he will,"[61] Frankfurter, whom Nixon held up as the model of the strict-constructionist judge, explained that the words of the Constitution are so unrestricted by their intrinsic meanings, or by history, or by tradition, or by prior decisions, "that they leave the individual justice free, if indeed they do not compel him, to gather meaning not from reading the Constitution but from reading life. ... The process of constitutional interpretation compels the translation of policy into judgment, and the controlling conceptions of the justices are their 'idealized political picture' of the existing social order."[62] Nixon's search for conservative strict constructionists was more than a candid attempt to alter the trend of decision; it was an acknowledgment that at the very apex of our system of government of laws and not of men, the men who interpret the laws, rather than the laws themselves, are the decisive factors. Warren showed his understanding of that fact when, on the occasion of his retirement, he noted that the Court consisted of nine independent men "who have no one to be responsible to except their own consciences." Strict constructionism can be a balm for the judicial conscience, but not much more.

The imprecision of the constitutional text makes strict constructionism a faintly ridiculous usage; indeed, our national experience makes it slightly sinister in its implications. The term originated in the pre-Civil War era as an argument in the armory of state's rightists who opposed the development of a strong Union detrimental to the proslavery interests. If words have symbolic value, strict constructionism means reversing the decision of Appomattox, crippling government regulation of the economy, a return to the legal order of Jim Crow, and letting the police have their way with suspects in the basement of the station house.

Notwithstanding Nixon's professed admiration for strict constructionism, his presidency stood for a promiscuous expansion of national powers, especially of the executive powers of the United States. Strict construction in the mouth of President Nixon was like the word love in the mouth of a whore, except that Nixon deceived only the public, not himself. As a lawyer and politician, he knew that inherently vague words cannot be strictly construed. He acknowledged that constitutional lawyers honestly disagree "as to where and how" to maintain "that delicate balance between the rights of society and the rights of defendants accused of crimes against society."[63] Nixon knew too that strict construction-ism can be an instrumentalist tactic for reaching desired results under a judicial guise of objectivity. It is a form of judicial laissez-faireism by which the judge acquiesces, as if in humility, to the status quo and defers to the other branches of the government, or to the states, or to law-enforcement agencies, as the case may be.

In the Alabama preliminary-hearing case, Douglas and Burger were on opposite sides, yet both purported to pursue a strict construction of the Sixth Amendment's right-to-counsel clause. That Douglas, a liberal activist, should have taken a strict-constructionist stance, was not really a surprise; after all, the law-and-order critics of the Warren Court bitterly complained that it enforced the Bill of Rights too strictly against law-enforcement officials. Nevertheless, both Douglas and Burger were pursuing an elusive will-o'-the-wisp when seeking a strict-constructionist interpretation. Each reasoned from unques-tioned premises to a foregone conclusion that had some logical form, yet represented, at bottom, a choice of competing values. Each relied on the rhetoric of strict constructionism to bolster the pretense that he was being impersonal in his judgment. Either would scrap that rhetoric if it stood in his way. Burger's rhetorical stance in effect proclaimed: "Whatever my personal wishes may be, I find nothing in the language of the Constitution that actually says that the accused must have counsel at a preliminary hearing." Nevertheless, in voting to deny trial by jury to accused persons if they are juveniles[64] or if they face imprisonment for not more than six months,[65] Burger abandoned strict con-structionism because it did not ease the way to the desired result. The Sixth Amendment, which requires a trial by jury in "all" criminal prosecutions, makes no exception for juveniles or petty offenders. But even words like "all" are malleable.

Burger is no more a strict constructionist than Douglas. The Chief Justice is, rather, a "judicial conservative" in Nixon's usage of that term. He meant a judge who sides with law-enforcement officials. When nominating Lewis F. Powell Jr. and William H. Rehnquist, Nixon both clarified and obscured his objective. His nominees, he conceded, "are conservatives . . . but only in a judicial, not a political sense." He wanted men on the Supreme Court who would share "my judicial philosophy, which is basically a conservative philosophy." To explain his meaning, he declared:

> As a judicial conservative, I believe some court decisions have gone too far in the past in weakening the peace forces as against the criminal forces in our society. In maintaining, as it must be maintained, the delicate balance between the rights of society and defendants accused of crimes, I believe the peace forces must not be denied the legal tools they need to protect the innocent from criminal elements.

There was no doubt about which way Nixon wanted his nominees to vote in criminal-justice cases, but he used a political standard, not a judicial one, just as he confounded the meanings of "judicial philosophy" and "judicial conservative." He said, quite properly, that a judge "should not twist or bend the Constitution in order to perpetuate his personal political and social views," but he knowingly chose men who, he hoped, would do exactly that in criminal-justice cases.[66] The term "judicial philosophy" refers to a concept of the judicial function and of the role of the Court in a political democracy. Frankfurter, for example, was a judicial passivist because he believed that the Court was inherently oligarchic in character. By the exercise of its power it could frustrate the representative institutions that are the product of the electoral process. The Court may be responsive to the people, but it need not be, and it is not responsible in a political sense. Majorities make mistakes, but the Court is also liable to err, and when it checks the majority Frankfurter believed that it has sapped the capacity of the people to learn from experience and correct their own mistakes. Frankfurter also worked out sophisticated theories about the judicial craft of interpreting statutes, the role of precedents in constitutional decisions, the jurisdiction of the Court, and the constitutional relationship between the nation and the states. He did not speak of supporting one side to a controversy over another, nor did he endorse a "conservative" judicial philosophy. Like Harlan, to whom he was close, Frankfurter had a due regard for the adjudicatory process of the Court. He did not express contempt for precedents, as Burger does. Frankfurter emulated Brandeis in adhering to a series of rules by which the Court avoids passing on constitutional questions when it can, avoids doctrines broader than required to settle a case, and avoids nullifying an act of government that can be given a constitutional construction.

A member of the Court who has a judicial philosophy of self-restraint is not one who will vote in an easily predictable way in a given case. He will differ from the liberal activist who sees the Court as one of democracy's institutions and the Constitution as a hedge against the excesses of majorities and of law-enforcement officials, clads himself in the armor of the Bill of Rights, and sets out to intervene as much as his judicial position will permit. The liberal activist is St. George or Don Quixote who tries to use his position to make the nation a better place or a fairer one by righting wrongs against the poor, the unpopular, and the disadvantaged. His votes are fairly predictable. So are the votes of the conservative activist or alleged strict constructionist of the Nixon sort. But a judge with a judicial philosophy like Holmes, Brandeis, Hughes, Frankfurter, or Harlan regularly defies the crystal ball of professional Court-watchers because he has abandoned his role as an advocate and does not sit on the bench to represent any particular interests or causes.

The members of the Court should, to the extent humanly possible, be aware of their own predilections and attempt to decide cases without consciously yielding to their own sympathies or deliberately reading the Constitution in the light of their own policy preferences. Yet even the best and most impartial of judges, those in whom the judicial temperament is most finely cultivated, cannot escape the currents that have tugged at them throughout their lives and inescapably color their judgment. Personality, the beliefs that make the man, has always made the difference in the Supreme Court's constitutional adjudication. There has never been a constitutional case before the Court in which room was lacking for personal discretion to express itself. In constitutional law there simply are no legal rules that are objective or neutral or value-free, enabling every judge, regardless of his identity and without regard to the litigants, to apply those rules in the same way with the same results. The rules themselves reflect considerations of policy and social advantage.

Legal erudition, legal rules, legal logic, legal research, and legal precedents do not decide cases involving the ambiguous clauses of the Constitution, the very clauses usually involved in those cases whose outcome helps to determine justice, the shape of public policy, and the degree of liberty or equality that exists in this country. Although some judges can intoxicate themselves with the belief that precedents control their decisions, decisions by the post-Warren Court, like decisions by its predecessors, prove that the Justices are intellectually supple enough to find their way around encumbering precedents. Moreover, the Court always has available to it alternative principles of constitutional construction—broad or narrow—as well as alternative lines of precedent, with the result that the Court has "a freedom" in the words of Edward S. Corwin, "virtually legislative in scope in choosing the values which it shall promote through its reading of the Constitution."[67] The Lord High Chancellor in *Iolanthe* might have characterized the Constitution and the Supreme Court when he humorously asserted, "The Law is the embodiment of everything that's excellent. . . . And I, my Lords, embody the Law."

The most gifted judge who has a deep understanding of himself and a deeper strain of self-skepticism cannot avoid the fact that every case presents a choice of competing considerations that are necessarily value-laden. His idealized picture of the social order, or his conception of the public interest, or his vision of the future, swerve his judgment one way or the other. "We may try to see things as objectively as we please," Justice Cardozo wrote. "Nonetheless, we can never see them with any eyes except our own."[68] Inevitably, then, our constitutional law is subjective in character and to a great degree result-oriented. We may not want judges who start with the answer rather than with the problem. We may not want such judges, but as long as mere mortals sit on the Court and must construe that majestic but muddy Constitution, we will rarely get any other kind. Not that the Justices knowingly or deliberately read their prejudices into law. There has probably never been a member of the Supreme Court who consciously decided against the Constitution or was unable, in his own mind, to square his opinions with it. Most judges convince themselves, or at least profess to believe the fiction, that they respond in the main to the clarity of words on parchment, illuminated, of course, by historical or social imperatives. The illusion may be good for their psyches or for the public's need to believe that the men who sit on the nation's highest tribunal really are Olympians, untainted by the considerations that move lesser beings. Even those Justices who start with the problem rather than with the result cannot transcend themselves nor transmogrify the obscure and inexact into simon-pure truth or impersonal principle. Even they cannot avoid the fact that constitutional law, more than any other branch of law, is a reflection of great public policies enshrined in the form of supreme and fundamental commands. It is truer of constitutional law than of any other branch that "what the courts declare to have always been the law," as Holmes put it, "is in fact new. It is legislative in its grounds. The very considerations which judges most rarely mention, and always with an apology, are the secret root from which the law draws all the juices of life. I mean, of course, consideration of what is expedient for the community concerned."[69] That applies as well to the realm of criminal justice. Judicial self-restraint and strict constructionism are at best factors that merely temper the ineluctible activism requisite for constitutional adjudication. Self-restraint and strict constructionism can also enable a member of the Court to achieve a pose which permits him to reach a preferred end in an apparently impersonal way. The judicial process is overwhelmingly a means of rationalizing preferred ends.

The Court under Burger has not veered dramatically away from the Court under Warren in criminal-justice cases. Criminal justice is the one field that Nixon expressly desired to influence by appointing men who shared his law-and-order philosophy. Cases that deal with the rights of the criminally accused under the Fourth, Fifth, and Sixth Amendments are the largest category of cases on constitutional law decided by the Court. The trend of decision in such cases by mid-1972 was abundantly clear. By then the four Nixon appointees had been together for six months. When the term of the Court closed, in June 1972, a reporter at a press conference, referring to the President's objective of balancing the Court to strengthen the "peace forces" against the "criminal forces," asked him whether the Court was balanced yet or needed "another dose of strict constructionism if that occasion should arise." Nixon replied, " . . . I feel at the present time that the Court is as balanced as I have had an opportunity to make it." But for the death-penalty decisions—and he clearly hoped Congress would remedy these—he seemed satisfied for the time being with the criminal-justice work of the Court.[70]

That the Court favored law-enforcement values is no surprise. Burger, Blackmun, Powell, and Rehnquist got their seats on the bench because of their supposed or known lack of sympathy for the rights of the criminally accused. In one respect they have been remarkably forbearing to date—and shrewd. They have avoided dramatic overrulings of precedents in the area of criminal justice. Precipitous repudiations of established doctrines would appear too much as an act of arbitrary will; decisions should not look like the obvious result of subjective choices. In the art of judging, a proper regard for appearances counts. One must seem to appreciate the values of coherence, stability, and continuity with the past. Judges, especially judges who are reputedly conservative, ought to avoid sudden, radical shifts in constitutional doctrine. Any man who reaches the highest court is sophisticated enough to appreciate the strategic and political values of achieving desired objectives by indirection. Overruling is a device of last resort, employed when other alternatives have failed. The Burger Court has raised the use of alternative routes to a high art by relying on more subtle means than overruling in order to alter the course of the law. It reinterprets precedents, distinguishes them away, blunts them, obliterates them, ignores them, and makes new law without the need of overruling or being bound by the past. It nourishes the impression that it is a standpat Court, which merely refuses to endorse further expansions of the rights of the criminally accused. It cultivates the illusion, suitable to the image of a conservative court, of having some respect for precedents; at the same time, it narrows them until they become meaningless and moribund. When new cases arise it finds factual distinctions, always available, that allegedly warrant watering down the constitutional right at issue. New decisions have a corrosive effect on previous ones. While the Burger Court goes about its quiet business of creating its own regressive "revolution" in the criminal law, striking a pose of doing no more than refusing to open new frontiers, it has systematically closed old frontiers and made daring incursions that cripple many rights of the criminally accused. . . .

The way the Court reasons or reaches its result is as important as the result itself; in the long run, perhaps, the Court's reasoning is even more important because a decision based on an unsound rationale is not likely to survive. A rationale may be unsound because it plays fast and loose with the relevant precedents or with truth; it may be overbroad, illogical, or biased; or, it may be one-dimensional by ignoring opposing arguments. The Court's respect for the judicial process, for the need to strive for objectivity even if unattainable, and for the requirements of professional expertise, in short, its craftsmanship, is a vital aspect of its work. Assessment of the Burger Court's craftsmanship is as subjective as the art of judging, and experts will doubtless disagree, as they have about the Warren Court's craftsmanship. Concern for the validity of the route by which the Court reached its decisions is a major theme of Archibald Cox's book *The Warren Court*, the most sympathetic account yet published. Again and again, Cox subjects the Court's opinions to the scrutiny of an analytical, questioning mind, and again and again he fretted because the Court, though having reached the just result, failed to convince its critics. Nevertheless, Charles Alan Wright, a conservative constitutional lawyer, writing when criticism of the Warren Court reached a fever pitch, asked, "What Court in the past achieved a higher level of professional craftsmanship than the present Court? The great opinions of Chief Justice Marshall surely fail the test. . . . Has any later Court done better?"[71]

The Burger Court has done a lot worse in its criminal-justice opinions. It does not confront complicated constitutional questions with appropriate disinterestedness. Its opinions do not provide intellectually convincing explanations for its results. Far too often the majority simply issues edicts. Its fiat cannot command respect when the majority abuses or ignores precedents or refuses to consider fairly and seriously the arguments advanced by dissenting opinions. The majority faces away from, instead of facing, opposing views. There is too little debate in majority opinions. They fail to weigh criticisms. In brief, they do not develop carefully reasoned judgments. The majority seems to engage in result-oriented adjudication which is a corruption of the judicial process that leaves too far behind the idea of the rule of law enforced by impersonal and impartial judges. In constitutional cases, as in any other, the judge who first chooses what the outcome should be and then reasons backwards to supply a rationalization, replete with rules and precedents, has betrayed his calling: Having decided on the basis of prejudice or prejudgment, he has made constitutional law little more than the embodiment of his own policy preferences.

The Burger Court writes opinions that have the sound of stump speeches for the prosecution. The majority Justices stand for law and order, but there is little reason to respect their work when they do not respect their dissenting brethren or critics who ask if there is something called law and the Constitution to which decisions should conform. The decisions of the Court represent what the majority at the moment happen to think is best for the country, but they do not persuade anyone who believes that a judge who does his job faithfully will with some regularity reach judgments that conflict with his personal views as a private citizen. Blackmun's anguish in the death-penalty case is almost unique for a Nixon appointee. All four, and White too, vote for the rights of the criminally accused about as often as snarks are sighted alighting on the roof of the Supreme Court building. Worse, their opinions lack cogency, rigor, and on more occasions than are fitting, intellectual rectitude. The heirs of the Warren Court, Brennan, Douglas, and Marshall, are by no means above judicial sin, but they commit it with considerably less frequency and are no longer in a position that makes its commisson count. Everyone makes mistakes. Even Frankfurter and Harlan had their lapses and gaffes. But the majority that now controls the Court in criminal-justice cases has elevated the lapse and the gaffe to familiar events on decision day. Their opinions tend to make bad law in the sense of being badly crafted, as well as in the sense of tarnishing the Bill of Rights. The Court, as Professor Kurland declared, "ought to be able to explain why it is doing what it is doing." If it changes constitutional law, "it ought to state the reasons why it thinks the change is appropriate or necessary. . . . And when it does say why, it ought to do so honestly and not disingenuously or fraudulently."[72]

Justice Holmes is supposed to have said of his Chief Justice, William Howard Taft, that he honored him as former President and respected him as Chief Justice, but thought that as a lawyer he was no damn good. The lawyers who today constitute the majority of the Court in most criminal-justice cases are no damn good as judges. They are more like advocates for law enforcement's cause. The national press oversimplifies the work of the Court by characterizing its decisions and the Justices themselves as liberal or conservative. Even the *Harvard Law Review* divided the members of the Court into liberal and conservative voting blocs.[73] If Brennan, Douglas, and Marshall were liberal activists, the Nixon four and White are conservative activists. To attribute their opinions to strict construction of the Constitution is either foolish or deceptive.

The Bill of Rights requires an ardently sympathetic if not a liberal activist Court. There is no way for the guarantees of the Bill of Rights to have real meaning if not enforced by unstinting judicial affirmations that keep restraints upon government. No one wants to hobble law enforcement, no one wants the Bill of Rights to rot, and no one has ever proved that law enforcement cannot be effective against crime and be observant of the Bill of Rights at the same time. The fundamental law is an instrument of society, existing not as art does for art's sake but as a means for the sake of society's ends. Society requires a risky degree of freedom as well as an unremitting attack on the causes of crime and on law-breakers, even when the culprit is a policeman, a prosecutor, or a President. If officials protect society by any means at hand, they trade freedom for security. Any means to a justifiable end is, in a free society, a noxious and dangerous doctrine.

The Burger Court surrendered to that doctrine when it condoned admittedly illegal police practices, sanctioned the use of illegal evidence, allowed warrantless searches and seizures unrelated to the cause of arrest, upheld the prosecution's failure to disclose evidence of value to the accused, permitted unknowing waivers of rights, and denied the effective assistance of counsel. Regrettably, one can expand this list showing the Court's determination to find means to sanitize or legitimate law-enforcement conduct that brings shame on the administration of the criminal-justice system. Stunting the Fourth, Fifth, and Sixth Amendment rights of the criminally accused may increase the prison population but will not have any effect on crime nor help solve its causes, any more than the Nixon Administration's habitual juggling of crime statistics can prove that crime is no longer a problem.

The trouble with the Administration's reports of crime statistics is, as *Time* said, that they are "like a set of crooked corporate books—deceptive." The President himself assured the nation that "the hour of crisis has passed" because of the dip in the urban crime rate. He did not mention that the cities to which he referred declined in population or that violent crime was still on the increase, especially in the suburbs, although the rate of increase is slowing down. Only a week later, in another speech scorning "soft-headed judges," Nixon recommended extremely harsh penalties for criminals. Despite the supposed passing of the crime crisis, there has been an unprecedented government crime wave, prompting a wag to suggest that Nixon took crime off the streets and put it in the White House.[74]

There is a subtle danger that the Nixonian ethic has penetrated the chambers of the Supreme Court. After the close of the 1972–73 term, one Washington lawyer ominously remarked, "The Court has been Nixonized." He meant only that "Nixon has left his stamp on the Court, and consequently on American law. It could last for a generation."[75] But the Court's fidelity to the Bill of Rights has become dangerously attenuated. Its integrity is at issue when it winks at official lawlessness, warps precedents, or reasons woefully.

A hieromancer can read the entrails of a sacrificial chicken for portents of the future. Anyone adept at that art knows that the Burger Court will continue to undermine many criminal-justice achievements of the Warren Court. Those not skilled at reading entrails predicted that the Nixon appointees, being conservative jurists, would respect not subvert precedents. All of us who possess perfect hindsight can now decipher the writings in the ashes of an increasing number of opinions that for all practical purposes are dead.

NOTES

2. John Lilburne and the Rights of Englishmen

1. There are two good biographies of Lilburne, both of which were invaluable to me. M. A. Gibb, *John Lilburne, The Leveller: A Christian Democrat* (London, 1947), and Pauline Gregg, *Free-Born John, A Biography of John Lilburne* (London, 1961). Gregg is more detailed; Gibb is more philosophical. Harold W. Wolfram's "John Lilburne: Democracy's Pillar of Fire," *Syracuse Law Review*, III (Spring 1952), 213–58, proved useful on legal points.

2. Trial of John Lilburne and John Wharton (1637), *State Trials*, III, 1315, at 1318. This account was written by Lilburne.

3. My account of Star Chamber procedure is based on William Hudson, *Treatise of the Court of Star Chamber*, in Francis Hargrave, *Collectanea Juridica*, (London, 1791–92, 2 vols.), II, 64, 127, 152.

4. *State Trials*, III, 1320.

5. *Ibid.*, 1321–3. Lilburne's remark that no one had ever before refused the Star Chamber oath is quoted in Gibb, 48, from Lilburne's *The Christian Mans Triall*, 6. Gregg, 57, stated that Lilburne had the distinction of being the first to refuse the Star Chamber oath. It seems most unlikely; indeed, in the account by Lilburne, printed in *State Trials*, 1315, at 1322, he stated that the Star Chamber compared him to "some that had harboured Jesuits and Seminary-priests (those traitors) who refused to be examined upon oath. . . ." Of course, the court's statement may have been untrue; it was certainly a tactic to shame the two Puritans by comparing them to those whom they despised and thereby persuade them to change their minds about refusing the oath. In any case, both Gregg and Gibb reflect naïve views about Star Chamber procedure. On Wharton's wars against the High Commission, see *State Trials*, III, 1324; P.R.O. 908, S.P.D. Car. I, 16/324, fol. 4b; and a letter by Wharton, in *ibid.*, 16/373, dated Dec. 1637.

6. *State Trials*, III, 1323–8.

7. *Ibid.*, 1345 and 1349–50 for eye-witness accounts of Lilburne's punishment and physical condition; his speech in the pillory is reprinted in *ibid.*, III, 1329–40. His account of his punishment is also described in his *A Worke of the Beast* (1638), reprinted in William Haller, ed., *Tracts on Liberty in the Puritan Revolution 1638–1647*. (New York, 1933–34, 3 vols.), II, 3–24. For secondary accounts of his Star Chamber trial and punishment, see Gregg, 52–74, and Gibb, 45–56.

8. *State Trials*, 1350–52.

9. There is a chronological list of Lilburne's works in Gregg, 400–403. Clarendon's statement is in *State Trials*, IV, 1418.

10. Lord's Bill on Church Reform, July 1, 1641, in Samuel R. Gardiner, ed., *Constitutional Documents of the Puritan Revolution, 1625–1660* (Oxford, 1906, 3rd ed. rev.), 177.

11. Act for Abolition of the Court of Star Chamber, July 5, 1641, in *ibid.*, 179–86.

12. Act for Abolition of the Court of High Commission, July 5, 1641, in *ibid.*, 186–9; reconfirmed in 1661, 13 Car. II, ch. 12, sect. 4.

13. Trial of Fitzpatrick (1631), *State Trials*, III, 419, at 420.

14. James Fitzjames Stephen, *A History of the Criminal Law of England* (London, 1883, 3 vols.), I, 358; see also 369–70, and *cf.* Stephen's remarks at p. 382. See also Sir John Pollock, *The Popish Plot: A Study in the History of the Reign of Charles II* (Cambridge, Eng., 1944), 296, 298.

15. On the oath of the accused at common law, see John H. Wigmore, *A Treatise on the Anglo-American System of Evidence in Trials at Common Law* (Boston, 1940, 3rd ed., 10 vols.), II, sect. 575(5), 681–2, and Sir William Holdsworth, *A History of English Law* (London and Boston, 1903–66, 16 vols.), IX, 194.

16. For the Commons' censure of Lilburne's sentence, *State Trials*, III, 1342; for Clarendon, *ibid.*, IV, 1419; for the remark by Lilburne, Gibb, 93.

17. Jordan, III (1640–60), 42–57; Gregg, 113–14. For the number of newspapers, see Frederick Seaton Siebert, *Freedom of the Press in England, 1476–1776* (Urbana, Ill., 1952), 203; for the number of pamphlets, see *ibid.*, 191, and Gregg, 94. Gregg and Siebert do not agree on the exact statistics, though both counted the pamphlets in the Thomason collection in the British Museum. For Siebert's remark on Lilburne, see pp. 198–9. See *ibid.*, 173–212, for a discussion of Parliament and censorship.

18. On the Levellers generally, see Joseph Frank, *The Levellers, A History of the Writings of Three Seventeenth-Century Democrats: John Lilburne, Richard Overton, William Walwyn* (Cambridge, Mass., 1955); Theodore Calvin Pease, *The Leveller Movement: A Study in the History and Political Theory of the English Great Civil War* (Washington, 1916); H. N. Brailsford, *The Levellers and the English Revolution*, ed. by Christopher Hill (London, 1961); the introduction by Don M. Wolfe in his edition of *Leveller Manifestoes of the Puritan Revolution* (New York, 1944); and the introduction by William Haller, in Haller and Godfrey Davies, eds. *The Leveller Tracts, 1647–1653* (New York, 1944), 1–50. For the information in my paragraph, see Gregg, 115, 117, 124; Gibb, 102, 103, 111, 122–3.

19. For Lilburne's examination before the committee, see his *A Copy of a Letter from Lieutenant-Colonel John Lilburne to a friend* (London, 1645), 2, 14. Italics added. The episode is recounted in Gregg, 119–21, and Gibb, 127–9.

20. Quoted in Gibb, 129, citing *Commons Journal*, IV, 235–7.

21. On Lilburne's reading, see Gibb, 130–33, and Gregg, 58, 94–5, 127, 133. Prynne's remark is in Gibb, 130. *Englands Birth-Right Justified* is reprinted in Haller, ed, *Tracts on Liberty*, III, 258–307; the quoted statement is at p. 263.

22. *Englands Birth-Right*, in Haller, III, 262–6.

23. *Englands Lamentable Slaverie* (1645) is reprinted in Haller, III, 311–35; the quoted matter is at p. 311. Cromwell's letter to Parliament is quoted by Lord Clarendon, in *State Trials*, IV, 1419.

24. Larner is quoted in Gregg, 136–7. See also William M. Clyde, *The Struggle for the Freedom of the Press from Caxton to Cromwell* (London, 1934), 109. On Lilburne, see Gregg, 137–42, and Gibb, 144–9.

25. Gibb, 150; Wolfe, 109, for the characterization of Overton's *Remonstrance;* Wolfe, 121, for the quotation from the document, which is reprinted at pp. 109–130.

26. Overton, *An Appeale, From the Degenerate Representative Body of the Commons of England Assembled at Westminster. To the Body Represented, The free people* (1647), reprinted in Wolfe, 156–95; quoted matter is at pp. 164–6, 192. Wolfe's description of the pamphlet as a "classic statement" is at p. 155. Gregg, 145, quotes Lord Hunsdon's "Lilburne-like" comment. See Gregg, 144–51, for the episode involving Overton and his family. See also Overton's *The Commoner's Complaint* (1647), in Haller, *Tracts*, III, 393. In 1647 Nicholas Tew, the Leveller printer, also refused to

answer questions before the Parliamentary committee on ground that he was not bound to accuse himself, *State Trials*, IV, 871, at 887.

27. Thomas Edwards, *Gangraena*, Part III (London, 1646), 169–70.

28. Gregg, 152–3.

29. G. P. Gooch, *Democratic Ideas in the Seventeenth Century* (Cambridge, Eng., 1926, 2nd ed.), 124, called Lilburne "the most popular man in England." Baxter and the anonymous newswriter are quoted in Gibb, 178.

30. Walwyn's *To the right honourable and supreme Authority of this Nation, the Commons in Parliament assembled. The humble Petition of many thousands* (1647) is reprinted in Wolfe, 135–41; the quoted lines are at p. 139. Gibb, 163. Margaret Atwood Judson, *The Crisis of the Constitution*, (New Brunswick, N.J., 1949), 381. For other Leveller documents demanding the right, see *The Case of the Armie Truly Stated* (1647), *To the Supream Authority* (1648), *To the Right Honorable, the Commons of England* (1648), *Foundations of Freedom* (the "2nd Agreement of the People," 1648), and *An Agreement of the Free People* (the "3rd Agreement of the people," 1649), in Wolfe, 38, 216, 266, 287, 301, 406. See also *Heads of the Proposals* (1647) and *Putney Projects* (1647), in A. S. P. Woodhouse, ed., *Puritanism and Liberty. Being the Army Debates (1647–49) from the Clarke Manuscripts with Supplementary Documents* (Chicago, 1951), 425 and 427. Additionally, see *A Declaration of Some Proceedings of Lt. Col. John Lilburn* (1648), *The Bloody Project* (1648), *Englands New Chains Discovered* (1649), *The Legall Fundamental Liberties of the People* (1649), *The Fountain of Slaunder* (1649), and *The Just Defense of John Lilburn* (1653), in Haller and Davies, *Leveller Tracts*, 109, 137–8, 163, 246, 410, 454, 457.

31. Theodorus Verax [Clement Walker], *Anarchia Anglicana: or, The History of Independency* (London, 1648), 53–60, quoted matter at pp. 55, 57.

32. J. Howldin [John Holden], *The Lawes Subversion: or, Sir John Maynards Case truly stated* (London, 1648), 6; at p. 16, Holden warned readers: "You may be imperiously commanded to fall upon the point of your own sword, i.e. to answer interrogatories propounded by degrees from a Command, to accuse yourselfe to an Oath *Ex Officio*."

33. *To the Right Honorable, The Commons of England In Parliament Assembled. The humble Petition of divers wel affected Persons* (1648), reprinted in Wolfe, 287. "We pray you . . ." is in *The Hunting of the Foxes* (1649), in *ibid.*, 371. The same pamphlet gives the soldier's reply to the General Council of the Army at p. 375; see also 372, 377, 378, 379. Lilburne's authorship of this pamphlet is uncertain. Gregg, 389, n. 2, attributes it to him; Wolfe, 356, attributes it to Overton. See Gregg, 269, for Parliament's condemnation of *Englands New Chains*, Part Two. Haller and Davies print *Englands New Chains*, 156–70, and the second part, 171–89.

34. For Bradshaw's remarks as Lilburne's counsel in 1645, see *State Trials*, III, 1349. The four prisoners co-authored an account of their arrest and examination in *The Picture of the Councel of State* (1649), reprinted in Haller and Davies, 190–246. See also the accounts in Gibb, 256–8, and Gregg, 269–70.

35. *Picture of the Councel*, in Haller and Davies, 201–2, 204, 224, 237.

36. Gregg, 274–94; Gibb, 258–77.

37. The report of Lilburne's trial in 1649, with related documents, is in *State Trials*, IV, 1269–1470. Quoted matter is at p. 1466.

38. *Ibid.*, 1281, 1283, 1386, 1294, 1299, 1306.

39. *Ibid.*, 1270–83.

40. *Ibid.*, 1281, 1286, 1293.

41. *Ibid.*, 1291, 1292, 1301, 1320–29.

42. *Ibid.*, 1292–6. In a treason case, refusal to plead to the indictment could be taken *pro confesso;* Stephen, *History of the Criminal Law of England*, I, 298.

43. *State Trials*, IV, 1295–1306; quoted matter at pp. 1297, 1298, 1300, 1305.

44. *Ibid.*, 1307, 1309–10.

248 Notes

45. *Ibid.*, 1310–14.

46. *Ibid.*, 1340–42. Extracts from Lilburne's pamphlets cover pp. 1352–72.

47. Lilburne's defense spreads over pp. 1373–95 in *ibid.*

48. *Ibid.*, 1377.

49. *Ibid.*, 1395, 1402.

50. *Ibid.*, 1405–6. See also the trial of Christopher Love (1651), *State Trials*, V, 43, who consciously emulated Lilburne, whose trial he had witnessed. At V, 76–7, the prosecutor complained that Love would not answer any questions to accuse himself.

51. Gregg, *Free-Born John*, 303–11; Gibb, *John Lilburne*, 295–302.

52. Quoted in Gibb, 315.

53. Lilburne's trial of 1653 is reported poorly and incompletely in *State Trials*, V, 407–46. Clarendon's remark is in *State Trials*, IV, 1420. See also Gibb, 308–20; Gregg, 324–32.

54. The examination of the jury is reported in *State Trials*, V, 445–50.

55. Gibb, 321–45; Gregg, 333–46.

3. Quaker Blasphemy and Toleration

1. *The Journal of George Fox*, ed. Norman Penney (Cambridge, 1911, 2 vols.), I, 249–50. This edition is the unexpurgated text, *verbatim* and *literatim*. But this edition and *The Short Journal and Itinerary Journals of George Fox*, ed. Norman Penney (Cambridge, 1925), are extremely difficult to read if only because Fox's style and eccentricities in spelling compound the problems presented by seventeenth-century orthography. *The Journal of George Fox*, ed. John T. Nickalls (Cambridge, 1952), presents in modern English most but not all of the 1911 *Journal* with valuable additions from the 1925 *Short Journal*. As a convenience to the reader I have used, whenever possible, Nickall's 1952 edition and cited it as *Journal* (1952). On occasion the earlier, definitive editions by Penney, which contain invaluable scholarly notes, must be used.

2. Burrough's remarks are from his introduction to Fox, *The Great Mistery of the Great Whore Unfolded* (1659), reprinted in *The Works of George Fox* (Philadelphia, 1831, 3 vols.), III, 14, and Burrough, *A Word of Reproof* (1659), quoted in Christopher Hill, *The World Turned Upside down* (New York, 1973), 197. Hill's eagerness to turn the early Quakers into "political radicals" (p. 195), turns the matter upside down; they were nonpolitical and wholly religious. Dewsbury's statement of 1665 is in William C. Braithwaite, *The Beginnings of Early Quakerism* (London, 1912), 280. Braithwaite's is the classic treatment for the period to 1660. Hugh Barbour, *The Quakers in Puritan England* (New Haven, 1964), is the only modern monograph that adds anything of value to Braithwaite.

3. *Journal* (1952), 14, 27, 68. On lamenting the army's failure, see Mabel Richmond Brailsford, *A Quaker from Cromwell's Army: James Nayler* (London, 1927), 24. Nayler's *Lamb's War Against the Man of Sin* (1657) is in his *A Collection of Sundry Books, Epistles and Papers*, ed. George Whitehead (London, 1716), 375–400.

4. *Journal* (1952), 182, 244–5; Braithwaite, *Beginnings*, 195, 446.

5. *Journal* (1952), 36, 92, 242–9; *Journal*, ed. Penney (1911), I, 217–9. Braithwaite, *Beginnings*, 486–99.

6. Barbour, *Quakers*, 257–8, quotes Audland; Braithwaite, *Beginnings*, 136, and on the woman, 199. For the Fox quote, Braithwaite, *Beginnings* 451; *Journal* (1952), 280, gives a variant quotation.

7. *Journal* (1952), 24, 39–40, 51; Braithwaite, *Beginnings*, 444–5.

8. *Journal* (1952), 35. Barbour, *Quakers*, 211, gives the quotations from E. Burrough and George Bishop; his ch. 8 on persecution of Quakers and their theory of toleration is very good.

9. *Journal* (1952), 7, 8, 11, 19–20; Barbour, *Quakers*, 154–7.

10. On Fox's railing as love, see *Journal*, ed. Penney (1911), I, 10, 90–2, 116. For the

first Baxter quote, Braithwaite, *Beginnings*, 284; the second, *Reliquae Baxterianae* (London, 1696), 77. On vituperative conduct, see Braithwaite, *Beginnings*, ch. 12.

11. Proclamation of 1655, reprinted in Samuel R. Gardiner, *History of the Commonwealth and Protectorate* (London, 1903, 4 vols.), III, 260–1.

12. *Reliquae Baxterianae*, 77; *Journal*, ed. Penney (1911), I, 89; *Journal* (1952), 15, 18, 27. On going naked for a sign, see Braithwaite, *Beginnings*, 148–51.

13. On the name "Quaker," *Journal*, ed. Penney (1911), I, 5–9; II, 395; Barclay, *Apology*, proposition xi, sect. 8 of any edition; I used the 8th ed. (Providence, 1940), 359; Braithwaite, *Beginnings*, 57. For the quote of Nayler, see James Gough, *Memoirs* (Dublin, 1781), 56.

14. *Journal* (1952), 8, 10–28.

15. *Diary of Thomas Burton*, ed. John Towill Rutt (London, 1828, 4 vols.), I, 62 (hereafter cited as *Diary of Burton*). On the social backgrounds of the early Quakers and their geographic strengths, see Barbour, *Quakerism*, ch. 3. On religious precursors, see generally Rufus M. Jones, *Spiritual Reformers of the 16th and 17th Centuries* (1914; Boston, 1959 reprint); Rufus M. Jones, *Studies in Mystical Religion* (London, 1909); Robert Barclay, *The Inner Life of the Religious Societies of the Commonwealth* (London, 1876), chs. 5, 9–10.

16. *Journal*, ed. Penney (1911), I, 2; *Journal* (1952), 51–2.

17. For Fox on the Ranters, *Journal* (1952), 47, 81, 181–3, 195. For the tract of 1652 and More's statement, see Braithwaite, *Beginnings*, 40, 58. G. H., *The Declaration of John Robins* (London, 1651), I, 6, identified Ranters as Shakers; J. M. (a former Ranter), *The Ranters Last Sermon* (London, 1654), 6, referred to "Ranters, Quakers, Shakers, and the rest of their atheistical crew." See also *The Ranters Creed* (1651), 6. R. Forneworth, *The Ranters Principles* (London, 1654), a Quaker tract censuring Ranters was written to distinguish Quakers from Ranters. On Hotham, *Journal* (1952), 75, 90, and on the identification of Hotham, *Short Journal*, ed. Penney (1925), 277. Dr. Robert Gell made a similar statement to William Penn about the Quakers' having prevented England from being overrun by the Ranters; see Jones, *Studies in Mystical Religion*, 481. The "leveller" remark, and many like it, is in *Diary of Burton*, I, 169. On the grand jury, Hill, *World Upside Down*, 192; Hill, 195, calls the Quakers "political radicals" to make them fit his ideological straitjacket.

18. *Journal* (1952), 61.

19. Braithwaite, *Beginnings*, 6; *Journal* (1952), 73, 100–1; Brailsford, *Quaker from Cromwell's Army*, 38–9, 41–2, 46–8, 67. Nayler, *A Collection of Sundry Books*, 12, for his "call."

20. *Reliquae Baxterianae*, 76; Braithwaite, *Beginnings*, 241; Alexander Gordon, on Nayler, *D.N.B.*, XIV, 133.

21. *Journal* (1952), 129–30; on Fell, see Braithwaite, *Beginnings*, 105–6. See Barbour, *Quakers*, 148, for Nayler on Fox and Fox's reply to a judge.

22. On Fox's blasphemy case of 1652, see *Journal* (1952), 129–39. On "Sonne of God," see *Short Journal*, ed. Penney (1925), xx, 5, 17, 479 n. 2. On "My Father and I are one," *Journal*, ed. Penney (1911), I, 66, and for Penney's comment, I, 425.

23. *Journal* (1952), 132–9; *Journal*, ed. Penney (1911), I, 62–7; on the petition, *Short Journal*, ed. Penney (1925), 283–4; Braithwaite, *Beginnings*, 108–9, and especially Fox, *Works (The Great Mystery)*, III, 585–97.

24. Nayler, *Diverse Particulars of the Persecutions of James Nayler, by the Priests of Westmorland* (1652), reprinted in *A Collection of Sundry Books, Epistles and Papers Written by James Nayler*, 1–10.

25. *The Examination of James Nayler, upon an Indictment for Blasphemy, at the Sessions at Appleby*, in *ibid.*, 11–16. On Pearson, see Brailsford, *Quaker from Cromwell's Army*, 28–9, and Braithwaite, *Beginnings*, 112–13.

26. *Journal* (1952), 158–9; *Short Journal*, ed. Penney (1925), 32–3.

27. *Journal* (1952), 160.

28. *Ibid.*, 160–4. On Cromwell and the Quakers, see W. K. Jordan, *The Development of Religious Toleration in England (1640–1660)*, III, 176–9, and Braithwaite, *Beginnings*, ch. 17 on Quaker "Relations with the State." On the Nominated Parliament of 1653, see Gardiner, *Commonwealth and Protectorate*, II, 272–92.

29. *Journal* (1952), 233. Brailsford, *Quaker from Cromwell's Army*, 85–9; Braithwaite, *Beginnings*, 170–200; Emilia Fogelklou, *James Nayler* (London, 1931), 131–7.

30. Brailsford, *Quaker from Cromwell's Army*, 76; Braithwaite, *Beginnings*, 172–3, 178–80, 446, Gardiner, *Commonwealth and Protectorate*, III, 263. For Fox's account, *Journal* (1952), 191–9.

31. *Journal* (1952), 242–66.

32. *Ibid.*, 267–9; Braithwaite, *Beginnings*, 245–8; Brailsford, *Quaker from Cromwell's Army;* 93–100, which on p. 97 includes the Fox letter on "unclean spirits." For an eyewitness account of the Fox–Nayler schism at Exeter, see Hubberthorne's letter reprinted in Fogelklou, *James Nayler*, 164–7.

33. James Deacon, *The grand Impostor examined, Or, the Life, Trial, and Examination of James Nayler* (1656), reprinted in Howell's *State Trials*, V, 826–42, of which pp. 830–2 includes some of the letters to Nayler. Deacon was an interrogator at the Bristol examination. In addition to his account, other eyewitness reports are Ra[lph] Farmer, *Sathan Inthron'd in his Chair of Pestilence* (1657) and William Grigge, *The Quakers Jesus* (1658). Grigge took the shorthand notes of the Bristol interrogation, *ibid.*, Epistle, answer 2. Farmer's *Sathan Inthron'd*, 4–10, includes a good selection of the letters. Another valuable primary source is Anon., *A True Narrative of the Examination, Tryall, and Sufferings of James Nayler* (1657). Anon, *Memoirs of the Life, Ministry, Tryal and Sufferings of that Very Eminent Person James Nailer, the Quaker's Great Apostle* (1729), is a later collection of the documents of the case, but unique because the long preface is favorable to Nayler and the documents are studded with notes pointing out distortions in the presentation of evidence against him; the author also reprinted some eloquent letters by Nayler on his religious beliefs (*ibid.*, pp. 71–80).

34. On the Dorcas Erbury incident, see Deacon, *Grand Impostor*, in *State Trials*, V, 834, 837. Henry J. Cadbury, *Fox's Book of Miracles* (Cambridge, 1948), is best on "miraculous" cures by Quaker preachers. There are some one hundred fifty entries on cures attributed to Fox; on Howgill and the lame boy, *ibid.*, 12. See also Braithwaite, *Beginnings*, 247, 341. Fox's letter is in Farmer, *Sathan Inthron'd*, 9–10.

35. Most of the primary sources mentioned in note 33 above include accounts of the entry into Bristol. Fogelklou, *James Nayler*, 157–73, contains an excellent account of the Fox–Nayler schism and its effect upon Nayler. See also Brailsford, *Quaker from Cromwell's Army*, 116–18. On Fox's recommendations to the Bristol Quakers, see his *Journal* (1952), 281–2.

36. The primary sources for the Bristol examinations are referred to in note 33 above. "Proceedings in the House of Commons against James Nayler for Blasphemy and Misdemeanours," *State Trials*, V, 801–20, of which p. 806 refers to Nayler's resemblance to Jesus. On the same point, see Grigge, *Quakers Jesus*, 68–9, and Farmer, *Sathan Inthron'd*, 25–7. *A True Narrative*, 1–28, reproduces the complete record of the parliamentary committee's interrogations and report. For judgments that Nayler was mad, see the account by David Hume, quoted in *State Trials*, V, 804; David Masson, *The Life of John Milton* (London, 1859–94, 7 vols.), V, 68; Thomas Carlyle, *Oliver Cromwell's Letters and Speeches* (London, 1904, 3 vols.), III, 213; Barclay, *The Inner Life*, 427; Charles H. Firth, *The Last Years of the Protectorate* (London, 1909, 2 vols.), I, 96; Jordan, *Religious Toleration (1640–1660)*, III, 221, 223, 226; Theodore A. Wilson and Frank J. Merli, "Nayler's Case and the Dilemma of the Protectorate," University of Birmingham *Historical Journal*, X (1965–6), 46, 47; and, to a lesser extent, Fogelklou, *James Nayler*, 163, 172, 176, 179–80.

37. The Bristol examinations are reprinted in Grigge, *Quakers Jesus*, 4–6. Barbour,

Quakers, 185, quotes the Fell letter in the context of the prevailing Quaker apocalyptic view.

38. Deacon, *Grand Imposter*, in *State Trials*, V, 832, 834. For a variant report of the same interrogation, see Grigge, *Quakers Jesus*, 7.

39. *State Trials*, V, 834. The woman supposedly called "mother" was Martha Symonds; for her examination, *ibid.*, 835–6. On her, see Fogelklou, *James Nayler*, 151–5; Farmer, *Sathan Inthron'd*, 9–10, for Fox's letter to Nayler about her.

40. For the Bristol examinations of Nayler's companions, see Deacon, *Grand Imposter*, in *State Trials*, V, 833–8.

41. *Journals of the House of Commons*, VII, 448, Oct. 31, 1656 (hereafter *Journals H.C.*); *State Trials*, V, 805.

42. *State Trials*, V, 805–15; *Journals H. C.*, VII, 448.

43. The Instrument of Government is reprinted in S. R. Gardiner, ed., *Constitutional Documents of the Puritan Revolution* (London, 1906, 3rd ed.), 405–17; the religion clauses, 416. My summary of the religious policy of the Protectorate is from Jordan, *Religious Toleration*, III, 144–202.

44. Jordan, *Religious Toleration*, III, 164–5; *ibid.*, 450–1, on the growth of Congregationalism.

45. *Ibid.*, 156–8; for the quote from the ambassador, 171.

46. *Journals H. C.*, VII, 399; Jordan, *Religious Toleration*, III, 166, 170.

47. Firth, *Last Years*, I, 11–21; Jordan, *Religious Toleration*, III, 188–90. The constitution of 1657 was "The Humble Petition and Advice," reprinted in Gardiner, ed., *Constitutional Documents*; see 454–5, for the religious clause. For the political situation leading to the new constitution, see Firth, *Last Years*, I, 128–200.

48. Carlyle, *Cromwell's Speeches and Letters*, III, 213.

49. Rex v. Taylor, 3 Keble 607 (1676), and 1 Ventris 293 (1676).

50. Instrument of Government, in Gardiner, ed., *Constitutional Documents*, 405–17. *Diary of Burton*, I, 29, 112, 118, 123, 141.

51. *Diary of Burton*, I, 25, 59, 68, 88, 90, 97. On the no-law theme, *ibid.*, 38, 57–8, 87, 120–1, 125, 128, 152, 163, 174; on the omnipotence of Parliament, 58, 108, 125; for Howard, 78; for Sydenham, 86; for Strickland, 88, and see also Wolsey, 89; for Kelsey, 164. Some claimed that the jurisdiction of the defunct ecclesiastical courts devolved upon Parliament, 35, 108, 125, 141–2.

52. On vindicating the honor of God and blasphemy as treason against God, *ibid.*, 25–6, 39, 48, 51, 55, 59–60, 63, 68, 86, 89, 96, 109, 114, 122, 125, 132, 139, 150. On merciful, 90; on Richard Cromwell, 126.

53. *Ibid.*, 62–3.

54. *Ibid.*, 25, 49–50, 63, 107. On Skippon, see Firth, *Last Years*, I, 86, 92.

55. For examples of biblical speeches by major generals, see *Diary of Burton*, I, 99–100 (Packer), 101–4 (Walley), 108–10 (Goffe), 113–14 (Boteler), 122–4 (Kelsey). A note showing all references to the Bible during the course of the debates would have to read *ibid.*, 25–150 *passim*. On Smith, *ibid.*, 87, and Masson, *Life of Milton*, V, 92.

56. *Diary of Burton*, I, 170, 173, 174; Grigge, *Quakers Jesus*, 35.

57. *Diary of Burton*, I, 98, 97, 108–9, 86, 124, 146, 169, in the sequence for the quotations in my text. For other anti-Quaker remarks, see pp. 70, 76, 128, 132, 137 ("they will level the foundations of all government"), and 170. Farmer, *Sathan Inthron'd*, 28, called Quakerism a "medly of Popery, Socinianism, Arianisme, Arminianisme, Anabaptisme, and all that is nought."

58. For statements sympathetic to Quakers, see *Diary of Burton*, 56, 62–3, 65, 69, 86, 88, 99, 120; for Baynes, White, and Goffe, 59, 60, 110.

59. *Ibid.*, 88, 120.

60. *Ibid.*, 33.

61. *Ibid.*, 46–8. Burton's prejudice shows even in the reporting of the debate. In

addition to his omission of Nayler's orthodox answers and his stating that Nayler had confessed, Burton omitted a tolerationist speech with the comment that the member, Walter Waller, "said a good deal more to extenuate the crime but I minded it not" (p. 152). At another point Burton gave a few terse lines to several tolerationist speeches, saying it was too dark to take notes, but still later that night he gave ample space to a "very large and handsome speech" by Bampfield against "the merciful men," in which Bampfield advocated death (pp. 90–92). The fullest analysis of the debate by a historian is Jordan, *Religious Toleration*, III, 221–43. Jordan's four volumes are in many respects invaluable and definitive, but he was wholly uninterested in the subject of blasphemy and never treated it as a special problem. To Jordan, blasphemy was merely an aspect of heresy, although he never distinguished the two. He reported the opinions of an extraordinary range of people and sects on toleration, but omitted Quaker opinions. His account of Nayler's case was unreliable and ununderstanding. He simplistically identified the revengers as the Presbyterians, never mentioning Congregationalists and Independents, without whom the revengers would not have been a political force. Jordan gave the impression that the government stood for toleration against the dominant Presbyterian party in Parliament. The government, in fact, was divided, as were Oliver and Richard Cromwell. The protector, having taken no position during the debate, offered no leadership; his councillors who sat in Parliament represented every viewpoint on every question during the Nayler debate. Jordan declared that the Nayler case was of great importance to the development of religious toleration, but without understanding early Quakerism and the differences between heresy and blasphemy, he could not understand the reasons. He regarded Nayler as "obviously mad," "obviously demented," and "plainly unbalanced," and said that he had "messianic delusions." He also said that Nayler had been worshipped "as" the Lamb, rather than that the worship had been directed to the Lamb in Nayler. The distinction is crucial. Jordan declared that Nayler offended "all religious men," yet some who defended him were not offended. More to the point, Nayler himself was a devout Christian, as religious as any member of Parliament, and so were his followers. Jordan saw Nayler as an undoubted blasphemer and claimed that his blasphemy was "universally admitted." Yet many of Nayler's defenders in Parliament denied that he was guilty of blasphemy. Like Burton, Jordan thought that Nayler was "determined to hang himself. He confessed to all the committee's charges against him. . . ." Jordan stated that insanity was not a defense to the charge of blasphemy; but Nayler did not plead insanity; it *was* a defense under the act of 1650, and it was a defense even in Scotland where the Presbyterians were in complete control. The Scottish Act against Blasphemy of 1661 exempted anyone "distracted in his wits" (Baron David Hume, *Commentaries on the Law of Scotland, respecting the Description and Punishment of Crimes* [Edinburgh, 1797, 2 vols.], II, 514). Without considering the cursing of God or atheistic denial and contempt of God, Jordan declared that "no severer test for the principle of religious toleration could have been devised by a satanic mind." Such a statement, from a specialist on toleration, was exaggerated as well as wrong. Firth, *Last Years*, I, 83–106, treats the Nayler case without glaring error; Firth was not interested in the subject of blasphemy. Braithwaite, *Beginnings*, 241–78, has a fascinating account of the Nayler case within the context of early Quaker thought; Braithwaite too was uninterested in blasphemy as a problem for religious toleration or as a legal or religious concept. He cared about the Quaker mind and the impact of the case on subsequent Quaker behavior and development. The two biographers of Nayler, Brailsford and Fogelklou, stressed colorful details, such as the entrance into Bristol and the execution of the punishment, but they were innocent of any concern for procedure, jurisdiction, or the substantive offense.

62. *Diary of Burton*, I, 53, 79.
63. *Ibid.*, 118–19; see also p. 123.
64. *Ibid.*, 56, 59–61.
65. *Ibid.*, 128–31, much of which consists of notes by Rutt, the editor of the *Diary of*

Burton, from *State Trials.* Whitelocke's speech of Dec. 12 is fully reported there, V, 821–8.

66. *Diary of Burton,* I, 47, 65.

67. *Ibid.,* 66–8, 74, 101–4, 124, 132, 151, 164, for the revengers; for Cooper and Packer, 96–7, 99–101.

68. *Journals H. C.,* VII, 468–9, Dec. 16, 1656; *Diary of Burton,* I, 152–8. Both sources include the vote and the sentence, but Burton provided additional detail on the debate concerning the lesser sentence. *The Diary of Burton,* pp. 161–3, also includes the debate giving the rationale for Parliament's choosing to act judicially rather than legislatively. Boring through the tongue with a hot iron, however cruel, was a humane refinement of the ancient punishment of cutting the tongue off. See John Godolphin, *Reportorium Canonicum; or An Abridgment of the Ecclesiastical Laws of this Realm* (London, 1678), 559. During the Nayler debate a Major Audley said that boring through the tongue "is an ordinary punishment for swearing [profanity], I have known twenty bored through the tongue" (*Diary of Burton,* I, 154).

69. *Diary of Burton,* I, 163, 167, 246.

70. *Ibid.,* 38, 137, 247. For the lashing scene, see *A True Narrative of the . . . Sufferings of James Nayler,* 34–8, written before Nayler underwent the last third of his punishment in Bristol. See also "The Testimony of Rebecca Travers," in *Memoirs of the Life, Ministry, Tryal and Sufferings,* 58–9.

71. *Diary of Burton,* I, 167–73; *Journals H. C.,* VII, 470, Dec. 18, 1656. On the toleration issue and the constitution of 1657, see above, text for note 47 of this chapter.

72. *Diary of Burton,* I, 182–3, 217–21; *State Papers Domestic, Commonwealth and Protectorate,* CXXXI, 1656, Dec. 20. No. 45; *Journals H. C.,* VII, 471; *True Narrative,* 49–56, includes the petitions of the one hundred to Parliament and to Cromwell, prefaced by a plea for religious liberty for Nayler and all Quakers. A copy of the petition to Cromwell, endorsed by him on Dec. 25, 1656, is reprinted in Norman Penney, *Extracts from State Papers Relating to Friends, 1654 to 1672* (London, 1913), 21–3, bearing eighty-eight signatures, including: Joshua Sprigge, a former New Model Army chaplain; Giles Calvert, the printer of Ranter, Leveller, and Quaker tracts; and Edward Bushell, one of the minor heroes in the history of English liberty. In 1670 Bushell was the foreman of the jury that refused, against fierce judicial browbeating, to return a verdict of guilty in the trial of Penn and Mead for inciting a riot—practicing their religion in violation of the act against conventicles. Bushell and his jury were fined, refused to pay, and were sent to jail where they stayed some months before a higher court ruled in favor of the right of the jury to return an honest verdict. See William S. Holdsworth, *A History of English Law* (London, 1938–66, 16 vols., 6th ed., rev.), I, 344–6.

73. *Journal,* ed. Penney (1911), I, 266; *True Narrative,* 55; *Diary of Burton,* I, 217–18, 263; Grigge, *Quakers Jesus,* 16–18.

74. *Diary of Burton,* I, 265–6; *True Narrative,* 42, for the size and behavior of the crowd and for Rich's conduct at the branding.

75. Grigge, *Quakers Jesus,* 19–22.

76. On Nayler's change of attitude, see his "Confessions" written from Bridewell prison, 1658, in Whitehead's introduction to Nayler's *A Collection,* xxv-xxxix; the words quoted are in *ibid.,* xxxv.

4. Did the Zenger Case Really Matter?

1. John P. Roche, "American Liberty: An Examination of the 'Tradition' of Freedom," in *Aspects of Liberty,* ed. M. R. Konvitz and Clinton Rossiter (Ithaca, 1958), 137.

2. My account of the Zenger case is based primarily on Livingston Rutherfurd, *John*

Peter Zenger, His Press, His Trial and a Bibliography of Zenger Imprints. Also a reprint of the First Edition of the Trial (New York, 1904), still the best and most detailed book, now rare. My own abridged version of the trial, based on Rutherfurd's literal reprint, is in Levy, ed. *Freedom of the Press from Zenger to Jefferson* (Indianapolis, 1966), 43–61. I have read every issue of Zenger's *New-York Weekly Journal*. The best modern account, which parallels Rutherfurd, is Stanley Nider Katz, ed., *A Brief Narrative of the Case and Trial of John Peter Zenger*, by James Alexander (Cambridge, Mass., 1972, 2nd ed.). Katz's introduction and critical annotations are excellent, and his volume includes valuable supplementary documents such as Alexander's brief. Because of the easy availability of Katz's modernized edition of the trial, I have referred to it in my notes. My own essay, "Did the Zenger Case Really Matter?" *William and Mary Quarterly*, 3rd ser., 17 (1960): 35–50, stressed the continued suppressive role of the popular Assembly of New York, a subject ignored by Paul Finkelman's putative reply, "The Zenger Case: Prototype of a Political Trial," an otherwise worthwhile essay, in Michal R. Belknap, ed., *American Political Trials* (Westport, Conn., 1981), 21–42. All background facts are from Livingston's prefatory chapters, pp. 3–132, as corroborated by Katz's introduction, pp. 1–38.

3. *Philadelphia Gazette*, May 18, 1738.

4. *New-York Weekly Journal*, Nov. 12, 1733, essay reprinted in Levy, ed., *Freedom of the Press*, 26–32, quotation at 28. For "rogue," *Weekly Journal*, Jan. 21, 1734.

5. For the charge, see Katz, ed. *Brief Narrative*, 41–42.

6. *Ibid.*, 45.

7. *Ibid.*, 50.

8. *Ibid.*, 51–54, 56.

9. On Hamilton, see Burton Alva Konkle, *The Life of Andrew Hamilton, 1676–1741* (Philadelphia, 1941). The briefs of both Alexander and Chambers are in Katz, ed., *Brief Narrative*, 139–51.

10. Katz, ed., *Brief Narrative*, 62.

11. *Ibid.*, 69–70, for the quotation, and pp. 41–42 and 74 for the reliance on Hawkins. See William Hawkins, *A Treatise of the Pleas of the Crown* (London, 1716, 2 vols), 1: 184.

12. Katz, ed., *Brief Narrative*, 70–74.

13. *Ibid.*, 75.

14. *Ibid.*, 78.

15. *Ibid.*, 78–79, 84, 96.

16. *Ibid.*, 99.

17. *Ibid.*, 101.

18. The principle that truth should be a defense, sometimes attributed to the Zenger defense, can be found earlier in *The Thoughts of a Tory Author, concerning the Press* (London, 1712), 25–26, a tract uncertainly ascribed to Joseph Addison. The principle was popularized by John Trenchard and William Gordon in "Reflections upon Libelling," London *Journal*, June 10, 1721, and reprinted in their very popular *Cato's Letters: Or, Essays on Liberty, Civil and Religious, and Other Important Subjects* (London, 1723–24), 6th ed., I (London, 1755), 247.

19. The principle that the jury should decide the law as well as the facts in a case of seditious libel, sometimes attributed to the Zenger defense, was explicitly stated in 1692 by William Bradford in his trial for seditious libel in Philadelphia. See *New-England's Spirit of Persecution Transmitted to Pennsilvania . . . in the Tryal of Peter Boss, George Keith, Thomas Budd, and William Bradford . . . 1692* (Philadelphia, 1693), 33–34. Thomas Maule, who was tried for seditious libel in Boston in 1696, also claimed that the jury should decide the law as well as the facts. See Theo. Philanthes [Thomas Maule], *New-England Persecutors Mauld with Their Own Weapons. . . . Together with a Brief Account of the Imprisonment and Tryal of Thomas Maule of Salem, for Publishing a Book . . .* (New York, 1697), 61–62.

20. There are more trials for seditious utterances reported in *A Complete Collection of State Trials . . .*, ed. T. B. Howell, 33 vols. (London, 1809–26), for the two years following Fox's Libel Act than the total number reported for the whole of the eighteenth century before that time. Within a year of the statute the attorney general declared that he had on file 200 informations for seditious libel, Thomas Erskine May, *The Constitutional History of England . . . 1760–1860* (New York, 1880), II, 142*n*. The most notorious conviction was that against Thomas Paine for publishing his *Rights of Man*, Rex *v.* Paine (1792), Howell, *State Trials*, XXII, 357. Duffin and Lloyd were convicted of seditious libel for having pasted a placard on the door of their debtor's prison alleging that liberty would commence in Great Britain when infamous bastilles, as France had shown, were no longer necessary, Rex *v.* Duffin and Lloyd (1792), *ibid.*, p. 318. A jury voted guilty against attorney John Frost for his remarks, probably uttered when tipsy, that he was for equality, no king, and a better constitution. Frost was disbarred and pilloried as well as imprisoned for his conversation, Rex *v.* Frost (1793), *ibid.*, 471. Winterbotham, a Baptist minister, commented favorably on the French Revolution and condemned oppressive taxes in his sermons. This resulted in his conviction for seditious words, a sentence of four years, and steep fines. In this case, the jury convicted against the court's recommendation of an acquittal, Rex *v.* Winterbotham (1793), *ibid.*, 875. The cases of Briellat, Hudson, Muir, Palmer, Skirving, Margarot, and Gerrald in 1793 and 1794 were similar to those already mentioned. In each the jury returned a verdict of guilty for seditious words, oral or printed, that were harmless and hardly even intemperate. Each of these cases, with citations to Howell, *State Trials*, is discussed by May, *Constitutional History*, II, 142–150.

21. The American Sedition Act cases are too familiar to require review. For an excellent treatment, see James Morton Smith, *Freedom's Fetters: The Alien and Sedition Laws and American Civil Liberties* (Ithaca, 1956). Smith reports the single acquittal on p. 185.

22. People *v.* Croswell, 3 Johnson (N.Y.), 336 (1804). Lewis's opinion is reported *ibid.*, 394–411.

23. MS Minutes, New York Court of Quarter Sessions, 1732–62, p. 181, cited in Julius Goebel, Jr. and T. Raymond Naughton, *Law Enforcement in Colonial New York, a Study in Criminal Procedure (1664–1776)* (New York, 1944), 99*n*.

24. Isaiah Thomas, *The History of Printing in America* (Worcester, 1810), II, 143–44. The case ended in an acquittal.

25. In the McDougall case of 1770, discussed below, the common-law prosecution, which was never brought to trial, was instigated by the legislature.

26. There were probably a greater number of prosecutions for oral utterances of a seditious nature than there were for seditious libels or publications, but there is no way of estimating the number of the former since most were tried before inferior courts whose records are, with few exceptions, unpublished. However, Goebel and Naughton systematically examined the manuscript records of the inferior courts of New York and reported that there were only "occasional exceptional" cases of seditious words during the whole of the colonial period up to 1776. See their *Law Enforcement in New York*, 98–99.

27. Between 1706 and 1720 there were four such cases in New York, one involving the arrest of nine citizens and another of seventeen grand jurors for seditious reflections on the assembly. In each of the other two cases, the victim of the assembly's wrath was one of its own members, Lewis Morris in 1710 and Samuel Mulford in 1720, *Journal of the Voters and Proceedings of the General Assembly of the Colony of New York . . .* [1691–1765] (New York, 1764–66), I, 211 (1706), 283 (1710), 411 (1717), 443 (1720). In a guarded understatement, Mary Patterson Clarke states: "Literally scores of persons, probably hundreds, throughout the colonies were tracked down by the various messengers and sergeants and brought into the house to make inglorious submission for words spoken in the heat of anger or for writings which intentionally or otherwise had given

offense." See her *Parliamentary Privilege in the American Colonies* (New Haven, 1943), 117.

28. Katz, ed., *Brief Narrative*, 46.

29. *New York Assembly Journal*, II, 173, 192, 193.

30. *Ibid.*, 198.

31. *Ibid.*, 358–59.

32. *Ibid.*, 487–89.

33. *Ibid.*, 551–55, passim.

34. Rutherfurd, *Trial of Zenger*, 206, 223.

35. *Minutes of the Provincial Council of Pennsylvania* (Harrisburg, 1838–40), III, 392.

36. Alexander, who had been a member of the council of both New Jersey and New York and attorney general of New York, was Zenger's editor and his first counsel. Summarily disbarred in the pre-trial stage of the case for accusing the presiding judge of bias, he brought in Hamilton to argue the cause and provided him with a detailed brief of the argument that proved victorious. The brief is reprinted in Goebel and Naughton, *Law Enforcement in New York*, 782–86. On Alexander, see Vincent Buranelli, "Peter Zenger's Editor," *American Quarterly*, VII (1955), 174–81.

37. The untitled essay, originally, published in four parts in the *Pennsylvania Gazette* (Philadelphia), Nov. 17–Dec. 8, 1737, was republished in Zenger's *Weekly Journal* (New York), Dec. 19, 1737–Jan. 9, 1738.

38. *Pennsylvania Gazette*, Dec. 1, ₹737.

39. The *Independent Reflector* (New York), Aug. 30, 1753, quoted in *The Journals of Hugh Gaine, Printer*, ed. Paul Leicester Ford (New York, 1902), I, 12–13.

40. November 1759, quoted in "James Parker *versus* New York Province," ed. Beverly McAnear, *New York History*, XXXII (1941), 322.

41. Thomas, *Printing in America*, II, 302–3.

42. Becker, *Parties in New York*, 77–78.

43. E. B. O'Callaghan, ed., *Documentary History of the State of New York* (Albany, 1849–51), 3:528–36, reproduces the broadsides and Colden's proclamations which quote the Assembly's resolutions. According to the proclamations the Assembly vote was unanimous. Isaac Q. Leake, *Memoir of the Life and Times of General John Lamb* (Albany, 1850), 51, claimed that one member, Philip Schuyler, voted against the resolutions, E. Wilder Spaulding, *His Excellency, George Clinton* (New York, 1938), 27, supported Leake. However, the diary of William Smith, a member of the Council, also showed that the Assembly's vote was unanimous. See William H. W. Sabine, ed., *Historical Memoirs from 16 March 1763 to 9 July 1776 of William Smith* (New York, 1956), 71. The MS Journal, cited in the next note for Dec. 19, 1769, is conclusive; the vote was unanimous.

44. For the McDougall case, I have read every issue of the *New York Journal*, the *New York Gazette, or Weekly Post-Boy* from December 1769 through March 1771, and the *New York Chronicle* through its last issue, Jan. 4, 1770. Another indispensable source was a microfilm copy of the manuscript *Journal of Votes and Proceedings of the General Assembly of the Colony of New-York* for the years 1769–71, obtained from the Public Records Office in London, Doc. #953. C.O. 5/1219. For additional accounts see "McDougall's Account," in a letter to the *New York Journal*, Feb. 15, 1770, and his statement in *ibid.*, Jan. 29, 1771. See also *Historical Memoirs of William Smith*, 73–75; Leake, *Lamb*, 60–61; Thomas, *History of Printing in America*, II, 479–81; and Dorothy Rita Dillon, *The New York Triumvirate* (New York, 1949), 106–7, and Roger J. Champagne, *Alexander McDougall and the American Revolution* (Schenectady, N.Y., 1975), 27–44.

45. *Dictionary of American Biography*.

46. "McDougall's Account," and Colden to Lord Hillsborough, Feb. 20, 1770, in Thomas Jones, *History of New York During the Revolutionary War* (New York, 1879, 2

vols.), I, 432–34. See also Thomas, *History of Printing in America*, II, 4812; Julius Goebel, Jr., and T. Raymond Naughton, *Law Enforcement in Colonial New York* (New York, 1944), 506 n. 89.

 47. See, for example, the *Post-Boy*, April 9, 1770, and *New York Journal*, March 15, 1770.

 48. Between April 9 and June 25, 1770, the *Mercury* published the twelve-part "Dougliad," a continuing attack on McDougall and a defense of the government and the prosecution. See also *Historical Memoirs of William Smith*, 75–76; Schlesinger, *Prelude to Independence*, 115–16; Dillon, *New York Triumvirate*, 112.

 49. *New York Mercury*, April 26, 1770.

 50. Jones, *History of New York*, I, 27–28, 435; *New York Post-Boy*, Feb. 19, 1770, and *New York Journal*, March 22 and, for the Tory's letter, March 29, 1770; Leake, *Lamb*, 62; John C. Miller, *Origins of the American Revolution* (Boston, 1943), 306.

 51. Good accounts of the events leading to the aborted trial are in the *New York Post-Boy*, May 7, 1770; *New York Journal*, May 3, 1770; and *New York Mercury*, April 30, 1770.

 52. On *peine forte et dure*, see Sir James Fitzjames Stephen, *A History of the Criminal Law of England* (London, 1883), I, 297–99; E. M. Morgan, "The Privilege Against Self-Incrimination," *Minnesota Law Review* 34:12–14, 20–21 (1949). England abolished this barbaric practice by a statute of 1772 which provided that a refusal to plead was equivalent to a plea of guilty which, by a statute of 1827, was changed to a plea of not guilty. The only known instance of *peine* having been inflicted in the colonies occurred in Giles Corey's case in 1692 in Salem on a charge of witchcraft; he was pressed to death. Goebel, *Law Enforcement in Colonial New York*, 582, questionably assert that a "modification" of *peine* was used in 1691 when Jacob Leisler was ordered "tyed up and putt in irons" after his refusal to plead to a charge of treason. There is no record in England or America of *peine* having been used in a legislative trial; moreover at common law it might be used only in a felony case. Seditious libel was misdemeanor. Thus De Noyelle's threat was illegally based.

 53. For accounts of McDougall's appearance and trial before the Assembly, see *Journal of Votes and Proceedings*, Dec. 13, 1770, p. 8; and McDougall's own account in *New York Weekly Mercury*, Dec. 24, 1770; and (New York) *Weekly Post-Boy* of the same date, reprinted in Leonard W. Levy, ed., *Freedom of the Press*, 117–27; McDougall's account is an invaluable source for the entire episode. See also, Leake, *Lamb*, 71–73; Spaulding, *George Clinton*, 28–29; Thomas, *History of Printing in America*, II, 482–83; Dillon, *New York Triumvirate*, 119–21; Schlesinger, *Prelude to Independence*, 116.

7. *The Original Meaning of the Establishment Clause*

 1. 330 U.S. 1:15–16 (1947).

 2. *Ibid.*, 31–32.

 3. J. M. O'Neill, *Religion and Education Under the Constitution* (New York: Harper and Row, 1949), 56. See also Edwin S. Corwin, "The Supreme Court As National School Board," *Law and Contemporary Problems* 14 (1949):10, 20. Chester James Antieau, Arthur L. Downey, and Edward C. Roberts, *Freedom from Federal Establishment. Formation and Early History of the First Amendment Religion Clauses* (Milwaukee: Bruce Publishing Company, 1964), is the most completely documented presentation of this point of view, which can also be found in Walter Berns, *The First Amendment and the Future of American Democracy* (New York: Basic Books, 1976); Michael J. Malbin, *Religion and Politics: The Intentions of the Authors of the First Amendment* (Washington: American Enterprise Institute, 1978); and Robert L. Cord, *Separation of Church and State: Historical Fact and Current Fiction* (New York: Lambeth Press, 1982).

 4. Several scholars declare that the germ of the no-establishment clause derived from a proposal allegedly advanced by Charles Pinckney of South Carolina on May 29: "The

legislature of the United States shall pass no law on the subject of religion." See Leo Pfeffer, *Church, State, and Freedom* (Boston: Beacon Press, 1967), 123; Anson Phelps Stokes, *Church and State in the United States* (New York: Harper & Brothers, 1950), 1:526–527. Pinckney's proposal appears in Madison's *Notes* as part of a comprehensive plan of Union submitted to the Convention by Pinckney. Jonathan Elliot, ed., *The Debates in the Several State Conventions on the Adoption of the Federal Constitution in Five Volumes* (Philadelphia: J. B. Lippincott, 1941), 5:131. However, the Pinckney plan has been revealed to be spurious. Neither it nor the proposal banning laws on religion was ever presented to the Convention; in 1818 or later a copy of the Pinckney plan was added by Madison to his original *Notes*, which were not published until 1840. Charles Warren, *The Making of the Constitution* (Boston: Little, Brown, 1928), 142–43. Pfeffer's book, mentioned above, is particularly recommended to readers as the most authoritative constitutional history of America's experience with the double-faceted principle of religious liberty and separation of government and religion.

5. Elliot, *Debates*, 5:446.

6. *Ibid.*, 498.

7. *Ibid.*

8. Stokes, *Church and State*, 1:527. See also Pfeffer, *Church, State, and Freedom*, 123.

9. See letter of Madison to Edmund Randolph, April 10, 1788, in James Madison, *The Papers of James Madison*, eds. Robert A. Rutland *et al.* (Charlottesville: University of Virginia Press, 1976), 11:19.

10. Elliot is in error on this point; see Charles C. Tansill, ed., *Documents Illustrative of the Formation of the Union of the American States* (Washington: Government Printing Office, 1927), 716.

11. For example: Elliot, *Debates*, 3:203–204, 450, 600 (Randolph and Nicholas in Virginia); 4:149 (Iredell in North Carolina); 4:315–316 (C. C. Pinckney in South Carolina); and 2:78 (Varnum in Massachusetts). For the very influential statements by Wilson of Pennsylvania, see *ibid.*, 2:436 and 453; also *Pennsylvania and the Federal Constitution, 1787–1788*, John Bach McMaster and Frederick D. Stone, eds. (Lancaster, Pa.: History Society of Pennsylvania, 1888): 313–314. See also McKean in *ibid.*, 377; Ellsworth in *Essays on the Constitution of the United States*, Paul L. Ford, ed. (Brooklyn: The Historical Printing Club, 1892), 163–164; Williamson, "Remarks," *ibid.*, 398 (N.C.); and Hanson, "Remarks on the Proposed Plan," in *Pamphlets on the Constitution of the United States*, Paul L. Ford, ed. (Brooklyn: The Historical Printing Club, 1888), 241–42 (Md.). See also *The Documentary History of the Ratification of the Constitution*, eds. Merrill Jensen *et al.*, 4 vols. to date (Madison: State Historical Society of Wisconsin, 1976–   ); the volumes published to date cover Pennsylvania, Delaware, New Jersey, Georgia, and Connecticut.

12. *The Federalist*, any edition, #84.

13. The whole concept of a federal system of distributed powers, with the national government possessing only limited, delegated powers, forms the principal evidence. In addition consider the following specific comments which are illustrative rather than exhaustive. Wilson of Pennsylvania in response to the allegation that there was no security for the rights of conscience: "I ask the honorable gentlemen, what part of this system puts it in the power of Congress to attack those rights? When there is no power to attack, it is idle to prepare the means of defense." Elliot, *Debates*, 2:455. Randolph of Virginia asserted that "no power is given expressly to Congress over religion," and added that only powers "constitutionally given" could be exercised. Elliot, *Debates*, 3:204 and 469. Madison of Virginia: "There is not a shadow of right in the general government to intermeddle with religion." Elliot, *Debates*, 3:330. Iredell of North Carolina: "If any future Congress should pass an act concerning the religion of the country, it would be an act which they are not authorized to pass, by the Constitution, and which the people would not obey." Elliot, *Debates*, 4:194. Spaight of North Carolina: "As to the subject of

religion . . . No power is given to the general government to interfere with it at all. Any act of Congress on this subject would be a usurpation." Elliot, *Debates*, 4:208.

14. Massachusetts, New Hampshire, Virginia, New York, North Carolina, and Rhode Island.

15. See Elliot, *Debates*, 2:112, 114 (Gore and Davis in Massachusetts); 3:468 (Randolph in Virginia); 4: 145, 150 (Iredell and Johnston in North Carolina); see also Wilson of Pennsylvania in McMaster and Stone, eds., *Pennsylvania and the Constitution*, 309, 353, 406. On the variety of early state procedures concerning the rights of accused persons, see generally Charles Fairman, "The Supreme Court and Constitutional Limitations on State Government Authority," *University of Chicago Law Review* 21 (Autumn 1953): 40–78 passim. Charles Warren points out that in civil cases, the citizens of four states had been deprived of jury trial in the seven-year period before the Constitution was framed, in *Congress, the Constitution and the Supreme Court* (Boston: Little, Brown, 1925), 81.

16. For example, only seven of the thirteen states had separate Bills of Rights in their constitutions; several states maintained establishments of religion which were prohibited by others; six states did not constitutionally provide for the right to the writ of habeas corpus. See generally Francis Newton Thorpe, *The Constitutional History of the United States* (Chicago: Callaghan & Co., 1901), 2:199–211, for a table on state precedents for the federal Bill of Rights.

17. For example, Massachusetts recommended the right to indictment by grand jury but did not provide for it in its own constitution; Virginia and North Carolina recommended constitutional protection for freedom of speech which they did not protect in their respective constitutions; and New York recommended protections against compulsory self-incrimination and double jeopardy, neither of which was constitutionally protected by New York.

18. Elliot, *Debates* reports in detail the debates of five states (Massachusetts, New York, Virginia, North Carolina, and South Carolina) and in very fragmentary fashion the debates of three others (Maryland, Pennsylvania, and Connecticut). McMaster and Stone collected the extant Pennsylvania debates, together with pamphlets and essays from that state, while P. L. Ford collected important essays and pamphlets from all the states. See also Jensen *et al.*, eds., *Ratification*.

19. Elliot, *Debates*, 2:202.

20. Ford, *Essays*, 168.

21. McMaster and Stone, *Pennsylvania*, 421, 424, 461, 480.

22. *Ibid.*, 502.

23. *Ibid.*, 589. "Centinel" was probably Samuel Bryan.

24. Tansill, *Documents*, 1018–20.

25. Elliott, *Debates*, 2:236.

26. *Ibid.*, 553.

27. Philip A. Crowl, *Maryland During and After the Revolution* (Baltimore: Johns Hopkins University Press, 1943): 156; Albert W. Werline, *Problems of Church and State in Maryland* (South Lancaster, Mass.: The College Press, 1948): 143–68.

28. Werline, *Problems*, ch. 6, passim.

29. *City Gazette or Daily Advertiser of Charleston*, May 26, 1788. Quoted in Antieau *et al.*, *Freedom*, 106.

30. Tansill, *Documents*, 1022–24.

31. *The Federal and State Constitutions, Colonial Charters, and Other Organic Laws of the States, Territories, and Colonies*, ed. Francis Newton Thorpe, 7 vols. (Washington: Government Printing Office, 1909), 6:3255. *South Carolina Laws, Charleston, 1785, 1786, 1787, 1790*, in Charles Evans, *American Bibliography: A Chronological Dictionary of All Books, Pamphlets and Periodical Publications Printed in the United States of America from the Genesis of Printing in 1639 down to and Including the Year 1820*, 14 vols. (Chicago: Charles Evans, 1903–1959, microcard): #19750, p. 8; #19998, p. 43;

#20715, p. 48; #22895, pp. 11–11 (this source will hereinafter be cited as Evans, *Early American Imprints*). John Wesley Brinsfield, *Religion and Politics in South Carolina* (Easley, S. C.: Southern Historical Press, 1983), 122–27.

32. Tansill, *Documents*, 1026.
33. Elliot, *Debates*, 3:204.
34. *Ibid.*, 330. See also the similar statement by Zachariah Johnson at 645–46.
35. *Ibid.*, 593.
36. *Ibid.*, 659 and Tansill, *Documents*, 1031.
37. Elliot, *Debates*, 2:399.
38. *Ibid.*, 410–412.
39. Tansill, *Documents*, 1035.
40. *Ibid.*, 1047, and Elliot, *Debates*, 4:244.
41. Elliot, *Debates*, 4:191–92.
42. *Ibid.*, 194.
43. *Ibid.*, 198–99.
44. *Ibid.*, 199.
45. *Ibid.*, 200.
46. *Ibid.*, 203.
47. *Ibid.*, 208.
48. Tansill, *Documents*, 1053.
49. For Madison's persistence, see *The Debates and Proceedings in the Congress of the United States. Compiled from Authentic Materials*, comp. Joseph Gales (Washington: Joseph Gales, 1834), 2:444, 459, 460, 733 (hereafter cited as *Annals*).
50. James Madison to Thomas Jefferson, Oct. 17 and Dec. 8, 1788, in *Madison Papers*, 11:295, 381; *The Federalist, #51; Annals*, 1:456.
51. James Madison to Thomas Jefferson, Dec. 8, 1788, James Madison to Tench Coxe, June 24, 1789, James Madison to George Eve, Jan. 2, 1789, in *Madison Papers*, 11:390, 12, 257, 11, 404.
52. Thomas Jefferson to James Madison, July 31, 1788, in *Madison Papers*, 11:213.
53. *The Statutes at Large*, ed., W. W. Henning, 13 vols. (Richmond, 1809–1823), 12:84–86.
54. Quoted in *Stokes*, 1:335. Available in any edition of Jefferson's writings.
55. "Declaration of the Virginia Association of Baptists," in Thomas Jefferson, *The Papers of Thomas Jefferson*, ed. Julian P. Boyd (Princeton: Princeton University Press, 1950–   ), 1:660–661.
56. James Madison, *The Writings of James Madison*, ed. Gaillard Hunt, 9 vols. (New York: G. P. Putnam's Sons, 1900–1910), 5:105. Madison to George Eve, George Nicholas to James Madison, Benjamin Johnson to James Madison (hereafter cited as *Madison Papers*), 11:404, 405, 408, 424, 442. L. H. Butterfield, "Elder John Leland, Jeffersonian Itinerant," *American Antiquarian Society Proceedings* 62 (1952):188.
57. *Annals*, 1:441.
58. *Madison Papers*, 12:453.
59. *Annals*, 1:448–49.
60. *Annals*, 1:451.
61. *Madison Papers*, 8:298–306.
62. Madison to Monroe, May 29, 1785, *Madison Papers*, 8:280. Irving Brant, *James Madison, the Nationalist* (Indianapolis: Bobbs-Merrill, 1948), 353.
63. *A Compilation of the Messages and Papers of the Presidents*, comp. James D. Richardson, 10 vols. (Washington: Government Printing Office, 1896–1899), 1:490.
64. "Madison's 'Detached Memoranda'," ed. Elizabeth Fleet, *William and Mary Quarterly* 3 (1946):554–59.
65. *Madison Papers*, 11:130.
66. *Annals*, 1:452.
67. In addition to Madison the committee included three other signers of the

Constitution: Abraham Baldwin of Georgia, Roger Sherman of Connecticut, and George Clymer of Pennsylvania. Also on the committee were Aedanus Burke of South Carolina, the only Anti-Federalist; Nicholas Gilman of New Hampshire; Egbert Benson of New York; Benjamin Goodhue of Massachusetts; Elias Boudinot of New Jersey; and John Vining of Delaware, who was chairman. *Annals*, 1:691.

68. *Annals*, 1:757.

69. *Ibid.*, 757–59.

70. *Ibid.*, 796.

71. *Documentary History of the First Federal Congress of the United States of America*, ed. Linda Grant DePauw, 3 vols. (Baltimore: Johns Hopkins University Press, 1977), 1:151.

72. *Ibid.*, 166. It is interesting, however, to note that a Baptist memorial of 1774 used similar language: "The magistrate's power extends not to the establishing any articles of faith or forms of worship, by force of laws." Yet the Baptists opposed nondiscriminatory government aid to all sects—proving once again how infuriatingly ambiguous language can be. For the Baptist statement, see Pfeffer, *Church, State*, 91. For Baptist views, see Stokes, *Church and State*, 1:306–10, 353–57, 368–75.

73. DePauw, *Documentary History*, 1:186, 189, 192.

74. *Annals*, 1:454.

75. Madison to Jefferson, Oct. 17, 1788, in *Madison Papers*, 11:295.

76. David M. Matteson, "The Organization of the Government under the Constitution," in Sol Bloom, Director General, *History of the Formation of the Union Under the Constitution*: (Washington: United States Sesquicentennial Commission, 1943), 317–19.

77. *Ibid.*, 325–28.

78. *Journal of the Senate of the Commonwealth of Virginia; Begun and Held in the City of Richmond, on Monday, the 18th Day of October, 1789* (Richmond, 1828) [*Binder's title, Journal of the Senate, 1785 to 1790*], 62. Quoted by John Courtney Murray, in "Law or Prepossessions," *Law and Contemporary Problems*, 14:43, and quoted by Corwin, "Supreme Court as National School Board," *ibid.*, 12. See also, Antieau *et al.*, *Freedom*, 144. The statement by the eight Virginia senators was revived and quoted by an advocate of the narrow interpretation of the no-establishment clause in "Brief for Appellees," 51–54, filed in the case of *McCollum v. Board of Education*, 333 U.S. 203 (1948). Both Murray and Corwin drew their conclusions on this matter from the brief alone, without investigating the context of the statement by the eight senators.

79. E. Randolph to Washington, Dec. 6, 1789, quoted by Matteson, "The Organization of the Government," 321.

80. Hardin Burnley to Madison, Dec. 5, 1789, *Madison Papers*, 12:460.

81. Matteson, "The Organization of the Government," 321–22; Madison to Washington, Nov. 20, 1789, quoted in Irving Brant, *Madison, Father of the Constitution* (Indianapolis: Bobbs-Merrill, 1948), 287.

82. Brant, *Madison, Father of the Constitution*, 287.

83. *Ibid.*, 286–87 and 491, note 16, for the voting records.

84. O'Neill, *Religion and Education*, 204.

85. Antieau, *et al.*, *Freedom*, 202 and passim. Cord, *Separation of Church and State*, 3–15.

86. Sanford Cobb, *The Rise of Religious Liberty in America* (New York: Macmillan, 1902), 236. John Webb Pratt, *Religion, Politics, and Diversity. The Church–State Theme in New York History* (Ithaca: Cornell University Press, 1967), 27–29.

87. *Ecclesiastical Records of the State of New York*, eds. Hugh Hastings and Edward T. Corwin, 7 vols. (Albany: J. B. Lyon, State Printer, 1901–1906), 1:571.

88. Pratt, *Religion*, 39.

89. *Ecclesiastical Records*, 2:1073–1078. Pratt, *Religion*, 40–42. Carl Bridenbaugh,

Mitre and Sceptre. Transatlantic Faiths, Ideas, Personalities, and Politics 1689–1775 (New York: Oxford University Press, 1962), 117–118.

90. *Ecclesiastical Records*, 2:1114.

91. E. B. O'Callaghan, ed., *Documents Relative to the Colonial History of the State of New York*, ed., E. B. O'Callaghan, 15 vols. (Albany: Weed, Parsons, Printers, 1853–1887), 5:323. Bridenbaugh, *Mitre*, 118.

92. *The Documentary History of the State of New York*, ed., E. B. O'Callaghan, 4 vols. (Albany: Weed, Parsons, Printers, 1848–1849), 3:278.

93. *Ibid.*, 309–311. The Jamaica controversy can be followed in this work, 205–302. See also Pratt, *Religion*, 54, 61–62.

94. O'Callaghan, ed., *Documentary History*, 3:311, 330. Pratt, *Politics*, 62.

95. *Ecclesiastical Records*, 2:1392, 3:1589, 1591, 1695, 2141.

96. William Smith, *A General Idea of the College of Mirania* (New York, 1753. Evans, *Early American Imprints*, #7121, microcard), 84. Pratt, *Politics*: 67–71.

97. *The Independent Reflector*, ed. Milton Klein (Cambridge, Mass.: Harvard University Press, 1963), 171–178 and passim. William Smith, Jr., *The History of the Province of New York*, ed. Michael Kammen (Cambridge, Mass.: Harvard University Press, 1972).

98. Klein, ed., *Independent Reflector, New York Mercury*, May 26, 1755: 26; William Livingston, *Address to Sir Charles Hardy* (New York, 1755), vii–viii.

99. "Remarks on the Quebec Bill," *Works of Alexander Hamilton*, ed. J. C. Hamilton, 2:131, quoted in Stokes, 1:510.

100. *Acts and Resolves, Public and Private of the Province of Massachusetts Bay (1692–1786)*, 21 vols. (Boston: Wright and Potter, 1869–1922), 1:62. Susan M. Reed, *Church and State in Massachusetts 1691–1740* (Urbana: University of Illinois Press, 1914): 19–35. William G. McLoughlin, *New England Dissent 1630–1833. The Baptists and the Separation of Church and State*, 2 vols. (Cambridge, Mass.: Harvard University Press, 1971), 1:113–27.

101. Reed, *Church and State*, 180. McLoughlin, *New England Dissent*, 1:221.

102. M. Louise Greene, *The Development of Religious Liberty in Connecticut* (Boston: Houghton, Mifflin, 1905), 200–201; McLoughlin, *New England Dissent*, 1:269.

103. McLoughlin, *New England Dissent*, 1:225–243.

104. Cotton Mather, *Ratio Discipline* (Boston, 1726. Evans, *Early American Imprints* #2775, microcard), 20.

105. Ebenezer Turell, *The Life and Character of Benjamin Colman* (Boston, 1749. Evans, *Early American Imprints* #6434, microcard), 138.

106. Jonathan Mayhew, *A Defense of the Observations* (Boston, 1763. Evans, *Early American Imprints*, #9442), 46–47.

107. Charles B. Kinney, *Church and State: The Struggle for Separation in New Hampshire, 1630–1900* (New York: Teachers College, Columbia University, 1955), 58–62, 72–82. McLoughlin, *New England Dissent*, 2:833–43.

108. Thorpe, *Federal and State Constitutions*, 5:2597.

109. *Delaware Convention Proceedings* (Wilmington, 1776. Evans, *Early American Imprints*, #43018, microcard), 14.

110. Thorpe, *Federal and State Constitutions*, 1:567, 5:2597.

111. *Ibid.*, 5:3082.

112. *Ibid.*, 2636. Italics added.

113. *Ibid.*, 3:1890–91.

114. See Meyer, *Church and State in Massachusetts to 1833* (Cleveland: Western Reserve University Press, 1930), for details, beginning with ch. 4. McLoughlin, *New England Dissent*, 2:697–722.

115. Thorpe, *Federal and State Constitutions*, 4:2454. see Kinney, *Separation*, 83–108. McLoughlin, *New England Dissent*, 2:844.

116. McLoughlin, *New England Dissent*, 2:923.

117. Thorpe, *Federal and State Constitutions*, 3:1689.

118. Allan Nevins, *The American States During and After the Revolution* (New York: Macmillan, 1927), 431; Werline, *Problems of Church and State*, 169–186. John C. Rainbolt, "The Struggle To Define 'Religious Liberty' in Maryland, 1776–1785," *Journal of Church and State* 17 (1975):448.

119. Thorpe, *Federal and State Constitutions*, 3:1705.

120. *Ibid.*, 2:784.

121. Reba C. Strickland, *Religion and the State in Georgia in the Eighteenth Century* (New York: Columbia University Press, 1939), 164, 166.

122. Thorpe, *Federal and State Constitutions*, 2:789.

123. *Ibid.*, 2:801. Evans, *Early American Imprints*, microcard: #19750, p. 8; #19998, p. 43; #20715, p. 48; #22895, pp. 11–12. Brinsfield, *Religion and Politics*, 122–127.

124. Thorpe, *Federal and State Constitutions*, 6:3253–3257. Brinsfield, *Religion and Politics*, 134.

125. Thorpe, *Federal and State Constitutions*, 6:3264.

126. *Ibid.*, 5:2793. Thomas Buckley, *Church and State in Revolutionary Virginia, 1776–1787* (Charlottesville: University of Virginia Press, 1977).

127. Stokes, *Church and State*, 1:393. Jefferson in 1776 had written a draft of a constitution for Virginia which included a similar provision: "Nor shall any be compelled to frequent or maintain any religious institution." Boyd, ed., *Jefferson Papers*, 1:344.

128. Hamilton J. Eckenrode, *The Separation of Church and State in Virginia* (Richmond, 1910), 58–61. For the actual bills, see Buckley, *Church and State*, 185–88, 190–91.

129. Eckenrode, *Separation*, 86. Buckley, *Church and State*, 188–89 for the text of the bill.

130. *Madison Papers*, 8:197. See Brant, *James Madison, the Nationalist*, 344–345.

131. In 1785, the same year the general assessment bill was debated in Virginia, both Maryland and Georgia also considered general assessment bills; comparatively little is known about their history.

8. *Liberty and the First Amendment: 1790–1800*

1. Some reviewers of my book, *Legacy of Suppression: Freedom of Speech and Press in Early American History* (Cambridge, Mass., 1960), have criticized my failure to define the words, "libertarian" and "libertarianism." The words derive from a Latin root meaning "free" and, like "liberty" or "freedom," cannot be defined with precision. I use them to signify those persons, or their thought, who advocated the widest measure of unrestricted freedom for speech and press. The meanings of the terms are relative to time and place.

2. Most recently expressed by Justice Black in *Communist Party of the US v. Subversive Activities Control Board*, 81 S. Ct. 1357, at 1443, n. 46 (1961). Black quotes the statement by Holmes, Brandeis concurring, in *Abrams* v. *US*, 250 US 616, at 630 (1919): "I wholly disagree with the argument of the Government that the First Amendment left the common law as to seditious libel in force. History seems to me against the notion." See also *Beauharnais* v. *Ill.*, 343 US 250, at 272 and 289 (1951). The leading scholarly statement of the accepted view is Zechariah Chafee, Jr., *Free Speech in the United States* (Cambridge, Mass., 1948), 21. The most recent restatements are James Morton Smith, *Freedom's Fetters: The Alien and Sedition Laws and American Civil Liberties* (Ithaca, N.Y., 1956), 427–31; C. Herman Pritchett, *The American Constitution* (New York, 1959), 430; and David Fellman, *The Limits of Freedom* (New Brunswick, N.J., 1959), 97.

3. Thomas Jefferson, *Notes on the State of Virginia*, ed. William Peden (Chapel Hill, N. C., 1955), 159.

4. "A Bill for new modelling the form of government and for establishing the Fundamental principles of our future Constitution," dated by Julian Boyd as "before 13 June 1776," in *The Papers of Thomas Jefferson*, ed. Julian P. Boyd *et al.* (16 vols., Princeton, N.J., 1950–   ), I, 353. Jefferson copied this provision from a similar one in an earlier draft, then bracketed it out, and finally omitted it from a third draft. (*Ibid.*, 347.)

5. "That the mere utterance of a political opinion is being penalized in these cases becomes even clearer in a statute such as that in Virginia, which declared the utterance of the opinion, or action upon it, to be equally offensive, providing a fine not exceeding £20,000 and imprisonment not exceeding five years 'if any person residing or being within this commonwealth shall ... by any word, open deed, or act, advisedly and willingly maintain and defend the authority, jurisdiction, or power, of the king or parliament of Great Britain, heretofore claimed and exercised within this colony, or shall attribute any such authority, jurisdiction, or power, to the king or parliament of Great Britain.' " (Willard Hurst, "Treason in the United States," *Harvard Law Review*, LVIII (Dec. 1944), 267, quoting *The Statutes at Large Being a Collection of All the Laws of Virginia* (1619–1792), ed. William Waller Hening [13 vols., Richmond, Va., 1809–23], IX, 170). For Jefferson's role, see Hurst, "Treason in the United States," 251, and *Papers of Jefferson*, ed. Boyd *et al.*, I, 598.

6. The standard authority on the meaning of freedom of the press was William Blackstone, the oracle of the common law to the American framers, who summarized the law of criminal libels as follows: "where blasphemous, immoral, treasonable, schismatical, seditious, or scandalous libels are punished by the English law ... the liberty of the press, properly understood, is by no means infringed or violated. The *liberty of the press* is indeed essential to the nature of a free state; but this consists in laying no *previous* restraints upon publications, and not in freedom from censure for criminal matter when published. Every freeman has an undoubted right to lay what sentiments he pleases before the public: to forbid this is to destroy the freedom of the press: but if he publishes what is improper, mischievous, or illegal, he must take the consequences of his own temerity. ... But to punish (as the law does at present) any dangerous or offensive writings, which, when published, shall on a fair and impartial trial be adjudged of a pernicious tendency, is necessary for the preservation of peace and good order, a government and religion, the only solid foundations of civil liberty. Thus the will of individuals is still left free; the abuse only of that free-will is the object of legal punishment. Neither is any restraint hereby laid upon freedom of thought or enquiry; liberty of private sentiment is still left; the disseminating, or making public, of bad sentiments, destructive of the ends of society, is the crime which society corrects." (Sir William Blackstone, *Commentaries on the Laws of England* [4 vols., London, 1765–69], Bk. IV, Chap. xi, 151–52; or, in the 18th ed., which I used [2 vols., New York, 1836] II, 112–13.)

7. *A Complete Collection of State Trials to 1783*, comp. Thomas Bayly Howell, continued by T. J. Howell to 1820 (34 vols., London, 1816–28), XVII, 675; see also Livingston Rutherford, *John Peter Zenger, His Press, His Trial and a Bibliography of Zenger Imprints. Also a Reprint of the First Edition of the Trial* (New York, 1904). On the contemporary significance of the trial and its questionable influence in "freeing" the press, see Leonard W. Levy, "Did the Zenger Case Really Matter? Freedom of the Press in Colonial New York," *William and Mary Quarterly*, XVII (Jan. 1960), 35–50.

8. "That the printing-presses shall be free to every person who undertakes to examine the proceedings of the legislature, or any branch of government, and no law shall ever be made to restrain the right thereof. The free communication of thoughts and opinions is one of the invaluable rights of man; and every citizen may freely speak, write, and print on any subject, *being responsible for the abuse of that liberty*. In *prosecutions* for the publication of papers investigating the official conduct of officers or men in a public

capacity, or where the matter published is proper for public information, the truth thereof may be given in evidence; and in all indictments for libels the jury shall have a right to determine the law and the facts, under the direction of the court, as in other cases." (Pennsylvania Constitution of 1790 [Art. IX, Sec. 7], in *The Federal and State Constitutions, Colonial Charters, and Other Organic Laws*, ed. Francis Newton Thorpe [7 vols., Washington, D.C., 1909], V, 3100. Italics mine.)

9. *Pennsylvania and the Federal Constitution, 1787–1788*, ed. John Bach McMaster and Frederick D. Stone (Philadelphia, 1888), 308–09.

10. *Respublica v. Oswald*, 1 Dallas (Pa.) Reports 319 (1788); "Trial of William Cobbett," Nov. 1797, in *State Trials of the United States during the Administrations of Washington and Adams*, ed. Francis Wharton (Philadelphia, 1849), 323–24; *Respublica v. Dennie*, 4 Yeates (Pa.) Reports 267 (1805).

11. Delaware Constitution of 1792 (Art. I, Sec. 5), in *Constitutions*, ed. Thorpe, I, 569, and Kentucky Constitution of 1792 (Art. XII, Sec. 7–8), *ibid.*, III, 1274.

12. "Hitherto Unpublished Correspondence between Chief Justice Cushing and John Adams in 1789," ed. Frank W. Grinnell, *Massachusetts Law Quarterly*, XXVII (Oct. 1942), 12–16. Adams, of course, signed the Sedition Act into law and urged its enforcement; Cushing, as a Supreme Court judge, presided over some of the Sedition Act trials and charged juries on its constitutionality. (See Smith, *Freedom's Fetters*, 97–98, 152, 242, 267, 268, 271, 284, 311, 363, and 371.)

13. See cases cited above in note 10. The judges in Oswald's case were Thomas McKean, then a Federalist but subsequently a Republican, and George Bryan, an Antifederalist and libertarian advocate of a national bill of rights.

14. *Commonwealth v. Freeman*, reported in the Boston *Independent Chronicle*, Feb. 24, Mar. 3, 10, 17, and 24, 1791.

15. "Draught of a Fundamental Constitution for the Commonwealth of Virginia," in *Papers of Jefferson*, ed. Boyd *et al.*, VI, 304: "PRINTING PRESS shall be subject to no other restraint than liableness to legal prosecution for false facts printed and published." Boyd dates this document between May 15 and June 17, 1783.

16. "A declaration that the federal government will never restrain the press from printing any thing they please, will not take away the liability of the printers for false facts printed." (Jefferson to Madison, July 31, 1788, in *ibid.*, XIII, 442.)

17. "Madison's Observations on Jefferson's Draft of a Constitution for Virginia," Oct. 1788, in *ibid.*, VI, 316.

18. Madison's original proposal was: "The people shall not be deprived or abridged of their right to speak, to write, or to publish their sentiments; and the freedom of the press, as one of the great bulwarks of liberty, shall be inviolable." (*The Debates and Proceedings in the Congress of the United States* [hereafter cited as *Annals of Congress*], 1 Cong., 1 sess., I, 451 [June 8, 1789].

19. Jefferson to Madison, Aug. 28, 1789, *Papers of Jefferson*, ed. Boyd *et al.*, XV, 367.

20. "The liberty of the press is secured. . . . In the time of King William, there passed an act for licensing the press. That was repealed. Since that time it has been looked upon as safe." (*The Debates in the Several State Conventions on the Adoption of the Federal Constitution . . . and Other Illustrations of the Constitution*, ed. Jonathan Elliot [2d. rev. ed., 5 vols. in 2, Philadelphia, 1941], III, 247.)

21. *Ibid.*, 560.

22. Jefferson to Madison, July 31, 1788, in *Papers of Jefferson*, ed. Boyd *et al.*, XIII, 422–23.

23. Madison to Jefferson, Oct. 17, 1788, in *ibid.*, XIV, 20.

24. *Debates*, ed. Elliot, III, 656.

25. See note 18, above.

26. "There was a time in England when neither book, pamphlet, nor paper could be published without a license from government. That restraint was finally removed in the year 1694; and, by such removal, the press became perfectly free, for it is not under the

restraint of any license. Certainly the new government can have no power to impose restraints." (Hugh Williamson, "Remarks on the New Plan of Government," in *Essays on the Constitution of the United States, Published during Its Discussion by the People*, ed. Paul Leicester Ford [Brooklyn, N.Y., 1892], 398.)

27. Melancthon Smith, "An Address to the People of the State of New York" (1788), in *Pamphlets on the Constitution of the United States, Published during Its Discussion by the People*, ed. Paul Leicester Ford (Brooklyn, N.Y., 1888), 114.

28. The brief and vague statement by Eleazar Oswald in 1788 may be regarded by some as an exception to this proposition. Oswald, having been indicted for a criminal libel on a private party, published an address to the public in which he stated: "The doctrine of libel being a doctrine incompatible with law and liberty, and at once destructive of the privileges of a free country, in the communication of our thoughts, has not hitherto gained any footing in *Pennsylvania. . . .*" (Quoted in *Respublica* v. *Oswald*, 1 Dallas 319, at 320 [1788].)

29. Wilson's statement in the Pennsylvania ratifying convention, quoted in *Pennsylvania and the Federal Constitution*, ed. McMaster and Stone, 308; Hamilton in *The Federalist*, No. 84.

30. In my book, *Legacy of Suppression*, I missed the significance of the reference to Article III, Section 2, and therefore misconstrued Wilson's statement to mean that criminal libels against the United States could be tried only in the *state* courts. I am indebted to Professor John J. Cound for calling attention to my error in his review, *New York University Law Review*, XXXVI (Jan. 1961), 256–57. The corrected reading of Wilson's statement strengthens the thesis of the book regarding the restrictive views of the framers.

31. "Trial of Joseph Ravara" (1792), in *State Trials*, ed. Wharton, 90–92; "Trial of Gideon Henfield" (1793), in *ibid.*, 49–92; *US* v. *Worrall*, 2 Dallas 384 (1798), in *ibid.*, 188–99; "Trial of the Northampton Insurgents" (1799), in *ibid.*, 476; "Trial of Isaac Williams" (1799), in *ibid.*, 652–54. See also *US* v *Smith* (1797), MSS Final Record of the United States Circuit Courts of Massachusetts, 1790–99, I, 242, 244 (Federal Records Center, Dorchester, Mass.). Smith's case is reported in 27 *Federal Cases*, No. 16323, where the date is erroneously given as 1792. Justice Samuel Chase in Worrall's case, mentioned above, disagreed with his associate, Judge Richard Peters, who supported the jurisdiction of the federal courts in cases of common-law crime. Chase, however, changed his opinion in *US* v *Sylvester* (1799), MSS Final Record, I, 303, an unreported case.

32. A federal grand jury in Richmond presented Congressman Samuel J. Cabell for seditious libel in 1797. Prosecutions for seditious libel were also begun against Benjamin F. Bache of the Philadelphia *Aurora* and John Daly Burk of the New York *Time Piece* in 1798, shortly before the enactment of the Sedition Act. See Smith, *Freedom's Fetters*, 95, 183–84, 188–220.

33. Supreme Court justices known to have accepted jurisdiction in cases of common-law crimes included James Wilson, Oliver Ellsworth, William Paterson, John Jay, James Iredell, and Samuel Chase. See cases mentioned in note 31, above.

34. *US* v. *Hudson and Goodwin*, 7 Cranch 32, at 34 (1812). Justice William Johnson, speaking for the "majority," gave an unreasoned opinion. The case had been decided without arguments of counsel. William W. Crosskey, *Politics and the Constitution* (2 vols., Chicago, 1953), II, 782, claims that Chief Justice Marshall and Justices Story and Washington dissented from Johnson's opinion without noting the fact of their dissent on the record.

35. On the English legislation of the 1790's, see Sir Thomas Erskine May, *The Constitutional History of England since the Accession of George Third, 1760–1860* (2 vols., New York, 1880), II, 161–74. the parliamentary debates and the texts of the Treasonable Practices Act and of the Sedition Act of 1795, known together as "The Two Acts," were published in London in 1796 under the title *The History of the Two Acts* and were imported into the United States and advertised under the title *History of the Treason*

and Sedition Bills lately passed in Great Britain. For the influence of the English experience and legislation on Federalist thought, see Manning J. Dauer, *The Adams Federalists* (Baltimore, 1953), 157–59.

36. *Annals of Congress,* 5 Cong., 2 sess., 2152 (July 10, 1798); see also *ibid.,* Gallatin at 2163, Nicholas at 2142, and Livingston at 2153.

37. *Debates,* ed. Elliot, IV, 540–41.

38. *The Writings of James Madison,* ed. Gaillard Hunt (9 vols., New York, 1900–10), VI, 333–34.

39. *People* v. *Croswell,* 3 Johnson's (N.Y.) Cases 336 (1804).

40. Chief Justice Morgan Lewis, joined by Judge Brockholst Livingston, whom Jefferson appointed to the United States Supreme Court in 1806, explicitly defined freedom of the press in common-law terms, relying on Blackstone and Mansfield for precedents. Ambrose Spencer, a Republican newly appointed to the New York Court of Errors, disqualified himself because as attorney general he had represented the state in the Croswell case. Lewis' opinion was based on Spencer's argument. Hamilton defended Croswell, arguing Zengerian principles which were accepted by Judge James Kent, a Federalist, joined by Smith Thompson, a Republican who had studied law with Kent. In 1805 the state legislature enacted a bill allowing truth as a defense if published "with good motives and for justifiable ends," and allowing the jury to decide the whole issue. The statute is reported at 3 Johnson's (N.Y.) Cases 336, at 411–13, following the arguments of counsel and the opinions of Kent and Lewis.

41. Jefferson to Governor Thomas McKean, Feb. 19, 1803, in *The Writings of Thomas Jefferson,* ed. Paul Leicester Ford (10 vols., New York, 1892–99), VIII, 218–19.

42. Jefferson to Abigail Adams, Sept. 4, 1804, in *ibid.,* 311. In the eloquent First Inaugural Address, Jefferson declared, in a deservedly much-quoted passage: "If there be any among us who would wish to dissolve this Union or to change its republican form, let them stand undisturbed as monuments of the safety with which error of opinion may be tolerated where reason is left free to combat it." But in the Second Inaugural Address, he spoke of the "licentiousness" with which the "artillery of the press has been levelled against us," alleged that the "abuses" of the press lessened its "usefulness," and stated, "they might, indeed, have been corrected by the wholesome punishments reserved and provided by the laws of the several States against falsehood and defamation. . . ." He declared that the pressure of public duties prevent prosecution of the offenders and that his re-election demonstrated that the people could be trusted to choose truth in a conflict with falsehood. But he added, "No inference is here intended, that the laws, provided by the State against false and defamatory publications, should not be enforced; he who has time, renders a service to public morals and public tranquility, in reforming these abuses by the salutary coercions of the law. . . ." (*Ibid.,* VIII, 346.)

43. "Hampden," *A Letter to the President of the United States, Touching the Prosecutions under His Patronage, before the Circuit Court in the District of Connecticut* (New Haven, Conn., 1808), 28.

44. *Ibid.,* 8–12.

45. Jefferson to Thomas Seymour, Feb. 11, 1807, in *Writings of Jefferson,* ed. Ford, IX, 30.

46. Sir James Fitzjames Stephen, *A History of the Criminal Law of England* (3 vols., London, 1883), II, 383; Frank Thayer, *Legal Control of the Press* (Brooklyn, N.Y., 1950), 17, 25, 178.

47. *Annals of Congress,* 5 Cong., 2 sess., 2103–11 (July 5, 1798); 2139–43, 2153–54, 2160–66 (July 10, 1798).

48. Boston *Independent Chronicle,* Mar. 4–7, Apr. 8–15, Apr. 29–May 2, 1799, reporting the trial of Abijah Adams, editor of the *Chronicle,* for seditious libel against the state legislature of Massachusetts.

49. George Hay ["Hortensius"], *An Essay on the Liberty of the Press. Respectfully Inscribed to the Republican Printers throughout the United States* (reprint, Richmond,

Va., 1803). In 1803 Hay also published a different tract with a similar title, *An Essay on the Liberty of the Press, Shewing, That the Requisition of Security for Good Behaviour from Libellers, is Perfectly Compatible with the Constitution and Laws of Virginia* (Richmond, Va., 1803). Hay, who was Monroe's son-in-law, served in the Virginia House of Delegates, was appointed United States attorney for Virginia by President Jefferson, conducted the prosecution of Burr for treason, and concluded his public career as a United States district judge.

50. The *Report* originally appeared as a tract of over eighty pages. The copy in the Langdell Treasure Room, Harvard Law Library, is bound together with the 1799 issue of Hay's *Essay*. Madison wrote the *Report* at the close of 1799; it was adopted by the Virginia legislature on January 11, 1800, which immediately published it. It is reproduced in *Debates*, ed. Elliot, IV, 546–80, under the title "Madison's Report on the Virginia Resolutions . . . Report of the Committee to whom were referred the Communications of various States, relative to the Resolutions of the last General Assembly of this State, concerning the Alien and Sedition Laws." The *Report* is also available in *Writings of Madison*, ed. Hunt, VI, 341–406. The edition cited here is *The Virginia Report of 1799–1800, Touching the Alien and Sedition Laws; together with the Virginia Resolutions of December 21, 1798, The Debates and Proceedings thereon, in the House of Delegates in Virginia* (Richmond, Va., 1850), 189–237, a book of great value for its inclusion of the Virginia debates on the Sedition Act (pp. 22–161). While those debates added little to the debates of the House of Representatives, the remarks of Republican speakers constitute another example of the new libertarianism.

51. Tunis Wortman, *A Treatise Concerning Political Enquiry, and the Liberty of the Press* (New York, 1800). Wortman, one of the leading democratic theoreticians of his time, was a New York lawyer prominent in Tammany politics. From 1801 to 1807 he served as clerk of the city and county of New York. He was the author of several important tracts, one of which outlined a democratic philosophy of social reform, *An Oration on the Influence of Social Institutions upon Human Morals and Happiness* (New York, 1796), and another which was a leading defense of Jefferson against charges of atheism in the election of 1800. See *A Solemn Address, to Christians and Patriots, upon the approaching Election of a President of the United States* (New York, 1800). Gallatin supported the publication of Wortman's *Enquiry* by undertaking to secure subscriptions to the book among Republican members of Congress. (Wortman to Gallatin, Dec. 24, 30, 1799, Albert Gallatin Papers, 1799, Nos. 47, 49, New York Historical Society.) In 1813–14 Wortman published a newspaper in New York, the *Standard of Union*, to which Jefferson subscribed in the hope that it would counteract the "abandoned spirit of falsehood" of the newspapers of the country. (Jefferson to Wortman, Aug. 15, 1813, Thomas Jefferson Papers, Henry E. Huntingdon Library.)

52. John Thomson, *An Enquiry, Concerning the Liberty, and Licentiousness of the Press* (New York, 1801). I have not been able to identify John Thomson.

53. Sir William Blackstone, *Commentaries on the Laws of England*, ed. St. George Tucker (5 vols., Philadelphia, 1803), I, pt. 2, n. G, 11–30 of Appendix. Tucker, a professor of law at William and Mary, was elected to the high court of Virginia in 1803. President Madison appointed him a United States district judge in 1813.

54. [Madison,] *Virginia Reports of 1799–1800*, 220.

55. Hay, *Essay on the Liberty of the Press* (1803 ed. of the 1799 tract), 29; *Essay on the Liberty of the Press* (1803), 32. See note 49, above, for a distinction between the two tracts.

56. Thomson, *Enquiry, Concerning the Liberty, and Licentiousness of the Press*, 6–7.

57. Wortman, *Treatise Concerning Political Enquiry*, 173.

58. [Madison,] *Virginia Report of 1799–1800*, 226–27.

59. Wortman, *Treatise Concerning Political Enquiry*, 253.

60. Hay, *Essay on the Liberty of the Press* (1803, ed. of 1799 tract), 28.

61. *Annals of Congress*, 5 Cong., 2 sess., 2162 (July 10, 1798).

62. Thomson, *Enquiry, Concerning the Liberty, and Licentiousness of the Press*, 68.

63. [Madison,] *Virginia Report of 1799–1800*, 226.

64. Wortman, *Treatise Concerning Political Enquiry*, 262.

65. Hay, Essay on the Liberty of the Press (1803 ed. of 1799 tract), 23–24.

66. *Ibid.*, 25.

67. Hay, *Essay on the Liberty of the Press* (1803 tract), 29.

68. Wortman, *Treatise Concerning Political Enquiry*, 140, 253; Thomson, *Enquiry, Concerning the Liberty, and Licentiousness of the Pres*, 79.

69. *Ibid.*, 22.

70. [Madison,] *Virginia Report of 1799–1800*, 222.

71. Wortman, *Treatise Concerning Political Enquiry*, 29.

72. Thomson, *Enquiry, Concerning the Liberty, and Licentiousness of the Press*, 20, 22; Hay, *Essay on the Liberty of the Press* (1803 ed. of 1799 tract), 26.

73. "Originality" refers to the American scene. American libertarian thought lagged behind its British counterpart which very likely provided a model for the Republicans in the same way that British thought advocating suppression influenced Federalist opinion. For British precursors of the new American libertarianism, see "Father of Candor," *A Letter Concerning Libels, Warrants, the Seizure of Papers, and Sureties for the Peace of Behaviour* (7th ed., London, 1771), 20, 34, 71, 161; Ebenezer Ratcliffe, *Two Letters Addressed to the Right Rev. Prelates* (London, 1773), 100; Andrew Kippis, *A Vindication of the Protestant Dissenting Ministers* (London, 1773), 98–99; Francis Maseres, *An Enquiry into the Extent of the Power of Juries* (1776) (Dublin, 1792), 6, 13, 18, 22, 24, 28; Jeremy Bentham, *A Fragment on Government* (London, 1776), 154; Capel Lofft, *An Essay on the Law of Libels* (London, 1785), 60–61; James Adair, *Discussions of the Law of Libels as at Present Received* (London, 1785), 27–28; Manasseh Dawes, *The Deformity of the Doctrine of Libels, and Informations Ex-Officio* (London, 1785), 11–24, 28; the celebrated argument of Thomas Erskine in a defense of Tom Paine, in a trial for seditious libel, 1792, published as a contemporary tract and available in *Speeches of Thomas Lord Erskine, Reprinted from the Five Volume Octavo Edition of 1810*, in ed. Edward Walford (2 vols., London, 1870), I, 309, 313; Robert Hall, "An Apology for the Freedom of the Press and for General Liberty" (1793) in *The Miscellaneous Works and Remains of the Reverend Robert Hall*, ed. John Foster (London, 1846), 172–79.

11. Subversion of *Miranda*

1. 401 U.S. 222. An indispensable article on the Harris case, to which I am greatly indebted, is Alan M. Dershowitz and John H. Ely, "*Harris v. New York*: Some Anxious Observations on the Candor and Logic of the Emerging Nixon Majority," *Yale Law J.*, Vol. 80 (May 1971), 1198–1227. For other comments on the case, see Erwin Davis, "Statements Obtained in Violation of Miranda May Be Used for Impeachment," *Arkansas Law Rev.*, Vol. 25 (Summer 1971), 190–200; Stanley B. Kent, "Harris v. New York: The Death Knell of Miranda and Walder?" *Brooklyn Law Rev.*, Vol. 38 (Fall 1971), 357–70.

2. Miranda v. Ariz., 384 U.S. 436 (1966).

3. Escobedo v. Ill., 378 U.S. 478 (1964).

4. Quoted in Dershowitz and Ely, p. 1203, citing Transcript of Oral Argument, p. 12.

5. *Ibid.*, p. 1203 note 31, citing Transcript, p. 19.

6. *Ibid.*, p. 1206, citing Transcript, p. 25.

7. *Ibid.*, p. 1206 note 42, citing Transcript, pp. 25–26.

8. *Ibid.*, p. 1222, citing Brief of the D.A. of N.Y. County, p. 12.

9. 401 U.S. 222, 224.

10. Dershowitz and Ely, p. 1199, speak of "the intolerability, of what is, at best, gross negligence concerning the state of the record and the controlling precedents."

11. 401 U.S. 222, 229 note 2.

12. *Ibid.*, 224.

13. 384 U.S. 436, 476–77.

14. 401 U.S. 222, 230.

15. *Ibid.*, 224.

16. *Ibid.*, 225.

17. *Ibid.*, 226.

18. *Ibid.*, 226 note 2.

19. 347 U.S. 62 (1954).

20. Weeks v. U.S., 232 U.S. 383 (1914). Mapp v. Ohio, 367 U.S. 643 (1961) applied the rule to the states.

21. 401 U.S. 222, 224.

22. 347 U.S. 62, 64.

23. *Ibid.*, 65. Italics added.

24. Agnello v. U.S., 269 U.S. 20 (1925).

25. *Ibid.*, 35.

26. 401 U.S. 222, 225.

27. Charles T. McCormick, *Handbook of the Law of Evidence* (St. Paul, 1954), sect. 39, p. 77.

28. Bruton v. U.S., 391 U.S. 123, 135.

29. 401 U.S. 222, 225.

30. *Ibid.*, 232.

31. Olmstead v. U.S., 277 U.S. 438, 485 (1928).

32. See Riddell v Rhay, 404 U.S. 974 (1971), for a case similar to Harris v. N.Y. in which the Court denied a petition for a writ of certiorari, over the dissenting opinion of Douglas, joined by Brennan, who declared: "Yet, after *Harris*, there is no longer any real incentive for police to obey *Miranda*." Ibid., 976.

33. Olmstead v. U.S., 277 U.S. 438, 479 (1927).

12. *Judicial Activism and Strict Construction*

1. The best general works on the Warren Court are Archibald Cox, *The Warren Court* (Cambridge, Mass., 1968); Alexander M. Bickel, *The Supreme Court and the Idea of Progress* (New York, 1970); Alfred M. Kelly and Winfred A Harbison, *The American Constitution*, 4th ed. (New York, 1970), chs. 33–35; Philip B. Kurland, *Politics, the Constitution, and the Warren Court* (Chicago, 1970); and, Anthony Lewis, ed., *The Warren Court: A Critical Evaluation* (New York, 1970).

2. Quotation from John D. Weaver, *Warren: The Man, the Court, the Era* (Boston, 1967), pp. 335–36, 342–43.

3. "Retirement of Mr. Chief Justice Warren," June 23, 1969, 89 S. Ct. 17, 18, 19.

4. Aug. 8, 1968, in *Vital Speeches of the Day*, Vol. 34 (Sept. 1, 1968), p. 676.

5. Sept. 29, 1968, quoted in Richard Harris, *Justice: The Crisis of Law, Order and Freedom in America* (New York, 1970), p. 23.

6. *New York Times*, June 15, 1969, p. 43, col. 1.

7. Strunk v. U.S., 412 U.S. 434 (1973).

8. McNabb v. U.S., 318 U.S. 332, 347 (1943). See also Malinski v. N.Y., 324 U.S. 401, 414 (1945).

9. Shaughnessy v. U.S., 345 U.S. 206, 224.

10. *Crime in the United States: 1972.* Uniform Crime Reports (Washington, 1973), pp. 1–4. For a discussion of crime statistics, see below, last chapter.

11. Charles Nott, "Coddling the Criminal," *Atlantic Monthly* (1911), discussed in Yale Kamisar, "When the Police Were Not 'Handcuffed,' " *New York Times Magazine*, Nov. 7, 1965, reprinted in Donald R. Cressy, ed., *Crime and Criminal Justice* (Chicago, 1971), pp. 46–57.

12. Escobedo v. Ill., 378 U.S. 478, 490 (1964).

13. Miranda v. Ariz., 384 U.S. 436, 483 note 54 (1966), quoting Hoover, "Civil Liberties and Law Enforcement: The Role of the F.B.I.," *Iowa Law Rev.*, Vol. 37 (Winter 1952), 175, 177–82.

14. See generally, Leonard Downey, *Justice Denied: The Case for the Reform of the Courts* (New York, 1971), and James Mills, "I Have Nothing to Do With Justice," *Life*, Vol. 70 (March 12, 1971), 57–68.

15. David Fellman, *The Defendant's Rights* (New York, 1958) is the best summary of the contitutional law of criminal justice for the pre-Warren Court. The only book on the Warren Court and criminal justice is Fred P. Graham, *The Self-Inflicted Wound* (New York, 1970).

16. Rochin v. Cal., 342 U.S. 165, 172–73 (1952).

17. Powell v. Ala., 287 U.S. 45 (1932). See also Palko v. Conn., 302 U.S. 319 (1937).

18. Rochin v. Cal., 342 U.S. 165.

19. Brown v. Allen, 344 U.S. 443 (1953).

20. Mapp v. Ohio, 367 U.S. 643.

21. Robinson v. Cal., 370 U.S. 660 (1962).

22. Gideon v. Wainwright, 372 U.S. 335.

23. Malloy v. Hogan, 378 U.S. 1 (1964).

24. Pointer v. Tex., 380 U.S. 400 (1965), Klopfer v. N. Car., 386 U.S. 213 (1967), Washington v. Tex., 388 U.S. 14 (1967).

25. Duncan v. La., 391 U.S. 145, and Benton v. Md., 395 U.S. 784 (1969).

26. Griffin v. Ill., 351 U.S. 12, 19.

27. Smith v. Bennett, 365 U.S. 708 (1961) and Douglas v. Cal., 372 U.S. 353 (1963).

28. Townsend v. Sain, 372 U.S. 293 (1963) and Fay v. Noia, 372 U.S. 391 (1963).

29. In re Gault, 387 U.S. 1 (1967).

30. Hamilton v. Ala., 368 U.S. 52 (1961); White v Md., 373 U.S. 59 (1963); Massiah v. U.S., 377 U.S. 201 (1964); Escobedo v. Ill., 378 U.S. 478 (1964); U.S. v. Wade, 388 U.S. 218 (1967).

31. Miranda v. Ariz., 383 U.S. 436 (1966).

32. See Earl Warren, "The Law and the Future," pamphlet reprint from *Fortune* (Nov. 1955), p. 11.

33. Ullmann v. U.S., 350 U.S. 422 (1956).

34. Belan v. Bd. of Ed., 357 U.S. 399 (1958); Lerner v. Casey, 357 U.S. 468 (1958); Nelson v. County of Los Angeles, 362 U.S. 1 (1960). The Court also upheld against First Amendment claims the denial of membership in a state bar association to a person who refused answer to questions concerning Communist affiliations. Konigsberg v. State Bar of Cal., 366 U.S. 36 (1961). The Warren Court sustained the government in numerous internal-security cases involving the First Amendment.

35. Breithaupt v. Abram, 352 U.S. 432 (1957) and Schmerber v. Cal., 384 U.S. 757 (1966).

36. U.S. v. Wade, 388 U.S. 218 (1967) and Gilbert v. Cal., 388 U.S. 263 (1967).

37. Hoffa v. U.S., 385 U.S. 293 (1966).

38. Lewis v. U.S., 385 U.S. 206 (1966).

39. Osborn v. U.S., 385 U.S. 323 (1966).

40. McCray v. Ill., 386 U.S. 300 (1967).

41. Warden v. Hayden, 387 U.S. 294 (1967), overruling Gouled v. U.S., 255 U.S. 298 (1921).

42. Katz v. U.S., 389 U.S. 347 (1967), overruling Olmstead v. U.S., 277 U.S. 438 (1928).

43. Terry v. Ohio, 392 U.S. 1 (1968).

44. "Retirement of Mr. Chief Justice Warren," June 23, 1969, 89 S. Ct. 17, 18.

45. *Ibid.*, 19–20, for Warren's response.

46. Wilson, *Constitutional Government in the United States* (New York, 1908), p. 57.

47. Warren, "The Law and the Future," pamphlet reprint from *Fortune* (Nov. 1955), pp. 6–11, *passim*.

48. *New York Times*, July 4, 1971, p. 1, col. 5, and p. 24.

49. McCollum v. Bd. of Ed., 333 U.S. 203, 237–38 (1948).

50. Coleman v. Ala., 399 U.S. 1 (1970).

51. Powell v. Ala., 287 U.S. 45, 69 (1932).

52. 399 U.S. 1, 9.

53. *Ibid.*, 12.

54. *Ibid.*, 14.

55. *Ibid.*, 19.

56. *Ibid.*, 22–23.

57. *Ibid.*, 23.

58. "Fundamental Constitutions of Carolina," 1669, sections 80 and 120, in Francis N. Thorpe, ed., *The Federal and State Constitutions, Colonial Charters, and Other Organic Laws* (Washington, 1909), Vol. 6, pp. 2782,. 2786.

59. James M. Beck, *The Constitution of the United States* (New York, 1922), p. 221.

60. To Spencer Roane, Sept. 6, 1819, in *The Writings of Thomas Jefferson*, Andrew A. Lipscomb and Albert Ellery Burgh, eds. (Washington, 1904–07), Vol. 15, p. 278.

61. Irving Dilliard, ed., *The Spirit of Liberty: Papers and Addresses of Learned Hand* (New York, 1953), p. 81.

62. Frankfurter, "Supreme Court, United States," *Encyclopaedia of Social Science.* (New York, 1934), Vol. 14, p. 480.

63. Oct. 21, 1971, *Public Papers of the Presidents of the United States. Richard Nixon: 1971* (Washington, 1972), p. 1055.

64. McKeiver v. Pa., 403, U.S. 528 (1971).

65. Baldwin v. N.Y., 399 U.S. 66 (1970).

66. Oct. 21, 1971, *Public Papers . . . Nixon*, pp. 1054–1055.

67. Edward S. Corwin, *Twilight of the Supreme Court* (New Haven, 1934), p. 117.

68. "The Nature of the Judicial Process," (1921), in *Selected Writings of Benjamin Nathan Cardozo*, Margaret E. Hall, ed. (New York, 1947), p. 110.

69. Holmes, *The Common Law* (Boston, 1881), p. 35.

70. *New York Times*, July 1, 1972, p. 8, col. 8.

71. Wright, "The Supreme Court Today," *Trial*, Vol. 3 (April–May 1967), 1, 10–11

72. Kurland, "1970 Term: Notes on the Emergence of the Burger Court," in *The Supreme Court Review: 1971* (Chicago, 1971), p. 267.

73. "The Supreme Court, 1971 Term," *Harvard Law Rev.*, Vol. 86 (Nov. 1972) pp. 298–99.

74. *Time*, Oct. 18, 1971, p. 34. See also *ibid.*, March 26, 1973, p. 69, and *New York Times*, Sept. 8, 1971, pt. 2, p. 1, col. 1, and *ibid.*, Jan. 17, 1972, editorial, "The Washington Crime Story," p. 30, col. 2. *New York Times*, March 5, 1973, p. 1, col. 3 *ibid.*, March 11, 1973, p. 1, col. 8, and *ibid.*, "News of the Week" section, Oct. 22, 197: p. 6, col. 1. For the most recent official statistics, see *Crime in the United States, 1972* Uniform Crime Reports (Washington, 1973).

75. *Los Angeles Times*, July 1, 1973, p. 1, col. 8.

DATE DUE

SEP 3 0 1997			
OCT 0 9 1997			
GAYLORD			PRINTED IN U.S.A.